Advances *in* Motor Learning *and* Control

Howard N. Zelaznik
Purdue University

Editor

Human Kinetics

Library of Congress Cataloging-in-Publication Data

Advances in motor learning and control / Howard N. Zelaznik, editor.
  p.   cm.
  Includes bibliographical references and index.
  ISBN 0-87322-947-9
  1. Motor learning.   2. Perceptual-motor learning.   3. Movement,
  Psychology.   I. Zelaznik, Howard N., 1952-   .
  BF295.A28   1996
  152.3'34--dc20   96-8063
                                                          CIP

ISBN: 0-87322-947-9

Acquisitions Editor: Richard Frey, PhD; **Developmental Editor**: Holly Gilly; **Assistant Editors**: Lynn M. Hooper, Chad Johnson; **Editorial Assistant**: Amy Carnes; **Copyeditor**: Denelle Eknes; **Proofreader**: Myla Smith; **Indexer**: Norman Duren; **Production Manager**: Judy Rademaker; **Graphic Artists**: Sandra Meier, Tara Welsch; **Text Designer**: Keith Blomberg; **Photo Editor**: Boyd LaFoon; **Cover Designer**: Jack Davis; **Illustrators**: Jennifer Delmotte, Craig Ronto, Tom Janowski, and Keith Blomberg; **Printer**: Edwards Brothers

Human Kinetics books are available at special discounts for bulk purchase. Special editions or book excerpts can also be created to specification. For details, contact the Special Sales Manager at Human Kinetics.

Printed in the United States of America

10   9   8   7   6   5   4   3   2   1

Human Kinetics
Web site: http://www.humankinetics.com/

United States: Human Kinetics, P.O. Box 5076, Champaign, IL 61825-5076
1-800-747-4457
humank@hkusa.com

Canada: Human Kinetics, Box 24040, Windsor, ON N8Y 4Y9
1-800-465-7301 (in Canada only)
humank@hkcanada.com

Europe: Human Kinetics, P.O. Box IW14, Leeds LS16 6TR, United Kingdom
(44) 1132 781708
humank@hkeurope.com

Australia: Human Kinetics, 57A Price Avenue, Lower Mitcham, South Australia
(08) 277 1555
humank@hkaustralia.com

New Zealand: Human Kinetics, P.O. Box 105-231, Auckland 1
(09) 523 3462
humank@hknewz.com

Contents

Contributors

Daniel Bullock
Daniel M. Corcos
Carol L. Cross
Paula Fitzpatrick
Melvyn A. Goodale
Gerald L. Gottlieb
Stephen Grossberg
Frank Guenther
Slobodan Jaric
Mitsuo Kawato

Kyoung-nae Kim
Stuart T. Klapp
Monique McMillan
R.C. Schmidt
Philip Servos
Ann L. Smiley-Oyen
Stephan P. Swinnen
Stephen A. Wallace
Charles J. Worringham
Howard N. Zelaznik

Preface

Over the past 20 years the area of motor behavior has emerged as an important discipline in kinesiology/physical education, psychology, and neuroscience. We can trace the birth of this new era in kinesiology/physical education to the publication of the Adams theory of motor learning in the *Journal of Motor Behavior* (Adams 1971) along with the very influential paper published by Keele (1968). Since that time we have had many new books, as well as theory and review papers that have advanced the field. However, current graduate students in motor learning and control are at times overwhelmed with the number of new articles published each year, and the number of books that are the result of conferences and workshops. It is fair to state that 15 to 20 years ago most students of motor behavior could have mastered the major concepts of the field during their graduate student experience. Such is not the case at the present time. The area of study of motor behavior and control has become very specialized. The present volume was prepared to provide individuals working in motor behavior and control with the necessary foundations to understand some of these specialized areas.

The present volume is designed to provide an in-depth historical perspective on some traditional and/or current areas of motor learning and control. My goal in editing this edition is to provide the graduate student, as well as the faculty member, a resource where some of the more difficult areas of inquiry are presented in a more tutorial fashion. Each chapter should serve as a springboard for future readings. One of my hopes is that this book can serve as the primer for a graduate seminar in motor behavior and control.

I also tried to avoid taking a particular philosophical stand concerning the nature of motor behavior and control. Currently the field is becoming divided into those who take an information-processing approach and those who utilize a dynamical systems approach to study motor behavior. Furthermore, many researchers are now attempting to determine the neurological underpinnings or substrates of motor performance and learning. These latter scholars are not necessarily aligned with either of the two behavioral perspectives. Instead they believe that particular mechanisms or processes can be uncovered in the neuroanatomy or neural organization of the nervous system. In the present volume I have tried to select scholars who would provide representation from many different approaches and perspectives.

Although the chapters were designed to stand alone, the book is organized so that if an individual wanted to read the book in chapter order there would be some organization to the book. Chapter 1 by Kim, McMillan, and Zelaznik provides a brief tutorial describing how well-known empirical findings can be used as a tool to open a window to processes in trajectory formation as well as in motor development. The second chapter by Klapp was included to remind all of us that there still is room in motor behavior and control for a line of research that is behavioral in nature and that this type of research can discover principles of organization of the central nervous system. Chapter 3 by Swinnen and 4 by Worringham provide sweeping reviews of learning issues from an analysis of the laws of knowledge of results and feedback (Swinnen) and from a review of central nervous system cites for motor learning (Worringham). Chapter 5 by Goodale and Servos highlights the continuing search for understanding the processes of visual motor control. Goodale and Servos present a strong case for two modes of visual motor control. This chapter is must reading for students of prehension and visual motor control.

Chapters 6 through 10 can be considered the second portion of the book. In these chapters the reader will learn about several different dynamical approaches to the study of central motor control. Corcos, Jaric, and Gottlieb (chapter 6) describe the development of a speed-sensitive and speed-insensitive strategy for the control of movement. They then apply this model to different motor tasks and different subject populations. In chapter 7, Wallace provides a wonderful tutorial of the dynamical pattern perspective from the view of the uninitiated. This chapter is designed to provide an interested reader with the necessary background to appreciate this perspective. R.C. Schmidt and P. Fitzpatrick show how a dynamical systems approach can be utilized to study learning. In their view learning is not the imposition of an external pattern of control, but rather the adaptation of the natural intrinsic dynamics of the performer. In the last two chapters Kawato (9) and Bullock, Grossberg, and Guenther (10) describe two different types of mathematical approaches to motor control. Kawato describes minimization principles while Bullock et al. utilize a connectionist approach, constrained by the known physiology, to model limb trajectory.

In all of the chapters the authors have attempted to present only the sparsest mathematics. However it is clear that a working knowledge of calculus is important for capturing the richness of many of the models discussed in the present volume. This does not mean that the reader must be able to solve a differential equation (that is why we have computers), but the reader should intuitively understand a derivative and an integral. One of the goals of each author is to provide the reader with some of the intuitions for understanding the value of employing mathematics for an analysis of motor behavior.

I would like to first thank all of the authors for providing excellent chapters and taking the review suggestions to heart. Jack Halbert and Rick Frey have my special thanks. They hounded me to agree to edit a volume such as this. Without their constant prodding and encouragement this edition would not have been possible. Finally, my wife, Lorraine Kisselburgh, and our two sons Steven and Michael have my special thanks for always providing enthusiasm, love and support for my silly academic endeavors.

Howard N. Zelaznik
Purdue University

Chapter 1

Behavioral Analysis of Trajectory Formation: The Speed-Accuracy Trade-Off as a Tool to Understand Strategies of Movement Control

Kyoung-nae Kim
Yonsei University, Seoul, (South) Korea

Monique McMillan and Howard N. Zelaznik
Purdue University

As a child growing up you heard many times that "there are many ways to skin a cat." In other words, you can achieve the goal of your task by various means. Each method presents unique benefits (perhaps time and money), but each method also presents unique costs (energy consumed and level of difficulty). How we solved problems as children, and now as adults, partly depends on our personal view of the costs and benefits associated with the method we chose. In motor behavior Hebb (1949) termed a similar process as "motor equivalence." You can solve a motoric problem by various methods; each can achieve the intended goal. For example, the way a child grasps an object depends on the size and shape of the object. The method chosen to capture the object is driven by the object itself. This example is one of many that demonstrates motor equivalence. The purpose of this chapter pertains to the analysis level of motor skill performance we need to comprehend the nature of the processes we use for understanding motor behavior.

We argue that research in motor behavior and control should recognize that an equivalence exists in the study of processes and strategies of control and performance. In the same manner that there is not a correct way to pick up a glass of water or wine, there is not one method for study that has a privileged status. The chapters in this tutorial edition attest to that. In this introductory chapter we highlight an area of research that our laboratory has been active in, the speed-accuracy trade-off. We show how we can use this phenomenon to ask questions about producing movement trajectories and developing skill as a result of maturation. Because of our belief that students of scientific inquiry should have a sense of history, we begin this chapter with a discussion of a classic paper by Woodworth (1899), who was one of the first scientists to use the speed-accuracy phenomenon to infer underlying processes of motor control.

WOODWORTH (1899)

In 1899 Woodworth published his dissertation, an epic work, in which he systematically examined "the accuracy of voluntary movement." Woodworth believed that to understand the workings of the mind, the output of mental activity, movement, must be examined in its own right. Woodworth proceeded to claim that the accuracy of movement is an important aspect to examine.

> The movement must have a particular direction, a definite extent or goal, a definite force, a definite duration, a definite relation to other movements, contemporaneous, preceding and following. Even in comparatively unskilled movements it is remarkable how many groups of muscles must cooperate, and with what accuracy each must do just so much and no more. (P. 4)

Woodworth then laid out what he believed to be the research agenda: Examine the conditions that affect movement accuracy. These findings would lead to an understanding of the will.

Woodworth's findings are still relevant today. He proposed that a movement toward a target consists of two components, an initial impulse followed by current control. The initial impulse is a ballistic movement not dependent on feedback. Current control is dependent primarily on vision to home in on the target. This model is probably one of the most important, well-documented, and essentially correct descriptions of movement control. Crossman and Goodeve (1963), Keele (1968), and most recently Meyer et al. (1988) have used Woodworth's idea to explain the logarithmic relation between movement speed and accuracy known as Fitts' Law (Fitts 1954). The work on grasping has derived much of its theoretical impetus from the work of Woodworth (see Jeannerod 1981, for example).

In his first experiment, Woodworth had subjects make repetitive movements at rates of 20 to 200 movements per min (expected duration being 3.0 to 0.3 s per movement). Woodworth noted that there appeared to be a monotonically increasing error as the rate of movement increased (or time decreased). Woodworth was interested in explaining the reasons for this relationship, which is called a speed-accuracy trade-off—as speed increases accuracy decreases. First, he observed that movements produced with the eyes closed exhibited a relatively constant level of accuracy as a function of speed, but movements produced with the eyes opened showed a gradual increase in error as speed increased. Woodworth deduced that processing visual information reduced error to a greater extent as the speed decreased.

After examining the movement trajectories (by very clever techniques, before the advent of laboratory computers!), Woodworth proposed that two processes controlled the trajectory of the movement: an *initial impulse* propelled the limb toward the end location and *current control* homed in on the end location. Although Woodward did not use these words, in modern jargon we call the initial impulse the *open-loop control strategy* (feedback is not used) and current control the *closed-loop control strategy* (feedback is used). According to Woodworth, the reason error decreased as the time per movement increased (speed decreased) resided in the increased effectiveness of current control to nullify the error of the initial impulse. Servos and Goodale (this volume) show how far we have progressed in understanding visual motor control.

Woodworth also entertained the notion that the initial adjustment could decrease its accuracy as movement speed increased:

> We have been all along overlooking one possible bad effect of speed. We have urged that speed would interfere with the current control of a movement, but have quietly assumed that it would not interfere with the initial adjustment. Yet it is not hard to conceive that the initial adjustment might become more difficult as speed increased. *A slight error in the duration of a movement would mean a greater error in extent, when the velocity is greater.* (P. 52, emphasis added)

Woodworth then argued that the accuracy of the initial impulse would be independent of movement time. Again, the conclusion from his work is that the increase in error as speed increases resides in the current control processes.

Numerous studies and models have been reported since Woodworth's classic study. Clearly, the essence of Woodworth's work is correct today, but some details need to be revised (see Meyer et al. 1988; Meyer et al. 1990). The model proposed by Woodworth must be seen on its own level of analysis, the behavioral one. This model does not explain the strategy used to control the initial adjustment. It assumes than an open-loop portion of a movement exists. Jeannerod (1992) and MacKenzie (1992) have used these constructs to explain the modification of a movement trajectory during the act of grasping.

However, these studies beg the question of how the limb is controlled. What strategy controls the activity of the musculature driving the movement? Chapters in this volume, such as those of Kawato, Corcos, and Bullock, attempt to answer these questions. These works do not negate Woodworth's analysis, but provide different answers to different questions. All the answers possess motor control equivalence.

FITTS' LAW AND
THE LINEAR SPEED-ACCURACY TRADE-OFF

Fitts (1954) described the relationship between the movement distance (D), spatial accuracy (defined as the width of a target, W), and the resulting movement time (T), in the now-famous Fitts' Law. It states that $T = a + b \, Log_2 \, (2D/W)$, in which a and b are empirically determined constants. This relationship has been explained by the idea that the change in T is required to meet the demands of the current control processes. Specifically, it has been proposed that following the initial adjustment toward the target, current control executes a series of successive approximations to the target. As the width of the target decreases or the distance to be moved increases, more submovements are required to achieve the desired movement accuracy (Crossman and Goodeve 1963; Keele 1968). The Fitts relationship has stood the test of time and has captured a fundamental limitation in the control of movement.

However, it has been shown that for very small movements to large targets Fitts' Law does not hold (Klapp 1975). The explanation for the "violation" of Fitts' Law is that current control is not needed for controlling movements that require little spatial accuracy or use small movement durations. Schmidt, Zelaznik, and Frank

(1978; Schmidt et al. 1979) then examined the relationship between speed and accuracy for rapid movements, where Fitts' Law does not hold.

In these experiments, much like Woodworth's, T and D are controlled by the experimenter. The measure of accuracy was called the effective target width, W_e, which is defined as the within-subject standard deviation in movement distance. This measure is calculated within a particular D/T condition. In this type of task, we hypothesized that the entire movement would be controlled by the initial adjustment, or in modern parlance, the motor program (Keele 1968; Schmidt 1975). Furthermore, we hypothesized that the motor program directly controlled the duration and intensity of the muscular forces responsible for positively accelerating, then negatively accelerating the limb toward the target. With these assumptions and additional theoretical work, we predicted that the relationship between speed and accuracy should be linear. In other words, W_e should be proportional to the average velocity of the movement D/T. In fact it is (see Meyer, Smith, and Wright 1982; Wright and Meyer 1983 for additional evidence).

It is not the goal of this chapter to discuss the underlying mechanisms of the linear speed-accuracy trade-off (see Meyer, Smith, and Wright 1982; and Zelaznik 1993 for a more thorough discussion), but to highlight how this relationship can be a tool to understand other aspects of control strategies and skill development. The original formulation of Schmidt et al. (1979) was flawed mathematically, although the premises of the model have held up well. In fact, they were used by Meyer, Smith, and Wright (1982) in their theoretical accounts for the linear speed-accuracy trade-off.

Meyer et al. (1988, 1990) have demonstrated how the linear relation between speed and accuracy for programmed movements can be used to explain the Fitts relationship. The performer is attempting to optimize the speed *and* accuracy of a movement. The subject chooses a time for the first movement toward the target so a small proportion of the trials require a correction (i.e., an additional submovement). If the subject produced an initial adjustment that was too slow, corrections would not be required, but T would be too large. On the other hand, an initial adjustment that was too fast would demand a high proportion of trials with submovements, also causing an increase in average T. Meyer and colleagues have shown that the optimal solution for a performer is to modify T in a way that approximates Fitts' Law. This work is truly a crowning achievement in motor control. Future work is needed to evaluate the strength of the details of this model.

We now turn our attention to how we can use the Fitts relation and the linear speed-accuracy trade-off to understand processes of skill development and performance.

PROCESSES IN MOTOR DEVELOPMENT

Obviously, as children mature, their motor skills improve. This improvement in fundamental skills has been well documented (Wickstrom 1983). It is also true that children's skilled performance becomes more adult-like as they mature. Again this is not a surprising finding. Many researchers have used the Fitts' Law paradigm to study the locus and nature of these developmental changes (Hay 1981; Kerr 1975; Salmoni and McIlwain 1979; Salmoni and Pascoe 1978; Wallace, Newell, and Wade 1978). We were interested in using Fitts' Law to determine whether motor development produced a change in degree versus a change in kind. In other words, do children control their movements with the same strategy and control processes adults use, or does maturation produce a change in their strategy or control processes? We borrowed a technique used in developmental cognitive psychology to examine this issue.

Kail (1991) has found that in speed-stressed cognitive tasks, such as mental rotation and memory scanning, children exhibit reaction time values larger than the adult measures. However, adults and children are affected proportionally by an independent variable. In other words, mean reaction time of a set of children at a particular age is a constant proportion of the same value as that of a set of adults on those tasks. The value of this proportion, called a slowing coefficient (Kail 1991), is greater than one, and it is task independent (obviously the children's values are greater than the adults). Regardless of the task, a set of eight-year-old children will exhibit reaction time values that are a constant proportion longer than a set of adult reaction time values. Kail also has discovered that there is a lawful decrease in the slowing coefficient as maturation progresses. The decrease follows an exponential function similar to exponential growth curves observed in many biological systems (Smith 1968).

The implication is that children and adults perform these cognitive tasks in fundamentally the same fashion. In other words, their cognitive architecture is the same. What changes over maturation is the speed in which these cognitive processes function. For these types of tasks we can conclude that maturation involves a change in degree, but not in the nature of the mental processes.

We attempted (McMillan 1992) to examine this hypothesis in the motoric domain. In one part of this study we had a group of six-year-old children ($n = 27$) and a group of adults perform a reciprocal Fitts movement task. A subject moved a handheld pen across a tabletop, reversing the direction of motion within a well-defined target. The width of the target was always 2.0 cm. Difficulty of the task was manipulated by D, which had four levels: 5.0, 10.0, 20.0, and 30.0 cm. The corresponding index of difficulty values ($Log_2 2D/W$) were 2.32, 3.32, 4.32, and 4.91 bits for the 5.0-, 10.0-, 20.0-, and 30.0-cm movement distance conditions, respectively. The movement trajectory was recorded with an infrared recording technique (Watsmart) so movement time and spatial accuracy could be determined.

As expected, the children produced movement time values that were greater than the adults. The adults were less careful in meeting the accuracy demands for the task. Thus, we determined the relationship between T and the index of difficulty for the children and the adults, correcting for the standard deviation in the movement end point. The target width was computed to be twice the standard deviation in movement end point. The T values were predicted at each prescribed level of index of difficulty for the adults and the children. Plotted in fig. 1.1 is the relationship between the adults' movement time (on the abscissa) and the children's movement time (on the ordinate) for the 2.32, 3.32, 4.32, and 4.91 levels of index of difficulty.

As we can see in this figure, a strong linear relationship exists between adults' movement times and those of children. It clearly is not proportional because the y-intercept value is about 308 ms. Strictly speaking the children's reaction times are not a constant proportion of the adults' values. We are encouraged that the strong linear relation between these scores ($r > 0.99$) suggests that children perform the Fitts task as adults do. Future work needs to evaluate the factors producing the nonzero intercept.

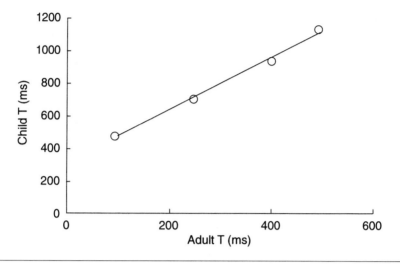

Fig. 1.1   Relationship between average movement time (T) of adults (abscissa) and children (ordinate) on a reciprocal Fitts' Law movement task.

This work, which has been on the behavioral level, shows that you can use a well-known relationship to ask fundamental questions about motor control from a developmental perspective. With this start, we can ask whether the underlying kinematic characteristics of Fitts' Law movements of children and adults show the same qualitative structure. One interesting aspect to examine is whether children produce initial adjustments that require more corrections, or whether the current control processes require additional time. Furthermore, one can study the mixture of initial adjustment movement, to movements with one, two, or more submovements produced via current control. Our current data is too limited (only four trials per index of difficulty) to perform such detailed analyses.

We view this study as a start. Clearly, the developmental functions must be mapped across the age span; then those functions should be compared across tasks. Kail (1991) shows that RT decreases in a lawful fashion across ages, regardless of task. It would be interesting to determine whether the same were true for motor tasks. For example, Williams, Woollacott, and Ivry (1992) show that children identified as clumsy exhibit poorer timekeeping skill than children with normal motor development. If the developmental function for timekeeping skill were mapped, would it be isomorphic with the developmental function for a different skill that uses timing skill? We believe mapping developmental functions, not on the descriptive level (Wickstrom 1983), but examining the growth of performance, can result in new insights in development.

LINEAR SPEED-ACCURACY TRADE-OFF AND TRAJECTORY FORMATION

A basic question asked by motor control scientists concerns trajectory formation. In this volume, many chapters are concerned with the rules and processes engaged when a person moves his or her limb from one place to another. Kawato is concerned with the minimization problem that can be solved by the nervous system to allow a trajectory to be formed. He shows that by minimizing the motor command change, a model-person produces trajectories similar to those produced by actual subjects. Wallace asks how the principles of nonlinear dynamical systems can be applied to trajectory formation. Schmidt is concerned with the development of new rules of coordination via a dynamical systems approach.

Historically, the production of a trajectory from one point to another has been conceived as driven by one of two possible systems. The first system, commonly called mass-spring, drives the limb by the control of the mechanical properties, such as stiffness, damping, and resting length, of the bone-muscle system (see Latash and Gottlieb 1991 for advances in this area). Another view of movement control is highlighted in the chapter by Corcos. In this approach the duration and intensity of a muscular contraction is under the direct control of the central nervous system. These models, of which impulse timing (Schmidt et al. 1979; Wallach 1981) is one, posit the existence of some prescriptive plan for movement that produces the desired trajectory.

The tractable movements handled by these models can be classified as point to point: they can occur in a straight path. What strategies might a subject use to produce a curved trajectory? Hollerbach (1981), in his model of handwriting, provides some clues about how a curved trajectory is produced. He posited that in writing cursive letters a person controls two orthogonal oscillators—one in the horizontal dimension and the other in the lateral dimension.

These oscillators can be envisioned as two independent mass-spring systems. By manipulating the intensity of each oscillatory mechanism, one can produce a straight line (one oscillatory mechanism is set to zero), or an elliptical to a circular trajectory. We can turn our attention to trigonometry to provide additional intuition to this process.

We remember from trigonometry that the unit circle can be described by the following equation: $\sin^2 + \cos^2 = 1$. We also know that the sine and cosine functions are 90° ($\prod/2$ radians) out of phase. A limb can produce a circular trajectory if there is a driving force in the horizontal dimension, and an identical driving force in the lateral dimension but 90° out of phase.

The above discussion assumes that a trajectory can be decomposed into its vector-like components. Rather than a spatiotemporal representation of the trajectory, the trajectory is constructed from elementary units—in this case orthogonal oscillatory processes. How might we provide evidence that is consistent with this idea?

Some authors in this volume would have generated a two-dimensional model to produce a trajectory, then determined how well a human subject fit the data from the model. Work could be conducted to determine the mass-spring coefficients in both dimensions of motion, then determine whether they were equal and the functions were 90° out of phase.

The approach taken here (Kim 1992) was to determine whether there were consistent behavioral consequences to show that trajectories are constructed from basic units (i.e., elements). The tool we used was the robust linear speed-accuracy trade-off. We hypothesized that if a circular movement was comprised from two elementary and orthogonal processes, one process controlling the horizontal motion and the other the lateral motion, then we should be able to distill a speed-accuracy trade-off in each orthogonal direction of motion indistinguishable from a linear motion along the same axis.

Five university subjects performed repetitive movements that were either linear, along the x or the y dimension, or circular. The diameter for the circle-drawing task was 10, 15, and 20 cm, as were the amplitudes of the lines in the x and y dimensions. Goal values of movement time, T, were 250, 275, 300, and 325 ms. T was controlled via a computer-driven metronome. The pacing signal was presented for 20 beats; then the subject attempted to move at the prescribed rate without the metronome for 20 more beats.

To equate the circle-drawing tasks with the line-drawing tasks, the metronome beat in the former specified the time to be at either the y or x target during the circular motion. Thus, there were two types of circle tasks, circle-x and circle-y. The x or y designation specified the location where the subject had to be on the beat.

Subjects performed these tasks by drawing repetitively with a dry china marker (Expo, fine point) over a Plexiglas-covered desk. An infrared light-emitting diode was attached to the pen, and the location of the diode was recorded by a Watsmart system. After standard data-reduction techniques and numerical differentiation, we computed the average distance, average movement time, and their respective within-subject variabilities for each dimension of motion for the circle and for the major dimension of motion of the line. In fig. 1.2 the relation between speed (D/T) and W_e in the x (horizontal dimension) is presented.

As we can see in the figure, there was a strong linear speed-accuracy trade-off for the linear task, as well as for the linear components of both circular tasks.

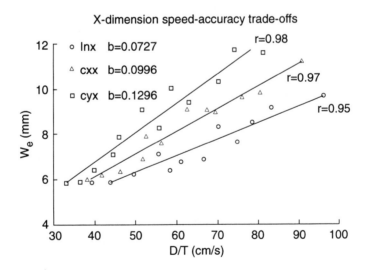

Fig. 1.2   Relationship between average velocity (D/T) and effective target width (W_e) in the x dimension for line movements (lnx), in the x dimension for circles that were to be on time in the x dimension (cxx), and for the x dimension of circles that were to be on time in the y dimension (cyx).

However, as is clear from the figure, the slope of the speed-accuracy relation in each of the circle tasks was greater than the slope for the linear-movement task. In other words, we could not distill the circle into an x-dimension speed-accuracy trade-off that was the same as the speed-accuracy trade-off for the linear movement in the x dimension.

However, in the y dimension the results were much different. As shown in fig. 1.3, there were strong linear speed-accuracy trade-offs in all three conditions. Contrary to the results in the x dimension, the three individual speed-accuracy trade-offs were the same. In other words, we were successful in distilling the y component of the line in terms of a linear speed-accuracy trade-off in that dimension.

One reason we could not distill both the x and y components of the speed-accuracy trade-off of the circle concerns the interactions of forces driving the limb. Our framework assumed that the forces operate on a point mass; however, the limb is not a point. Furthermore, as Hollerbach and Flash (1982) have pointed out, multidegree-of-freedom arm movements have interaction forces from the transfer of momentum and the viscous-elastic properties of muscle. Thus, it is quite possible that although the subject is attempting to produce an x and y oscillation 90° out of phase, the nonlinearity of the muscle-bone system prevents that observation from being made. Heuer (1988) made a similar point when he discussed some reasons relative timing might not be seen as invariant across changes in rate, even if the commands to drive the movement were invariant across rate.

The purpose of the previous description of the Kim experiment was not to delve into possible reasons for the discrepancy between the results within each dimension, but to show how one can use stable robust relations between independent and dependent variables to examine additional issues in motor behavior and control.

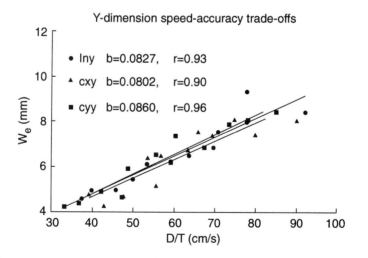

Fig. 1.3   Relationship between average velocity (D/T) and effective target width (W_e) in the y dimension for line movements (lny), in the y dimension for circles that were to be on time in the y dimension (cyy), and for the y dimension of circles that were to be on time in the x dimension (cxy).

SUMMARY AND RECOMMENDATIONS

In this introductory chapter our goal was not to espouse a particular position about motor control. Rather we wanted to demonstrate how we can use some well-known facts about motor behavior (i.e., the relation between speed and accuracy) to question the workings of developmental processes and the nature of the control strategies in circular movements.

The speed-accuracy trade-off work for circular movements, we believe, is particularly enlightening. The linear speed-accuracy trade-off models were born out of a belief in the generalized motor program (Schmidt 1988). Proponents of this construct believe that movements are governed as units (see Young and Schmidt 1990 for limits to this notion). Variability in movement end point is the result of variability in the motor programming processes. The work that we described in this chapter is not compatible with that idea. We set out to examine whether movements are constructed from elements—elements that could be conceptualized as oscillatory processes. Thus, in this work we have borrowed from the two dominant theoretical frameworks for motor control, the motor program and the dynamical pattern perspective, to ask a fundamental question about trajectory control. This approach was only partially successful because we could only decompose the trajectory into the lateral (y) component. We have planned research to decompose joint trajectories responsible for the x and y components of the circle, then to determine whether we can find the corresponding speed-accuracy trade-offs.

We used a similar approach to begin our studies of motor development. The questions were not of specific processes or mechanisms slower or less adept in children, but whether there was a stable relationship between children's performance and adults' performance. In general there was. This approach can be expanded to ask about the course of maturation in children who are developmentally disabled.

In fact Williams, Woollacott, and Ivry (1992) have used this approach to examine whether children who are clumsy exhibit a general deficit in timing. Children identified as clumsy and those considered normal motorically were given a timing-production task and various other tasks. Children who are clumsy appear to have a generalized deficit in central timing processes. In this experiment the concern was whether there was a deficit in a process associated with many motor skills. We believe that approaches such as those described in this chapter can further our understanding of skilled motor performance.

REFERENCES

Crossman, E.R.F., and Goodeve, C. 1963. Feedback control of hand-movement and Fitts' law. *Quarterly Journal of Experimental Psychology* 35A:251-278.

Fitts, P.M. 1954. The information capacity of the human motor system in controlling the amplitude of movement. *Journal of Experimental Psychology* 47:381-391.

Hay, L. 1981. The effect of amplitude and accuracy requirements on movement time in children. *Journal of Motor Behavior* 13:177-186.

Hebb, D.O. 1949. *The organization of behavior: A neurophysiological theory.* New York: Wiley.

Heuer, H. 1988. Testing the invariance of relative timing: Comment on Gentner (1987). *Psychological Review* 95:552-557.

Hollerbach, J.M. 1981. An oscillation theory of handwriting. *Biological Cybernetics* 39:139-156.

Hollerbach, J.M., and Flash, T. 1982. Dynamic interaction between limb segments during planar arm movements. *Biological Cybernetics* 44:67-77.

Jeannerod, M. 1981. Intersegmental coordination during reaching at natural visual objects. P. 153-168 in *Attention and performance IX*, edited by J. Long and A. Baddely. Hillsdale, NJ: Erlbaum.

Jeannerod, M. 1992. Coordination mechanisms in prehension movements. P. 265-286 in *Tutorials in motor behavior II*, edited by G.E. Stelmach and J. Requin. Amsterdam: North-Holland.

Kail, R. 1991. Developmental change in speed of processing during childhood and adolescence. *Psychological Bulletin* 109:490-501.

Keele, S.W. 1968. Movement control in skilled motor performance. *Psychological Bulletin* 70:387-403.

Kerr, R. 1975. Movement control and maturation in elementary-grade children. *Perceptual and Motor Skills* 41:151-154.

Kim, K.N. 1992. Speed-accuracy trade-offs in linear and circular movements. PhD diss., Purdue University, West Lafayette, Indiana.

Klapp, S.T. 1975. Feedback versus motor programming in the control of aimed movements. *Journal of Experimental Psychology: Human Perception and Performance* 1:147-153.

Latash, M.L., and Gottlieb, G.L. 1991. An equilibrium-point model of dynamic regulation for fast single-joint movements: I. Emergence of strategy-dependent EMG patterns. *Journal of Motor Behavior* 23:163-177.

MacKenzie, C.L. 1992. Constraints, phases and sensorimotor processing in prehension. P. 371-400 in *Tutorials in motor behavior II*, edited by G.E. Stelmach and J. Requin. Amsterdam: North-Holland.

McMillan, M.C. 1992. Differences in movement speed between six year old children and adults on three motor tasks. Master's thesis, Purdue University, West Lafayette, Indiana.

Meyer, D.E., Abrams, R.A., Kornblum, S., Wright, C.E., and Smith, J.E.K. 1988. Optimality in human motor performance: Ideal control of rapid aimed movements. *Psychological Review* 95:340-370.

Meyer, D.E., Smith, J.E.K., Kornblum, S., Abrams, R.A., and Wright, C.E. 1990. Speed-accuracy tradeoffs in aimed movements: Toward a theory of rapid voluntary action. P. 173-226 in *Attention and performance XIII*, edited by M. Jeannerod. Hillsdale, NJ: Erlbaum.

Meyer, D.E., Smith, J.E.K., and Wright, C.E. 1982. Models for the speed and accuracy of aimed movements. *Psychological Review* 89:449-482.

Salmoni, A.W., and McIlwain, J.S. 1979. Fitts' reciprocal tapping task, a measure of motor capacity? *Perceptual and Motor Skills* 49:403-413.

Salmoni, A.W., and Pascoe, C. 1978. Fitts' reciprocal tapping task: A developmental study. P. 288-294 in *Psychology of motor behavior and sport*, edited by C.G. Roberts and K.M. Newell. Champaign, IL: Human Kinetics.

Schmidt, R.A. 1975. A schema theory of discrete motor skill learning. *Psychological Review* 82:225-260.

Schmidt, R.A. 1988. *Motor control and learning: A behavioral emphasis.* 2d ed. Champaign, IL: Human Kinetics.

Schmidt, R.A., Zelaznik, H.N., and Frank, J.S. 1978. Sources of inaccuracy in rapid motor acts. P. 323-345 in *Information processing in motor control and learning,* edited by G.E. Stelmach. New York: Academic Press.

Schmidt, R.A., Zelaznik, H.N., Hawkins, B., Frank, J.S., and Quinn, J.T., Jr. 1979. Motor-output variability: A theory for the accuracy of rapid motor acts. *Psychological Review* 86: 415-451.

Smith, J.M. 1968. *Mathematical ideas in biology.* Cambridge, U.K.: Cambridge University Press.

Wallace, S.A. 1981. An impulse-timing theory for reciprocal control of muscular activity in rapid, discrete movements. *Journal of Motor Behavior* 13:144-160.

Wallace, S.A., Newell, K.A., and Wade, M.G. 1978. Decision and response times as a function of movement difficulty in preschool children. *Child Development* 49:509-512.

Wickstrom, R.L. 1983. *Fundamental motor patterns.* 3d ed. Philadelphia: Lea & Febiger.

Williams, H.G., Woollacott, M.H., and Ivry, R. 1992. Timing and motor control in clumsy children. *Journal of Motor Behavior* 24:165-172.

Woodworth, R.S. 1899. The accuracy of voluntary movement. *Psychological Review* 3:1-114.

Wright, C.E., and Meyer, D.E. 1983. Conditions for a linear speed-accuracy trade-off in aimed movements. *Quarterly Journal of Experimental Psychology* 35A:279-296.

Young, D.E., and Schmidt, R.A. 1990. Units of motor behavior: Modifications with practice and feedback. P. 763-795 in *Attention and performance XII: Motor representation and control,* edited by M. Jeannerod. Hillsdale, NJ: Erlbaum.

Zelaznik, H.N. 1993. Necessary and sufficient conditions for the production of linear speed-accuracy trade-offs in aimed hand movements. P. 91-116 in *Variability and motor control,* edited by K.M. Newell and D. Corcos. Champaign, IL: Human Kinetics.

Chapter 2

Reaction Time Analysis of Central Motor Control

Stuart T. Klapp
California State University, Hayward

FOUNDATION CONCEPTS

This section introduces fundamental concepts and their history.

Historical Origins of the Motor Program Concept

We can trace the notion of a motor program to the classical "serial order of behavior" paper of Lashley (1951). A frequently cited aspect of Lashley's analysis is that the time delay in neural transmission between proprioception (and other senses) to the central nervous system, then back to the muscular effectors, is too long to permit feedback (response chaining) during rapid-response sequences. Therefore, these responses must be organized centrally (programmed) before their initiation.

Consistent with this analysis, the most widely quoted definition of a motor program is "a set of muscle commands that [is] structured before a movement sequence begins, and that allows the entire sequence to be carried out uninfluenced by peripheral feedback" (Keele 1968, 387). This definition has two components: prior planning and freedom from reliance on feedback control during execution. (We need not take the term "muscle commands" literally; a program probably is more abstract in representation.) The logical relationship between the two aspects of Keele's definition rests on the term "allows." When an action sequence is planned, the program allows it to be executed without feedback. But a programmed action might also be subject to modification (changes in the program) if unanticipated events occur during its execution. Thus, planning, rather than lack of concurrent control by feedback, may be the more fundamental criterion for motor programming.

Reaction Time Analysis of Response Programming

This review focuses on a reaction time (RT) technique for investigating planning (programming) of motor responses. For a more general review see Keele (1986). The RT approach is based on the assumption that the time required to plan a response depends on some parameters characterizing the response. Because programming is assumed to occur during the RT interval (from imperative signal to response onset), differences in programming time should influence RT.

The RT approach was introduced by Henry and Rogers (1960), who compared the RT before three-movement sequences differing in duration and in complexity. These responses were (a) lifting the finger; (b) lifting the finger, then reaching forward to grasp a ball; and (c) these actions followed by pushing a button, then contacting a second ball. The RT increased as a function of response complexity—longest RT before movement (c) and shortest before movement (a). This was interpreted as showing that longer, or more complex, movements require a more extensive program, which requires more time to establish before movement onset. Replications of some aspects of this experiment have been reported (Christina et al. 1985; Fischman and Lim 1991).

It is important to distinguish this method from other RT paradigms. In particular, the experiments considered here investigate response programming rather than response selection. The concepts of response selection and response programming can be related in a sequential stage model. Selection must be completed first; then the selected response can be programmed. The difficulty of the selection processes is varied by independent variables such as response uncertainty (e.g., the number of possible alternative responses) or stimulus-response compatibility. The imperative signal at the beginning of the RT interval resolves response uncertainty by informing the subject which of the alternative responses is required on that trial. Processing this information influences RT. A considerable literature relates RT and aspects of response selection (e.g., Rosenbaum 1980, 1990). This type of study is not reviewed here; we will consider the experiments in which RT depends on the *value* of some parameter of the response (e.g., its duration or complexity) with the degree of uncertainty concerning this value (and compatibility) held constant. This is because the focus of this review is on response programming rather than on response selection.

An alternative approach to the study of programming involves movement-related brain potentials recorded from surface electrodes (see Coles, Gratton, and Donchin 1988; Miller and Hackley 1992). This approach is not reviewed here; we limit this review to the RT method.

Programming as Retrieval in the Sense of Reconstruction

In the Henry and Rogers (1960) experiment, and in most RT experiments we review here, subjects were performing well-practiced responses. Thus, the relation between RT and the values of response parameters may not represent variation in the time required to *invent* programs for novel action sequences. Instead, RT may depend on the time required to *retrieve* programs from long-term memory (LTM). Differences in retrieval time are not attributed to differences in difficulty of memory search because response uncertainty was held constant in these experiments. However, retrieval time may increase as a function of the complexity or duration of the response because of differences in the time required to reconstruct a response representation from a code in LTM.

Simple and Choice RT Methods

An important distinction concerns the sequence of events when RT is measured as a function of response complexity. In the *simple RT* method, the required response is identified first; then, after a delay, an imperative signal indicates that the response should be produced. Simple RT is measured from the imperative signal until the start of the response. By contrast, the *choice RT* method does not include any informative precue; instead a neutral warning signal may precede the imperative signal. Only the imperative signal informs the subject about which response to make. Choice RT is measured from this signal until the start of the response.

Of course, choice RT is longer than simple RT; our analysis does not rest on this finding. Instead, we consider the interaction involving the method variable (simple versus choice) and response complexity. We consider two cases. In case 1, response complexity influences choice RT more than it influences simple RT. In case 2, response complexity influences simple RT more than choice RT. This contrast in findings has been a major challenge to developing a theory of response programming (Klapp 1995).

CASE 1: RESPONSE COMPLEXITY INFLUENCES CHOICE RT MORE THAN SIMPLE RT

In the simple RT method, the required response is precued before the measured RT interval. Therefore, programming might be completed before RT starts, so simple RT would not depend on the response complexity. By contrast, for choice RT this advance programming (preprogramming) is not possible because the required response is not identified until the RT interval begins. Because programming must occur during RT, choice RT should depend on the complexity of the response (if more complex responses take longer to program). These considerations lead to the prediction of the case 1 pattern in which choice RT depends on response complexity and simple RT does not.

Preprogramming in simple RT requires a buffer memory when, as often occurs in these experiments, the time that the response is to be produced is unpredictable. After preprogramming is completed, the programmed (retrieved) representation may be retained in a buffer until the imperative signal occurs and the response is initiated. This buffer may correspond in some ways to short-term memory (Klapp 1976).

Programming Speech Articulation

An early study from our laboratory (Klapp, Anderson, and Berrian 1973) illustrates the case 1 data pattern, thereby supporting the claims that (1) programming is an aspect of retrieval from LTM, (2) preprogramming can occur under some circumstances, and (3) the retrieved program is retained in a buffer. The subjects pronounced (articulated) words. These were one-syllable and two-syllable words with the number of letters and frequency of occurrence matched across syllable conditions. As is apparent in table 2.1, when a word was presented visually as the imperative signal, choice RT (from presentation of the word to initial speech sound) was longer before two-syllable than before one-syllable words. Similar findings have been reported in other studies (Eriksen, Pollack, and Montague 1970; Jared and Seidenberg 1990). We could interpret this result as showing that it takes longer to program two-syllable

Table 2.1   Reaction Time (RT) and Speech Duration (ms)

Task	Number of syllables		Difference
	1	2	
Choice RT			
Pronounce word based on:			
Lexical stimulus	518	533	15
Pictorial stimulus	619	633	14
Lexical decision			
Animal or object	696	697	1
Simple RT			
Pronounce word	311	313	2
Response duration			
Time to pronounce	495	494	(−1)

than it does one-syllable articulatory responses. Because these were common words, *programming* must refer to retrieval of response programs from LTM, not to development of novel programs.

The data just described is for choice RT; the pattern of data we identify as case 1 also includes simple RT. In the simple RT condition, the word to be pronounced in each trial was identified before the imperative signal from which RT was measured. Simple RT was short and independent of the number of syllables. We interpreted this result as indicating the subjects could preprogram the articulatory response before the beginning of the simple RT interval, then retain the program in buffer storage awaiting the imperative signal.

An alternative to the response programming interpretation of the simple and choice RT results attributes the effect of syllables on choice RT to perceptual processing for recognizing letter strings as words (Eriksen, Pollack, and Montague 1970). Two additional results argue against this word-perception interpretation and support the response programming view (see table 2.1): (1) The effect of syllables on choice RT appeared when the words were presented as pictures rather than as letter strings; word perception could not be a factor in this task, and (2) the choice RT to determine whether a word represented an animal or an object was independent of the number of syllables; if word perception were the origin of the effect of syllables on RT, this effect also should have appeared for the decision task. Thus, we concluded that it takes longer to retrieve the programs to articulate two-syllable than it does one-syllable words.

Klapp and Erwin (1976, Experiment 1) measured the duration of pronunciation of the words used by Klapp, Anderson, and Berrian (1973). The average durations did not differ as a function of the number of syllables for these words (see table 2.1). This suggests that the effects of response complexity (here syllables) on choice RT can occur even for responses that do not differ in average duration. (The similarity of these word durations is attributable to elongation of vowel sounds in the one-syllable words. This tended to expand the duration of these words to equal that of the two-syllable words.)

Klapp (1974) reported a corresponding effect of number of syllables on choice RT, with no effect on simple RT, for pronunciation of three-syllable numbers (e.g., 36, 54) compared to four-syllable numbers (e.g., 37, 57). This effect on choice RT cannot be attributed to recognition of words presented as letters, because digits were used as stimuli. This experiment permitted balancing the initial sound (e.g., 30, 50) across syllable conditions. However, there was a necessary confounding with the digit "7," which appeared in all four-syllable numbers (e.g., 37), but in no three-syllable numbers (e.g., 36). This was necessary because 7 is the only two-syllable digit.

Programming Press Durations (Dit-Dah)

The next example of the case 1 data pattern involves responses that are simpler than speech articulation. The subject merely pressed a switch, holding it down for either a short or a long duration. This may be thought of as generating a Morse code dit or dah. We caused a tone to sound while the switch was held down, and we sometimes used a telegraph key as the response device. Whereas the speech articulation data may involve manipulation of response complexity (number of syllables) but not duration, the dit-dah key-press task appears to manipulate duration but not complexity. Nevertheless, we obtained a similar pattern of results (Klapp, Wyatt, and Lingo 1974). For choice RT the subject was not informed until the imperative stimulus at the beginning of the RT interval whether to make a short or a long press; here RT was longer before the longer response. By contrast, for simple RT the subject was informed in advance which response to make so preprogramming could be possible; here RT did not differ between the two responses (see table 2.2).

Because only two responses (dit and dah) were involved and tested repetitively, we concluded that programming must be retrieval from memory rather than invention of novel response sequences. The lack of effect of duration on simple RT suggests that preprogramming is possible. However, preprogramming is assumed to be impossible for choice RT; even though there were only two responses, these cannot both be preprogrammed. This interpretation implies a severe limit on preprogramming or on the buffer memory for program storage.

Aspects of these findings have been replicated (Carlton, Carlton, and Newell 1987; Klapp 1977b; Klapp 1995; Klapp, McRae, and Long 1978; Klapp and

Table 2.2   RT (ms) as a Function of Response Duration

Procedure	Response duration		Difference
	Short	Long	
Choice RT	358	382	24
Simple RT	246	245	(−1)

Rodriguez 1982; Klapp and Wyatt 1976; Spijkers and Steyvers 1984; Vidal, Bonnet, and Macar 1991; Zelaznik, Shapiro, and Carter 1982). However, this dit-dah effect is not entirely robust; failures to replicate have also been reported (Kerr 1979). One identified problem concerns how response duration feedback is provided to the subject (Klapp and Greim 1981). If this feedback causes one response to be perceived as having a stricter accuracy requirement (i.e., a tighter tolerance), speed-accuracy trade-off effects may contaminate the results. In particular, if the shorter response is perceived as having a tighter tolerance, its RT may become longer because of the accuracy demand. Then the RT for dit may become the same as, or longer than, the RT for dah.

Another potential difficulty is that subjects may guess which stimulus, signaling dit (short) or dah (long), will appear in the choice RT condition. The more frequently guessed alternative would have a shorter RT. This could enhance a weak (or non-existent) programming effect (if dit were the more frequent guess), or it could bias against detecting a real programming effect (if dah were the more frequent guess). This guessing interpretation also handles the lack of a response duration effect on simple RT; subjects would not need to guess because they would have been informed which response will be required. We next consider two ways to evaluate guessing.

Klapp and Rodriguez (1982) developed a dit-dah paradigm that prevents biased guessing. Subjects responded by moving a handle left or right, making a 150-ms (dit) response in one direction or a 300-ms (dah) in the other direction. In any block of trials, one direction was designated high probability; the stimulus for this response occurred on 80% of the trials. Subjects were instructed to anticipate and plan for (preprogram) the high probability response; this corresponded to simple RT in the previous analysis. The unanticipated direction corresponded to choice RT in that preprogramming would not occur. For each subject, blocks of trials alternated the assignment of dit and dah to probability and direction conditions, so each subject was tested with high probability dit and dah, and with low probability dit and dah. (Subjects require considerable training before they master these contingencies.) The results support the validity of the previous findings (see table 2.3). For anticipated responses, RT did not depend on duration; this corresponds to simple RT for which preprogramming is possible. For unanticipated responses, RT did depend on duration; this corresponds to choice RT for which preprogramming is not possible. (A recent attempt to replicate this experiment in our laboratory was not successful; there were no significant differences in RT as a function of duration for either high or low probability responses. Whereas the high probability RT values showed minimal

Table 2.3   RT (ms) as a Function of Response Duration and Probability

| Probability | Duration | | Difference |
	Short	Long	
Low	408	446	38
High	254	257	3

variability, the low probability RTs were quite variable, both within subject and between subjects for each of the long and short responses.)

A simpler way to handle the possible guessing artifact for the press-duration (dit-dah) task is to use more than two durations. Klapp, McRae, and Long (1978) reported that choice RT increased systematically as a function of duration for short (150-ms), medium (300-ms), and long (600-ms) presses. It is difficult to interpret this result in terms of guessing; to do so would require that the probability of guessing that each alternative would appear must also vary systematically with duration. A similar approach involves using four alternatives in choice RT, only two of which are single dit and dah responses (Klapp 1995).

Programming for Target Aiming

A well-known example of speed-accuracy trade-off is the classical Fitts' Law target-aiming task (Fitts and Peterson 1964). Although movement duration is the usual dependent variable in Fitts' Law studies, we have also examined RT (Klapp 1975). For movements of short distance, choice RT increased as the targets became smaller, thereby increasing the required accuracy (see table 2.4). This accuracy effect on choice RT was not reflected in simple RT, indicating that preprogramming is possible (Klapp and Greim 1979). However, there is a report suggesting that accuracy can influence simple RT (Sidaway 1991).

Unfortunately it was not clear which underlying response parameter produced the increase in choice RT. Perhaps accuracy itself influenced RT, or perhaps accuracy influenced other parameters that in turn influenced RT. More accurate movements also (1) require more gestures (as in the speech data), (2) take longer to complete (as in the key-press data), and (3) proceed at a slower velocity (Falkenberg and Newell 1980). All three are confounded with accuracy in the Klapp (1975) study. A subsequent series of experiments reported that target size did not influence choice RT when duration was controlled, but duration influenced choice RT when target size was controlled (Quinn et al. 1980). Thus, in my study, target size may have affected choice RT indirectly through its effect on duration or velocity.

Programming Within a Sequence

We conclude that case 1 data fit a theory in which the programming time increases with the duration or complexity of the response; this produces a corresponding

Table 2.4   RT (ms) as a Function of Movement Length and Target Diameter

	Movement length	
Target diameter	2 mm	336 mm
Small (2 and 4 mm)	374	327
Medium (8 and 16 mm)	327	329
Large (32 and 64 mm)	304	323

increase in choice RT. However, there must be a limit to the applicability of this theory. If it applied for very long response sequences, the theory would predict an absurdly long choice RT before initiation of extended actions, such as everyday tasks. We can handle this problem by assuming that a long response consists of a sequence of individually programmed chunks, only the first of which is programmed during RT. Programming for later chunks occurs parallel to execution of earlier chunks or during pauses between response chunks.

To illustrate, consider an additional aspect of our target-aiming study (Klapp 1975). The accuracy effect on choice RT was moderated by the distance moved from start to target contact. Whereas choice RT increased with accuracy for short-distance movements, it was independent of accuracy for longer movements (see table 2.4). This suggests that the longer movements consisted of chunks, only the first of which was programmed during the RT interval. The action involved in executing the first chunk may be independent of target size because this segment of the response did not include target contact; thus, RT for these long-distance movements was independent of accuracy. However, segmentation was not involved for short-distance movements; the initially programmed response segment included target contact, so target size influenced programming time and therefore choice RT.

If long-distance movements consist of a sequence of individually programmed chunks (as we assume in this analysis), then it is reasonable to suppose that feedback from the earlier movement chunk guides programming of the next chunk. Thus, long-distance movements, but not short-distance (single-segment) movements, should be dependent on feedback. Consistent with this assumption, elimination of visual feedback was much more disruptive for movements over longer distances (Klapp 1975, Experiment 2).

This analysis of the longer movements is consistent with the classical interpretation of Fitts' Law (Crossman and Goodeve 1963), which relates movement duration to accuracy. According to this interpretation, target-aiming responses consist of a series of successive segments, only the first of which is programmed before movement initiation. Subsequent segments are programmed on the basis of feedback during the movement. Fitts' Law can be derived from this assumption (Keele 1968). Movement durations in the Klapp (1975) study corresponded to Fitts' Law for long-distance movements, for which the segmentation assumption seems to apply. But Fitts' Law did not hold for short-distance movements, which may fail to meet the assumption of segmentation. Although supported by these findings, the Crossman and Goodeve interpretation may not account for the mathematical relation of Fitts' Law in detail (Jagacinski et al. 1980; Meyer et al. 1988).

The notion that longer response sequences are not entirely programmed before their initiation can be applied also to the press-duration (dit-dah) task. As expected, the relation between response duration and choice RT is eliminated for very long durations (Carlton, Carlton, and Newell 1987; Ivry 1986). A second application of this notion is that, for sequences of two presses, programming only the first press duration would be expected during the initial RT, with programming for the second press deferred until later. This also appears to be the case. For practiced subjects, the duration of the second press in a two-press sequence influenced the duration of the inter-response interval, but not the initial RT. However, the duration of the first press of the sequence did influence choice RT (Klapp and Wyatt 1976).

As a final example of distributed programming for longer responses, consider a task in which subjects produced sequences of successive taps, with one tap stressed by pressing harder. As the temporal position of the stressed tap was delayed, the RT decreased. This is as expected if subjects could initiate the longer sequence without programming a late-occurring stress (Garcia-Colera and Semjen 1988; Semjen and Garcia-Colera 1986).

A THEORY FOR CASE 1

We conclude that some type of programming process causes choice RT to be longer before more complex responses. However, simple RT is independent of response complexity because programming can be completed before the simple RT interval. This section reviews attempts to understand the programming function in more detail. We begin with an appealing possibility that fails to fit the data.

Are the Responding Muscles Referenced in Buffer Storage?

The notion of preprogramming (for simple RT) assumes that the program can be stored in a buffer memory until the imperative signal occurs at the beginning of the RT interval. We now consider how codes used to represent responses may differ between long-term memory (LTM) and buffer storage. In particular, a programming function may transform from an abstract code in LTM to a representation of specific muscular actions in the buffer.

There is considerable evidence suggesting that the representations of action sequences in LTM are not referenced to particular muscles. For example, one's handwritten signature is similar in overall shape, although differing in details, whether executed with finger muscles to make a small signature or with arm muscles to write on a blackboard (Merton 1972; Wright 1990). This suggests that the underlying learning is not limited to the more frequently used effectors (fingers). This conclusion is not restricted to long-established responses; recently acquired responses also transfer between finger and arm muscles (Cohen, Ivry, and Keele 1990). Even classically conditioned withdrawal of a finger transfers across reversal of the roles of muscles as agonist and antagonist (Wickens 1939).

One function of programming might be transformation from a code in LTM that represents goals, but not muscles, into a different code (in buffer storage) that does refer to muscles. In that way, one LTM code could contain the information for many distinct muscular actions, as in the example of the code for a signature, which can be used for finger responses or for arm responses. This notion could explain why programming is needed and what it accomplishes; programming particularizes the code for the muscles that are to execute the response on each occasion.

However attractive this view might seem, evidence from the RT method does not support it. One way this notion has been tested is in a binary choice RT paradigm, which varies the way the two responses differ from each other. Whereas RT increased as a function of whether the two responses differed or did not differ in timing and in form, it was independent of whether they differed in the muscle involved (Heuer 1984). This suggests that requiring a choice between muscles failed to complicate the programming process, as would be expected if muscles were specified during programming.

Another prediction of the view that muscles are specified during programming is that preprogramming would be possible only if both the response and the responding muscle had been identified. But, for key-press responses, preprogramming appears to occur (simple RT identical for dit and dah) even when only duration, and not responding muscle, is precued (Klapp 1977b; Spijkers and Steyvers 1984; Vidal, Bonnet, and Macar 1991; Zelaznik, Shapiro, and Carter 1982). We conclude that, for many responses, either buffer storage does not include a representation of muscles, or multiple programs can be stored in the buffer—one for each possible responding muscle—provided the responses are the same duration. It might be possible to distinguish these possibilities by requiring infrequent use of an unexpected muscle to execute a precued and expected duration. If duration only is stored in the buffer, then RT should be independent of duration for both expected and unexpected muscles. If multiple muscle-specific programs are stored, then requiring an unexpected muscle would necessitate programming for that muscle. Hence, the effect of response duration on RT for the unexpected muscle (but expected duration) should be restored to equal that observed when duration is not precued.

Conveyer Belt Analogy

If programming of motor responses does not generate commands for muscles, then what does it do? An analogy that may suggest a function for programming is that response sequences are controlled by a conveyer belt (a.k.a. the "memory drum" of Henry and Rogers 1960) moving at constant speed. This conveyer belt transports triggers that determine the time and order of the gestures in the response. Programming can be viewed as setting up the triggers, based on a compactly coded representation in LTM. As the number of gestures increases, more triggers are required and more time is required for programming. As the duration increases, the triggers must be spaced over more of the conveyer belt, also requiring more programming time. The conveyer belt with its triggers represents the buffer storage of a programmed (or preprogrammed) action. This notion fits the conclusion that the buffer storage does not represent specific muscles, because these triggers are associated only with the times that gestures are to occur.

The conveyer belt analogy also provides a way to think about the problem of generating complex responses involving more than one muscle. Consider the task of tapping a polyrhythm (e.g., the two-against-three pattern that frequently occurs in music). This can be quite difficult when viewed as independent generation of three taps with one hand and two taps with the other hand (Deutsch 1983; Klapp 1979; Peters 1981). However, if the two tapping responses are perceptually organized as one rhythmic sequence to be executed by two hands, the action becomes facilitated (Klapp et al. 1985). This may explain how musicians can produce polyrhythms (Jagacinski et al. 1988). In the conveyer belt analogy, the system can have only one belt. If the polyrhythm task is conceived as two independent rhythms, the need for two independently timed belts is implied and the task is not possible. This difficulty is overcome when the task is restructured as one response sequence involving triggers for both hands on the same conveyer belt.

Neural Implementation

Presumably any neural implementation of a "conveyer belt" would involve a nonmoving mechanism for introducing timed delays. One possibility, based on a computer analogy, would be counting clock pulses; responses are triggered at particular counts. The response program would be a table of clock pulse counts associated with response gestures. However, this does not easily handle the behavioral data on programming. Why would the time required to program (i.e., to generate a table of trigger count numbers) be longer for longer responses of an unchanged number of gestures (as suggested by the RT results of the dit-dah experiments)? Why couldn't the LTM code and the buffer storage code be the same table, thereby eliminating the need for programming responses that were previously learned (such as articulation of common words)?

Earlier we (Klapp 1977a; Klapp and Erwin 1976) proposed a neural network implementation for a response program that is consistent with the behavioral data and that corresponds functionally to the conveyer belt analogy. In this view, transmission along a long neural pathway provides timing delays, and nodes along the pathway act as the trigger points for initiation of response gestures. Because these circuits would commit a considerable amount of neural tissue, it is not economical to retain a large population of responses in a programmed state. In fact, we assume that only one such circuit can be activated at any time. Thus, it is not possible to preprogram two responses that differ in temporal patterning, even if both are simple. In particular, it is not possible to preprogram both a dit and a dah button press. However, this does not limit the number of nodes that may be present on a single pathway. Therefore, complex actions, such as speech articulation or a polyrhythm structured as a single response involving two hands, can be preprogrammed when the response elements are represented in a unitary temporal framework.

In this view, retrieval involves not only selection and search for the code in LTM but also construction of the neural circuits, including the trigger nodes, from the blueprint compactly represented in LTM. The relation between choice RT and response duration or complexity is attributed to the second, construction aspect of retrieval. Increasing the response duration increases the time required for retrieval (programming) because of the additional time needed to activate longer neural circuits with longer delay. Hence, RT is longer for the long (dah) press than for the short (dit) press even though the number of gestures is constant. Adding more gestures also complicates activation of neural circuits because more trigger nodes are needed. Thus RT is longer for more complex responses even if duration is constant, as in the speech articulation data.

Recent evidence suggests that timing networks, not unlike those just described, are implemented in the cerebellum (Ivry and Keele 1989; Keele and Ivry 1991). Injury to the cerebellum reduces performance in generation of timed motor action and in perception of durations, but performance in control tasks, such as force production and intensity perception, is relatively unaffected. The notion that circuits in the cerebellum compute timing for both action and perception may encourage the view that these circuits correspond to those we propose for buffer storage of preprogrammed responses. These are abstract in that they represent timing for both perception and action, rather than commands to effector muscles. Thus, a motor program may be a dynamic sensory-motor imagelike template for the response (Greenwald 1970; Klapp, Porter-Graham, and Hoifjeld 1991). This template can be compared with sensory events to permit time perception, and it can be used to generate a timed action.

It is important to note that this theory cannot be the entire story; after programming in this sense is completed, commands to muscles remain to be generated. Although this is a theory of motor response programming, it tells us nothing about muscles.

METHODOLOGY

Methodological issues are described as they apply to the case 1 pattern of results.

Motivation to Preprogram

When the required response has been precued, subjects are assumed to preprogram before the imperative signal, so simple RT is independent of response duration and complexity. However, preprogramming is optional; the unmotivated subject might wait until after the imperative signal has occurred, then program the response just before its initiation. Because programming would then be done during the RT interval, simple RT would depend on response duration and complexity. Support for the prediction that motivation level to preprogram should interact with the response duration for simple RT was demonstrated in the dit-dah paradigm (Klapp, Wyatt, and Lingo 1974). For unmotivated subjects, simple RT varied between dit and dah; when subjects were motivated to attend to the precue and shorten RT, this effect was eliminated. Also, the use of a preprogramming strategy may develop as the result of practice (Jagacinski, Shulman, and Burke 1980). Therefore, failure to employ a preprogramming strategy is a possible interpretation of reports in which simple RT depends on response complexity or duration (see also Klapp 1977a).

In the simple RT paradigm, the subject is informed in advance which response is required. This is also true of the Go versus No Go (Donders C) paradigm in which the final stimulus indicates whether to produce or withold a precued response. Many simple RT studies reviewed here are similar to Go versus No Go in that they included a low proportion of "catch" trials in which no stimulus for responding occurred (e.g., Sternberg et al. 1978). Baba and Marteniuk (1983, 326) assume that this "minimizes the possibility of subjects preprogramming the movement." Preprogramming is possible because the response has been precued. However, as the proportion of No Go or of catch trials is increased, the motivation to preprogram may be reduced. In this way the Go versus No Go paradigm might approach the effectiveness of choice RT in reducing preprogramming. Nevertheless, I prefer to use less ambiguous paradigms—choice RT to prevent preprogramming and simple

RT with no catch trials to encourage preprogramming. To discourage anticipatory responses in simple RT, one can use a randomly varied foreperiod duration rather than catch trials; even further reduction in anticipations could be achieved if the random-duration foreperiod was nonaging.

Simple RT as a Control

Simple RT can be regarded as a control to assess the influence of potential artifacts on RT (Klapp 1977a). For example, consider the case of RT before speech onset as a function of the number of syllables (Klapp, Anderson, and Berrian 1973). Because the initial vocalization sound was not constant as a function of the number of syllables, differential sensitivity of the voice detection apparatus to differing sounds might account for the observed differences in choice RT. But the simple RT condition served as a control. Because simple RT was independent of syllables, we know that this potential bias was not present and could not be the source of the effect of syllables on choice RT (Eriksen, Pollack, and Montague 1970; Klapp, Anderson, and Berrian 1973).

The simple RT control is also important for the press-duration (dit-dah) experiments. There may be a fundamental incompatibility between responding quickly (minimizing RT) and producing the longer duration, as has been suggested within a different context (Newell et al. 1979, 53). This lack of speed compatibility would occur for both simple and choice RT. That the effect of dit-dah (duration) on RT appeared only for choice RT argues against this explanation.

These examples illustrate how simple RT can be used as a control for artifacts that can be confused with effects predicted by any version of central programming theory. These artifacts will occur in both simple and choice RT. Therefore, if an effect appears only for choice RT, it cannot be attributable to this type of artifact.

Fractionated RT

In the fractionated RT technique, overall RT is divided into two components—time from the stimulus to the start of electromyographic (EMG) activity (premotor time) and time from EMG onset to movement onset. The first of these intervals is considered to be of central origin, the latter of peripheral origin. Anson (1989) applied this technique to demonstrate peripheral artifacts in simple RT. Simple RT increased as a function of the moment of inertia of the apparatus. However, there was no effect of inertia on the (premotor) latency before the initial EMG activity. This indicates that the differences in simple RT can reflect peripheral recruitment of force needed to overcome inertia, rather than central programming (see Sidaway 1988 for a similar analysis). Earlier Anson (1982) had applied the fractionated RT method to a portion of the original Henry and Rogers (1960) experiment, concluding that at least part of the simple RT effects reported could be due to peripheral factors. However, Christina and Rose (1985) used evidence based on this technique to conclude that other contrasts in that classical experiment are attributable to central processing.

As another example of the usefulness of the fractionated RT technique in distinguishing central from peripheral factors, consider the study of the effect of "response dynamics" on RT. Carlton, Carlton, and Newell (1987, Experiment 3) reported shorter simple RT for responses requiring a faster increase of force rate. But this effect was not reflected in the premotor time before initial EMG (353-354); rather the major increase was in the fraction of RT between initial EMG and response onset. Clearly, as the authors note (357), this result suggests a peripheral rather than central interpretation. It is also interesting that, whereas rate of force production influenced simple RT, force intensity itself often has no effect on either simple or choice RT (see also Ivry 1986).

CASE 2: RESPONSE COMPLEXITY INFLUENCES SIMPLE RT MORE THAN CHOICE RT

Whereas the examples of case 1 indicate that response complexity influences choice RT more than it influences simple RT, the examples of case 2 show that response complexity influences simple RT more than choice RT. Whereas both case 1 and case 2 display an interaction of response complexity by procedure (simple RT versus choice RT), the interaction of case 2 is opposite that of case 1. This contrast represents an empirical challenge—under what conditions will each case appear? Case 2 is also a challenge for interpretation. Why would complexity influence simple RT, for which the response is precued (and preprogramming is at least logically possible), but not choice RT, for which response programming must be deferred to occur during RT? Thus, case 2 seems counterintuitive. Note that choice RT can be viewed as a control in case 2, analogous to the role of simple RT as a control in case 1 (see methodology section earlier in this chapter). Thus, artifacts involving apparatus activation, and so forth, cannot be the cause of the case 2 results because these artifacts would also influence choice RT.

Examples of Case 2

A particularly clear example of case 2 was reported by Allan Netick and his students at California State University, Hayward. Subjects pressed a key on the computer one, two, or three times under simple RT or choice RT procedures. As indicated in fig. 2.1, simple RT increased systematically as a function of the number of presses, but choice RT was independent of presses. Several other experiments display the case 2 data pattern (Garcia-Colera and Semjen 1987; Klapp 1995; Klapp et al. 1979).

Jagacinski, Shulman, and Burke (1980) compared choice and simple RT for a single-key press and two presses with different fingers of the same hand. A feedback signal encouraged subjects to produce an inter-tap interval of 250 ms. The result had aspects of both case 1 and case 2. Performance in simple RT was observed as a function of practice. Early in practice, simple RT was longer before the two-press response; this difference vanished late in practice. (The role of practice is discussed later.) Choice RT, observed only early in practice, was longer

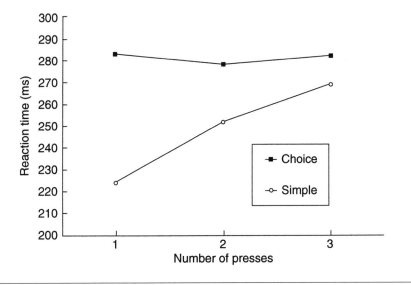

Fig. 2.1   This is an example of the case 2 pattern of results.

before the two-press response; this might be attributed to the stringent limits on the delay between taps.

Other Reports Consistent With Case 2

There are many studies using only simple RT for which RT increased with response complexity. These include the original report of Henry and Rogers (1960). These findings, of course, are consistent with case 2 and contrast with case 1 for which simple RT is independent of response complexity. One study (Fischman 1984) measured the time before EMG activation (the premotor time) in a simple RT paradigm. Because this measure increased with response complexity, we can assume that the effect is of central origin (see earlier discussion of this methodological point). Examples in which simple RT depended on the number of key presses were reported by Canic and Franks (1989) and by Franks and Van Donkelaar (1990).

Perhaps the best-known demonstrations of robust effects of response complexity on simple RT are those reported by Sternberg et al. (1978) for speech and typing sequences; see Sternberg, Knoll, and Turock (1990) for related work. In one example of this research, subjects were given a sequence of words in advance. At the start signal, they were to speak the words rapidly. One feature of the resulting data is that simple RT increased linearly as a function of the number of words, with a slope of about 10 ms per word. If this effect represents response programming, why didn't the subjects preprogram before the start signal? The problem of lack of motivation, discussed in the methodology section, is not a likely explanation even though there was a low rate of catch trials. The instructions and feedback used would seem to ensure that these subjects were highly motivated to minimize RT, and the short overall RT indicates that this was the case.

WHAT DETERMINES
WHETHER CASE 1 OR CASE 2 APPLIES

Comparison of the examples for case 1 and case 2 suggests a way to determine when each case applies. If a complex response is represented as a string of chunks, the following empirical principle indicates the circumstances leading to each case: *Choice RT depends on the complexity of a single chunk; this has little or no influence on simple RT (case 1). Simple RT depends on the number of chunks; this has little or no influence on choice RT (case 2).*

For example, consider RT before speech articulation. Each word can be regarded as a chunk. Experiments for which choice RT (but not simple RT) depended on complexity manipulated the number of syllables for a single word (Klapp, Anderson, and Berrian 1973), but the experiments for which simple RT depended on complexity manipulated the number of words to be articulated in sequence (e.g., Sternberg et al. 1978).

Recently, I extended this principle to apply to strings of dit or dah presses, and thereby obtained both case 1 and case 2 results using a common procedure (Klapp 1995). Comparing single dit and dah responses (i.e., varying the complexity of a single chunk) produced case 1 results. Choice RT depended on complexity (longer RT before dah), but simple RT was relatively independent of complexity. However, when the number of chunks (either dits or dahs) in the sequence was varied, simple RT depended on the number of response chunks more than choice RT—the case 2 pattern.

Performance was observed as a function of practice (8 one-hour sessions on different days). The pattern of results just described appeared on day 1; this gradually shifted to a different pattern with practice. Specifically, by day 8, simple RT became independent of the number of dits and dahs in the sequence, but choice RT was significantly longer before the longer strings. How can we account for the effect of practice? My subjects (all advanced psychology majors) claimed that, after practice, a string of elements (e.g., dit-dah-dah-dit) becomes integrated into a single unit (chunk). In this view, the sequence of four dits and dahs is four chunks early in practice, and only one chunk late in practice. This introspection (modestly supported by additional analyses in this report) suggests a way to accommodate the results found both early and late in practice to the previous descriptive principle. Early in practice, when the four-element sequences are each represented as four chunks, simple RT was longer before the four-element sequences. Late in practice, the four-element responses become represented as one chunk; then simple RT no longer depends on the number of elements in the sequence. All responses are now represented as one chunk, and simple RT is assumed to depend on the number of chunks. By contrast, choice RT depended on the number of elements (one vs. four) at high levels of practice. This may be because each of the four-element responses (e.g., dit-dah-dah-dit) becomes represented as one complex chunk after practice. Choice RT is assumed to depend on the complexity of a single chunk.

This analysis of the role of practice is based on the assumption that subjects may encode a response in fewer but longer chunks after practice. This assumption was tested for pen movements through a maze (VanMier, Hulstijn, and Petersen 1993).

A chunk was defined as a movement episode free of halts or errors at choice points in the maze. These chunks lengthened with practice. If simple RT depends on the number of chunks, this observation could explain why the relation between simple RT and response complexity in writing and drawing is reduced with practice (Hulstijn and Van Galen 1983; VanMier and Hulstijn 1993). Finally consider the paradox that, whereas repeating articulation of the same number produced increasing simple RT as a function of the number of repetitions, counting from 1 to a particular number produced a much smaller relation between simple RT and the number of items spoken (Klapp et al. 1979). These results correspond to the earlier principle if we assume that a sequence of ordered numbers (e.g., 1 2 3) tends to be represented as one chunk because of extensive practice, but repetition (e.g., 1, 1, 1) is represented as a string of chunks.

THEORETICAL INTERPRETATION FOR CONTRASTING CASES

Two ways to interpret the empirical principle distinguishing cases 1 and 2 are now considered. I argue that one approach, previously proposed for the simple RT aspect of case 2, is not adequate. A viable alternative is proposed.

Why Might Preprogramming Fail to Occur?

The unsuccessful approach to handling the difference between case 1 and case 2 focuses on simple RT and asks why preprogramming may fail to occur (leading to an effect of complexity on simple RT). Two examples of this approach follow:

1. Perhaps responding follows automatically after programming (preprogramming) is completed. Thus, the subject is obligated not to complete preprogramming before the imperative signal because to do so might lead to responding on catch trials, or to responding prematurely. One prediction of this view is that the complexity effects on simple RT should vanish when uncertainty regarding the start signal is removed. However, when catch trials were eliminated and the interval from warning signal to start signal was held constant, the relation between the number of finger taps and simple RT remained (Canic and Franks 1989). Using a stop-action paradigm, Osman, Kornblum, and Meyer (1990) found that changes in response complexity affect processes before the "point of no return" and suggest that "motor programming does not necessitate response execution" (183).

2. Perhaps preprogrammed responses are retained in a buffer storage of limited capacity. Short responses (for example, single words and dit-dah presses) can be stored in the buffer, but longer responses exceed the capacity of the buffer and cannot be stored. Thus, preprogramming is possible for brief responses but not for longer responses. One problem with this view is that, if preprogramming can occur for short responses, the slope of the relation between simple RT and response complexity should be shallow or zero for comparisons between short responses (e.g., one versus two words) and larger for comparisons between longer responses

(e.g., four versus five words). This is generally not found; see for example, fig. 2.1, Canic and Franks (1989), Klapp et al. (1979), and Sternberg et al. (1978).

An overriding problem with both proposals (and with any attempt to understand the differences between case 1 and case 2 in terms of failure to preprogram) is that choice RT is relatively independent of the complexity variable that influences simple RT in case 2. Even if the assumption of failure to preprogram could handle the result that simple RT depends on response complexity, it cannot handle the finding that choice RT fails to depend on complexity. By itself, this approach would be useful only to account for findings in which both simple and choice RT depend on complexity.

Two-Process Interpretation

Elsewhere (Klapp 1995) I have considered several alternative models that might encompass case 1 and case 2; here I present the model I consider most promising. This assumes two processes that might be identified with response programming. Both must be completed before initiation of a response. One process (INT) programs the internal features of a chunk. The time to complete INT depends on the complexity (number of internal gestures or duration) of the chunk. The other process (SEQ) sequences chunks into the proper order. The time to complete SEQ depends on the number of chunks. The other assumptions of this model are:

- INT can be done before simple RT (i.e., preprogramming of INT is possible),
- SEQ must be completed during RT just before the release of the response (i.e., preprogramming of SEQ is not possible),
- INT and SEQ can occur in parallel, and
- INT takes longer to complete than SEQ.

The model accounts for case 1 findings directly. The time to complete process SEQ is constant because only one chunk is involved; we can ignore SEQ. Because INT can be preprogrammed, simple RT is independent of chunk complexity. However, preprogramming is not possible in choice RT; this depends on the time to complete INT. Thus, choice RT depends on chunk complexity. A theory of process INT was described in the section on case 1.

The account for case 2 is more elaborate. Both INT and SEQ must occur during choice RT; these occur in parallel and a "race" model applies. Because INT is slower, SEQ is completed first and any effect of number of chunks on the duration of SEQ will not appear as an increase in choice RT. Therefore, choice RT does not depend on the number of chunks even though process SEQ occurs during choice RT. This race model does not apply for simple RT because INT occurred earlier rather than parallel to SEQ. Thus, simple RT does depend on the time needed to complete SEQ.

Process SEQ relates to ordering of chunks; this cannot be completed before the simple RT interval. The interpretation proposed by Sternberg et al. (1978) assumes that the entire response sequence is retrieved from LTM and loaded into a buffer before the imperative signal. (This might correspond to preprogramming in some ways.) However, before the response can begin, the buffer must be searched (serial exhaustive search) to position a pointer at the starting chunk just before initiation of the response. Search time, and therefore simple RT, increases as a function of the number of chunks in the buffer. This interpretation cannot be accommodated with the parallel model considered here because process INT could not start until the first chunk was located. A way to modify the Sternberg theory to permit parallel processing is suggested by the result that the inter-response intervals also depend on the number of chunks in the sequence (Sternberg et al. 1978). Perhaps SEQ is related to sequencing only the chunks following the first. Thus, INT could be applied to the first chunk in parallel with applying SEQ to the remaining chunks of the sequence. An alternative to the parallel model (Klapp 1995) can also account for the finding that choice RT is independent of the number of chunks by modifying the Sternberg model so the search need not occur for choice RT.

CONCLUSION

Experiments in which reaction time (RT) was shown to vary as a function of the nature of the response were reviewed. These effects may be attributed to processing required to program a response before it can be initiated. Two patterns of results have been reported: case 1 in which choice RT depends on the complexity of the response with little or no effect on simple RT, and case 2 in which simple RT depends on the complexity of the response with little or no effect on choice RT. These apparently inconsistent results can be reconciled by the principle that the complexity of a single response chunk influences choice RT more than simple RT, but the number of chunks in a response sequence influences simple RT more than choice RT.

Interpretation of case 1 was based on an assumption that the time required to program a response increases as a function of the complexity of a single response chunk (e.g., its duration or the number of gestures it contains). Because programming must occur during choice RT, an increase in time required for programming produces an increase in choice RT. However, the response can be programmed in advance when the response has been precued. Thus, simple RT can become independent of the response parameters that influence choice RT. Interpretation of case 2 is more challenging. In addition to the type of programming responsible for the case 1 pattern, a second type of programming is also postulated; the case 2 pattern can be predicted on the basis of the way these two programming processes combine to determine simple and choice RT.

REFERENCES

Anson, J.G. 1982. Memory Drum Theory: Alternative tests and explanations for the complexity effects on simple reaction time. *Journal of Motor Behavior* 14:228-246.

Anson, J.G. 1989. Effects of moment of inertia on simple reaction time. *Journal of Motor Behavior* 21:60-71.

Baba, D.M., and Marteniuk, R.G. 1983. Timing and torque involvement in the organization of a rapid forearm flexion. *Quarterly Journal of Experimental Psychology* 35A:323-331.

Canic, M.J., and Franks, I.M. 1989. Response preparation and latency in patterns of tapping movements. *Human Movement Science* 8:123-139.

Carlton, L.G., Carlton, M.J., and Newell, K.M. 1987. Reaction time and response dynamics. *Quarterly Journal of Experimental Psychology* 39A:337-360.

Christina, R.W., Fischman, M.G., Lambert, A.L., and Moore, J.F. 1985. Simple reaction time as a function of response complexity: Christina et al. (1982) revisited. *Research Quarterly for Exercise and Sport* 56:316-322.

Christina, R.W., and Rose, D.J. 1985. Premotor and motor reaction time as a function of response complexity. *Research Quarterly for Exercise and Sport* 56:306-315.

Cohen, A., Ivry, R.I., and Keele, S.W. 1990. Attention and structure in sequence learning. *Journal of Experimental Psychology: Learning Memory and Cognition* 16:17-30.

Coles, M.G.H., Gratton, G., and Donchin, E. 1988. Detecting early communication: Using measures of movement-related potentials to illuminate human information processing. *Biological Psychology* 26:69-89.

Crossman, E.R.F.W., and Goodeve, P.J. 1963. Feedback control of hand movements and Fitts' law. *Proceedings of the Experimental Society*, Oxford, England.

Deutsch, D. 1983. The generation of two isochronous sequences in parallel. *Perception & Psychophysics* 34:331-337.

Eriksen, C., Pollack, M., and Montague, W. 1970. Implicit speech: Mechanism in perceptual encoding? *Journal of Experimental Psychology* 84:502-507.

Falkenberg, L.E., and Newell, K.M. 1980. Relative contribution of movement time, amplitude, and velocity to response initiation. *Journal of Experimental Psychology: Human Perception and Performance* 6:760-768.

Fischman, M.G. 1984. Programming time as a function of number of movement parts and changes in movement direction. *Journal of Motor Behavior* 16:405-423.

Fischman, M.G., and Lim, C. 1991. Influence of extended practice on programming time, movement time and transfer in simple target-striking responses. *Journal of Motor Behavior* 23:39-50.

Fitts, P.M., and Peterson, J.R. 1964. Information capacity of discrete motor responses. *Journal of Experimental Psychology* 67:103-112.

Franks, I.M., and Van Donkelaar, P. 1990. The effects of demanding temporal accuracy on the programming of simple tapping sequences. *Acta Psychologica* 74:1-14.

Garcia-Colera, A., and Semjen, A. 1987. The organization of rapid movement sequences as a function of sequence length. *Acta Psychologica* 66:237-250.

Garcia-Colera, A., and Semjen, A. 1988. Distributed planning of movement sequences. *Journal of Motor Behavior* 20:341-367.

Greenwald, A.S. 1970. A choice reaction time test of ideomotor theory. *Journal of Experimental Psychology* 86:20-25.

Henry, F.M., and Rogers, D.E. 1960. Increased response latency for complicated movements and a "memory drum" theory of neuromotor reaction. *Research Quarterly* 31:448-458.

Heuer, H. 1984. Binary choice reaction time as a function of the relationship between durations and forms of responses. *Journal of Motor Behavior* 16:392-404.

Hulstijn, W., and Van Galen, G.P. 1983. Programming in handwriting: Reaction time and movement time as a function of required length. *Acta Psychologica* 54:23-49.

Ivry, R.B. 1986. Force and timing components of the motor program. *Journal of Motor Behavior* 18:449-474.

Ivry, R.B., and Keele, S.W. 1989. Timing functions of the cerebellum. *Journal of Cognitive Neuroscience* 1:136-151.

Jagacinski, R.J., Marshburn, E., Klapp, S.T., and Jones, M.R. 1988. Tests of parallel versus integrated structure in polyrhythmic tapping. *Journal of Motor Behavior* 20:416-442.

Jagacinski, R.J., Repperger, D.W., Ward, S.L., and Moran, M.S. 1980. A test of Fitt's Law with moving targets. *Human Factors* 22:225-233.

Jagacinski, R.J., Shulman, H.G., and Burke, M.W. 1980. Motor programming and alerting. *Journal of Human Movement Studies* 6:151-164.

Jared, D., and Seidenberg, M.S. 1990. Naming multisyllabic words. *Journal of Experimental Psychology: Human Perception and Performance* 16:92-105.

Keele, S.W. 1968. Movement control in skilled motor performance. *Psychological Bulletin* 70:387-403.

Keele, S.W. 1986. Motor control. In *Handbook of perception and human performance, Vol II. Cognitive processes and performance,* edited by K.R. Boll, L. Kaufman, and J.P. Thomas. New York: Wiley.

Keele, S.W., and Ivry, R. 1991. Does the cerebellum provide a common computation for diverse tasks? Vol. 68 in *The development and neural bases of higher cognitive functions,* edited by A. Diamond. Annals of the New York Academy of Sciences.

Kerr, B. 1979. Is reaction time different for long and short response durations in simple and choice conditions? *Journal of Motor Behavior* 11:269-274.

Klapp, S.T. 1974. Syllable dependent pronunciation latencies in number-naming, a replication. *Journal of Experimental Psychology* 102:1138-1140.

Klapp, S.T. 1975. Feedback versus motor programming in the control of aimed movements. *Journal of Experimental Psychology: Human Perception and Performance* 1:147-153.

Klapp, S.T. 1976. Short-term memory as a response preparation state. *Memory & Cognition* 4:721-729.

Klapp, S.T. 1977a. Reaction time analysis of programmed control. In *Exercise and sports sciences reviews,* edited by R. Hutton. Santa Barbara, CA: Journal Publishing Affiliates.

Klapp, S.T. 1977b. Response programming, as assessed by reaction time, does not establish commands for particular muscles. *Journal of Motor Behavior* 9:301-312.

Klapp, S.T. 1979. Doing two things at once: The role of temporal compatibility. *Memory & Cognition* 7:375-381.

Klapp, S.T. 1995. Motor response programming during simple and choice reaction time: The role of practice. *Journal of Experimental Psychology: Human Perception and Performance* 21:1015-1027.

Klapp, S.T., Abbott, J., Coffman, K., Snider, R., and Young, F. 1979. Simple and choice reaction time methods in the study of motor programming. *Journal of Motor Behavior* 11:91-101.

Klapp, S.T., Anderson, W.G., and Berrian, R.W. 1973. Implicit speech in reading, reconsidered. *Journal of Experimental Psychology,* 100:368-374.

Klapp, S.T., and Erwin, C.I. 1976. Relation between programming time and duration of the response being programmed. *Journal of Experimental Psychology: Human Perception and Performance* 2:591-598.

Klapp, S.T., and Greim, D.M. 1979. Programmed control of aimed movements revisited: The role of target visibility and symmetry. *Journal of Experimental Psychology: Human Perception and Performance* 5:509-521.

Klapp, S.T., and Greim, D.M. 1981. Technical considerations regarding the short (dit)-long (dah) key press paradigm. *Journal of Motor Behavior* 13:1-8.

Klapp, S.T., Hill, M.D., Tyler, J.G., Martin, Z.E., Jagacinski, R.J., and Jones, M.R. 1985. On marching to two different drummers: Perceptual aspects of the difficulties. *Journal of Experimental Psychology: Human Perception and Performance* 11:814-827.

Klapp, S.T., McRae, J., and Long, W. 1978. Response programming versus alternative interpretations of the "dit-dah" reaction time effect. *Bulletin of the Psychonomic Society* 11:5-6.

Klapp, S.T., Porter-Graham, K.A., and Hoifjeld, A.R. 1991. The relation of perception and motor action: Ideomotor compatibility and interference in divided attention. *Journal of Motor Behavior* 23:155-162.

Klapp, S.T., and Rodriguez, G. 1982. Programming time as a function of response duration: A replication of "dit-dah" without possible guessing artifacts. *Journal of Motor Behavior* 14:46-56.

Klapp, S.T., and Wyatt, E.P. 1976. Motor programming within a sequence of responses. *Journal of Motor Behavior* 8:19-26.

Klapp, S.T., Wyatt, E.P., and Lingo, W.M. 1974. Response programming in simple and choice reactions. *Journal of Motor Behavior* 6:263-271.

Lashley, K.S. 1951. The problem of serial order in behavior. In *Cerebral mechanisms in behavior: The Hixon Symposium,* edited by L.S. Jeffress. New York: Wiley.

Merton, P.P. 1972. How we control the contraction of our muscles. *Scientific American* 226:30-37.

Meyer, D.E., Abrahms, R.A., Kornblum, S., Wright, C.E., and Smith, J.K. 1988. Optimality in human motor performance: Ideal control of rapid aimed movements. *Psychological Review* 95:310-370.

Miller, J., and Hackley, S.A. 1992. Electrophysiological evidence for temporal overlap among contingent mental processes. *Journal of Experimental Psychology: General* 121:195-209.

Newell, K.M., Hoshizaki, L.E.F., Carlton, M.J., and Halbert, J.A. 1979. Movement time and velocity as determinants of movement timing and accuracy. *Journal of Motor Behavior* 11:49-58.

Osman, A., Kornblum, S., and Meyer, D. 1990. Does motor programming necessitate response execution? *Journal of Experimental Psychology: Human Perception and Performance* 16:183-198.

Peters, M. 1981. Attention asymmetries during concurrent bimanual performance. *Quarterly Journal of Experimental Psychology* 33A:95-103.

Quinn, J.T., Schmidt, R.A., Zelaznik, H.N., Hawkins, B., and McFarquhar, R. 1980. Target-size influences on reaction time with movement time controlled. *Journal of Motor Behavior* 12:239-261.

Rosenbaum, D.A. 1980. Human movement initiation: specification of arm, direction, and extent. *Journal of Experimental Psychology: General* 109:444-474.

Rosenbaum, D.A. 1990. On choosing between movement sequences: Comments on Rose (1988). *Journal of Experimental Psychology: Human Perception and Performance* 16:439-444.

Semjen, A., and Garcia-Colera, A. 1986. Planning and timing of finger-tapping sequences with a stressed element. *Journal of Motor Behavior* 18:287-322.

Sidaway, B. 1988. Fractionated reaction time in lower leg responses: A note on response programming time. *Research Quarterly for Exercise and Sport* 59: 248-251.

Sidaway, B. 1991. Motor programming as a function of constraints of movement initiation. *Journal of Motor Behavior* 23:120-130.

Spijkers, W.A.C., and Steyvers, F. 1984. Specification of direction and duration during programming of discrete sliding movements. *Psychological Research* 46:59-71.

Sternberg, S., Knoll, R.L., and Turock, D.L. 1990. Hierarchical control in the execution of action sequences: Tests of two invariance properties. In *Attention and performance XIII: Motor representation and control*, edited by M. Jeannerod. Hillsdale, NJ: Erlbaum.

Sternberg, S., Monsell, S., Knoll, R.L., and Wright, C.E. 1978. The latency and duration of rapid movement sequences: Comparisons of speech and typewriting. In *Information processing in motor control and learning*, edited by G.E. Stelmach. New York: Academic.

VanMier, H., and Hulstijn, W. 1993. The effects of motor complexity and practice on initiation time in writing and drawing. *Acta Psychologica* 84:231-251.

VanMier, H., Hulstijn, W., and Petersen, S. 1993. Changes in motor planning during the acquisition of movement patterns in a continuous task. *Acta Psychologica* 82:291-312.

Vidal, F., Bonnet, M.L., and Macar, F. 1991. Programming response duration in a precueing reaction time paradigm. *Journal of Motor Behavior* 23:226-234.

Wickens, D.D. 1939. The simultaneous transfer of conditioned excitation and conditioned inhibition. *Journal of Experimental Psychology* 24:332-338.

Wright, C.E. 1990. Generalized motor programs: Reexamining claims of effector independence in writing. In *Attention and performance XIII: Motor representation and control,* edited by M. Jeannerod. Hillsdale, NJ: Erlbaum.

Zelaznik, H.N., Shapiro, D.C., and Carter, M.C. 1982. The specification of digit and duration during motor programming: A new method of precueing. *Journal of Motor Behavior* 14:57-68.

Acknowledgment

A draft of this chapter was prepared while the author held a "Research, Scholarship, and Creative Activity" award at California State University, Hayward.

Chapter 3

Information Feedback for Motor Skill Learning: A Review

Stephan P. Swinnen

Katholieke Universiteit, Leuven

Since the beginning of the 20th century, augmented information feedback has been considered critically important for learning motor skills. This viewpoint was the basis for the proliferation of feedback research that characterized the field of motor behavior for many years. Recently, more qualified statements about the importance of feedback have been proposed. At least two reasons underlie this change in appreciation. First, learning can occur without augmented information feedback through intrinsic feedback sources. When learners know what they should do through prescriptive task information, self-initiated error detection and correction can occur, if the intrinsic feedback sources are intact. Second, augmented feedback has some pitfalls in that it can be too directive, discouraging learners from processing intrinsic information feedback sources. The theme of this chapter is to identify and discuss the benefits and pitfalls of augmented information feedback. I propose that future research on motor learning focus on all the task-related information that enhances motor proficiency (i.e., information about what should be done as well as what was done).

WHAT IS LEARNED?

When dealing with information feedback, it is important to first address *what is being learned*. The answer to that question has important implications for the role of information feedback in motor learning.

Throughout the history of motor learning, this issue has never been sufficiently addressed. It was often implied by the characteristics of the tasks investigated. Because of the increasing complexity of the tasks used for experimentation in the past decade, motor behavior scientists have gradually come to grips with this problem. The distinction between nonessential and essential variables played a central role in this debate (Gelfand and Tsetlin 1971; Langley and Zelaznik 1984). Depending on the theoretical framework one follows, alternative but related concepts are in use: parameters and invariant features (Schmidt 1988), metrical and structural movement specifications (Newell 1985), and so forth.

This distinction pertains to the motor control system's ability to scale the movement according to specific environmental contingencies while leaving the movement signature or its underlying structure intact (or at least within certain boundaries).

This capability allows adaptability and consistency in movement behavior. With this distinction in mind, one can appreciate the task dimensions focused on throughout the history of motor learning science.

A research overview reveals that scientists have predominantly addressed movement parameterization, whereas acquiring the signature of movement has been underresearched. Traditionally, learning a skill often implied producing an available movement pattern with a new or specific timing or force requirement (i.e., make the movement in 500-ms movement time or move 50 cm). Thus, acquiring the movement topology, which often precedes parameterization and fine tuning, has largely been ignored in experimental learning research. In recent years, an increased interest in the learning of new movement topologies involving the production of particular spatiotemporal structures and patterns of interlimb coordination has been evident. This research has prompted questions about the role of innate or intrinsic coordination patterns while learning new movement forms (Schöner, Zanone, and Kelso 1992; Swinnen and Walter 1988; Walter and Swinnen 1994; Zanone and Kelso 1992), a question at the heart of the processes underlying motor learning and the errors performers cope with when acquiring new skills. In addition, questions emerge about what types of information feedback should be provided to optimize the learning process. However, before one can efficiently deal with issues about optimizing learning, one needs to address what is being learned. Sometimes, the answer to that question is straightforward. For example, recent studies on interlimb coordination have addressed the acquisition of new coordination modes (i.e., a 90° out-of-phase pattern) against the background of preexisting modes (Lee, Swinnen, and Verschueren 1995; Swinnen, Lee, et al. 1995; Zanone and Kelso 1992, 1994). The strength of this approach is that both the initial state and the end state are described by the same variable that captures the coordination pattern (e.g., relative phase). The evolution between the initial and end states can then be traced. On the other hand, there exist many tasks in which the characteristics of the end state need to be identified by analyzing skilled performance. Following this task analysis, the stages of learning are set out. Beek and Van Santvoord (1992) have applied this strategy to learning cascade juggling.

In summary, the first 80 years of motor skill research have mainly addressed acquiring movement parameters, whereas the qualitative structure of movement has become the focus of investigation more recently. Given that learning may entail issues as diverse as developing a perception-action linkage, acquiring a new movement topology, or fine tuning a movement parameter, we can now address the role of information feedback with respect to these goals more specifically.

HOW DOES LEARNING OCCUR?
ON THE NECESSITY
OF AUGMENTED INFORMATION FEEDBACK

Few would doubt that we require information when learning a new task. The role of intrinsic information sources like vision and proprioception is indispensable for performance and learning. This is apparent from the difficulties that deafferented patients experience when producing motor tasks, and it becomes more obvious when their normal vision is prohibited (Teasdale et al. 1994). However, this chapter focuses on the role of augmented information feedback provided in addition to the normally available information sources.

Intrinsic Information, Extrinsic Information, and Learning

Augmented information feedback refers to extrinsic feedback provided to a learner. It supplements the information that is naturally available. Two types have been most commonly used: knowledge of results (KR) and knowledge of performance (KP). KR refers to verbalizable extrinsic information about the performance outcome. KP is information about the action pattern underlying the movement outcome (Gentile 1972; Magill 1993b; Schmidt 1988). Typically, these information sources are provided after the motor task is completed. However, augmented information can be provided during the movement, like a kinematic or kinetic movement representation, biofeedback about the degree of muscle contraction, or a real-time relative motion plot of a coordination pattern (Lee et al. 1995; Swinnen, Lee, et al. 1995).

Early work strongly implied the importance of augmented information feedback for motor learning. For example, Thorndike (1931) stated that subjects failed to improve on a line-drawing task unless they were informed about their performance. This finding established a mind-set about the role of information feedback in learning for the next 50 years. The persistence of this preoccupation is striking because a reanalysis of Thorndike's experiment by Seashore and Bavelas, as early as 1941, showed more consistent responses across practice, although no improvement toward the prescribed target length was made. In addition, Annett (1969) showed some early examples of learning without KR, and more have followed.

Recent experimental evidence forces us to adopt a more qualified statement concerning the necessity of augmented feedback for learning. First, performance changes occur without augmented information feedback, indicating the learner's involvement in error-detection and correction processes. Second, when augmented information does aid learning, the learner does not require it on every trial. Third, under certain circumstances, this augmented information can become detrimental to learning. These and related issues will be further discussed in this chapter. Clearly, general statements about the role of augmented information feedback for motor learning, without reference to the task characteristics, are misleading and oversimplified (see Magill 1993a for a similar argument). Whereas the ultimate search for general laws of learning characterized traditional learning psychology, I believe a selective task-based inductive approach toward theory construction better serves the current state of movement science.

Evidence for Learning in the Absence of Augmented Information Feedback

Convincing experimental evidence exists for performance improvements without augmented feedback in humans and in animals. For example, birds learn species-specific songs by listening to their peers without receiving augmented information feedback from them (at least we think they don't). Although it has been argued that birdsong is represented centrally, experiments with birds reared from an early nestling stage without hearing the species-specific songs have underscored the learned contributions to developing the normal song template. Such findings point to the importance of sensory (auditory) experience in developing the species-specific template (Johnston 1988).

In human experimental work, learning without augmented information feedback has been demonstrated through establishing a (prepractice) reference-of-correctness. Zelaznik and colleagues gave subjects recorded sounds of a correct ballistic timing task, resulting in more accurate performance without knowledge of results (Zelaznik and Spring 1976; Zelaznik, Shapiro, and Newell 1978). Before and during the acquisition of a gymnastic task, Swinnen, Vandenberghe, and Van Assche (1985) gave subjects visual and verbal information about optimal performance. Dramatic improvements in skill became evident although subjects never received augmented information about their actual performance. Magill and coworkers studied the role of augmented information feedback during the learning of a coincidence-anticipation timing task. One group did not receive augmented information feedback, whereas the other group received information about the temporal deviation between the movement produced and arrival of the stimulus at the coincidence point. Verbal knowledge of results was found redundant for learning this anticipation timing skill because it did not produce any benefit over that provided by intrinsic information feedback (Magill, Chamberlin, and Hall 1991).

In all these studies, learners were able to detect their own errors with the help of a reference-of-correctness that enabled them to evaluate performance themselves. They established this reference during the experiment through visual and verbal information, or it was already available from previous experiences. To these examples we can add the daily learning experiences all of us have encountered in the absence of extrinsic augmented information feedback. In view of this evidence, it is striking that the field of motor behavior has emphasized the role of augmented information feedback for learning so strongly and has largely ignored other instructional techniques.

Overrating KR as a Feedback Variable

As often happens in (movement) science, experiments are designed to maximize chances to demonstrate the effectiveness of the manipulations under investigation. Apparently, the success of KR manipulations was largely a result of the nature of the experimental setup, often characterized by deprivation of intrinsic information sources. In addition, traditional work often failed to tell subjects what they should do, so augmented information was the only resource for information about the task to be learned. Few experiments established the learning goal through visual and verbal instructions before or during practice. This is in contrast to the real learning environments in which these information sources are frequently used. It is conceivable that the well-documented effects of KR on learning in laboratory environments were not solely a result of KR's role as a provider of feedback information, but also as an indirect aid in establishing the reference-of-correctness. In other words, subjects probably used the error information to become acquainted with the task goal whenever it was not clearly defined.

This situation is a source of confusion because KR is usually defined as augmented information *feedback* about the response outcome, and its effects have predominantly been accounted for in reference to that function. This is not to deny the important role that feedback plays in refining the reference-of-correctness. However, the omission of more direct instructional means, whenever they are suitable to building the reference-of-correctness, provides an exaggeration of the role of augmented information effects.

Thus, we can make a distinction between two effects of KR, that is, KR as an indirect means to specify the learning goal or standard (prescriptive information), and KR as outcome feedback, providing information about the correctness of the just-completed response (feedback information). Traditional learning research has often failed to provide the learning goal through alternative instructional means, thereby disrupting the learner's involvement in the learning process, particularly the ability to detect errors. This capability is critically dependent on the availability of a reference-of-correctness. Consequently, research has overrated KR's role in motor learning as a feedback technique. The overemphasis on KR manipulations has detracted from other learning aids, such as demonstrations and verbal instructions. However, a revival of the latter work is expected soon (Adams 1987; McCullagh and Caird 1990; Pollock and Lee 1992). This would provide opportunities for a more unconfounded assessment of the role of feedback information by comparing groups that receive information about what should be done with groups that receive information about what should be and what was done. In this respect, the recent studies by Newell and collaborators, in which they provide prescriptive information and feedback information about the criterion, can be considered a good design move (Newell, Carlton, and Antoniou 1990).

Although the previous section may have left us with a pessimistic view of KR's role in motor learning, there are clearly circumstances in which providing external information, in the form of KR or KP, is important. Performance errors may not be obvious to learners during complex skill learning, because of failure to detect them, or because of intrusion of preexisting movement tendencies into performance of the new task. The pattern of errors may be so intertwined that the learner needs priorities assigned and a strategy for correction, developed with the help of an instructor. This points to another source of instructional aid, called "transitional information." Even though performers know how they should perform a movement and how they actually performed it, they may still fail to improve performance. Transitional information may help here because it provides information about what and how to change a movement to modify the movement pattern (Newell 1991; Newell, Morris, and Scully 1985).

In summary, voluntary learning takes place in various ways, but the following conditions seem essential: On one hand, learners ought to know how to perform the task. The establishment of the reference-of-correctness can be self-evident to the subject or acquired through visual and verbal information. On the other hand, learners should obtain information about how they actually performed the task. They can accomplish this either by self-evaluation of the response-produced feedback, by augmented information feedback (provided by a teacher, therapist, or trainer), or by a combination of these. To the extent that learners establish a solid reference-of-correctness and have access to reliable response-produced sensory information, they are able to detect and correct errors themselves. When the task-intrinsic information sources are blocked and the learner is not well informed about the task to accomplish—two conditions that were present in traditional KR research—the importance of extrinsic information sources increases substantially.

CHANGING VIEWPOINTS
ABOUT THE ROLE OF KR THROUGH
THE HISTORY OF MOTOR LEARNING RESEARCH:
THE GUIDANCE HYPOTHESIS

Whereas the traditional perspective held that KR should be given as detailed, as frequently, and as quickly as possible, recent experimental evidence has unveiled some pitfalls associated with KR and has pointed to several limitations. I will review some of this work next.

Guidance Hypothesis of KR

In the past years, Schmidt and associates conducted a series of experiments on the role of information feedback in learning to uncover the principles underlying its functioning. Unlike some previous work, they separated the temporary performance effects from the more permanent learning effects of KR. A goal was to obtain evidence concerning optimal ways to schedule KR during acquisition. These studies have provided converging evidence for the so-called guidance hypothesis of KR. This hypothesis implies that KR guides the learner to the proper response when it is available, but it may detract from attention to other information sources that may be crucial for future performance without KR. Schmidt hinted at this phenomenon in his 1982 textbook, and the ideas were further developed in subsequent publications (Salmoni, Schmidt and Walter 1984; Schmidt et al. 1989; Swinnen, Nicholson, et al. 1990; Winstein and Schmidt 1990; Winstein, Pohl, and Lewthwaite 1994). To better understand the guidance hypothesis of KR, it is useful to elaborate on guidance in relation to information feedback.

Evidence in Favor of the Guiding Effects of Information Feedback

First discussions of the guidance effects of information feedback go back at least 40 years (Annett 1969; Seashore et al. 1949; Stockbridge and Chambers 1958). There exists a rich tradition on the guiding effects of concurrent information feedback during performance in tracking tasks. The idea is that augmented information feedback guides the learner to the correct performance, just as a road map guides the driver to the intended town or geographical spot. Information is provided about how to accomplish the goal. Nevertheless, when interested in retaining the skill, one needs to ask what happens when this augmented information is withheld. Just as there is no guarantee that the driver could find the right location again without the road map, performance with augmented feedback often does not reliably predict performance after information withdrawal. It will depend on the driver's effort to process all the information available from the environment. Similarly, learners should process the sensory information associated with task execution, instead of relying solely on augmented information. Even though receiving this augmented information feedback may be invaluable for the learner, it is important also to learn to do without it, at least when it will not normally be available at future performance conditions.

Some decades ago, Annett (1969) noted that hit scores, time-on-target scores, and other measures could be added to intrinsic information feedback, but he doubted their value in relation to transfer performance. He noted, "There is a strong suggestion that whilst giving a temporary boost there are no long-lasting effects" (Annett 1969, 60). This conclusion was based on his review of early tracking studies, some of which showed that various augmented devices only produced temporary effects. More recently, Winstein and collaborators (1994) demonstrated that frequent physical guidance during target location hampered retention and transfer performance, relative to conditions that produced less guidance. Vander Linden, Cauraugh, and Greene (1993) found that concurrent kinetic (force) feedback during an isometric elbow contraction, compared to posttrial kinetic feedback, was also detrimental to retention performance.

Augmented information feedback can benefit learning if learners do not become dependent on it. A study by Kinkade (1963) is revealing in this respect. He examined a tracking task with poor intrinsic feedback compared with one that had clear intrinsic feedback. Two control and two augmented groups performed with either a perturbed or unperturbed null indicator. Subsequently, he transferred them to a nonaugmented feedback test with the same type of intrinsic feedback experienced during acquisition. Kinkade found that both augmented feedback groups outperformed their respective control groups during acquisition. However, only the group trained with a high degree of intrinsic feedback maintained this advantage in transfer trials. What appeared crucial here was that the subject learned to use augmented feedback to generate appropriate behavior, but not as a substitute for intrinsic feedback.

More recently, we have investigated the effects of real-time relative motion information on learning a new bimanual coordination pattern. When performing upper-limb movements in space, a natural tendency is to coordinate them, either according to the in-phase mode (homologous muscles contracting simultaneously) or the anti-phase mode (nonhomologous muscles contracting simultaneously) (Kelso 1984). Consequently, modes that deviate from these intrinsic patterns will require practice to attain stability. For that reason, we had subjects produce a coordination pattern that required the left limb to move 90° out of phase with the right limb and with a frequency ratio of either 1:1 or 2:1 (Lee et al. 1995; Swinnen, De Pooter, and Delrue 1991; Swinnen, Lee, et al. 1995). Augmented information in both experiments consisted of real-time relative motion information, provided on the oscilloscope or computer terminal, with the left limb displacement represented on the ordinate and the right limb displacement on the abscissa (Lissajous figures). We conducted various data analyses, of which the difference in phase angle between both limbs (relative phase) was the most important. These experiments revealed that subjects became very good at producing the required coordination pattern with real-time relative motion feedback. But the pattern deteriorated when this information was withdrawn. At first, it appears that removal of this guiding source of extra visual information feedback results in performance decrease. However, a recent experiment compared the performance of a group receiving real-time information with a group that did not receive this feedback (but had normal vision of the limbs) and with a blindfolded group. Findings revealed that the augmented (concurrent) feedback group was more successful than the other groups under real-time, normal vision, and blindfolded criterion test conditions (Swinnen, Lee, et al. 1995). In other words, the augmented feedback group outperformed the other groups, even under criterion conditions that the latter groups were more familiar with.

All together, these findings suggest that various sources of augmented (concurrent) information feedback can facilitate performance. However, it is not guaranteed that performers can sustain the accomplished level after withdrawal of these augmented information sources. This is not to deny the positive effects this information induced, and the previous examples provide clear evidence in this respect. Lintern (1991) and Lintern and Roscoe (1980) have reported additional evidence in ergonomics settings. However, when used inadvertently, augmented information feedback may induce temporary effects rather than the more permanent learning effects instructional settings pursue. One reason may be that subjects attend to augmented information at the expense of processing the intrinsic feedback sources, which become increasingly important for performance without augmented information. A second possibility is that information made available to the learner may become integrated with other information sources into a sensory motor representation of the task. When transferred to conditions in which these information sources are withdrawn, performance may deteriorate, especially when these sources are indispensable for achieving success (Proteau et al. 1987).

An important goal for future work is to explore possibilities for maximally exploiting the benefits of augmented information while reducing or eliminating its negative effects. One way is to warn learners about the negative side.effects and to inform them about future test conditions. Another way is to encourage them to pay attention to and process the available intrinsic information feedback. A third possibility is to expose subjects to nonaugmented test conditions at regular intervals during practice. These and other possibilities have not received much attention from motor behavior scientists so far, even though they are crucial in optimizing the use of feedback in skill learning (for exceptions, see Lintern and Roscoe 1980; Lintern, Roscoe, and Sivier 1990).

Based on this review of experimental studies, we can conclude that augmented (mostly concurrent) information feedback may be guiding and, for that reason, potentially misleading as a learning variable under certain circumstances. The question remains whether other feedback sources also suffer from these effects. Schmidt and coworkers have argued that this is the case for KR (Schmidt 1988; Salmoni, Schmidt, and Walter 1984), whereas Newell and associates have occasionally failed to demonstrate these crutch-like effects in kinematic and kinetic feedback studies (Newell, Carlton, and Antoniou 1990). We now turn to experimental evidence about this issue.

Experimental Evidence on the Guidance Effects of KR

Having demonstrated that information may guide learners toward correct performance as well as misguide them in the long run, I will address the guidance hypothesis within the framework of KR manipulations. At least four lines of research have directly or indirectly dealt with this hypothesis: relative frequency of KR, bandwidth KR, summary of KR, and the temporal locus of KR.

Before discussing these feedback manipulations, it is necessary to describe the methodology currently used in experiments on motor learning. Typically, a KR experiment consists of at least two phases: an acquisition and a retention/transfer phase. During the acquisition phase, groups are subjected to different KR manipulations. Following a rest period, one or more retention/transfer tests are administered in which the KR manipulations are withdrawn, so the experimental conditions are equated across groups. The latter tests disentangle the temporary performance effects from the more permanent learning effects. Based on our experience, we advise focus on a delayed retention test that is usually administered one or more days following acquisition. In spite of criticism, I believe performance assessment under feedback withdrawal conditions is a valid strategy. Withdrawal does not pertain to those information sources that are naturally available, only to those that are artificially augmented.

Relative Frequency of KR

When dealing with the amount of KR, a distinction is made between two measures: absolute and relative frequency of KR. Absolute frequency of KR refers to the number of KR presentations over the course of practice, whereas relative frequency refers to the percentage of trials on which KR is provided (Schmidt 1988). According to Thorndike's (1931) "Law of Effect," KR was to be provided immediately after a response, and as often as possible. These viewpoints did not change in the decennia that followed, though KR shifted from a reinforcement to an informational perspective (Adams 1971; Schmidt 1975). Reevaluating existing research within the framework of the learning-performance distinction, Salmoni, Schmidt, and Walter (1984) concluded that decreased relative frequency of KR increased learning. In summarizing the experimental evidence that has since been produced, I conclude that Salmoni, Schmidt, and Walter's hypothesis has not been invariably supported, though some interesting findings emerged from this work.

In learning a timing task with two direction reversals (MT = 1000 ms), we manipulated four experimental conditions: KR presented after every trial (100%), every second (50%), fifth (20%), and every tenth trial (10%) (Swinnen 1984). Findings revealed that the groups were ordered according to their relative frequency schedule during acquisition, with higher percentages of trials with KR resulting in higher performance accuracy. However, no differences in temporal accuracy (as measured by |CE|) and consistency (as measured by variable error—VE) were observed during the 10-min and 2-day no-KR retention tests. Relative frequency schedules failed to produce differential learning effects in this study, and this finding was supported in other work (Sparrow and Summers 1992, Experiment 1; Winstein and Schmidt 1990, Experiment 1).

Nevertheless, certain relative frequency procedures are supportive of Salmoni, Schmidt, and Walter's hypothesis. For example, Winstein and Schmidt (1990) used an interesting manipulation called "fading KR." Their subjects produced a forearm flexion-extension movement with a specific spatiotemporal configuration. One group received feedback after every trial (100%), whereas another group had KR faded across practice, resulting in an overall frequency schedule of 50%. KR was provided as root mean square (RMS) error. The fading schedule was based on the idea that subjects would need feedback more often in the initial stages (when they make many errors) than in later stages in practice. For that reason, the fading group received KR frequently early in learning, then KR was gradually diminished. The findings demonstrated that RMS error was not much different between groups during the acquisition phase. During the delayed no-KR retention test (after two days), the fading group performed with lower error than the 100% relative frequency group. The authors concluded that reduced frequency of information feedback facilitated learning, relative to feedback on every trial. Sparrow and Summers (1992, Experiment 2) also found qualified support for the relative frequency hypothesis. During a delayed retention test, their 10% relative frequency group performed with less error than the 100% and 33% groups. Wulf and Schmidt (1989) also found support for reducing relative frequency during the acquisition of three versions of a sequential timing task. Reduced relative frequency enhanced transfer to a task with a novel movement duration.

These findings do not invariably support the hypothesis that reduced relative frequency of KR is beneficial to learning, even though particular instructional conditions provide some credibility. What the studies do indicate is that more feedback is not necessarily better for learning, though it may boost performance temporarily when that information is present.

Bandwidth KR

Bandwidth feedback refers to the provision of feedback only if errors are outside a predetermined range of correctness. If a performance error lies within the bandwidth, no information is provided to the subject. However, this condition is informative because it indicates that no modifications are required or that performance is (approximately) correct. Recent studies have informed subjects that they can treat trials in which no information is provided as correct ones (Lee and Carnahan 1990; Sherwood 1988). If the error is outside the bandwidth, the subject receives precise information feedback about performance or performance error. Thus, it can be considered a combination of qualitative and quantitative information feedback.

One similarity between bandwidth feedback and relative frequency of KR manipulations is that information is not provided on every trial. It is also similar to a fading schedule of feedback provision because subjects typically produce fewer responses outside the bandwidth as practice proceeds. In contrast to the fading schedule, the learner's individual performance determines the rate and amount of information provided.

In Sherwood's study (1988), subjects learned a rapid timing task (MT = 200 ms) under one of three bandwidth conditions: KR on every trial (0% bandwidth), on trials that exceeded a 5% bandwidth (190-210 ms), and on trials that exceeded a

10% bandwidth (180-220 ms). Relative to a 100% feedback schedule, bandwidth feedback produced more stable behavior than during acquisition. During no-KR retention, Sherwood found that subjects given a 10% bandwidth were least variable, whereas those given a 0% bandwidth were most variable. These significant effects for performance consistency were not traded off for performance accuracy.

Lee and Carnahan (1990) followed up on this work by assessing the uniqueness of bandwidth KR compared with relative frequency manipulations. As mentioned before, these procedures bear similarities in that increases in bandwidth reduce the number of trials followed by KR (error KR). In other words, relative frequency of KR varies concomitantly with the extent of the bandwidth. However, both manipulations are distinct in that trials after which no information is provided can be interpreted as correct in bandwidth procedures (no-error KR or qualitative KR), whereas this is not the case for blank trials in relative frequency manipulations. This makes the no-KR trials in bandwidth conditions directive in that they inform performers not to change their behavior. In addition to the 5 and 10% bandwidth groups, two yoked groups were added, matched subject to subject with the bandwidth groups for relative frequency of error KR. Providing each yoked subject with error KR only when the matched bandwidth subject had received error KR accomplished this. Using this yoking procedure, each bandwidth and its matched control group were similar in terms of relative frequency of KR and when KR was provided during the acquisition trials.

Findings revealed that the bandwidth groups performed the sequential movement with higher accuracy (lower |CE|) and less variability (VE) than the yoked groups during acquisition. During no-KR retention, the bandwidth groups performed with significantly less variability. The conclusion was drawn that wider bandwidths and less frequent KR presentations combined to enhance movement stability. Moreover, bandwidth manipulations produced effects beyond those attributable to relative frequency manipulations. This would imply that the trials in which no error information was provided produced an additional effect on learning in the bandwidth groups, distinct from blank trial performances in the relative frequency conditions. A re-analysis of the data about absolute performance changes following trials with error KR versus no-error KR confirmed these speculations. For the bandwidth groups, these performance changes were smaller following a no-error KR trial than for the relative frequency groups following a blank trial. No differences were found among groups following error KR. As the effects of bandwidth KR on learning have usually been found for movement consistency (Lee and Carnahan 1990; Sherwood 1988), these findings may imply that the trials on which no KR is provided are critical for stabilizing performance. I will take up the issue of blank trials later in this chapter.

It appears from the previous studies that bandwidth KR affects performance stability as determined on immediate retention tests (for an exception, see Lee and Maraj 1994). Future studies must establish whether this effect will persist after longer retention intervals, because previous KR work has often demonstrated discrepancies between performance at immediate and delayed retention tests. Whereas the former test is usually applied a few minutes after acquisition, the latter is administered after one or more days. Though the reasons underlying this discrepancy are not yet clear, I suspect the processes accompanying sleep play an important role in memory consolidation.

Lintern and Roscoe (1980) have provided additional evidence for a bandwidth scheduling, but with respect to concurrent information feedback. They trained subjects on a simulated landing maneuver, which they considered a task with poor intrinsic feedback sources. There were four groups, two of which received augmented glide slope indicators (i.e., feedback that provides the trainee more precise information when he or she deviates from a desired flight path). In one group, these indicators switched on only when the learner departed from an optimum flight envelope (the adaptive augmentation group), whereas the indicators were provided continuously in another group, whatever the subjects' performance level (continuous augmentation group). As subjects of the adaptive augmentation group became more skilled, the glide slope indicators appeared less frequently because the envelope was broken less frequently. This adaptive manipulation draws similarities with fading KR and with bandwidth KR manipulations. Transfer to the simulated landing task without the augmented feedback was found better with practice under the performance-dependent augmented feedback cuing procedure compared with augmented feedback provided on all trials and no augmented feedback cuing at all.

Drawing further analogies with bandwidth manipulations in this tracking work, one can elaborate on whether augmented feedback should be provided when the subject is performing correctly (on target) or incorrectly (off-target manipulation). Based on a review of relevant work, Lintern and Roscoe (1980) concluded that predominantly the off-target manipulations showed transfer benefits. They argued that on-target manipulations would make the subject more dependent on the augmented information, at the expense of attention to intrinsic feedback. Inspired by the ecological perspective developed by Gibson (1977), Lintern (1991) proposed that, in contrast to on-target presentation of augmented feedback, off-target augmentation "would not distract attention from critical invariants that specify correct performance or that would support accurate tracking" (259). This appears to be a way to fully exploit the benefits of augmented information feedback while minimizing its drawbacks.

Summary KR

Summary feedback refers to providing feedback about a series of trials after the last trial has been performed. For example, a 5-trial summary manipulation implies that following completion of 5 trials, performers receive an overview of the errors made on each trial. Lavery (1962) did one of the early studies of this kind. Subjects practiced simple motor tasks according to 3 feedback manipulations: (a) the immediate condition received feedback after each trial, (b) the summary condition received summary feedback after each 20-trial set, and (c) the third condition (the both group) received feedback after each trial and summary feedback after each series of 20 trials. Following acquisition, subjects performed retention tests. Findings revealed that during acquisition the immediate group and the combined feedback group performed better than the summary group. However, this trend was reversed at retention. Here the summary group performed more successfully than the remaining two groups, although this effect diminished after a three-month retention interval. Because the immediate and both group performed more poorly at retention than the summary KR group, and because both former groups received feedback after each trial, it appears that receiving feedback on every trial was detrimental to retention performance.

Following up on Lavery's work, Schmidt and associates investigated various summary-KR lengths' influence on task complexity manipulations. The logic behind this idea was that increases in task complexity would decrease the optimal length of the summary. In the first series of experiments, they used summary lengths of 1, 5, 10, and 15 trials during the learning of a ballistic timing task that required two direction reversals (Schmidt et al. 1989). During acquisition (when KR was present), shorter summary lengths resulted in better performance. At the immediate retention test, they observed no performance differences. However, at the delayed retention test (after two days), the performance trend found during acquisition was reversed: the longer the summary lengths, the better the no-KR retention performance. Though these findings appear encouraging, some have failed to replicate them (Guay, Salmoni, and McIlwain 1992; Sidaway, Moore, and Schoenfelder-Zohdi 1991). Therefore, it is justified to say that summary KR currently lacks the robustness and generalizability we expect in the face of small variations in the experimental environment. However, there are studies that support this work.

Gable, Shea, and Wright (1991) used a 1-, 8-, and 16-trial summary condition during the learning of a simple isometric force production task. Retention performance was improved as the summary length of the trials increased. Both the Gable, Shea, and Wright and the Schmidt et al. experiments failed to show an optimal summary KR length. It was possibly at 15 or 16 trials or beyond. However, additional experimentation has demonstrated that summary length interacts with task complexity.

In studying a coincidence-anticipation timing task, Schmidt, Lange, and Young (1990) found an inverted-U relationship between summary length and performance at retention. The task consisted of moving a horizontal lever so it intercepted a visual target that moved downward toward the subject. The performance score represented a combination of spatial accuracy and velocity at which the lever passed the coincidence point. Four experimental groups received summary KR after 1, 5, 10, or 15 trials. During acquisition, performance was better with shorter summary lengths. However, during delayed retention, the 5-trial summary group demonstrated the best scores on coincident timing, followed by the 1-, 10-, and 15-trial summary groups, respectively. Yao, Fischman, and Wang (1994) generated similar evidence with respect to an aiming task involving temporal and spatial accuracy. They demonstrated a superiority for the 5-trial summary group compared with the 1-trial group at delayed retention.

Schmidt, Lange, and Young (1990) have argued that task complexity might be an important intervening variable in summary-KR feedback manipulations in that shorter summary lengths might be better for more complex tasks than longer summary lengths. If we take this argument further, the optimal summary-KR length should approach 1 (i.e., KR after every trial) as task complexity increases. The next experiment shows preliminary (though partial) evidence for this viewpoint.

We had subjects perform a sequential horizontal arm movement consistent of three segments (Swinnen, Schmidt, and Pauwels 1989). First we established the temporal structure that subjects would normally generate for this movement without imposed relative timing requirements. To ensure task learning, subjects were to produce a temporal structure that significantly deviated from their "natural" pattern. What made this task difficult was the change in speed, which was shifted rapidly among segments: 213, 84, and 290°/s for segment 1 to 3, respectively. A computer terminal provided summary KR after 1, 5, or 10 trials, showing the deviations from the target times for each segment in a different color. Following the 90 acquisition trials, we held no-KR retention tests after 10 min, 2 days, 1 month, and 5 months. During acquisition, shorter summary lengths resulted in significantly lower absolute constant error (|CE|) scores with respect to absolute timing. With respect to relative timing, we computed a deviation from the target proportion, similar to |CE| (called phasing bias). We found no significant differences in phasing bias among groups, although the 1-trial summary group performed with lower error than the 5-trial and 10-trial groups. These trends remained across retention intervals, although the differences failed to reach significance. The findings differed for response stability as indexed by variable error (VE). Although no group effect was found for VE in absolute timing during acquisition, phasing variability (the variability of the proportions around their mean) showed a significant group effect: the 10-trial summary group had the lowest error scores, followed by the 5-trial and 1-trial groups. This effect persisted across retention intervals up to five months. These findings demonstrated a trend for performance accuracy to decrease, but performance consistency to increase significantly with longer summary lengths. Again, no-KR trials or blank trials during acquisition developed a more stable temporal structure. Lee, White, and Carnahan (1990) provided similar evidence under different experimental circumstances for a reciprocal tapping task. They concluded that provision of KR leads to a homing-in strategy that results in improved accuracy at the expense of performance stability.

Temporal Position of KR

When information provides guidance, the sooner it is given following performance completion, the more guiding it should become. This was the major hypothesis of a series of investigations in which we manipulated the duration of the KR-delay interval during the learning of a sequential timing task and an anticipation timing task (Swinnen, Nicholson, et al. 1990). Compared with a group who received KR after 3 to 8 s, we gave one group KR right after performance completion. Findings revealed that instantaneous provision of KR was detrimental to retention performance. We hypothesized that immediate presentation of KR discourages evaluation of response-produced feedback information, and this may be invaluable for successful future performance without KR. Although these findings may carry more theoretical than practical relevance, they possibly support the guidance hypothesis of KR. Furthermore, they converge with the previously discussed directive effects of concurrent augmented information feedback.

Reevaluating the Hypothesis Put Forward by Salmoni, Schmidt, and Walter (1984)

When evaluating the predictions made by Salmoni, Schmidt, and Walter (1984) regarding KR manipulations, the following can be concluded.

1. It appears that reducing the relative frequency of KR is either detrimental or indifferent to performance during acquisition. During retention, relative frequency of KR schedules does not produce differential effects on performance. Exceptions are the fading KR manipulation, which leads to better retention performance than 100% KR (Winstein and Schmidt 1990) and the more successful transfer performance of the reduced relative frequency group during the combined acquisition of several sequential movements (Wulf and Schmidt 1989). In all, the reversal in performance order among groups between acquisition and retention, as predicted by Salmoni, Schmidt, and Walter (1984), is not invariably supported. The practical conclusion is that information feedback after every trial is not required during the learning of simple movements. This conclusion is corroborated by the bandwidth KR manipulations that have similarities to fading KR and some additional unique features. It may be that during the learning of complex movements involving new topologies, subjects need all the information they can obtain to improve performance.

2. The summary KR studies show that the length of summary KR on performance interacts with task complexity. When subjects perform a simple task, increasing summary-KR length appears beneficial to learning up to some level. As task complexity increases, a trade-off may occur between performance accuracy and consistency. Similar to the relative frequency studies, additional research on the acquisition of complex tasks is necessary. Currently, summary-KR research is plagued with discouraging inconsistencies.

To summarize, the studies conducted so far do not invariably support the guidance hypothesis of KR, although some findings point in that direction. Studies that support the guidance hypothesis demonstrate smaller retention losses for groups receiving KR less frequently or in a summary, relative to groups that receive KR on every trial. Further research is needed to validate this hypothesis. It would be interesting to see how the guidance hypothesis of KR will withstand the acquisition of more complex tasks involving new movement topologies and the control of more than one degree of freedom. The majority of studies conducted so far pertain to movement parameterization.

SEARCHING FOR A BALANCE BETWEEN THE POSITIVE AND NEGATIVE EFFECTS OF KR

In this section, we will discuss the potentially negative effects of information feedback and propose suggestions to organize the instructional environment to minimize the detrimental effects and maximize the benefits of information feedback.

Negative Faces of Augmented Information Feedback

The mixed support for the guidance hypothesis of KR is not surprising given the complex ways information feedback affects performance. In a review of the recent KR work, Schmidt (1991) has argued that at least two phenomena might be operating when information feedback is provided. On one hand, feedback contributes to learning, and this effect has received the most attention throughout the history of motor learning research. It contains information about success in goal achievement and allows subjects to know their error rate. In other words, feedback guides the subject toward correct performance. The second effect of feedback is negative and has received more attention in recent years (Schmidt 1991). These negative effects can be brought about in various ways, and it should be a goal of future research to validate the proposed hypotheses.

First, when feedback is provided frequently, the learner may develop some dependence on it, which may become an intrinsic part of the task. As mentioned previously, experimental evidence shows that concurrent information feedback aids performance when it is present. However, when it is withdrawn, performance deteriorates significantly (Annett 1969).

Second, when KR is presented frequently, the subject may rely on it so extensively that self-generated error detection based on evaluation of response-produced sensory information is not fully conducted. This may happen when subjects lack sufficient motivation for learning, as is often the case when confronted with contrived simple tasks. Furthermore, evidence shows that learners are unable to ignore augmented feedback, even when it is wrong and disagrees with intrinsic information feedback sources (Buekers, Magill, and Hall 1992). It has been demonstrated that subjects use KR to modify the task in spite of instructions not to correct for it (Nicholson and Schmidt 1991). These studies provide convergent evidence that KR is *directive* information for learners.

Third, whenever information feedback is presented, the learner will try to correct the behavior on the next trial, often making overcompensations. This causes performance to oscillate about the zero error line and may prevent developing stable movement production. As skill progresses, it becomes gradually more difficult to distinguish between real errors in movement generation and errors from inherent noise processes in the neuromuscular system. Whereas subjects should correct for the former, they should not correct for the latter type of error, labeled as "maladaptive short-term corrections." (Schmidt 1991). The bandwidth KR manipulation, discussed previously, is a potential way to obviate these maladaptive corrections. A similar argument holds for precision of KR. It probably does not make sense to provide error information with a precision beyond the subjects' level of control. Annett (1991) has argued that "providing more information than the learner can handle induces 'hunting' behaviour which could itself interfere with long-term storage" (36).

Information Feedback, Guidance, Arousal, and Motivation

When generalizing beyond the information feedback schedules, it may be that other variables mediate the role of information feedback in motor learning. Any manipulation that makes the task more difficult, say complicating the learning context by performing related tasks within the practice setting (Lee and Magill 1983; Shea and Morgan 1979), making information feedback harder to access, or reducing the frequency at which information is provided, results in greater involvement in the learning process that may benefit subsequent long-term retention (Lee, Swinnen, and Serrien 1994).

Arousal and motivation may be mediating variables in this respect. Experimental evidence in favor of this has been provided by Berlyne and associates regarding paired-associate learning (Berlyne 1967; Berlyne et al. 1965; Berlyne et al. 1966). They provided white noise to subjects during paired-associate learning to increase their arousal level and found that recall was worse for items presented with white noise during acquisition. However, at retention without white noise, the subjects better recalled the items accompanied by white noise during training (Berlyne et al. 1965). In another study, they demonstrated that the beneficial effects of white noise became apparent only on a delayed transfer test (after one day) and not during immediate retention (Berlyne et al. 1966). This is reminiscent of the KR manipulations discussed previously, which have often failed to show effects at immediate retention, but have demonstrated differences among experimental manipulations after one or more days. These differences were sometimes opposite those observed during the acquisition phase. The findings of Berlyne and collaborators possibly suggest that the more the subject is aroused (up to some optimal level), the more effort he or she is likely to spend in the training process, with better learning as a result (see Kahneman 1973 for links between arousal and effort). Although the role of these variables has not been well documented in motor learning research, there seems no compelling reason for ignoring them. Considering that frequent KR presentation does not prevent but rather discourages subjects from processing intrinsic task characteristics, it may be that the concomitant negative guidance effects decrease or even disappear with highly motivated learners confronted with challenging tasks.

Role of Blank Trials During Acquisition

The bulk of KR research that the guidance hypothesis has inspired has directed attention to trials after which no information feedback is provided and their potential role in performance. Although some have argued that these blank trials are unimportant for learning (Bilodeau 1966), recent work indicates otherwise. When learning a skill is dependent on augmented information feedback sources, trials without KR—be it under summary, relative frequency, or bandwidth manipulations—encourage subjects not to change their behavior. Externally provided information about a required performance change is lacking in the blank trials resulting from frequency and summary KR manipulations, whereas in the bandwidth study, there is no need to change performance because no-KR trials can be interpreted as correct. Levine, Leitenberg, and Richter (1964) observed that no-KR is, under certain circumstances, equivalent to right (qualitative KR) in paired-associate learning. They referred to this as the "blank trials law" and argued that blank trials are similar to positive reinforcement. With respect to motor performance, blank trials may foster performance stabilization, and some KR studies that have included variability measures converge toward this viewpoint. In addition, they invite performers to focus on and process intrinsic information feedback.

Prospections for the Future on the Guidance Hypothesis

This review of experimental work suggests that the guidance hypothesis of KR needs additional verification through experimental research. As it stands, the hypothesis pertains to the acquisition of simple tasks. The potential for generalization to more complex tasks remains open. Defining task complexity is a thorny problem. One way to conceptualize it is to identify the number of movement components, segments, or joint motions to be produced sequentially and/or simultaneously. This indirectly refers to the degrees-of-freedom problem. Clearly, task difficulty does not bear a simple linear relation with number of limbs or segments involved. The degree of compatibility (or the required degree of dissociation) among the action patterns performed simultaneously is a critical factor. In addition, I would like to entertain the hypothesis that the simple versus complex task continuum may refer to poor versus rich intrinsic information feedback. Tasks with poor intrinsic feedback are possibly more vulnerable to the negative effects of guidance than tasks rich in intrinsic information feedback.

The contention that the laws underlying the control and learning of simple tasks do not generalize to more complex motor tasks further corroborates the plea for studying more complex skills. With a few exceptions, laws of learning that are indifferent to task dimensions may be a utopia, left over from the heritage of traditional theories on human and animal learning. Whereas there is no problem with studying short learning periods, we should realize that findings from such work do not necessarily extrapolate to tasks requiring extensive practice. This is another argument that has often been made in recent years. The inertia of traditional habits needs to be overcome to tackle these objectives. Such strategy will possibly promote a healthy development of the field of motor learning.

KR IN RELATION TO OTHER SOURCES OF INFORMATION FEEDBACK

Previous sections demonstrated why recent findings have tempered the enthusiasm surrounding the role of KR in motor learning. There is another reason KR has been criticized, pertaining to its presumed limited usefulness in the learning of multiple degree-of-freedom tasks (Fowler and Turvey 1978; Newell and Walter 1981). The arguments are mainly built on the assumption that KR does not match the task characteristics to be controlled when task complexity increases. As mentioned, research has predominantly shown the powerful effects of KR with simple tasks (such as blind-lever positioning and ballistic timing) that require adjustments on one dimension (e.g., position or time). KR, conveyed as a single outcome score, provides all the information necessary for controlling that dimension. In contrast, many common actions consist of coordinating several body parts, often requiring a fundamental reorganization of the movement form or topology through practice. Under these circumstances, outcome information no longer implies *direct* suggestions about the task dimensions that need to be modified. It is often desirable to draw the learner's attention to the underlying movement patterns, the interrelationships among joints within and between limbs, or the kinematic- or kinetic-time histories that create movement outcomes. Another problem is that KR may be redundant information. Many circumstances have outcome information readily available through sensory information (e.g., basketball shooting). These problems have motivated motor learning scientists to focus on KP variables in recent years (Fowler and Turvey 1978; Newell, Morris, and Scully 1985; Newell, Sparrow, and Quinn 1985; Newell 1991; Schmidt and Young 1991).

This expansion in instructional techniques is welcomed. However, two additional points should be made. First, although KR provides only general outcome information, it can induce considerable changes in movement kinematics. Young and Schmidt (1990) emphasized this point in the acquisition of a coincidence-anticipation timing task, and we extended these results to learning a bimanual coordination task. We demonstrated changes in the coordination pattern with KR that were distinct from practice without KR (Swinnen et al. 1993). It is clear from these examples that performers do not invariably need kinematic information to induce profound kinematic changes in movement patterns. Second, Salmoni (1989) has argued that the number of task dimensions and the type of information feedback may be irrelevant, unless it can be shown that KP acts in a way that is qualitatively different from traditional KR.

In a series of experiments, Newell and associates have shown that some KP manipulations (kinematic-kinetic information) are superior to KR under certain conditions, even for single degree-of-freedom tasks (Newell and Carlton 1987; Newell, Carlton, and Antoniou 1990; Newell et al. 1983; Newell, Sparrow, and Quinn 1985). However, differences between both feedback variables have not always been found. Research by Newell and his group has demonstrated that when the subject was familiar with the task (drawing a circle in two-dimensional space) and it had a single parameter (such as circle radius), a group receiving KR or outcome information (absolute integrated error) was as effective as a group receiving a combination of KR and KP information (a computer-generated positional representation of the drawing produced), with or without the goal task or criterion. However, when the task was less familiar, consisting of an unfamiliar shape, performance of the experimental groups diverged during no-feedback retention performance: The group receiving KR + KP + criterion information performed better than the KR and KR + KP groups. A final experiment demonstrated that the availability of both the criterion task and kinematic information of the just-completed response produced the best learning results (Newell, Carlton, and Antoniou 1990). This implies that it did not suffice to inform subjects what movement they had produced. It was also important to link this with the criterion movement. The availability of the criterion movement was critical to build the reference-of-correctness. Only then could the subjects find out not only what they did, but also what they did wrong, by comparing performance with the criterion task.

Using an anticipation timing task in which subjects were to move a horizontal lever to a coincidence point, Young and Schmidt (1990, 1992) compared the performance of a group receiving KR and a group receiving KR and KP. KR referred to a performance score on a computer screen given after each trial. KP consisted of information about the maximum amplitude of the backswing, provided as an average score of five trials after completion of every fifth trial. During acquisition, the scores of the KR-KP group exceeded those of the KR-only group, and this effect persisted at a retention test with KR. Analyses of backswing amplitudes indicated that subjects of the KR-KP group had effectively modified this aspect of movement more than the KR-only group.

During the acquisition of a bimanual task, we compared the effectiveness of KR with augmented displacement information feedback (Swinnen et al. 1993). The task involved the simultaneous performance of a unidirectional elbow-flexion movement in the nondominant limb and a flexion-extension-flexion (reversal) movement in the dominant limb. This movement is difficult to perform because of a dominant interlimb synchronization tendency, causing patterns of mutual interference (Franz, Zelaznik, and McCabe 1991; Kelso, Southard, and Goodman 1979; Swinnen and Walter 1988, 1991; Walter, Swinnen, and Franz 1993). A major goal in acquiring the skill was to reduce or eliminate interlimb synchronization (i.e., to dissociate the limbs). The degree of coupling was quantified according to the metrical and structural features of movement (Swinnen, Walter, Beirinckx, and Meugens 1991). Dividing the amount of relative work generated by both limbs determined metrical coupling, whereas we measured structural coupling by cross correlating the acceleration-time profiles of the respective limb movements. The former measure provides information about the degree of differentiation of intensity specifications, whereas the latter refers to differentiation of the movement forms. There were four groups: one group did not receive information feedback about the degree of coupling; a second group received KR as an overall outcome measure of success in bimanual decoupling, which was based on the cross correlation of the limbs' acceleration profiles; a third group received KP with the displacement-time patterns of both limbs shown on a computer terminal; and a fourth group received a combination of both KR and KP. Findings revealed that the groups receiving augmented information feedback were more successful in dissociating the limbs than the groups not receiving this information, supporting earlier work (Swinnen and Walter 1991; Swinnen, Walter et al. 1990). However, no significant differences in degree of metrical and structural coupling were found between the KR, KP, and KR + KP groups.

These findings are striking considering that KP was much more detailed and provided more direct suggestions for improving performance than KR. Two preliminary suggestions follow from these findings. First, the strength of KR may lie in its simplicity. It contains information that can be easily interpreted, whereas kinematic information feedback may be less comprehensible, particularly the higher time derivatives of displacement. Second, it appears that KR may have more potential for acquiring tasks involving the control of more than one degree of freedom than originally conceived. In this study, KR may have encouraged learners to become aware of errors in performance, increasing their sensitivity to intrinsic response-produced information sources. This may have resulted in more elaborate detection and correction of errors. To the extent that learners can conduct these operations themselves and that they are well informed about the task goal or standard, KR and KP may have similar effects on performance. KR suggests that an error has been made and encourages the learner to search for the problem and its solution. Bear in mind that instructional settings exist in which KP may produce additional benefits for performance and learning beyond those KR provides.

FUTURE DEVELOPMENTS IN THE STUDY OF AUGMENTED INFORMATION FEEDBACK: SOME SPECULATIONS

In previous sections, I have pointed to an important evolution in the field of motor behavior pertaining to the study of more complex tasks. One is then prompted to ask whether this will result in the application of more complex and elaborated feedback techniques. This section will build on recent advances made in the field of motor control that will eventually find their way into the domain of motor learning.

Behavioral Complexity, Control Simplicity?

Although one might think that an increase in the complexity of the tasks studied will be associated with using increasingly complex feedback techniques, I believe this is not necessarily the case, and I build my argument on two lines of thinking. First, there are limitations in the learner's ability to process information about movement kinetics and kinematics, in particular the higher time derivatives. In tracking studies in which the order of control indicates the degree of complexity, acceleration control has been shown much more difficult than velocity or position control (Fracker and Wickens 1989; Hammerton 1989). This constitutes a problem of control and of interpreting incoming information and translating it into action. Even though higher time derivatives provide more detailed and sensitive information about performance, learners risk having difficulty evaluating it and using it to shape subsequent action.

Second, seemingly complex actions involving many limbs and body parts are often governed by elementary control principles, and these have recently become the major focus of attention in motor control research. Experimental studies have focused on what the system can get for free (i.e., with minimal reliance on representations). For a long time, Russian movement specialists have called attention to the important role of muscle collectives or synergies in movement control (Bernstein 1967; Gelfand, Gurfinkel, Tsetlin, and Shik 1971). This idea was subsequently promoted by Turvey (1977) in his influential paper on the role of coordinative structures in movement. Inspired by Easton (1972), coordinative structures were originally considered reflex based, whereas subsequent work underscored the goal-directed nature of these functional muscle linkages.

More recently, considerable efforts have been undertaken to unravel the organizing principles governing multilimb coordination. This research has identified preferred modes of movement coordination to which humans are (naturally) drawn when moving limbs simultaneously. Though this research has concentrated on what Von Holst called absolute coordination (e.g., moving the limbs in synchrony with a 1:1 frequency ratio), the search for a limited set of elementary though powerful coordination principles appears promising. Studies on cyclical finger or hand movements in the horizontal plane have pointed to two stable modes of movement coordination: in-phase (requiring the simultaneous contraction of homologous muscle groups) and anti-phase (requiring the simultaneous contraction of non-homologous muscle groups), with the former reaching higher degrees of stability than the latter (Kay, Saltzman, Kelso, and Schöner 1987; Kelso 1984; Yamanishi, Kawato, and Suzuki 1979). For (para)sagittal movements of the upper and lower limbs, isodirectional movements (in-phase—both limbs go up and down together) are produced with a higher degree of stability than anisodirectional movements (anti-phase—one limb goes up and the other goes down) (Baldissera, Cavallari, and Civaschi 1982; Kelso and Jeka 1992; Swinnen et al. 1995). These observations have been made during the production of cyclical actions. Nevertheless, a strong synchronization tendency has also been observed during the production of discrete movements (Kelso, Southard, and Goodman 1979; Swinnen, Walter, and Shapiro 1988; Walter, Swinnen, and Franz 1993). Thus, it appears that coordination principles exist that govern multilimb movements under a variety of task conditions.

Augmented Information Feedback and the Exploitation/Suppression of Preexisting Muscle Collectives

The aforementioned developments in the field of motor control may have consequences for elaborating principles of motor learning and the role of augmented information feedback herein. Learning does not involve constructing action patterns "de novo" but occurs against the backdrop of preexisting synergies, reflexes, or patterns of interlimb coordination. On one hand, augmented information feedback should be focused on the integration of preexisting movements with the new pattern to be acquired in case it suits the new task demands. On the other hand, augmented feedback should be focused on the errors caused by preexisting movement patterns when they interfere with the acquisition of the new task. If certain control principles are unique for multilimb coordination and cannot necessarily be inferred from the principles governing the control of the subcomponents, augmented information should focus on the principles that pertain to relationships among subsystems or to invariants between perception and action. I turn to each of these issues next.

Given that simple low-dimensional organizational principles govern complex coordination, augmented feedback should be directed at uncovering these principles. Relative motion information is one likely candidate (Newell 1985). It provides information about the relative positions of limbs or joints against each other. Recent research in our lab has demonstrated that difficult coordination tasks can be taught through real-time relative motion information (e.g., moving the upper limbs 90° out of phase in a 1:1 or 2:1 frequency ratio) (Lee et al. 1995; Swinnen, Dounskaia, Walter, and Serrien 1995). From relative motion plots, one can extract information about the frequency ratio in which the limbs move as well as about their relative phase.

If we view learning against the background of preexisting movement patterns or synergies, we can seek alternative ways to assist performers. Whenever preexisting preferred movement patterns suit the new task demands, learners should be aided in exploiting them and in integrating them with the new pattern of action. In addition to providing information feedback about the movements produced, instructors often rely on prescriptive information, telling learners what to do to improve performance. On the other hand, learning environments can be set up to maximize the probability of success. Simple instructions can evoke preexisting reflexes, synergies, or previously overlearned responses. Gymnastics teachers often focus on the performer's head position, thereby promoting the positive effects induced by tonic neck reflexes or labyrinthine reflexes during a somersault or handstand. For example, during a handstand, beginning performers will often generate increased extensor tone in the upper limbs when bending the head backward, in congruence with the symmetric tonic neck reflex. Fukuda (1961) has provided many examples of voluntary movements in which action patterns occur that converge on neck and labyrinthine reflexes. Not only reflexes but also previously acquired synergies can be used. When teaching a glide mill-up[1] on the uneven bars, my colleagues and I often used the instruction "pull on your shorts." This holistic type of instruction elicits a global pattern of relative motions in the arms, the hips, and the legs that resembles the well-known and overlearned pattern of putting on clothing. This way, a complex synergy was made available *almost for free*.

Even though these examples show how preexisting movement synergies can be exploited, sometimes such patterns need to be suppressed because they interfere with new task demands (Swinnen and Walter 1988; Walter and Swinnen 1994). This has been a major research focus in studies that Charles Walter and I have conducted in the past 10 years. Viewed this way, learning requires suppressing the attraction exhibited by preexisting preferred coordination modes. This has been clearly exemplified for discrete (Swinnen, Walter, and Shapiro 1988; Walter and Swinnen 1992) as well as cyclical bimanual task performance (Lee et al. 1995; Zanone and Kelso 1992). Because of a strong synchronization tendency, performers often experience difficulty learning to decouple the limbs when attempting to perform discrete movements with different spatiotemporal features. Augmented feedback plays an important role here by helping learners focus on performance errors that result from the attraction exhibited by preexisting coordination modes. To the extent that learners can solve these errors themselves, outcome information in the form of KR may be as effective as KP in alleviating the difficulties encountered (Swinnen et al. 1993).

Alternative Instructional Techniques to Guide Learners Toward Correct Performance

Instructors use various means to enhance success in motor performance. It would be a mistake to focus solely on augmented information feedback to help subjects build the new movement pattern or suppress the interference induced by preexisting preferred coordination modes. One example is the reduction of the speed of task execution to reduce the pull of attraction toward preferred (but incorrect) coordination modes. In the bimanual studies that Walter and I conducted, we demonstrated that increasing the torque (Walter and Swinnen 1990a, 1990b) or speed (Swinnen et al. 1992) requirements resulted in greater degrees of interlimb coupling, preventing the production of differentiated limb patterns. However, when subjects performed the bimanual skill at very low speeds after which the speed was gradually increased, they were more successful in interlimb decoupling than a group that produced the movements always at the target speed (Walter and Swinnen 1992). In a more general way, the probability of occurrence of a particular movement pattern can be increased,

---

[1]At completion of a glide on the low bar, the gymnast brings one leg between the hands (as backward momentum picks up) while pulling down the arms strongly. The legs are kept split during execution. The rear leg kips up as the move is completed. The gymnast ends in a split position above the low bar with one leg in front and one leg behind the bar.

or the shift from one coordination pattern to another can be induced through manipulation of certain parameters. This adaptive tuning technique (Walter and Swinnen 1992) is only one example of how to guide learners toward correct performance, but it shows that instructional techniques should not be limited to providing augmented information feedback.

CONCLUSION

In this contribution, I have discussed the role of KR in relation to other sources of augmented information feedback. KR has received the most attention throughout the history of motor behavior research. In spite of these efforts, the major message that arises from this overview is that the function of KR in relation to other instructional aids is still not well understood. Limitations are indicated that temper the enthusiasm surrounding the role of KR for motor learning. Nevertheless, KR has some strong features. Most appealing is its apparent simplicity in spite of the profound changes in underlying movement kinematics that it often induces. Therefore, it will remain a powerful feedback technique that will attract the attention of practitioners and researchers for many years. A potentially fruitful line of future research underscored in this review pertains to weighing the effect of KR in combination with visual and verbal instructions about the task to be learned. In addition to feedback manipulations, future research should deal with the broader array of instructional manipulations that can guide the learner toward correct performance.

REFERENCES

Adams, J.A. 1971. A closed-loop theory of motor learning. *Journal of Motor Behavior* 3:111-150.

Adams, J.A. 1987. Historical review and appraisal of research on the learning, retention, and transfer of human motor skills. *Psychological Bulletin* 101:41-74.

Annett, J. 1969. *Feedback and human behaviour.* Middlesex: Penguin Books.

Annett, J. 1991. Skill acquisition. P. 13-51 in *Training for performance. Principles of applied human learning,* edited by J.E. Morrison. Chichester: Wiley.

Baldissera, F., Cavallari, P., and Civaschi, P. 1982. Preferential coupling between voluntary movements of ipsilateral limbs. *Neuroscience Letters* 34:95-100.

Beek, P.J., and Van Santvoord, A.A.M. 1992. Learning the cascade juggle: a dynamical systems analysis. *Journal of Motor Behavior* 24:85-94.

Berlyne, D.E. 1967. Arousal and reinforcement. P. 110 in *Nebraska symposium on motivation,* edited by D. Levine. Lincoln: University of Nebraska Press.

Berlyne, D.E., Borsa, D.M., Craw, M.A., Gelman, R.S., and Mandell, E.E. 1965. Effects of stimulus complexity and induced arousal on paired-associate learning. *Journal of Verbal Learning and Verbal Behavior* 4:291-299.

Berlyne, D.E., Borsa, D.M., Hamacher, J.H., and Koenig, I.D.V. 1966. Paired-associate learning and the timing of arousal. *Journal of Experimental Psychology* 72:1-6.

Bernstein, N. 1967. *The co-ordination and regulation of movements.* Oxford: Pergamon Press.

Bilodeau, I.M. 1966. Information feedback. P. 225-296 in *Acquisition of skill*, edited by E.A. Bilodeau. New York: Academic Press.

Buekers, M.J.A., Magill, R.A., and Hall, K.G. 1992. The effect of erroneous knowledge of results on skill acquisition when augmented information is redundant. *Quarterly Journal of Experimental Psychology* 44A:105-117.

Easton, T.A. 1972. On the normal use of reflexes. *American Scientist* 60:591-599.

Fowler, C.A., and Turvey, M.T. 1978. Skill acquisition: an event approach with special reference to searching for the optimum of a function of several variables. P. 1-40 in *Information processing in motor control and learning,* edited by G.E. Stelmach. New York: Academic Press.

Fracker, M.L., and Wickens, C.D. 1989. Resources, confusions, and compatibility in dual-axis tracking: displays, controls, and dynamics. *Journal of Experimental Psychology: Human Perception and Performance* 15:80-96.

Franz, E.A., Zelaznik, H.N., and McCabe, G. 1991. Spatial topological constraints in a bimanual task. *Acta Psychologica* 77:137-151.

Fukuda, T. 1961. Studies on human dynamic postures from the viewpoint of postural reflexes. *Acta Oto-Laryngologica* 161:1-52.

Gable, C.D., Shea, C.H., and Wright, D.L. 1991. Summary knowledge of results. *Research Quarterly for Exercise and Sport* 62:285-292.

Gelfand, I.M., Gurfinkel, V.S., Tsetlin, M.L., and Shik, M.L. 1971. Some problems in the analysis of movements. P. 329-345 in *Models of the structural-functional organization of certain biological systems,* edited by I.M. Gelfand, V.S. Gurfinkel, S.V. Fomin, and M.L. Tsetlin. Cambridge, MA: MIT Press.

Gelfand, I.M., and Tsetlin, M. 1971. Mathematical modeling of mechanisms of the central nervous system. P. 1-22 in *Models of the structural-functional organization of certain biological systems*, edited by I.M. Gelfand, V.S. Gurfinkel, S.V. Fomin, and M.L. Tsetlin. Cambridge, MA: MIT Press.

Gentile, A.M. 1972. A working model of skill acquisition with application to teaching. *Quest* 17:3-23.

Gibson, J.J. 1977. The theory of affordances. P. 67-82 in *Perceiving, acting, and knowing. Toward an ecological psychology,* edited by R. Shaw and J. Bransford. Hillsdale, NJ: Erlbaum.

Guay, M., Salmoni, A., and McIlwain, J. 1992. Summary knowledge of results for skill acquisition: beyond Lavery and Schmidt. *Human Movement Science* 11:653-673.

Hammerton, M. 1989. Tracking. P. 171-195 in D.H. Holding, *Human skills.* 2d ed. Chichester: Wiley.

Johnston, T.D. 1988. Developmental explanation and the ontogeny of birdsong: Nature/nuture redux. *Behavioral and Brain Sciences* 11:617-663.

Kahneman, D. 1973. *Attention and effort.* Englewood Cliffs, NJ: Prentice Hall.

Kay, B.A., Saltzman, E.L., Kelso, J.A.S., and Schöner, G. 1987. Space-time behavior of single and bimanual rhythmical movements: data and limit cycle model. *Journal of Experimental Psychology: Human Perception and Performance* 13:178-192.

Kelso, J.A.S. 1984. Phase transitions and critical behavior in human bimanual coordination. *American Journal of Physiology: Regulatory, Integrative, and Comparative Physiology* 15:1000-1004.

Kelso, J.A.S., and Jeka, J.J. 1992. Symmetry breaking dynamics in human multilimb coordination. *Journal of Experimental Psychology: Human Perception and Performance* 18:645-668.

Kelso, J.A.S., Southard, D.L., and Goodman, D. 1979. On the coordination of two-handed movements. *Journal of Experimental Psychology: Human Perception and Performance* 2:229-238.

Kinkade, R.G. 1963. *A differential influence of augmented feedback on learning and on performance.* Wright-Patterson Air Force Base, Ohio: Tech. Doc. AMRL-TDR-63-12.

Langley, D.J., and Zelaznik, H.N. 1984. The acquisition of time properties associated with a sequential motor skill. *Journal of Motor Behavior* 16:275-301.

Lavery, J.J. 1962. Retention of simple motor skills as a function of type of knowledge of results. *Canadian Journal of Psychology* 16:300-311.

Lee, T.D., and Carnahan, H. 1990. Bandwidth knowledge of results and motor learning: more than just a relative frequency effect. *Quarterly Journal of Experimental Psychology* 42A:777-789.

Lee, T.D., and Magill, R.A. 1983. The locus of contextual interference in motor-skill acquisition. *Journal of Experimental Psychology: Learning, Memory, and Cognition* 9:730-746.

Lee, T.D., and Maraj, K.V. 1994. Effects of bandwidth goals and bandwidth knowledge of results on motor learning. *Research Quarterly for Exercise and Sport* 65:244-249.

Lee, T.D., Swinnen, S.P., and Serrien, D.J. 1994. Cognitive effort and motor learning. *Quest* 46:328-344.

Lee, T.D., Swinnen, S.P., and Verschueren, S. 1995. Relative phase alterations during bimanual skill acquisition. *Journal of Motor Behavior* 27:263-274.

Lee, T.D., White, M.A., and Carnahan, H. 1990. On the role of knowledge of results in motor learning: exploring the guidance hypothesis. *Journal of Motor Behavior* 22:191-208.

Levine, M., Leitenberg, H., and Richter, M. 1964. The blank trials law: the equivalence of positive reinforcement and non-reinforcement. *Psychological Review* 71:94-103.

Lintern, G. 1991. An informational perspective on skill transfer in human-machine systems. *Human Factors* 33:251-266.

Lintern, G., and Roscoe, S.N. 1980. Visual cue augmentation in contact flight simulation. P. 227-238 in *Aviation psychology,* edited by S.N. Roscoe. Ames, IA: Iowa State University Press.

Lintern, G., Roscoe, S.N., and Sivier, J.E. 1990. Display principles, control dynamics, and environmental factors in pilot training and transfer. *Human Factors* 32:299-317.

Magill, R.A. 1993a. Augmented feedback in skill acquisition. P. 193-212 in *Handbook of research on sport psychology,* edited by R.N. Singer, M. Murphy, and L.K. Tennant. New York: Macmillan.

Magill, R.A. 1993b. *Motor learning. Concepts and applications.* 4th ed. Dubuque, IA: Brown & Benchmark.

Magill, R.A., Chamberlin, C.J., and Hall, K.G. 1991. Verbal knowledge of results as redundant information for learning an anticipation timing skill. *Human Movement Science* 10:485-507.

McCullagh, P., and Caird, J. 1990. A comparison of exemplary and learning sequence models and the use of model knowledge of results to increase learning and performance. *Journal of Human Movement Studies* 18:107-116.

Newell, K.M. 1985. Coordination, control and skill. P. 295-317 in *Differing perspectives in motor learning, memory, and control,* edited by D. Goodman, R.B. Wilberg, and I.M. Franks. Amsterdam: North-Holland.

Newell, K.M. 1991. Motor skill acquisition. *Annual Review of Psychology* 42:213-237.

Newell, K.M., and Carlton, M.J. 1987. Augmented information and the acquisition of isometric tasks. *Journal of Motor Behavior* 19:4-12.

Newell, K.M., Carlton, M.J., and Antoniou, A. 1990. The interaction of criterion and feedback information in learning a drawing task. *Journal of Motor Behavior* 22:536-552.

Newell, K.M., Morris, L.R., and Scully, D.M. 1985. Augmented information and the acquisition of skill in physical activity. P. 235-291 in *Exercise and Sport Sciences Reviews 13,* edited by R.L. Terjung. New York: Macmillan.

Newell, K.M., Quinn, J.T., Sparrow, W.A., and Walter, C.B. 1983. Kinematic information feedback for learning a rapid arm movement. *Human Movement Science* 2:255-269.

Newell, K.M., Sparrow, W.A., and Quinn, J.T. 1985. Kinetic information feedback for learning isometric tasks. *Journal of Human Movement Studies* 11:113-123.

Newell, K.M., and Walter, C.B. 1981. Kinematic and kinetic parameters as information feedback in motor skill acquisition. *Journal of Human Movement Studies* 7:235-254.

Nicholson, D.E., and Schmidt, R.A. 1991. Feedback scheduling effects in skill acquisition. Manuscript. Motor Control Laboratory, University of California, Los Angeles.

Pollock, B.J., and Lee, T.D. 1992. Effects of the model's skill level on observational motor learning. *Research Quarterly for Exercise and Sport* 63:25-29.

Proteau, L., Marteniuk, R.G., Girouard, Y., and Dugas, C. 1987. On the type of information used to control and learn an aiming movement after moderate and extensive training. *Human Movement Science* 6:181-199.

Salmoni, A.W. 1989. Motor skill learning. P. 197-227 in *Human skills.* 2d ed., edited by D.H. Holding. Chichester: Wiley.

Salmoni, A.W., Schmidt, R.A., and Walter, C.B. 1984. Knowledge of results and motor learning: a review and critical reappraisal. *Psychological Bulletin* 95:355-386.

Schmidt, R.A. 1975. A schema theory of discrete motor learning. *Psychological Review* 82:225-260.

Schmidt, R.A. 1988. *Motor control and learning: A behavioral emphasis.* Champaign, IL: Human Kinetics.

Schmidt, R.A. 1991. Frequent augmented feedback can degrade learning: evidence and interpretations. P. 59-75 in *Tutorials in motor neuroscience,* edited by J. Requin and G.E. Stelmach. Dordrecht: Kluwer.

Schmidt, R.A., Lange, C., and Young, D.E. 1990. Optimizing summary knowledge of results for skill learning. *Human Movement Science* 9:325-348.

Schmidt, R.A., and Young, D.E. 1991. Methodology for motor learning: a paradigm for kinematic feedback. *Journal of Motor Behavior* 23:13-24.

Schmidt, R.A., Young, D.E., Swinnen, S., and Shapiro, D.C. 1989. Summary knowledge of results for skill acquisition: support for the guidance hypothesis. *Journal of Experimental Psychology: Learning, Memory, and Cognition* 15:352-359.

Schöner, G., Zanone, P.G., and Kelso, J.A.S. 1992. Learning as change of coordination dynamics: theory and experiment. *Journal of Motor Behavior* 24:29-48.

Seashore, R.H., and Bavelas, A. 1941. The functioning of knowledge of results in Thorndike's line-drawing experiment. *Psychological Review* 48:155-164.

Seashore, R.H., Underwood, B.J., Berks, J., and Houston, R.C. 1949. The effect of knowledge of results on performance in the SAM pedestal sight manipulation test. P. 414-417 in *Experimental Psychology,* edited by B.J. Underwood. Englewood Cliffs, NJ: Appleton-Century-Crofts.

Shea, J.B., and Morgan, R.L. 1979. Contextual interference effects on the acquisition, retention, and transfer of a motor skill. *Journal of Experimental Psychology: Human Learning and Memory* 5:179-187.

Sherwood, D.E. 1988. Effects of bandwidth knowledge of results on movement consistency. *Perceptual and Motor Skills* 66:535-542.

Sidaway, B., Moore, B., and Schoenfelder-Zohdi, B. 1991. Summary and frequency of KR presentation effects on retention of a motor skill. *Research Quarterly for Exercise and Sport* 62:27-32.

Sparrow, W.A., and Summers, J.J. 1992. Performance on trials without knowledge of results (KR) in reduced relative frequency presentations of KR. *Journal of Motor Behavior* 24:197-209.

Stockbridge, H.C.W., and Chambers, B. 1958. Aiming, transfer of training, and knowledge of results. *Journal of Applied Psychology* 42:148-153.

Swinnen, S.P. 1984. Relative frequency of KR and skill learning. Unpublished data. University of California, Los Angeles.

Swinnen, S.P., De Pooter, A., and Delrue, S. 1991. Moving away from the in-phase attractor during bimanual oscillations. Posters presented at the VIth International Conference on Event Perception and Action in *Studies in perception and action,* edited by P.J. Beek, R.J. Bootsma, and P.C.W. Van Wieringen. Amsterdam: Rodopi.

Swinnen, S.P., Dounskaia, N., Verschueren, S., Serrien, D.J., and Daelman, A. 1995. Relative phase destabilization during interlimb coordination: The disruptive role of kinesthetic afferences induced by passive movement. *Experimental Brain Research* 105:439-454.

Swinnen, S.P., Dounskaia, N., Walter, C.B., and Serrien, D.J. 1995. Unraveling the macrodynamics and microdynamics of preferred and induced coordination modes during the acquisition of bimanual movements with a 2:1 frequency ratio. Manuscript submitted for publication.

Swinnen, S.P., Lee, T.D., Verschueren, S., and Serrien, D.J. 1995. Interlimb coordination: learning and transfer under different feedback conditions. Manuscript submitted for publication.

Swinnen, S.P., Nicholson, D.E., Schmidt, R.A., and Shapiro, D.C. 1990. Information feedback for skill acquisition: instantaneous knowledge of results degrades learning. *Journal of Experimental Psychology: Learning, Memory, and Cognition* 16:706-716.

Swinnen, S.P., Schmidt, R.A., and Pauwels, J.M. 1989. The effects of summary KR manipulations on absolute and relative timing. Paper presented at the Naspspa annual conference. Knoxville, TN.

Swinnen, S.P., Vandenberghe, J., and Van Assche, E. 1985. Role of cognitive style constructs field dependence-independence and reflection-impulsivity in skill acquisition. *Journal of Sport Psychology* 8:51-69.

Swinnen, S.P., and Walter, C.B. 1988. Constraints in coordinating limb movements. P. 127-143 in *Cognition and action in skilled behaviour,* edited by A.M. Colley and R.J. Beech. Amsterdam: North-Holland.

Swinnen, S.P., and Walter, C.B. 1991. Toward a movement dynamics perspective on dual-task performance. *Human Factors* 33:367-387.

Swinnen, S.P., Walter, C.B., Beirinckx, M.B., and Meugens, P.F. 1991. Dissociating the structural and metrical specifications of bimanual movement. *Journal of Motor Behavior* 23:263-279.

Swinnen, S.P., Walter, C.B., Lee, T.D., and Serrien, D.J. 1993. Acquiring bimanual skills: contrasting forms of information feedback for interlimb decoupling. *Journal of Experimental Psychology: Learning, Memory, & Cognition* 19: 1328-1344.

Swinnen, S.P., Walter, C.B., Pauwels, J.M., Meugens, P.F., and Beirinckx, M.B. 1990. The dissociation of interlimb constraints. *Human Performance* 3:187-215.

Swinnen, S.P., Walter, C.B., Serrien, D.J., and Vandendriessche, C. 1992. The effect of movement speed on upper-limb coupling strength. *Human Movement Science* 11:615-636.

Swinnen, S.P., Walter, C.B., and Shapiro, D.C. 1988. The coordination of limb movements with different kinematic patterns. *Brain and Cognition* 8:326-347.

Teasdale, N., Bard, C., Fleury, M., Paillard, J., Forget, R., and Lamarre, Y. 1994. Bimanual interference in a deafferented patient and in control subjects. P. 243-258 in *Interlimb coordination: neural, dynamical, and cognitive constraints,* edited by S.P. Swinnen, H. Heuer, J. Massion, and P. Casaer. San Diego: Academic Press.

Thorndike, E.L. 1931. *Human learning.* New York: Century.

Turvey, M.T. 1977. Preliminaries to a theory of action with reference to vision. P. 211-265 in *Perceiving, acting, and knowing: Toward an ecological psychology,* edited by R. Shaw and J. Bransford. Hillsdale, NJ: Erlbaum.

Vander Linden, D.H., Cauraugh, J.H., and Greene, T.A. 1993. The effect of frequency of kinetic feedback on learning an isometric force production task in nondisabled subjects. *Physical Therapy* 73:79-87.

Walter, C.B., and Swinnen, S.P. 1990a. Asymmetric interlimb interference during the performance of a dynamic bimanual task. *Brain & Cognition* 14:185-200.

Walter, C.B., and Swinnen, S.P. 1990b. Kinetic attraction during bimanual coordination. *Journal of Motor Behavior* 22:451-473.

Walter, C.B., and Swinnen, S.P. 1992. Adaptive tuning of interlimb attraction to facilitate bimanual decoupling. *Journal of Motor Behavior* 24:95-104.

Walter, C.B., and Swinnen, S.P. 1994. The formation and dissolution of "bad habits" during the acquisition of coordination skills. P. 491-513 in *Interlimb coordination: neural, dynamical, and cognitive constraints,* edited by S.P. Swinnen, H. Heuer, J. Massion, and P. Casaer. San Diego: Academic Press.

Walter, C.B., Swinnen, S.P., and Franz, L. 1993. Stability of symmetric and asymmetric discrete bimanual actions. P. 359-380 in *Variability and motor control,* edited by K.M. Newell and D.M. Corcos. Champaign, IL: Human Kinetics.

Winstein, C.J., Pohl, P.S., and Lewthwaite, R. 1994. Effects of physical guidance and knowledge of results on motor learning: support for the guidance hypothesis. *Research Quarterly for Exercise and Sport* 65:316-323.

Winstein, C.J., and Schmidt, R.A. 1990. Reduced frequency of knowledge of results enhances motor skill learning. *Journal of Experimental Psychology: Learning, Memory, and Cognition* 16:677-691.

Wulf, G., and Schmidt, R.A. 1989. The learning of generalized motor programs: reducing the relative frequency of knowledge of results enhances memory. *Journal of Experimental Psychology: Learning, Memory, & Cognition* 15: 748-757.

Yamanishi, J., Kawato, M., and Suzuki, R. 1979. Studies on human finger tapping neural networks by phase transition curves. *Biological Cybernetics* 33:199-208.

Yao, W.X., Fischman, M.G., and Wang, Y.T. 1994. Motor skill acquisition and retention as a function of average feedback, summary feedback, and performance variability. *Journal of Motor Behavior* 26:273-282.

Young, D.E., and Schmidt, R.A. 1990. Units of motor behavior: modifications with practice and feedback. P. 763-795 in *Attention and performance XIII,* edited by M. Jeannerod. Hillsdale, NJ: Erlbaum.

Young, D.E., and Schmidt, R.A. 1992. Augmented kinematic feedback for motor learning. *Journal of Motor Behavior* 24:261-273.

Zanone, P.G., and Kelso, J.A.S. 1992. The evolution of behavioral attractors with learning: Nonequilibrium phase transitions. *Journal of Experimental Psychology: Human Perception and Performance* 18:403-421.

Zanone, P.G., and Kelso, J.A.S. 1994. The coordination dynamics of learning: Theoretical structure and experimental agenda. P. 461-490 in *Interlimb coordination: neural, dynamical, and cognitive constraints,* edited by S.P. Swinnen, H. Heuer, J. Massion, and P. Casaer. San Diego: Academic Press.

Zelaznik, H.N., Shapiro, D.C., and Newell, K.M. 1978. On the structure of motor recognition memory. *Journal of Motor Behavior* 10:313-323.

Zelaznik, H.N., and Spring, J. 1976. Feedback in response recognition and production. *Journal of Motor Behavior* 8:309-312.

Acknowledgments

Support for this study was provided through a grant from the Research Council of K.U. Leuven, Belgium (Contract No. OT/94/30) and from the National Fund for Scientific Research (S 2/5 - ND. E. 112 and S 2/5 - AB - D 12161). I am indebted to Prof. T.D. Lee and Prof. C.B. Walter for their insightful comments on an earlier draft of this chapter.

Requests for reprints should be sent to S.P. Swinnen, Motor Control Laboratory, Dept. of Kinesiology, FLOK, K.U. Leuven, Tervuurse Vest 101, 3001 Heverlee, Belgium.

Chapter 4

Neural Basis of Motor Learning in Humans

Charles J. Worringham, Ann L. Smiley-Oyen, and Carol L. Cross
The University of Michigan

The path to undertanding complex phenomena such as motor behavior is not a straight one. It is bounded on one side by behavioral observations and on the other by underlying mechanisms: ideally, those traveling the path should attend to both sides, because the long-term goal is to account for observations made at one level of analysis with mechanisms working at another. Motor learning research has attended more closely to the observable behavior side, making only occasional forays to the poorly mapped terrain of underlying mechanisms. We may liken the status of knowledge in motor learning to that of exercise physiology if only empirical training studies had been undertaken over the last 30 years: we would have developed a good conception of the time-course of training effects on performance; we would know something of the specificity and generality of different training regimens for particular types of performance; and we would have formulated some tentative theories of adaptation, relying heavily on inference to augment our skimpy knowledge of the underlying physiology. What we would not have, for example, is an understanding of the molecular basis of muscle hypertrophy, the adaptation that occurs in fuel substrate use, or changes in mitochondrial mass or fiber types with endurance training. In other words, we could *characterize*, but not *explain*, training effects. The field of motor learning is replete with studies of knowledge of results and practice distribution manipulations, mental practice and context effects, but has paid scant attention to where and how motor learning processes are instantiated in the nervous system.

The goal of this chapter is to review such information about the neural basis of human motor learning as does exist. Those who profess to understand motor learning cannot ignore questions about how and where such learning takes place: the lead has already been given in motor control, where the burgeoning of motor neuroscience has reached the point at which behavioral and neural perspectives are beginning to overlap. A good example of this is the work of Georgopoulos and his students concerning the means by which movement direction is coded neurally (Georgopoulos, Kalaska, and Caminiti 1985). The discovery that the vectorially summed activity of groups of motor cortical cells relates to the direction in which the forelimb moves has been followed by the observation that some cells in the parietal cortex appear to code the direction of limb movement independent of the muscles that carry it out (Kalaska et al. 1990). Thus overt motor behavior can in some cases be well correlated with meaningful patterns of neural activity. The challenge to find comparable structure-function relationships for motor learning will become an increasingly insistent one.

"Motor learning" is a term that encompasses an extraordinarily broad spectrum of behavioral and neural change. It is used to describe phenomena as diverse as classical conditioning of the rabbit nictitating membrane response (a third "eyelid" that reflexly covers the eye in response to, for example, a puff of air, but that can be paired with other stimuli)—a widely used model of motor learning in neurophysiology, and acquiring such complex skills as slalom skiing or the virtuoso performance of a violinist. In this chapter we mention some landmark animal studies, but restrict ourselves primarily to asking what we know, from direct human evidence, about the neural basis of motor learning in humans. We pose the question this way because it seems less than satisfactory to depend too heavily on animal data for an answer. This is not to detract from the important studies of, for example, the cerebellum and its inputs in animals (see Glickstein and Yeo 1990 for a recent review) or of multiple cortical and subcortical sites (e.g., Thompson et al. 1990). It is reasonable to suppose that many motor learning mechanisms will be manifest across phylogenetic levels—some human skill acquisition probably involves such low-level adaptation. Moreover, we make the assumption that neural plasticity, such as that seen in the reorganization of monkey motor cortical maps by changes in limb proprioception (Sanes, Wang, and Donoghue 1992), is a basic substrate of motor learning. The question is prompted by the recognition that human motor learning constitutes a qualitatively different set of phenomena. Consider, for example, some differences between the animal and human cases already given. In the classically conditioned nictitating membrane response, the task's motor component is simple, involving a muscle synergy normally part of the animal's repertoire. One need not invoke anthropomorphic notions of intent and goal-directed behavior to explain this type of change. Nor does the animal practice the task, or engage in any high-level information processing about performance or error. Yet an accomplished violinist does not attain proficiency in such a simple manner, for there has to be conscious consideration of the desired goal and persistent, attention-demanding, and cumulative practice. The fact that humans can acquire motor skills far outside the innate repertoire, and that these demand extensive and diligent rehearsal, seems to place human motor learning in a distinct class, hitherto the province of purely behavioral research.

As Eccles (1986) has stated, in contrasting the neural basis of motor learning at different phylogenetic levels, "the emerging story will be more fragmentary . . . for our enquiry into the learning of the much more complex *human* motor skills" (15, our italics). We can glean some evidence from movement disorder and brain imaging studies. We offer the following survey as a starting point for those wishing to think of motor learning in neural terms. To do so, we structure our review around three major brain areas: the cerebral cortex, the cerebellum, and the basal ganglia. (This does not exclude the possible contributions of other areas. For example, Brooks 1986 has suggested the limbic system as mediating the connection between motivation and insight into motor tasks in monkeys.) These are gross brain regions, of course, and some evidence comes from the study of specific nuclei or cytoarchitectonically defined areas within these regions. It is reasonable to suppose that motor learning must involve parts of the brain that participate directly in motor control, and such areas receive special consideration. To organize the sometimes patchy and incomplete data on this subject, we pose a series of questions and use the literature to attempt an answer to each.

CEREBRAL CORTEX

The primary motor cortex, premotor and supplementary motor areas, as well as parts of the parietal areas 5 and 7, are active in planning or executing many features of voluntary movement. In addition, areas in the frontal lobe are active in many cognitive functions. It is therefore reasonable to suppose that we could observe modulation of activity in these areas during motor learning.

Assuming the Cerebral Cortex Is Involved in Motor Learning, Is There a Special Role for One or the Other Hemisphere?

First, evidence shows that both left and right hemispheres can participate in motor learning processes. For example, Kimura (1977) found that a finger movement sequence task was more readily acquired by 16 patients with right hemisphere damage than by 29 patients with left hemisphere damage, hinting at a special contribution of the left hemisphere. Heilman, Schwartz, and Geschwind (1975) studied nine patients with apraxia and right hemiparesis resulting from left hemisphere cerebral infarction, and eight right hemiparetic patients without apraxia, on a rotary pursuit tracking task. Both groups improved over five trials, but on the sixth trial after a 15-min break, the apraxic group's performance had reverted to initial levels. Thus, parts of the left hemisphere may play a role in motor skill retention if apraxia is evident.

Balancing these observations is evidence that areas in the right hemisphere can contribute to motor learning, exemplified by the rotary pursuit data of Heap and Wyke (1972). They found that patients with right hemisphere damage showed no learning for either hand over 10 trials, whereas patients with left hemisphere damage did for both hands. Similarly, Chen et al. (1990) found that three of four patients with partial surgical section of the corpus callosum could learn a unimanual knotting task with the left hand but not with the right. As the two hemispheres were functionally separated, the ability to acquire proficiency in this task must be attributed to the right hemisphere for these patients. Questions about possible hemispheric specialization for motor learning are inevitably clouded by issues of handedness and the extent to which the skill to be learned requires left or right side movements, but there is no evidence that motor learning processes are exclusively the province of one or the other cerebral hemisphere.

Is Motor Learning Mediated by Particular Cortical Areas?

A starting point is the classic observations of Milner (1962) concerning the patient HM, whose severe epilepsy was treated with bilateral excision of the hippocampus and parts of the temporal lobes. Despite massive impairments of *declarative* or *explicit* memory (i.e., the storage and conscious recall of words, images, or events), HM successfully learned a mirror-tracing task over three days, despite protesting that he had not seen the apparatus before and needed to have the task explained anew each time! This dramatic dissociation for two types of memory suggests that motor learning is not primarily mediated by the temporal lobe and hippocampal circuits clearly involved in more cognitive memory. Subsequent replications of this finding include Yamashita's report of three amnesic patients with bilateral medial temporal lobe damage confirmed by magnetic resonance imaging, who learned a pursuit rotor task and retained the skill over a seven-day interval, without any acknowledgment of having been trained in the task (Yamashita 1993).

Other data are reasonably consistent with this. Heap and Wyke (1972) found that patients with frontal lobe damage were more often impaired in rotary pursuit learning than were patients with parietal and temporal lobe damage. Several reasons exist for this, including the possibility that this task's requirement for eye movements may have made it more difficult for frontal lobe patients because of damage to areas concerned with eye movement control.

A greater involvement of frontal lobe (including the supplementary motor area— SMA) in motor learning in humans was also reported in studies of tracking visual targets with a handheld stylus, by Lang et al. (1983, 1988), in which they measured cerebral potentials and regional cerebral blood flow (rCBF). They recorded more activity in the frontocentral areas than in parietal or occipital areas. Increased blood flow between the two conditions occurred in the middle front gyri, frontomedial cortex (including SMA), right basal ganglia (caudate-putamen), and left cerebellar hemisphere. A correlation of blood flow between the middle frontal gyri and basal ganglia is consistent with a functional relationship between these brain structures. These data indicate that as a visuomotor task requiring generation of new perceptual-motor rules is learned, the frontal lobe, including the SMA and the basal ganglia, is highly involved in the process, whereas the parietal, occipital, and precentral areas participate less.

Halsband and Freund (1990) hinted at possible motor learning contributions by the premotor cortex (PMC) and SMA in a study requiring subjects to associate six arm and hand movements with six sensory stimuli. Patients with PMC and SMA lesions either did not achieve the criterion score or did so more slowly than healthy controls, parietal patients, or patients with damage of the primary motor cortex. In this case, however, the task did not require any new movement to be learned, but merely pairing a stimulus and a movement.

How Does Learning Occur in the Cortex?

The boundary between accepted knowledge and speculation is necessarily crossed in attempting an answer. A compelling notion is that cerebral cortical areas less directly concerned with movement production have active learning roles but make themselves progressively redundant with practice. For example, a PET imaging study by Seitz et al. (1990) measured rCBF changes in the brain as a finger-sequencing task was being learned. Cortex involvement changed as the task shifted from closed-loop (sensory) control to open-loop (ballistic) control. Involvement of the somatosensory association cortices diminished, especially in the right hemisphere (ipsilateral to the moving hand). In addition, activity in inferior frontal gyri disappeared; subjects reported that during this stage they no longer needed to guide the sequence verbally. As the fingers moved faster, the left primary motor hand area increased in activity. This is consistent with the notion that cognitive, including verbal, strategies can be central to early learning of some tasks, but "fall out" as the task becomes automated. The concept that improvements in performance are accompanied by localizing brain activity in a decreasing set of structures is supported by another PET study, involving eight adults learning the visuospatially demanding game of Tetris (Haier et al. 1992).

Subsequently, Grafton et al. (1992) studied six normal humans at four stages in their acquisition of a pursuit rotor skill (using the right hand), during which their mean time on target improved from 17 to 66%. Over the four sessions they observed increased blood flow in the left primary motor cortex, left SMA, and left pulvinar thalamus. The areas within which change occurred over sessions were a subset of those involved in execution, which included additional cortical, cerebellar, and striatonigral sites (the latter being part of the basal ganglia). This seems to be at odds with the data of Seitz et al. (1990), but this task is less amenable to verbal or cognitive mediation than sequential movement task, the components of which can be rehearsed symbolically. The greater activation of primarily motor sites remains consistent with the idea that the progressive automation of a skill with practice is caused by the movement becoming represented more fully in primarily motor regions.

Animal evidence supports this position. For example, Asanuma and Keller (1991) have shown that the sensory cortex (at the anterior margin of the parietal lobe) is crucial for the acquisition of novel wrist supination skills in the cat (required to retrieve food from rotating a beaker through a slot). Once acquired, however, the skill is not lost even after the sensory cortex is removed. The authors suggest that the sensory cortex is producing long-term changes in motor cortex ("long-term potentiation") and becomes dispensible after learning is completed.

Finally, we need to be careful to avoid making general statements about cortical changes during motor learning. The PET findings of Schlaug, Knorr, and Seitz (1994) show that great variation exists among subjects in those areas that are activated as they acquire a skill.

We may assume that areas critical for learning early in acquisition can become redundant only through permanent modification of the functions of other, primarily motor structures. There is no reason to think that these changes are confined to motor areas of the cerebral cortex, and consideration of the principal subcortical motor structures, the cerebellum and the basal ganglia, is therefore justified.

CEREBELLUM

Of all areas of the brain, the cerebellum and its inputs from the inferior olive have received the greatest attention as likely mediators of motor learning. Human studies are heavily outnumbered by investigations using animals, and the latter fall outside the scope of this review. Briefly, interest in the cerebellum as a principal site of motor learning arose from theoretical analyses of the possible functions of the parallel cell architecture of the cerebellum and the ideas of Marr (1969) and Albus (1971), often labeled the Marr-Albus theory, in which cerebellar integration of incoming information through *mossy* fibers is modified by specific inputs from the inferior olive (via *climbing* fibers).

How is the Cerebellum Thought to Mediate Motor Learning?

The proposed mechanism for motor learning involves a signal from the inferior olive via climbing fibers, "teaching" Purkinje cells to respond differently to inputs from mossy fibers during motor learning. Purkinje cells are the cells of origin for all signals leaving the cerebellum. Because they receive weak, though massively converging, parallel fiber input and just a single climbing fiber input (but one strong enough to produce the Purkinje cell firing single-handedly), the highly uniform cerebellar circuitry seems well suited to having simple error signals modify the way the cerebellum integrates sensory and motor information. Thus its output could be modified to change movements that previously resulted in errors. Experimental data broadly supporting these views have followed. So far, there is evidence that simple reflex movements cannot be classically conditioned if the cerebellum is lesioned in animals, and that the gains of reflexes (such as the vestibular-ocular reflex) are not modified normally with cerebellar damage (e.g., Lisberger 1988; Yeo 1988).

The work of Gilbert and Thach (1977) on adaptation to unexpected loads in a monkey's wrist movements comes closest to human skill learning. These authors adduced evidence that, when a monkey trained to make wrist movements against a load adapted to unfamiliar loads and reduced error over 40 to 50 trials, climbing fiber activity was changing the response of Purkinje cells to other inputs—an observation made possible by the fact that the type of action potentials recorded in Purkinje cells is quite different depending on whether climbing fiber or parallel fiber inputs made that cell fire.

Such findings have not been replicated universally, however. Ojakangas and Ebner (1992) found no evidence of long-term alterations in Purkinje cell activity from olivary inputs. Kelly, Zuo, and Bloedel (1990) have reported that rabbits could both produce and acquire classically conditioned nictitating membrane responses even after removal of both the cerebrum and the cerebellum. In their view, the cerebellum's motor learning role is in optimizing performance, not in mediating adaptive changes. This is a major discrepancy with other studies, one that is not yet resolved.

Does Human Evidence Support a Learning Function for the Cerebellum?

The study of humans with cerebellar dysfunction, especially if the damage includes cerebellar afferents arising in the olive (as in olivopontocerebellar atrophy—OPCA), is obviously of special interest. Unfortunately, the evidence from human studies does not present a clear picture. Modest support comes from the adaptation experiments of Gauthier et al. (1979) and Weiner, Hallett, and Funkenstein (1983).

Gauthier et al. (1979) studied six cases of major cerebellar lesions confirmed by computerized tomography, resulting from tumors (five cases) or stroke (one case). In five of these cases, motor signs were in remission, but in a sixth, persistent cerebellar motor signs were still present. Subjects pointed to targets under normal visual conditions, but without seeing the arm and hand, then with 2.5x magnifying lenses. Normal subjects make pointing errors under these conditions, but soon rescale their movements. There followed an adaptation period with lenses, during which the subjects viewed their hands while they moved as rapidly as possible to a series of numbered points. A third test was conducted with lenses in place, but they were removed for a final test.

Patients with remission of motor signs showed normal performance in all phases, compared with normals. The patient with persistent cerebellar signs, however, had not adapted after 20 min of exposure to active hand movements through the magnifying lenses, nor had any significant aftereffect once these were removed. The authors report that visual-motor adaptation is normal in patients with major cerebellar lesions, provided motor signs are absent, but it is absent if motor signs persist. The authors further implicate the cerebellar olivary system as exercising a role in visual-motor gain calibration, given that the one affected patient had signs often associated with damage to the olive (palatal myoclonus).

Weiner, Hallett, and Funkenstein (1983) also used a visual-motor adaptation task in studying subjects with cerebellar dysfunction, Parkinson's disease (PD), Alzheimer's disease (AD), Korsakoff's syndrome, and left and right cerebral hemisphere lesions. The cerebellar group comprised two patients with olivopontocerebellar degeneration, and one each with spinocerebellar degeneration, vestibulocerebellar degeneration, and progressive cerebellar degeneration. Cerebral hemisphere lesions were a mix of tumors, infarcts, and hemorrhages.

The subjects undertook a pointing task with and without wearing goggles fitted with displacing prisms, with spatial error as the measure of performance. The first 5 trials were made without prism glasses, and the next 20 adaptation trials were made with them. Finally, 20 more trials were undertaken without the prism glasses to measure aftereffect.

All groups showed initial high errors in the adaptation phase and significant reduction in that error over the 20 trials. The Korsakoff group was quite normal, and the Alzheimer's group showed the least consistent and smallest degree of error reduction. The error reduction other groups showed was less than normal. The authors claimed that the degree of negative aftereffect was the best index of true adaptation, and found, by this measure, that only the cerebellar group was significantly impaired. The authors assert that this finding supports the idea that the cerebellum is involved in motor learning.

One recent case study that investigated the ability to generalize from a learned motor program indicated impairments with cerebellar damage (Keating and Thach 1990). A right-handed subject with a right cerebellar cortex infarct was trained to move a manipulandum such that a cursor on a computer screen moved to a target. After holding the cursor in a given position, another target was displayed. This required the subject to execute a flexion or extension movement at the wrist that moved the cursor in a steplike function to the new target. After some training trials, the gain was changed, altering the relationship between the extent of the limb and cursor movement. The subject made this adaptation one-third as fast with his right hand as with his left. The rate of change in his left hand was comparable to both hands of a control subject. This indicates that the right hand, affected by a right-sided infarct, exhibited learning, but did so more slowly. Rendering a clean interpretation somewhat harder is the fact that learning did occur. A change in the learning rate does not unequivocally indicate that the damaged structure mediates that learning.

Sanes, Dimitrov, and Hallett (1990) took a different approach to motor learning in a study of sequential hand movements. Using a digitizing tablet, these researchers studied cerebellar hemisphere degeneration, olivopontocerebellar atrophy (OPCA), and control groups. Subjects performed planar movement sequences, moving a stylus from a starting position to each of three or four small squares. They were to move as rapidly as possible, without missing the squares.

Over the course of 50 trials, both cerebellar groups and controls had significantly decreased normalized movement times (nMT), showing that learning can occur in this condition. Their decreases were smaller than controls, however, suggesting a relative impairment in learning. OPCA subjects had larger spatial errors than either controls or hemisphere subjects, and two of the four OPCA subjects showed deteriorating accuracy over trials. This is significant because the same two patients had the largest drop in nMT. This suggests that an altered speed-accuracy trade-off was occurring in the OPCA group. The authors point out that this does not demonstrate motor skill learning in this group, but merely an altered performance strategy. Hemisphere patients showed real improvement, though less than controls. Consistent with this, average error and nMT were significantly negatively correlated for OPCA and control groups. Hemisphere patients had neither a decline in accuracy over trials nor significant error/nMT correlations.

A second task with a different sequence was performed with mirror-reversed vision. All groups showed declines in MT, but now OPCA patients showed significantly less improvement than controls, from whom the hemisphere patients did not differ. A similar pattern was observed for reduction in acceleration-zero crossings—a simple index of the number of movement units needed to complete the figure. The study provides some support of motor learning deficits being more evident if degeneration includes brainstem projections to the cerebellum, and not just the cerebellar hemispheres. The speed-accuracy confound and the use of normalized data that differed considerably from performance prevent a clear interpretation, however.

Do Imaging Studies Indicate Cerebellar Mediation of Human Motor Learning?

In the study of Seitz et al. (1990) already discussed, in which subjects performed a finger-sequencing task with their right hands, an indirect confirmation of cerebellar participation arose. The authors found that the rCBF of the right anterior lobe was equally active in all phases of learning. Given that the frequency of finger movements increased greatly over the course of practice, they argue that normalized activity declined, that is, less metabolic activity in the right anterior cerebellum occurred during skilled performance than would be expected for the increased rate of finger movement. This they interpret as consistent with climbing fiber inputs modifying transmission in cerebellar cortex in initial learning. Of course, the resolution of the method does not permit distinction by cell type, and it is not clear what type of adaptation or modification analogous to VOR gain changes is necessary in this task. Unfortunately, the inferior olive was not within the PET camera range.

The Grafton et al. study (1992) mentioned earlier showed cerebellar activity correlated with execution, rather than learning, of the pursuit rotor task. The authors do not exclude the possibility that longer term practice might show cerebellar involvement, but given the significant improvements in performance, the failure to find obvious cerebellar changes is not consistent with this structure occupying a central functional role in motor learning, at least for this task. On the other hand, PET data has shown both an increase in cerebellar activity during learning a motor sequence compared with executing an overlearned one (Jenkins et al. 1994), and a decrease in cerebellar activity with the practice of a simple motor task (Friston et al. 1992).

Might the Cerebellum's Role Be Restricted to Unconscious Adaptation Rather Than Learning Mediated by the Conscious Use of Feedback?

An additional study reported by Thach, Goodkin, and Keating (1992) is of interest in this respect. Two patients with inferior olive hypertrophy (a degenerative disease) performed a dart-throwing task first without, then with, and again without wearing displacing prism spectacles. Normal subjects are fairly accurate without the prisms, make large errors on initial trials with prisms but rapidly adapt, then have an error in the opposite direction on restoration of normal vision (an aftereffect). The two olive hypertrophy patients neither adapted nor showed an aftereffect, fully consistent with an olivo-cerebellar role for adaptation. An interesting note is that one normal and one patient showed instances of cheating (i.e., making a deliberate offset to compensate for an error [personal communication]). The effects reported by Thach require the subjects to aim where they see the target and do not permit them to use such a strategy. Thus a consciously mediated change was possible, whereas automatic adaptation was not. In our laboratory (Smiley-Oyen, Cross, and Worringham 1991), we have found additional evidence for the normal deliberate feedback use despite cerebellar damage. Seven OPCA and seven age-matched control subjects performed a linear arm movement task in which a visually presented bar indicated the extent of the movement. Four bar lengths were used, corresponding to movements of 12, 16, 20, and 24 cm. Subjects practiced the task for 144 trials, receiving knowledge of results (KR) concerning the direction and size of error after every second trial. The bar length was changed every six trials. OPCA subjects reduced errors as much as controls. In subsequent phases they performed no worse on retention trials and could both extrapolate to new distances and adapt to a new gain. A specific focus, however, was on the use of KR.

Feedback use was assessed by examining the relationship between the error made on a trial on which feedback was given and the correction on the following trial.

If KR were used perfectly, the regression should have a slope of 1, an intercept of 0, and a correlation of 1; both should average 0 if there is a failure to use feedback (i.e., if the following movement differs randomly from the preceding one). The OPCA group and the control group mean slopes were 0.71 and 0.73, respectively, and the r-squared values were 45.8% and 44.7%. There was no indication that the OPCA patients were impaired in using error feedback to improve the subsequent movement. We analyzed in the same way pairs of trials in which the first was not followed by KR and the second one was. Here, the subject is entirely dependent on internal error detection and correction processes. The mean slopes were 0.45 (OPCA) and 0.39 (controls), and mean r-squared values were 21.3 (OPCA) and 18.9 (controls). All subjects in both groups performed significantly above chance levels in using KR, and similar proportions in each group (6/7 OPCA, 5/7 controls) did so for internal error detection and correction.

Overall, the results suggest that humans with damage to the cerebellum and its input structures, including the climbing fiber system, resulting from olivopontocerebellar atrophy, can learn movement scaling well, use KR normally, and detect and correct errors without objective feedback as well as normals.

When we take all the evidence together, the cerebellum appears to have a much smaller role in motor learning in humans than in animals, largely because human motor learning demands the conscious use of feedback or KR and less on automatic adaptation. Thus many constituent processes of human motor learning, particularly those involved in conscious strategy use, may be mediated by noncerebellar circuits.

BASAL GANGLIA

The basal ganglia, a set of nuclei deep within the brain that includes the caudate and putamen, internal and external globus pallidus, substantia nigra and subthalamic nucleus, are plausible candidates for mediating some motor learning functions in addition to their more obvious role in motor control. Animal work has pointed to possible roles of the caudate and putamen (Peeke and Herz 1971; Sanberg, Lehmann, and Fibiger 1978) and basal ganglia projections to the frontal cortex via the thalamus (Canavan, Nixon, and Passingham 1989) in learning. Research and clinical observations of patients with PD have led one observer to propose that the role of the basal ganglia is responsible for the "automatic execution of learned motor plans" (Marsden 1982). This implies that the basal ganglia serve, if not as the repository of acquired motor programs, then at least as a crucial structure for their retrieval and activation. One would therefore expect individuals with basal ganglia damage to have difficulty acquiring motor skills, bearing in mind the caveat that PD and other basal ganglia disorders are an imperfect window on normal basal ganglia function.

Is There an Impairment in Learning to Use Predictable Components of a Task in Parkinson's Disease?

We begin by considering the ability to use predictable features of task stimuli to plan open-loop movements. If individuals can incorporate prediction into their movement strategy, they are presumably learning some critical features of the task. More specifically, if they are tracking an object more accurately and with reduced time lag, they must be basing their movements less on current external sensory information and more on an internal model acquired through learning (shifting from closed-loop to more open-loop control).

Tracking tasks have been used extensively to answer this question, following an early observation that PD patients experience difficulty using a *feedforward* mode of control (Flowers 1978), that is, generating movements that anticipate the motion of the object being tracked. Flowers concluded that PD subjects could not use a predictive strategy, despite more practice than controls and the fact that they could accurately describe the cursor's movement patterns. They failed to match the pattern when the cursor disapeared for a 2-s interval. In addition, their performance was less disrupted than was that of controls when the cursor unexpectedly changed direction.

Subsequent studies have not been in full agreement, however. For example, Day, Dick, and Marsden (1984) found that PD subjects could reduce tracking lag in elbow and wrist tracking tasks. During the first 150 trials in which they were unaware of the target's predictable motion, 11 out of 12 PD patients reduced their mean tracking lag, and 8 out of 12 did so further after they were informed of its repetitive nature. This led to the conclusion that ''patients with Parkinson's disease are capable of learning a target motion and moving according to an 'internal plan' in a predictive fashion,'' although less well than controls.

Frith, Bloxham, and Carpenter (1986), who examined the ability of PD patients to acquire proficiency in two novel tracking tasks, used a variation on this approach. In both, a joystick controlled the two-dimensional position of a cursor on a computer screen. The goal was to track a target that moved both vertically and horizontally. In task one, the target's horizontal motion was fully predictable and its vertical motion was irregular and unpredictable. Although the unpredictable component per se could not be learned, improved performance indicated that attention necessary for the predictable component was decreasing and therefore, more attention was available to track the unpredictable component. In the second task both components were unpredictable and therefore unlearnable, but the relation between the movement and the cursor direction could be learned—the horizontal motion of the cursor was opposite that of the hand motion, yielding a directional incompatibility. Over two sets of 3-min sessions separated by a 10-min rest, PD subjects clearly improved their tracking, whether the motion was predictable or unpredictable and whether the response involved compatible or incompatible hand movements.

One difference the authors noted in the learning curves of the two groups was in performance during the first minute of each 3-min session. Control subjects improved rapidly while the PD group did so gradually. The authors argue that this difference indicates a PD deficit in the *temporary* component of motor learning. There is, however, an alternative explanation. Controls had more noticeable improvements within each session and began the second with poorer performance than at the end of the first. The latter effect resembles a ''warm-up decrement'' (Adams 1961). This difference in the first minute may be attributable not to a group difference in permanent and temporary components of learning, but to the fact that a slight drop in performance typically follows a rest period if the earlier performance is near a ceiling.

Two additional studies in which patient groups had to acquire a tracking skill are equivocal, partly because of possible nonlearning factors and partly because not all subjects exhibited less learning. Harrington et al. (1990) studied the effects of practice on the rotary pursuit apparatus, by PD and control subjects. PD subjects showed absolute improvement, but slightly less than control when judged across days. Improvement within sessions was similar between the two groups. Severity of symptoms, specifically bradykinesia, was related to impaired motor learning, especially at the fast speed. Even with initial performance equated between the two PD groups, there were still differences in the amount of improvement, which might suggest that the deficit is not merely a result of impairment in their primary motor skills. The advanced symptom PD group may have encountered a performance ceiling later in practice, attributable to motor control differences not evident at the outset.

Another study of pursuit tracking also found heterogeneity with the patient sample (Abdul-Malek et al. 1988). They had subjects rotate a handle that controlled the sequential illumination of a row of lights in response to that of a set of stimulus lights. As a group, PD patients improved (reduced variance unaccounted for by variance in the stimulus light pattern), but not to the same degree as controls. Whereas all but one control improved from the first to the second session, nearly half the PD subjects did not, indicating a possible learning deficit. No information was given that might distinguish those patients who did improve from those who did not.

Are Similar Results Found for Patients With Huntington's Disease?

Heindel et al. (1989) examined the learning of the pursuit rotor task by Huntington's disease (HD), Alzheimer's disease (AD), and PD patients. The AD subjects improved as much as age-matched controls, but the HD subjects exhibited significantly less learning—similar to the demented PD group—but they did improve over the course of practice.

Corkin et al. (1990) measured learning on both the rotary pursuit task and mirror tracing in HD, PD, and patients with unilateral caudate lesions. They also assessed spatial abilities, because both motor tasks incorporate a strong spatial component. The HD subjects exhibited impaired motor learning, but the PD and unilateral caudate lesion patients did not show deficits. The minimal research of motor learning in HD indicates that learning is impaired, at least in terms of tracking and rapid sequencing, both of which require a shift from closed- to open-loop control. Because a common feature of these studies is a strong spatial component, and HD patients in this study were shown to be severely impaired in spatial processing, their difficulty in learning these tasks may be a result of disrupted spatial abilities rather than a primary problem of motor learning.

What Evidence Exists for the Learning of Other Motor Tasks in Parkinson's or Huntington's Disease?

An early finding in the study of Parkinson's disease was that PD patients have prolonged simple reaction times. The implication is that they are unable to pre-program simple movements (i.e., cannot take advantage of advance information concerning a movement to initiate it more quickly) (Evarts, Teravainen, and Calne 1981). Worringham and Stelmach (1990) found that the selective impairment in simple RT was diminished over blocks of trials. Although controls showed most of their improvement in choice RT conditions, PD patients' simple RTs fell more than their choice RT times. This demonstrates an ability to learn how to capitalize on the availability of advance information. It also points to the danger in inferring that a movement disorder population has a deficit in a particular process or function if the evidence comes from only a small number of trials, because there is insufficient opportunity to display optimal performance. In a linear arm-movement task (identical to that described for OPCA patients), Worringham, Cross, and Smiley-Oyen (1990) found poorer PD performance than for controls, but no group differences in the degree of improvement, extrapolation to novel targets, retention with KR withdrawn, or adaptation to a new gain. PD use of KR and error detection were also not significantly impaired.

Using a sequencing task in which one of four lights were turned on and subjects were to push the button corresponding to it, Willingham and Koroshetz (1990) found that control subjects reduced their response times although they were not aware that a sequence was being repeated. When lights were turned on randomly, the control subjects' response times did not decrease. HD subjects did not exhibit this sequence-specific learning. They did improve when the task was to learn which button they were to match with a particular light (stimulus-response mapping incompatibility), with lights presented as individual trials rather than as part of a sequence. This dissociation indicates that striatal damage affects learning rapid sequential movements but leaves learning associations between visual cues and motor responses intact.

Soliveri et al. (1992) had PD patients learn a timed buttoning task, either alone or with a simultaneous foot-tapping action at various frequencies. PD patients improved as much as controls in either case, but had poorer overall performance and were more affected by the dual-task requirement. The authors interpret the outcome as a delay in the rate of learning, not as a direct impairment of the learning process.

Do the Basal Ganglia Appear to Participate in Motor Learning in Studies of Normal Individuals Using Brain Imaging Methods?

In the previously cited PET study of finger-sequence learning by Seitz et al. (1990) and in a second report (Seitz and Roland 1992), rCBF in areas including the midsectors of the putamen and globus pallidus decreased relative to rest during initial learning. Activity increased in these sites as learning progressed (as it did for other sites including brainstem regions near the red nucleus). The authors argue that this modulation is evidence that the corticostriatal circuit is one in which the motor program for the skilled movement is represented. They make a similar claim for a corticocerebellar circuit (see prior reference).

Among the changes noted by Lang et al. (1983, 1988) in their studies of visual tracking was an increased rCBF in the right caudate and putamen in the inverted version of the task (which required the subjects to produce a directionally in-compatible response), but not during normal tracking.

Taking account of the different task characteristics may reconcile an apparent contradiction between these studies. Seitz et al. (1990) note a decrease in rCBF in initial learning, which is subsequently reversed as the task becomes more open loop. One might expect rCBF to be higher in the normal tracking of the Lang et al. study than for inverted tracking, on the grounds that the former is more fully learned and automatic. However, the Lang normal tracking task used constant velocity move-ments that randomly changed every 1.5 s. This would preclude significant use of open-loop control. What remains inconsistent between the studies is the increased rCBF during inverted tracking, because its random nature would also seem to preclude much open-loop control, and as the authors state, requires attention and conscious awareness, the very stage during which Seitz et al. observed a reduction in rCBF in the finger-sequence task.

When we take lesion and imaging studies together, it is difficult to conclude that the basal ganglia are central to motor learning, although their functioning may become modified for certain tasks, perhaps those involving complex sequences, and they may be involved in representing movement skills once they have been learned. Unless dementia is present (which might prevent a patient from understanding the goal of a task), patients with basal ganglia damage learn motor tasks either at the same rate as controls or somewhat slower. Their control limitations can become evident during acquisition of a task and therefore limit the degree of proficiency that they can attain.

CONCLUSIONS

In the final section, we point to some areas of agreement that emerge from the existing literature, consider some of the literature's shortcomings, and explore some factors that may help experimentalists develop a clearer picture of the neural basis of human motor learning.

Can Any Clear Interpretation Be Made of These Diverse Studies?

We should first note that there are several serious obstacles in the way of this goal. The reader will have observed that the studies we reviewed used a bewildering range of tasks, measures, and procedures. Although some specific tasks have been widely used (e.g., the pursuit rotor), the studies call on widely differing processes and levels of complexity, and involve different types and amounts of practice, availability of KR, and movement feedback. All this would present sufficient prob-lems were it not for the fact that the results, too, employ different measures of what constitutes impaired learning. We further note that lesion studies—especially those of slow degenerative disease—have the potential difficulty that unaffected structures have assumed the motor learning functions of the damaged area in a functional, but atypical way.

In spite of these caveats, we can tentatively identify some common strands, and we enumerate these here.

1. No ''motor learning center'' exists. Specifically, no evidence exists from imaging or lesion studies that any single neural locus mediates motor learning. It has every appearance of consisting of a set of highly distributed functions. Although this should not be too surprising, given the multiplicity of processes comprising this complex phenomenon, it makes the search for the neural basis of motor learning qualitatively different from that for more narrowly defined functions. This view of motor learning as *essentially* distributed, and thus dissimilar to explicit memory (declarative learning) with its relatively defined temporal lobe-hippocampal basis, is becoming widely accepted (Halsband and Freund 1993).

2. A general shift occurs from widely distributed activity including circuits not primarily involved in motor control to those that are. It appears that the former have a role in modifying the action of the latter, which become increasingly redundant with the achievement of automaticity.

3. The basal ganglia appear to have no pivotal role in motor *learning*, although their control function may become modified, especially for more complex tasks such as sequences of movement. Skill representation may have a role in the basal ganglia, however. Both PD and HD patients can learn a range of tasks with, at most, an impairment in the rate of improvement. We are unable to determine if even this is not the consequence of a ceiling effect, in which performance becomes limited by the primary motor control limits imposed by the disease, rather than by any specific impairment of motor learning. PD patients seem able to improve, with practice, even functions hitherto considered among their greatest impairments (simultaneous movements, the use of advance information, and the use of predictive strategies).

4. In light of the much-studied phenomenon of cerebellar plasticity in classical conditioning and reflex gain adaptation, there is a surprising paucity of evidence that the cerebellum is critically involved in the acquisition of many human motor skills. A principal reason seems to be that the type of nonconscious adaptation so prominent in the tasks used in animal studies occupies a minor role in human motor learning. This is not to say that similar low-level adaptation may not also be mediated, at least in part, by the human cerebellum. We suggest that the cerebellum's contribution to motor learning has become considerably exaggerated, in part because similar types of long-term potentiation or depression elsewhere have yet to be as fully studied, but mostly because the tasks used as models for motor learning in animal studies are too low level to capture the diversity of processing manifest in human skill acquisition. Even on the narrower grounds of reassessment of animal studies of cerebellar function, others are questioning whether the view that the cerebellum occupies a central role in motor learning is really tenable (Llinas and Welsh 1993).

5. Several regions of the cerebral cortex show adaptive change during motor learning. This appears to be of two forms. Primarily motor areas, including the involved parts of the motor cortex and supplementary motor area, may show increased activation during learning. Other parts of the cerebral cortex become less

active, including nonmotor frontal lobe areas, and, possibly, the sensory cortex. Such regions may be crucial for processing KR, and for using verbal or other cognitive strategies essential at early stages of skill acquisition.

6. The foregoing must remain heavily qualified by the recognition that the detailed, cell-level mechanisms of motor learning cannot be captured at this coarse level of analysis (the tentative assignment of learning functions to gross anatomical subdivisions). The latter may be questioned in light of the evidence for neural plasticity, though various brain regions probably have specific motor learning functions just as they do for motor control.

What Approaches Are Needed to Advance Our Knowledge of the Neural Basis of Motor Learning?

Two strategies may prove useful. One is to find more common ground between conventional behavioral studies of motor learning in normals and movement disorders or imaging studies. For example, a great deal of knowledge has accumulated about the use of KR—including its content, precision, and frequency—in healthy individuals. Similar studies in patients with neurological damage may isolate specific features of, for example, feedback use that depend on the lesioned structures. In the studies we reviewed, for example, all but a few fail to use any test of retention by withdrawing KR. Motor behaviorists accept this practice as necessary for drawing distinctions about learning and performance factors in conventional motor learning research. Thus, motor behavior methods offer ample opportunity to find application in searching for the neural basis of motor learning.

Second, we must recognize that a computational framework for understanding learning is inexorably pushing to the forefront. It is not only desirable but inevitable that the tools of connectionism will be widely employed as the middle ground between nervous system function and observable characteristics of motor learning. Adaptive networks that can accomplish learning and are neurally realistic can be used to model neural subsystems, and thus guide behavioral and neural studies. Although this is not the place to review this burgeoning field, the reader may refer to Gluck and Granger (1993), who review models that include cognitive, perceptual, and motor learning phenomena, and Kawato and Gomi (1992), who model motor learning involving the cerebellum and its function during eye movements, for representative thinking on motor learning and neural networks. Motor behaviorists need to be part of this enterprise, because no neural network, however biologically realistic, can be devised without clear and comprehensive accounts of the behavior to be modeled.

Students of motor behavior should not feel discouraged by the challenge of such a basic question as how the brain acquires motor skills. Just as motor control has become the province of many disciplines—neuroscience, kinesiology, engineering, and psychology among them—so will motor learning become more completely understood as a more encompassing view is taken. The burden does not lie exclusively on any one discipline.

REFERENCES

Abdul-Malek, A., Markham, C.H., Marmarellis, P.Z., and Marmarmelis, V.Z. 1988. Quantifying deficiencies associated with Parkinson's disease by use of time-series analysis. *Electroencephaolography and Clinical Neurophysiology* 69: 24-33.

Adams, J.A. 1961. The second facet of forgetting: A review of the warm-up decrement. *Psychological Bulletin* 58:257-273.

Albus, J.S. 1971. A theory of cerebellar function. *Mathematical Bioscience* 10:25-61.

Asanuma, H., and Keller, A. 1991. Neuronal mechanisms of motor learning in mammals. *NeuroReport* 2:217-224.

Brooks, V.B. 1986. How does the limbic system assist motor learning? A limbic comparator hypothesis. *Brain, Behavior, and Evolution* 29:29-53.

Canavan, A.G., Nixon, P.D., and Passingham, R.E. 1989. Motor learning in monkeys (Macaca fascicularis) with lesions in motor thalamus. *Experimental Brain Research* 77:113-126.

Chen, Y.P., Campbell, R., Marshall, J.C., and Zaidel, W.W. 1990. Learning a unimanual motor skill by partial commissurotomy patients. *Journal of Neurology, Neurosurgery, & Psychiatry* 53:785-788.

Corkin, S., Growdon, J.H., Koroshetz, W., and Snow, M. 1990. Differential effects of striatal lesions on motor-skill learning. *Movement Disorders* 5, Supplement:35.

Day, B.L., Dick, J.P.R., and Marsden, C.D. 1984. Patients with Parkinson's disease can employ a predictive strategy. *Journal of Neurology, Neurosurgery, & Psychiatry* 47:1299-1306.

Eccles, J.C. 1986. Learning in the motor system. *Progress in Brain Research* 64:3-18.

Evarts, E., Teravainen, H., and Calne, D. 1981. Reaction time in Parkinson's disease. *Brain* 104:167-186.

Flowers, K.A. 1978. Lack of prediction in the motor behaviour of Parkinsonism. *Brain* 101:35-52.

Friston, K.J., Frith, C.D., Passingham, R.E., Liddle, P.F., and Frackowiak, R.S.J. 1992. Motor practice and neurophysiological adaptation in the cerebellum: a positron tomography study. *Proceedings of the Royal Society of London (Biology)* 248:223-228.

Frith, C.D., Bloxham, C.A., and Carpenter, K.N. 1986. Impairments in the learning and performance of a new manual skill in patients with Parkinson's disease. *Journal of Neurology, Neurosurgery, & Psychiatry* 49:661-668.

Gauthier, G.M., Hofferer, J.M., Hoyt, W.F., and Stark, L. 1979. Visual-motor adaptation: Quantitative demonstration in patients with posterior fossa involvement. *Archives of Neurology* 36:155-160.

Georgopoulos, A.P., Kalaska, J.F., and Caminiti, R. 1985. Relations between two-dimensional arm movements and single cell discharge in motor cortex and area 5: Movement direction versus movement end point. *Experimental Brain Research* Supplementum 10:175-183.

Gilbert, P.F.C., and Thach, W.T. 1977. Purkinje cell activity during motor learning. *Brain Research* 128:309-328.

Glickstein, M., and Yeo, C. 1990. The cerebellum and motor learning. *Journal of Cognitive Neuroscience* 2:69-80.

Gluck, M.A., and Granger, R. 1993. Computational models of the neural bases of learning and memory. *Annual Review of Neuroscience* 16:667-706.

Grafton, S.T., Mazziotta, J.C., Presty, S., Friston, K.J., Frackowiak, S.J., and Phelps, M.E. 1992. Functional anatomy of human procedural learning determined with regional cerebral blood flow and PET. *Journal of Neuroscience* 12:2542-2548.

Haier, R.J., Siegel, B.V., MacLachlan, A., Soderling, E., Lottenberg, S., and Buchsbaum, M.S. 1992. Regional glucose metabolic changes after learning a complex, visuospatial/motor task. *Brain Research* 570:134-143.

Halsband, U., and Freund, H.-J. 1990. Premotor cortex and conditional motor learning in man. *Brain* 113:207-222.

Halsband, U., and Freund, H.-J. 1993. Motor Learning. *Current Opinion in Neurobiology* 3:940-949.

Harrington, D.L., Haaland, K.Y., Yeo, R.A., and Marder, E. 1990. Procedural memory in Parkinson's disease: Impaired motor but not visuoperceptual learning. *Journal of Clinical and Experimental Neuropsychology* 12:323-339.

Heap, M., and Wyke, M. 1972. Learning of a unimanual motor skill by patients with brain lesions: an experimental study. *Cortex* 8:1-18.

Heilman, K.M., Schwartz, H.D., and Geschwind, N. 1975. Defective motor learning in ideomotor apraxia. *Neurobiology* 25:1018-1020.

Heindel, W.C., Salmon, D.P., Shults, C.W., Walicke, P.A., and Butters, N. 1989. Neuropsychological evidence for multiple implicit memory systems. A comparison of Alzheimer's, Huntington's, and Parkinson's disease patients. *Journal of Neuroscience* 9:582-587.

Jenkins, I.H., Brooks, D.J., Nixon, P.D., Frackowiak, R.S.J., and Passingham, R.E. 1994. Motor sequence learning: a study with positron emission tomography. *Journal of Neuroscience* 14:3775-3790.

Kalaska, J.F., Cohen, D.A.D., Prud'homme, M., and Hyde, M.L. 1990. Parietal area 5 neuron activity encodes movement kinematics not movement dynamics. *Experimental Brain Research* 80:351-364.

Kawato, M., and Gomi, A. 1992. The cerebellum and VOR/OKR learning models. *Trends in Neuroscience* 15:445-453.

Keating, J.G., and Thach, W.T. 1990. Cerebellar motor learning: Quantitation of movement adaptation and performance in Rhesus monkeys and humans implicates cortex as the site of adaptation. *Society for Neuroscience Abstracts* 16:762.

Kelly, T.M., Zuo, C.-C., and Bloedel, J.R. 1990. Classical conditioning of the eyeblink reflex in the decerebrate-decerebellate rabbit. *Behavioral Brain Research* 38:7-18.

Kimura, D. 1977. Acquisition of a motor skill after left-hemisphere damage. *Brain* 100:527-542.

Lang, W., Lang, M., Kornhuber, A., Deecke, L., and Kornhuber, H.H. 1983. Human cerebral potentials and visuomotor learning. *Pflugers Archives* 399:342-344.

Lang, W., Lang, M., Podreka, I., Steiner, M., Uhl, F., Suess, E., Muller, C., and Deecke, L. 1988. DC-potential shifts and regional cerebral blood flow reveal frontal cortex involvement in human visuomotor learning. *Experimental Brain Research* 71:353-364.

Lisberger, S.G. 1988. The neural basis for learning of simple motor skills. *Science* (Washington, DC) 242:728-735.

Llinas, R., and Welsh, J.P. 1993. On the cerebellum and motor learning. *Current Opinion in Neurobiology* 3:958-965.

Marr, D. 1969. A theory of cerebellar cortex. *Journal of Physiology* (London) 202:437-470.

Marsden, C.D. 1982. The mysterious motor function of the basal ganglia: The Robert Wartenburg Lecture. *Neurology* 32:514-539.

Milner, B. 1962. Les troubles de la memoire accompagnant des lesions hippocampiques bilaterales. P. 257-272 in *Physiologie de l'Hippocampe*. Paris: Centre National de la Recherche Scientifique.

Ojakangas, C.L., and Ebner, T.J. 1992. Purkinje cell complex and simple spike changes during a voluntary arm movement learning task in the monkey. *Journal of Neurophysiology* 68:2222-2236.

Peeke, H.V.S., and Herz, M.J. 1971. Caudate nucleus stimulation retroactively impairs complex maze learning in the rat. *Science* 173:80-82.

Sanberg, P.R., Lehmann, J., and Fibiger, H.C. 1978. Impaired learning and memory after kainic acid lesions of the striatum: A behavioral model of Huntington's disease. *Brain Research* 149:546-551.

Sanes, J.N., Dimitrov, B., and Hallett, M. 1990. Motor learning in patients with cerebellar dysfunction. *Brain* 113:103-120.

Sanes, J.N., Wang, J., and Donoghue, J.P. 1992. Immediate and delayed changes of rat motor cortical output representation with new forelimb configurations. *Cerebral Cortex* 2:141-152.

Schlaug, G., Knorr, U., and Seitz, R. 1994. Inter-subject variability of cerebral activations in acquiring a motor skill: a study with positron emission tomography. *Experimental Brain Research* 98:523-534.

Seitz, R.J., and Roland, P.E. 1992. Learning of sequential finger movements in man: a combined kinematic and positron emission tomographic (PET) study. *European Journal of Neuroscience*, 4:154-165.

Seitz, R.J., Roland, P.E., Bohm, C., Greitz, T., and Stone-Elander, S. 1990. Motor learning in man: A positron emission tomographic study. *Neuroreport* 1:57-66.

Smiley-Oyen, A.L., Cross, C.L., and Worringham, C.J. 1991. Motor learning in olivo-pontocerebellar atrophy: schema formation, adaptation to altered gain, and use of error information. *Society for Neuroscience Abstracts* 17:1033.

Soliveri, P., Brown, R.G., Jahanshahi, M., and Marsden, C.D. 1992. Effects of practice on performance of a skilled motor task in patients with Parkinson's disease. *Journal of Neurology, Neurosurgery, & Psychiatry* 55:454-460.

Thach, W.T., Goodkin, H.P., and Keating, J.G. 1992. The cerebellum and the adaptive coordination of movement. *Annual Review of Neuroscience* 15:403-442.

Thompson, R., Huestis, C.W., Crinella, F.M., and Yu, J. 1990. Brain mechanisms underlying motor skill learning in the rat. *American Journal of Physical Medicine and Rehabilitation* 69:191-197.

Weiner, M.J., Hallett, M., and Funkenstein, H.H. 1983. Adaptation to lateral displacement of vision in patients with lesions of the central nervous system. *Neurology* 33:766-772.

Willingham, D.B., and Koroshetz, W. 1990. Huntington's patients learn motor associations, but not motor sequences. *Society for Neuroscience Abstracts* 16:1239.

Worringham, C.J., Cross, C.L., and Smiley-Oyen, A.L. 1990. Motor learning in Parkinson's Disease: schema formation, adaptation to altered gain, and limb kinematics. *Society for Neuroscience Abstracts* 16:1315.

Worringham, C.J., and Stelmach, G.E. 1990. Practice effects on the preprogramming of discrete movements in Parkinson's disease. *Journal of Neurology, Neurosurgery, & Psychiatry* 53:702-704.

Yamashita, H. 1993. Perceptual-motor learning in amnesic patients with medial temporal lobe lesions. *Perceptual and Motor Skills* 77:1311-1314.

Yeo, C.H. 1988. Cerebellum and classical conditioning. P. 321-333 in *Cerebellum and Neural Plasticity,* edited by M. Glickstein, C.H. Yeo, and J. Stein. New York: Plenum.

Acknowledgment

The authors wish to thank Graham Kerr for his helpful comments on an earlier draft. This review was supported by NIH grant NS27761.

Chapter 5

Visual Control of Prehension

Melvyn A. Goodale
University of Western Ontario

Philip Servos
Stanford University

Although most members of the primate order can reach out and grasp objects with considerable dexterity, this ability is most highly developed in human beings. Clearly, the human hand is capable of subtle and precise movements. The control of this remarkable instrument depends on information derived from several sensory systems. One of the most important of these is vision. As fig. 5.1 illustrates, when we initiate a grasping movement, not only do we reach toward the correct spatial location of the goal object, but the posture of our hand and fingers also anticipates the size, shape, and orientation of that object well before we make contact. In this chapter, we will explore the nature of this visual control and what we know of its neural architecture. Readers familiar with issues related to speed-accuracy trade-off and the role of visual feedback in the amendment of fast goal-directed aiming movements might be surprised to discover that we do not discuss these problems in any detail in this chapter. Instead, the focus is almost entirely on the precise nature of the

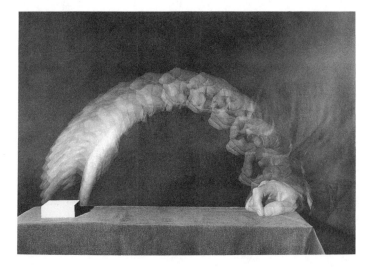

Fig. 5.1 Composite photograph of a prehensile movement directed at a goal object. Note that the hand achieves maximum opening well before it makes contact with the object.

visual information that controls the different elements of prehension, the neural substrates of that control, and the way this visual information differs from what is ordinarily described as *visual perception*. These are issues that are rarely addressed in discussions of motor control.

ELEMENTS OF PREHENSION

The act of prehension is complex. Not only does it involve movements of the arm and hand, but the eyes, head, and body also move so the image of the object to be grasped falls within the central portion of the visual field. Moreover, the movements of the arm and hand can be separated into at least three components: spatial positioning of the arm (the reaching or transport component), anticipatory posturing of the hand (the grasp component), and object manipulation (for review, see Jakobson and Goodale 1991; Jeannerod 1988). As we shall see, the available visual information affects the characteristics of all three components of prehension.

Transport and Grasp Components

Much of the work on the visual control of prehension has focused on the distinction drawn between the control of the reaching arm and the control of the hand and fingers during grip formation. As fig. 5.1 illustrates, these movements are not organized sequentially but instead unfold in parallel. Thus, as the hand leaves the substrate on its way to the object, the fingers have already begun to open and the hand has begun to rotate in the appropriate direction. There is a wealth of anatomical, physiological, and behavioral evidence in both monkeys and humans to suggest that the transport and grasp components depend on separate neural substrates. Although the neural innervation of the distal musculature controlling the grasping movements of the hand and fingers in monkeys is almost entirely crossed (Lawrence and Hopkins 1972; Muir 1985; Muir and Lemon 1983; Passingham, Perry, and Wilkinson 1978), the reaching or transport component can be controlled by either cerebral hemisphere (Brinkman and Kuypers 1973; Trevarthen 1965). These findings in the monkey are in agreement with observations made in patients in whom the two hemispheres have been surgically disconnected (e.g., Gazzaniga, Bogen, and Sperry 1967).

The two components of prehension also have different developmental profiles: young human infants can reach toward goal objects well before they can form an accurate grasp (e.g., von Hofsten 1990). It has been suggested that the developmental lag in the control of grasping may reflect the relatively late myelinization of the crossed corticospinal tract in the developing infant (see Jeannerod 1988). There is also evidence that lesions in different loci within the posterior parietal cortex of monkeys can have differential effects on these two components of prehension (e.g., Denny-Brown, Yanagisawa, and Kirk 1975; Haaxma and Kuypers 1975). We will return to this issue in the section on the neural substrates of visually guided prehension.

It was this kind of evidence that led Jeannerod (1981, 1984, 1986) to propose that the visual control of these two components of prehension might be relatively independent. He tested this idea directly by carrying out detailed analyses of the transport and grasp components in normal healthy adults. He found that the size of the opening between the index finger and thumb was directly related to the size of the object to be picked up and that this relationship could be clearly seen at the point of maximum grip aperture, which was achieved well before contact was made with the object. Despite these systematic changes in grip aperture as a function of object size, the resultant velocity profile of the reaching movement itself (measured by following the displacement of a point on the wrist) remained unaffected by trial-to-trial changes in the object size. Conversely, although the peak velocity of the reaching movement was affected by the distance of the object, the maximum grip aperture was not. In short, the transport component seemed sensitive to object distance and not size, whereas the grasp component seemed sensitive to object size but not distance. Consistent with these observations, Jeannerod also found that unexpected changes in the size of the object during the movement produced corresponding changes in opening between the finger and thumb but did not affect the trajectory of the reaching movement itself.

Based on these results, Jeannerod suggested that the transport and grasp components of prehension were generated by relatively independent visuomotor channels. The visuomotor channel mediating transport of the limb, Jeannerod suggested, is sensitive to the spatial location of objects, but the channel mediating the grasp is sensitive to more intrinsic object characteristics, such as shape, size, and local orientation. As we shall see later, Jeannerod has recently attempted to localize these two visuomotor channels in different regions of the cerebral cortex (Jeannerod and Decety 1990).

Although Jeannerod's initial analysis had shown that the visuomotor transformations for the reach and the grasp components are relatively independent, it soon became clear that these two components are closely coordinated during the execution of the movement. We can expect such synchrony if the hand is to close at the right moment during the reach trajectory. It would clearly be maladaptive if it were to close too soon or too late. Not surprisingly, Jeannerod observed that the beginning of the hand closure was tightly coupled with the final approach to the goal object, and that this relationship remained invariant over a range of object sizes and distances. Moreover, this was true even in so-called open-loop trials in which the subject could not see the hand or the target during the execution of the movement. Although Jeannerod was unclear whether this synchrony was achieved by a higher-order timing mechanism (Jeannerod 1986) or was simply a synergistic consequence of peripheral constraints on the two effector systems (Jeannerod and Biguer 1982), the problem was simplified by the movement time remaining largely invariant over the range of object distances used in these experiments. Whatever the nature of the mechanisms responsible for the temporal coupling between the reach and the grasp might be, Jeannerod originally maintained that the parameters for the two components are determined independently by separate transformations of different visual information.

More recent work, however, suggests that the temporal coordination between the reach and the grasp may be just one aspect of a more fundamental interaction between these two components of prehension. Jakobson and Goodale (1991) have recently shown that, although the opening of the hand during a grasping movement is closely correlated with the size of the object, it is also affected by the amplitude of the required reach (see also Chieffi and Gentilucci 1993). Thus as fig. 5.2A indicates, maximum grip aperture increases as a function of an increase in either object size or distance. Moreover, both object size and distance affect the transport component, with peak velocity increasing as a function of an increase in either variable (although, as we can see in fig. 5.2B, the effect of distance is more dramatic). These results suggest that object characteristics such as size and distance do not have independent effects on the grasp and the reach respectively. Although manipulations of either variable in these experiments affected both components of the reach, hand closure always occurred at approximately the same relative time during the reach, when approximately two-thirds of the movement time had elapsed. Thus, as

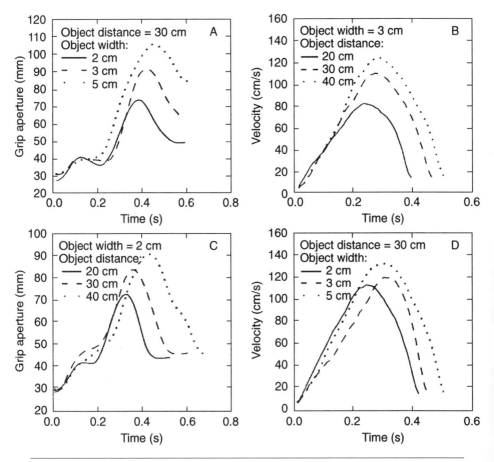

Fig. 5.2   Representative traces from one subject demonstrating (A) scaling of maximum grip aperture for object size; (B) scaling of acceleration, peak velocity, and duration for object distance; (C) scaling of maximum grip aperture for object distance; and (D) scaling of peak velocity and duration for object size.
Reprinted from Jakobson and Goodale 1991.

Jeannerod (1981, 1984) had observed earlier, there appeared to be a strong coupling of the two components during their execution. The coordination Jakobson and Goodale observed, however, was even more compelling because, unlike Jeannerod, they did not find that the movement time of the reach was invariant, but instead increased (along with peak velocity) as a function of object distance and size. Thus, the apparent synchrony between the grasp and the transport components in their experiments could not have been due to a simple temporal coupling in which the two components were synchronously triggered and then run off in the same time domain. A much more subtle integration was required. Furthermore, Jakobson and Goodale also observed small but reliable shifts in the relative timing of several kinematic markers as a function of both movement amplitude and object size, suggesting that the relationship between the two components is quite complex.

That object size and distance affected both the transport and grasp components of prehension in these experiments may have reflected an adaptive strategy invoked by the higher-order control mechanisms because, unlike Jeannerod (1981, 1984), Jakobson and Goodale randomized object size and object distance within a given block of trials. Varying object distance, for example, would presumably increase variability in the computation of the required amplitude of the reach. By increasing grip size, subjects could increase their margin of error, particularly for objects at the edge of the prehension work space. In other words, task constraints, such as the predictability of object size and distance, may shape the nature of the interaction between the different components of prehension. As will become evident later, the same kind of adaptive strategies may be at work in determining the characteristics of reaching and grasping movements made under visually open- and closed-loop conditions.

Several other studies have also revealed a more complex relationship between the transport and grasp components than Jeannerod originally proposed. Wing, Turton, and Fraser (1986) demonstrated that requiring subjects to reach more quickly produced a corresponding increase in the maximum aperture of the hand. More recently, Gentilucci et al. (1991) found, like Jakobson and Goodale (1991), that manipulations of object distance affect the size of the grasp as well as the velocity profile of the reach. In addition, they observed that the kind of grasp required (a precision grip with the index finger and thumb or a whole-hand grip) significantly affected the kinematics of the transport component. When subjects used a precision grip to pick up a small object, they accelerated more slowly, achieved a lower peak velocity, and spent more time in deceleration than when they used a whole-hand grip to pick up a larger object (see also Castiello, Bennett, and Stelmach 1993). These results are consistent with a large body of literature, ranging from the pioneering work of Woodworth (1899) to the formalism of Fitts' Law (1954), showing that the precision requirements of a task affects movement time in a predictable fashion. These results also suggest that the kinematic parameters of the reach and grasp components of prehension are not determined independently: different distal components (precision versus whole-hand grip, for example) appear to be associated with different patterns in the transport component, and increases in the required transport speeds (or times) are associated with increases in the amplitude of the grasp.

Additional evidence for a close interaction between the transport and grasp components of prehension is provided by the results of recent experiments carried out in

Jeannerod's laboratory in which either the location of the goal object or its size was unpredictably changed during the prehension movement. If the two components were truly independent and simply synchronized in time, then perturbing the location of the object should affect only the transport and not the grasp component, whereas perturbing the size of the object should affect only the grasp and not the transport component. This appeared to be the case, at least for manipulations of object size, in an early experiment Jeannerod (1981) reported. The results of more recent experiments, however, did not conform to these predictions. Instead when object location was perturbed, both the movement time of the reach and the formation of the grip were affected (Gentilucci et al. 1992; Paulignan et al. 1990, 1991). Similarly, when object size was perturbed, grip formation was altered to accommodate the perturbation. In addition the trajectories of the reach became more variable, peak velocity was reduced, and there was an increase in the low velocity phase of the movement (Castiello, Bennett, and Paulignan 1992; Castiello, Bennett, and Stelmach 1993; Paulignan et al. 1991). Indeed, with these findings, Jeannerod has abandoned the strong form of his original hypothesis and has proposed instead that the efficient coordination of the reaching and grasping components must involve some higher-order mechanism that consistently monitors movement-related signals and compares them with ongoing efferent commands to achieve the "resultant goal of the complete action" (Paulignan et al. 1991, 418).

Just as these behavioral studies challenge the original suggestion that the transport and grasp components of prehension are largely independent, several neuro-physiological studies are now showing that the pattern of innervation to the muscula-ture underlying these two components may be less distinct than was originally supposed. Recent functional neuroimaging studies in humans and work with patients with callosal agenesis indicate that the control of the shoulder and arm, at least for certain motor acts, may be as contralaterally organized as the control of the fingers and hand (Colebatch et al. 1991; Jakobson et al. 1994).

Open- and Closed-Loop Studies

The results of the perturbation experiments indicate that visual information is used for on-line control during the movement. Unlike target-directed aiming movements, however, there has been little work on the nature of this on-line control. Nevertheless, some studies have investigated the effects on reaching and grasping of removing visual feedback during the movement. One of the most consistent findings has been that removal of visual feedback, by requiring subjects to reach without seeing the hand or the target, results in an increase in maximum grip aperture (Chieffi and Gentilucci 1993; Jakobson and Goodale 1991; Wing, Turton, and Fraser 1986). Despite the unavailability of visual information during the movement, the grip aperture remains well correlated with the size of the object, suggesting that subjects can program their grasp based on the initial view of the object before they start the movement (see fig. 5.3). This conclusion is supported by the fact that when subjects are tested in open-loop conditions, in which vision of the hand and target becomes unavailable as soon as the hand leaves the start position, they take significantly longer to initiate the movement than they do when vision is continuously available

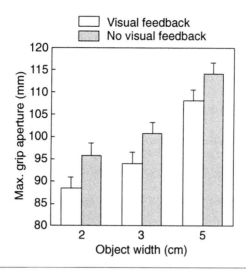

Fig. 5.3 Mean values of the maximum aperture (mm) between the index finger and thumb under visually open- or closed-loop conditions. Note that in both conditions subjects scale for object size.
Reprinted from Jakobson and Goodale 1991.

(Jakobson and Goodale 1991). Presumably, they take longer to initiate the movement under these conditions so they can *preprogram* the grasp amplitude accurately before the movement begins, because once they start to move all visual information will be gone. In addition, they build in a larger margin of error in the grasp by opening the hand more widely. Under conditions in which visual feedback remains available during the movement, subjects can afford to initiate their movements more quickly, then use vision on-line to make more precise adjustments to the size of the grasp. Indeed, when feedback is available, subjects reach maximum grip aperture significantly later during the reach than they do when it is not. It is interesting that the trajectory of the reach itself is largely unaffected by the imposition of either condition; neither the duration of the reach nor the peak velocity differs between closed- and open-loop testing.

These differences between reaches made under feedback and no-feedback conditions depend on vision being *predictably* available (or not) during the movement. As fig. 5.4 illustrates, when feedback and no-feedback trials are randomly interleaved, subjects adopt the same strategy they use on block no-feedback trials (i.e., they are slower to initiate their movements and they build a larger margin of error into the grasp by opening the hand more widely). This observation is consistent with the results of several studies on aiming movements. They have shown that when visual feedback is unpredictably available, subjects program their movements almost entirely at the outset and do not take advantage of vision to improve the accuracy of their pointing even if vision remains available during the movement (Zelaznik, Hawkins, and Kisselburgh 1983; Elliot and Allard 1985). This does not mean, of course, that movements made under these conditions are entirely ballistic; visual information available at the beginning of the movement can still be referred to

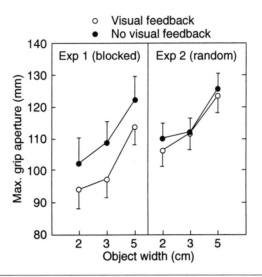

Fig. 5.4   A comparison of the mean maximum apertures (mm) between the index finger and thumb when subjects could (*Exp. 1*) or could not (*Exp. 2*) predict whether visual feedback would be available during the movement.
Reprinted from Jakobson and Goodale 1991.

nonvisual information (proprioceptive or kinesthetic feedback and/or motor-efference copy) about limb position and hand configuration during the movement. Jeannerod, Michel, and Prablanc (1984) observed that a patient with hemianesthesia (for whom proprioceptive and kinesthetic information about the moving limb was presumably unavailable) could grasp an object accurately *only* when vision was available. This suggests that such information normally guides prehension under conditions in which the moving limb cannot be seen. Nevertheless, high-level strategies for distributing control between the initial programming of movement parameters and their on-line modification exist, and the adoption of these strategies depends on perceived predictability of available visual feedback.

Object Manipulation

As we have seen, vision plays an important role in the initial programming and the on-line control of both the reach trajectory and the formation of the grasp. Vision also contributes to the control of movements (and forces) produced after contact is made with the goal object (i.e., during the object manipulation phase of prehension). Recent work on programming manipulative forces during a precision grip has shown that visual information about the size of an object is used to anticipate the forces required to lift it (Gordon et al. 1991a, 1991b). The forces used to grip, then lift an object are not only scaled for object size, but this scaling is achieved well before any feedback from the somatosensory system is available. The rapid application of these forces can only mean that visual information has been used to set the force parameters. When boxes of different sizes but the same weight are lifted, the grip and load forces remain correlated with the size of the boxes, although theoretically the same forces are required to lift them (Gordon et al. 1991a, 1991b). This suggests that visual information about the target object may access stored internal representations of the normal relationship between the physical properties of objects, such as size and weight (Johansson 1991). Visual information of this sort would be important in specifying the parameters of manipulative actions directed at unfamiliar objects. Moreover, even when the expected relationship between size and weight is violated by using objects of the same weight but different sizes, subjects continue to scale their grip and load forces according to the visual appearance of the object and not its weight, even after many trials (Gordon et al. 1991a, 1991b). In addition, subjects will persist in applying smaller forces when lifting the smaller box in the series although they report the smaller box is heavier than the larger one.

SOURCES OF VISUAL INFORMATION

Although it is clear that vision is critically important in the control of manual prehension, we know little about the kinds of visual information used. Substantial literature deals with the localization of targets in manual aiming tasks, but most of this work has concentrated on the relative contribution of retinal error signals and extra-retinal signals, such as eye position, to the computation of target position (for review, see Jeannerod 1988). Most paradigms employed in these studies either have assumed a completely two-dimensional case, or have used the term *retinal error signal* to refer to any visual information about target position that is independent of eye position.

Prehensile movements are not only directed at objects in three-dimensional space, but the objects themselves have three-dimensional structure that influences the kinematics of the grasp. Nevertheless, as we saw in the previous section, most studies that have investigated the contribution of visual information to the initial programming and on-line control of these movements have simply examined the effects of removing vision of the target and/or the moving limb on performance. There have been few attempts to tease apart the cues used either to locate the target object or to compute its size, shape, and local orientation.

Binocular Cues

Although it is likely that several cues are used in these computations, one possible set of cues is provided by binocular vision. The study of binocular vision in humans, like the study of depth cues in general, has concentrated almost entirely on perceptual judgments about the visual world, and has largely ignored the role of such cues in programming and executing skilled motor behaviors. In addition, the perceptual studies have been principally concerned with estimates of the relative depth of objects as opposed to their distance from the observer. Yet prehensile movements require precisely the latter type of estimate. For example, perceiving that the coffee cup is closer to you than the box of cornflakes will be of limited use in planning the movements required to pick up that cup. What you need is an accurate estimate of the distance of the cup so you can execute an efficient reaching movement without constant monitoring of the relative distances of the hand, cup, and cereal box.

Binocular cues, such as the convergence of the two eyes on the target object and the horizontal or vertical disparities in the visual array subtended by the two eyes, theoretically could provide the necessary information for programming such movements. Unfortunately, the few attempts to investigate the role of binocular vision in skilled motor performance have relied on indirect measures, such as time to complete a task and accuracy, and have not looked at the kinematics of the required movements. In addition, the role of absolute distance computation has been largely ignored. Sheedy et al. (1986), for example, compared the performance of subjects on several manual tasks (e.g., threading beads onto a string) under monocular versus binocular viewing conditions. They found that performance was better in the binocular condition. Tasks like threading beads, however, do not require computing absolute distance. Although one task used by Sheedy et al., tossing bean bags at targets, presumably did involve some estimation of distance, they provided only sketchy information about subjects' performance.

In a recent series of studies (Servos and Goodale 1990, 1992, 1994; Servos, Goodale, and Jakobson 1992), we assessed the contribution of binocular vision to the initial programming and the on-line control of prehensile movements. The first study we carried out was straightforward; we simply compared the kinematics of movements made under binocular and monocular viewing conditions. We required subjects to reach out and pick up, with the index finger and thumb, a small oblong block placed randomly at one of three distances in front of them. We used three blocks that varied in size from trial to trial. The subject's view of the object and the surrounding tabletop was unrestricted, and most normal distance cues were available, including static cues such as perspective, elevation, relative position to the table edge, accommodation, and possibly even familiar size, because the relative proportions of the three blocks differed systematically from one another. Furthermore, because the subjects were free to move their heads, retinal translation and loom cues were also available. Despite the rich array of distance and size cues, however, covering one eye had dramatic effects on the kinematics of the subjects' reaching and grasping movements.

Fig. 5.5 shows velocity profiles for two reaches made by the same subject—one reach was made under normal binocular control, the other with one eye covered. As these representative profiles illustrate, with binocular vision, the latency to begin the movement was shorter, the peak acceleration and velocity were higher, and the duration was shorter than it was under monocular viewing conditions. In addition, the deceleration phase of the movement was longer under binocular than monocular viewing, and the monocular profiles typically showed a long period of low-velocity movement near the end of the reach. When subjects grasped the block in the monocular condition they spent 150 ms longer in the low-velocity movement phase of the reach than they did under binocular viewing conditions. In short, monocular reaches were much less efficient than binocular ones.

As fig. 5.6 shows, despite clear differences in the kinematics, most measures remained correlated with distance under monocular viewing conditions. But not all the correlations were the same in both conditions. For example, peak velocity under monocular viewing did not increase as much with distance as it did under binocular

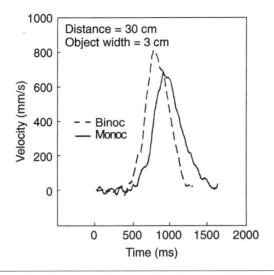

Fig. 5.5   Velocity profiles for two reaches made by the same subject—one reach was made under normal binocular control, the other under monocular control.
Reprinted from Servos, Goodale, and Jakobson 1992.

viewing. Similarly, the movement time of reaches made under monocular viewing increased more sharply with distance. That the correlations between kinematics and distance were still present, however, indicates that other distance cues can be used to scale the reach trajectory in the absence of binocular information.

Monocular viewing also affected the calibration of the grasp. As fig. 5.7 shows, with one eye covered, subjects did not open the hand as wide, although they did scale the grip aperture for object size. This again suggests that the subjects could use monocular cues to compute object size (by combining distance estimates with retinal image size), although that computation was not the same as the one carried out under binocular viewing.

The differences in the kinematics between the two viewing conditions demonstrate that removing binocular information, even in a viewing environment containing rich monocular cues, can interfere with performing a skilled prehensile movement. We cannot explain these differences by binocular summation arguments, in which two eyes are assumed to be more reliable at detecting and processing information than one (Jones and Lee 1981; Ueno 1977). If computations of object distance and size were simply less reliable under monocular than binocular viewing conditions, then one might have expected to see increases in the variability of performance but no change in the mean values of kinematic variables, such as peak velocity and acceleration. We observed quite the opposite pattern, however. Variability did not change as a function of viewing condition, but the mean values of these kinematic variables did.

One possible interpretation of the differences between the two conditions is that the kinematic changes evident in monocular viewing were the consequence of a visuomotor strategy that the subjects used to cope with a predicted reduction in the opportunity to fine-tune the movement during its execution. It is possible that

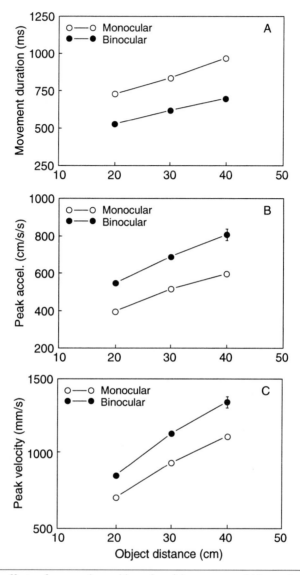

Fig. 5.6   The effects of monocular or binocular vision on several kinematic parameters: (*A*) movement duration (ms), (*B*) peak acceleration (cm/s/s), and (*C*) peak velocity (mm/s). Reprinted from Servos, Goodale, and Jakobson 1992.

subjects were treating the monocular task as an open-loop problem in which visual information was degraded during the movement. The observations of Jakobson and Goodale (1991) described earlier make this an unlikely possibility, however. In the open-loop condition of their experiment, they completely removed vision of the hand and target during the movement, and yet they found no differences between the kinematics of reaches made under this condition and those made under normal

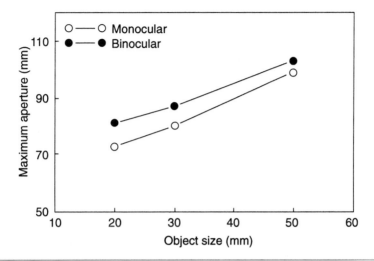

Fig. 5.7 The effects of monocular or binocular vision on maximum grip aperture (mm). Reprinted from Servos, Goodale, and Jakobson 1992.

closed-loop conditions (even when these conditions were run in separate blocks of trials). As fig. 5.8 illustrates, this lack of effect on the transport kinematics stands in striking contrast to the large differences we saw between binocular and monocular reaches. Of course, in the Jakobson and Goodale experiment, subjects had a binocular view of the object at the beginning of the movement. This initial binocular view determines a good deal about the kinematics of the reach, even if vision of the hand is denied during movement execution. Thus, it is unlikely that the slower movements we observed under monocular viewing conditions reflected a motor strategy designed to compensate for an anticipated degradation in visual control. Rather, the changes were more likely due to characteristics of the monocular array itself (i.e., an array lacking only binocular cues).

What was it about the nature of the monocular array that determined the differences we observed? Evidence from analysis of both the reach and the grasp components of prehension is consistent with the notion that when subjects viewed the object monocularly, they consistently underestimated its distance and thus its size. First, the peak velocities of reaches in the monocular condition were lower relative to the binocular condition, although subjects were still scaling for distance. In fact, the long period of deceleration evident in the monocular reaches could have reflected in part the need to adjust a trajectory programmed on the basis of an underestimate of object distance. Second, when subjects reached in the monocular condition, they generated smaller grip apertures although they still scaled their grips for object size. Such behavior is consistent with the idea that they were underestimating object distance, because the retinal image of the object combined with an underestimate of object distance would generate a corresponding underestimate of object size.

The smaller grip apertures we observed in monocular testing are opposite to the effect Jakobson and Goodale (1991) observed in their open-loop experiments in which subjects opened the hand wider when vision was unavailable during the

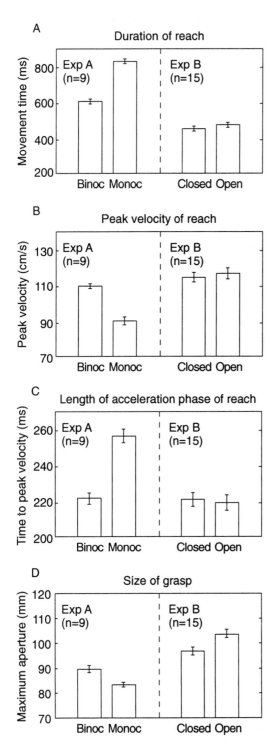

Fig. 5.8 Comparison of several kinematic variables under monocular and binocular viewing conditions (Exp. A, Servos, Goodale, and Jakobson 1992), and under visually closed- and open-loop conditions (Exp. B, Jakobson and Goodale 1991). (*A*) movement duration (ms), (*B*) peak velocity (cm/s), (*C*) duration of acceleration phase (ms), and (*D*) maximum grip aperture (mm). Reprinted from Jakobson and Goodale 1991.

movement (see fig. 5.3). This again suggests that the reaches made under monocular viewing are not simply a consequence of invoking a strategy designed to deal with reduced visual information during movement execution, but instead reflect a bias in computing the parameters for the required movements.

Although the superior performance of subjects under binocular viewing conditions suggests that binocular cues are important to the control of prehension, the question remains as to where in programming and executing the constituent movements binocular information is used. That binocular-monocular differences were evident early in the reach trajectory suggests that some differences, such as those observed in peak acceleration and velocity, were a consequence of initial programming rather than modifications during the movement. Peak acceleration, for example, was typically achieved 100 ms after movement onset—a time window in which there would have been little or no opportunity for on-line modification of the movement (for review, see Jeannerod 1988).

This conclusion is reinforced by the results of a study (Servos and Goodale 1994) in which binocular vision was permitted during the initial viewing of the object, but allowed only monocular viewing during the movement. This was achieved by having subjects wear modified goggles fitted with liquid crystal shutters that could be individually closed as soon as the hand left the start position. For some blocks of trials, vision remained binocular throughout the reach; for other blocks, only monocular feedback was allowed during the movement. Not surprisingly, because binocular viewing was available at the beginning of the movement in both conditions, there were no differences observed in the early portion of the reach. Indeed, as the representative profiles shown in fig. 5.9 illustrate, peak velocity and the time to peak velocity were identical. Removing binocular feedback did not affect maximum grip aperture—suggesting that this parameter too is largely computed during the premovement stage of the reach. All these results suggest that binocular cues make a critical contribution to the initial programming of prehensile movements.

Evidence shows that binocular cues also provide important feedback during the movement. Certainly, subjects spent more time decelerating under monocular than under binocular viewing, whether or not they had an initial binocular view (see figs. 5.5 and 5.9). When subjects were provided with only monocular views of the object before the movement began, then were switched to binocular viewing during the movement, the later portions of their reach were more efficient than when they were permitted only monocular viewing throughout (see fig. 5.10).

Binocular vision also appears to affect the time that subjects spend picking up the objects (see fig. 5.11). When subjects received an initial binocular view of the targets, they spent dramatically less time in contact with the objects than when they received only an initial monocular view of them. However, when the initial monocular view of the objects was followed by a binocular view, subjects spent significantly less time in contact with the objects than when they received a monocular view throughout the trial.

The differences in the time spent in contact with the objects in the two experiments could have been due, in part, to differences in the initial programming of the constituent movements. Possibly, an inaccurate estimate of the target distance when only initial monocular views were present could have caused the hand to be in a less than optimal position relative to the object just before contacting it. As reviewed

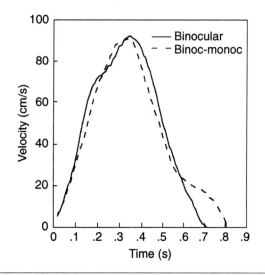

Fig. 5.9 Velocity profiles of two reaches made by the same subject—one under binocular feedback, the other under monocular feedback. Before movement initiation full binocular viewing was available in both reaches. Note the prolonged deceleration period in the reach made under monocular feedback.
Reprinted from Servos and Goodale 1994.

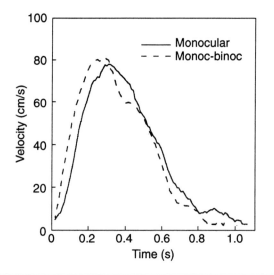

Fig. 5.10 Velocity profiles of two reaches made by the same subject—one under binocular feedback, the other under monocular feedback; both reaches having initial monocular viewing conditions. Note the prolonged deceleration period in the reach made under monocular feedback.
Reprinted from Servos and Goodale 1994.

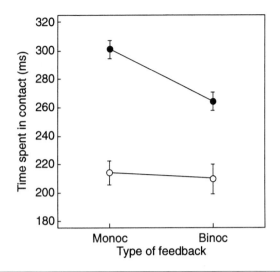

Fig. 5.11   Time spent in contact with the object as a function of viewing condition. *Open circles*—initial binocular view, *filled circles*—initial monocular view.
Reprinted from Servos and Goodale 1994.

earlier, size information can be used to set the force parameters needed to lift the goal object (Gordon et al. 1991a, 1991b). Thus, the extended time spent in contact with the object, when the initial view was monocular, might have been due to an initial inaccurate size estimate that interfered with the subsequent programming of the forces needed to lift the object. It is likely that the nature of the feedback available to subjects in both experiments was also a factor affecting the time spent in contact with the object. With the availability of binocular feedback in the experiment in which subjects had only an initial monocular view of the object, the hand appears to have compensated, to some degree, for diminished, and possibly inaccurate, information that the subjects had initially.

Taken together, these studies demonstrate that removing binocular cues has detrimental effects on planning and executing prehensile movements. Not only is there an apparent underestimation of target size and distance before movement onset, but there is also a reduction in the efficiency of feedback control of such movements. The contribution of individual binocular mechanisms to these different processes is an open question, because no attempt was made in these experiments to isolate particular binocular cues. It is possible that different sources of binocular information are used in movement planning and execution. The initial programming of the movement, for example, could rely on several different binocular cues, including stereopsis (and allied mechanisms such as vertical retinal disparity), convergence, or some combination of these mechanisms. These cues could also play a role in on-line control. In addition, other potential sources of binocular information are available for on-line control. When the subject foveates the target, stereomotion from the moving hand (Regan 1991; Regan, Erkelens, and Collewijn 1986) and possibly the extent of diplopia between the two eyes' images of the moving hand

(Hering 1861, cited in Hochberg 1971) could provide information about the hand's trajectory. It has been suggested that the lower part of the visual field in which these limb movements would normally occur is specialized for processing the disparate moving images in the two eyes (Previc 1990). Although the contribution of these mechanisms needs to be disentangled, it is clear that binocular vision plays an important role in the control of manual prehension.

Monocular Cues

Although most work summarized so far has stressed the importance of binocular cues in the control of reaching and grasping movements, certain monocular cues, such as optic expansion, opposite edge velocities of a moving target, and motion parallax, might also play a part.

An optically expanding (or looming) target will generate defensive reactions in a wide variety of animals including humans (Schiff, Caviness, and Gibson 1962; Bower, Broughton, and Moore 1970). Later work has shown that subjects can use information derived from the expanding visual image of an approaching target to intercept it (e.g., Lee et al. 1983). Lee (1976, 1980) has argued that time-to-contact can be derived directly from the inverse of the expansion rate of the object's image on the retina. Lee called this optic variable the *tau margin*. He further argued that the tau margin provides a reliable and rapidly available method for controlling an interception or avoidance movement (or for modulating an observer's movement speed through the visual world). The tau margin could theoretically be used to control a grasping movement directed at an approaching target. Two recent studies by Savelsbergh and his colleagues, employing a particularly clever manipulation, have demonstrated that this is indeed the case (Savelsbergh, Whiting, and Bootsma 1991; Savelsbergh et al. 1993). In these studies, subjects were required to grasp an approaching luminescent ball as it swung toward them on a pendulum. The ball was actually a balloon that could be deflated in flight. On trials in which the diameter of the balloon was suddenly reduced, resulting in a reduction in the optical expansion rate of its image on the retina, subjects delayed the time of the maximal closing velocity of their grasp. This work, which is the first to manipulate the optical expansion rate directly in this kind of motor task, provides strong support for Lee's suggestion that the relative expansion rate of the target image on the retina provides accurate time-to-contact information.

Velocity differences between the opposite edges of the retinal image of an object moving in depth provide accurate information about the trajectory of a moving object (see Regan 1986, 1993; Regan and Beverley 1980; Regan and Kaushal 1994). We have recently shown that under certain conditions, opposite edge velocities and time-to-contact information provide sufficient information for the control of interceptive grasping movements. When we required subjects to intercept moving balls, we found that the kinematics of their interceptive movements were comparable under monocular and binocular viewing conditions (Servos and Goodale 1995).

Motion parallax, produced by movements of the head, is another source of monocular information that could be of use to prehension. The retinal translation produced by such movements, combined with the magnitude of the head movements, could be used to compute absolute distance information (Ferris 1972; Gogel and Tietz 1979). Work by Steinbach and his colleagues has shown that subjects can be trained to use this source of depth information (Gonzalez et al. 1989; Steinbach, Ono, and Wolf 1991). A recent study conducted in our laboratory has demonstrated that patients who have had an eye removed due to disease make more translational head movements than normal subjects who have had their vision temporarily restricted to one eye during visually guided reaching and grasping movements (Marotta et al. 1995).

Motion Cues Versus Position Cues

A persistent idea in discussions of the visual control of prehension is that there are two separate channels for the control of the different phases of the movements involved (e.g., Georgopoulos 1986). Evidence for this idea is largely derived from experiments by Paillard and his colleagues (Beaubaton, Grangetto, and Paillard 1979; Paillard 1982; Paillard, Jordan, and Brouchon 1981). According to their two-channel model, which is similar to an idea put forward by Trevarthen (1968), one system analyzes positional or displacement cues and the other analyzes motion cues. The position channel uses central vision and is facilitated by the presence of a fixated target. This channel presumably provides information about the relative position of the hand and the target in the final stages of the prehensile movement. The motion channel employs peripheral vision and tracks the arm movement in the peripheral visual field during the movement (see Previc 1990). Not surprisingly, the motion channel is more sensitive to stroboscopic illumination than the position channel. Unfortunately, there have been few attempts to pursue this proposed distinction in the mechanisms of the visual control of prehension (but see Sivak and MacKenzie 1991).

Before leaving this topic, we should note that the two visual channels proposed by Paillard are quite different from the two visuomotor channels proposed by Jeannerod (1981, 1984, 1986) that we discussed earlier. Jeannerod's channels are mapped onto a distinction between the transport and grasp components of prehension, components that are presumably controlled in parallel by different high-level transformational algorithms. In contrast, Paillard's two-channel model refers to a distinction between the role of foveal and peripheral vision in different phases of a goal-directed reaching movement.

PERCEPTION VERSUS ACTION

Vision provides us with a rich source of information about the structure of the world and the objects and events within it. It is not surprising, therefore, that we see the function of vision as largely perceptual, providing an internal representation of the external world that can serve as the foundation for thought and action. There is much evidence to suggest that the kinds of visual processes that mediate what we commonly think of as *visual perception* may be quite distinct from those that mediate skilled actions such as manual prehension. In other words, evidence suggests that the visual mechanisms that allow us to identify our coffee cup and decide to pick it up are functionally and neurally distinct from those that control the grasping movement itself. In developing this argument, we will review the organization of the visual pathways in the primate cerebral hemispheres and some current ideas about their functional organization.

Two Cortical Visual Systems

The primate cerebral cortex contains a complex mosaic of interconnected visual areas (for review, see Felleman and Van Essen 1991; Maunsell and Newsome 1987). Most, though not all the visual input to these areas arrives via projections that arise from primary visual cortex (V1), which, in turn, receives projections from the dorsal lateral geniculate nucleus (LGNd). Despite the confusing pattern of interconnectivity between the different cortical visual areas, Ungerleider and Mishkin in 1982 distinguished two broad streams of projections from V1: a dorsal stream ultimately projecting to areas within posterior parietal cortex, and a ventral stream projecting eventually to inferior temporal cortex. As fig. 5.12 illustrates, recent anatomical studies have largely confirmed this basic anatomical subdivision in the cortical visual projections, although the degree of cross talk between the two systems is much greater than was originally thought.

Another important distinction between the inputs to primate visual cortex is based on a classification of the projections arising from the retina (for review, see Livingstone and Hubel 1988; Schiller and Logothetis 1990). The two main

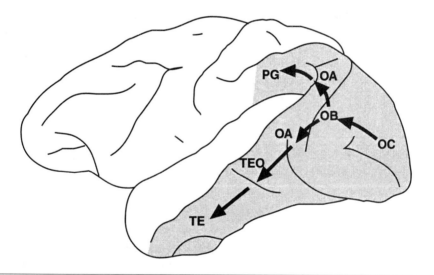

Fig. 5.12   Schematic diagram of the two cortical visual systems originally proposed by Ungerleider and Mishkin (1982). The dorsal stream projects from primary visual cortex (*OC*) to the posterior parietal lobule (*PG*), the ventral stream from primary visual cortex to inferotemporal cortex (*TE*).
Reprinted from Mishkin et al. 1983.

cytologically distinguishable subdivisions of ganglion cells (the small or *midget* ganglion cells and the larger *parasol* cells) in the primate retina are segregated in their projections to the LGNd, where they terminate selectively in the parvocellular (P) and magnocellular (M) layers respectively. The P system is color selective with low temporal but high spatial resolution; the M system is broadly tuned for wavelength with high temporal but low spatial resolution. These two pathways remain segregated in V1, in adjacent visual areas such as V2, and beyond. Although it has been suggested that the P and M pathways are linked to the ventral and dorsal streams of projections respectively (Livingstone and Hubel 1988), more recent electrophysiological studies have shown that both streams receive inputs from both the P and M pathways. The dorsal stream, although dominated by M inputs, also receives a significant P input (Maunsell, Nealey, and De Priest 1990); the ventral stream receives a large contribution from both the M and the P systems (Ferrera, Nealey, and Maunsell 1991). Although there are undoubtedly differences in emphasis between their visual inputs, the dorsal and ventral projection streams can presumably exploit a wide range of visual information in performing their functions.

In making their original distinction between the dorsal and ventral streams, Ungerleider and Mishkin (1982) ascribed different functions to these pathways. Based on a series of electrophysiological and behavioral studies in the monkey, they suggested that the dorsal stream of projections from V1 to the posterior parietal cortex was concerned with establishing the spatial location of an object, whereas the ventral stream of projections from V1 to inferotemporal cortex was concerned with identifying that object. This division of labor in the visual cortical pathways between one system mediating spatial vision and another mediating object vision (the *where* pathway versus the *what* pathway) has been one of the most influential accounts of higher visual function in recent times. The distinction between spatial vision and object vision, and their putative neural substrates, the dorsal and ventral streams, are often invoked in discussions of the visual control of prehension. In a recent paper, Jeannerod and Decety (1990) imply that the computations that specify stimulus location for the reach component of prehension are carried out in the dorsal stream, and the computations that identify the intrinsic object properties are carried out in the ventral stream.

Goodale and Milner (1992) have recently challenged the idea that there are two cortical systems, one for object vision and another for spatial vision. They do not dispute that there are anatomically separate projection systems from V1 to the inferotemporal and parietal regions, but take issue with the functional distinction put forward by Ungerleider and Mishkin (1982). The division of labor proposed by Ungerleider and Mishkin, they point out, is couched entirely in terms of perceptual representation. Thus, the dorsal stream of projections to posterior parietal cortex, according to the *where* versus *what* dichotomy, simply computes one aspect of an object, its location, but the ventral stream computes visual attributes such as size, shape, and orientation. Little attention is paid to the reason for this apparent separation in processing visual inputs. In contrast, the division of labor proposed by Goodale and Milner places less emphasis on input distinctions (object location versus object qualities) and more emphasis on the output requirements of the two systems. It seems plausible, they argue, that separate processing modules would have evolved to mediate the different uses to which vision can be put. This principle is accepted in relation to automatic types of behavior such as saccadic eye movements (Sparks and May 1990), and it could be extended to other systems for a range of behavioral skills such as prehension, in which close coordination is required between movements of the fingers, hands, upper limbs, head, and eyes. Goodale and Milner argue that the inputs and transformations these skilled visuomotor acts require differ in important respects from those leading to what we understand as *visual perception*. They propose that the dorsal stream of projections to the posterior parietal lobule, in close conjunction with areas in premotor and prefrontal cortex, provides a specialized set of semi-independent modules or expert systems for the control of skilled action, such as manual prehension, whereas the ventral stream of projections, although to some extent using similar visual information, is primarily concerned with more perceptual functions, such as visual learning and object recognition (Goodale and Milner 1992; Milner and Goodale 1993, 1995). In other words, the differences between the dorsal and ventral streams (and other modular subdivisions within the cortical elaboration of the visual pathways) reflect the requirements of the different output systems they serve rather than an arbitrary division in processing incoming visual information. In the following section, we review some neuropsychological evidence supporting this suggestion.

Neuropsychological Evidence

Neuropsychological studies of patients with damage to one projection system but not the other have often been cited in support of the model Ungerleider and Mishkin proposed. Patients with visual agnosia following brain damage that includes, for example, the occipitotemporal region are often unable to recognize or describe common objects, faces, pictures, or abstract designs, even though they can navigate through the everyday world—at least at a local level—with considerable skill. Conversely, patients suffering from optic ataxia following damage to the posterior parietal region are unable to reach accurately toward visual targets that they have no difficulty recognizing. Such observations provide support for an occipitotemporal system mediating object vision but not spatial vision, and a parietal system mediating spatial vision but not object vision.

Closer examination of the behavior of such patients, however, leads to a different conclusion. Observations in our laboratory and in several others have shown that patients with optic ataxia not only have difficulty reaching in the right direction, but also in positioning their fingers or adjusting the orientation of their hands to reflect the size, shape, and orientation of the object to be grasped (Jakobson et al. 1991; Perenin and Vighetto 1983, 1988). These findings suggest that damage to the parietal lobe can impair the ability of patients to use information about the structural features and local orientation of an object to control the posture of the hand during a grasping movement, although this information can still be used to identify and describe the objects. Clearly, a *disorder of spatial vision* fails to capture this range of visuomotor impairments. Instead, this pattern of deficits is consistent with the proposal put forward by Goodale and Milner (1992) that the posterior parietal cortex plays a critical role in the visuomotor transformations required for skilled actions such as visually guided prehension.

Similar complications arise when one examines in detail the behavior of patients with visual agnosia. Goodale et al. (1991) recently studied the behavior of one such patient (DF), who developed a profound visual form agnosia following carbon monoxide poisoning. Although medical imaging revealed a pattern of diffuse brain damage consistent with anoxia, most damage was evident in visual areas outside of primary visual cortex (V1). Despite her profound inability to recognize the shape, size, and orientation of visual objects, DF showed strikingly accurate guidance of hand and finger movements directed at the same objects. Thus, when she was presented with a pair of rectangular blocks of the same or different dimensions, she was unable to distinguish between them. Even when she was asked to indicate the width of a single block using her index finger and thumb, her matches bore no relationship to the dimensions of the object and showed considerable trial-to-trial variability (see fig. 5.13). In contrast, when she was asked to reach out and pick up the block, the aperture between her index finger and thumb changed systematically with the width of the object, just as in normal subjects (fig. 5.13). In other words, DF scaled her grip to the dimensions of the object she was about to pick up, even though she appeared unable to perceive those dimensions.

As fig. 5.14 illustrates, a similar dissociation was seen in her responses to the orientation of stimuli. When presented with a large slot that could be oriented in one of several ways, she showed great difficulty in indicating the orientation either verbally or manually (i.e., by rotating her hand or a handheld card). Nevertheless, she was as good as normal subjects at reaching out and placing her hand or the card into the slot—rotating her hand in the appropriate direction as soon as she began the movement.

Contrary to expectations based on the ideas of Ungerleider and Mishkin, a profound loss of shape perception in DF coexists with a preserved ability to use shape in guiding action. The distinction they make between object vision and spatial vision is unable to do justice to this dissociation. Such a dissociation is consistent with the idea that separate neural pathways transform incoming visual information into representations for action and perception respectively. Presumably it is the latter and not the former that is compromised in DF. Indeed, Goodale and Milner (1992) have postulated that it is the ventral stream of projections that is damaged in this patient.

Electrophysiological Evidence

Electrophysiological studies of the dorsal and ventral streams in the monkey show considerable support for the idea of relatively independent visual processing for action and perception (for a detailed account, see Goodale and Milner 1992; Milner and Goodale 1993, 1995). For example, in sharp contrast to the cell activity in the ventral stream, the responses of cells in the dorsal stream depend on the animal's behavior with respect to the visual stimulus. Separate subsets of cells in the posterior parietal cortex, the major terminal zone for the dorsal stream, have been implicated in visual fixation, pursuit and saccadic eye movements, visually guided reaching, and the manipulation of objects. In reviewing these studies, Andersen (1987) has pointed out that most neurons in these areas "exhibit both sensory-related and

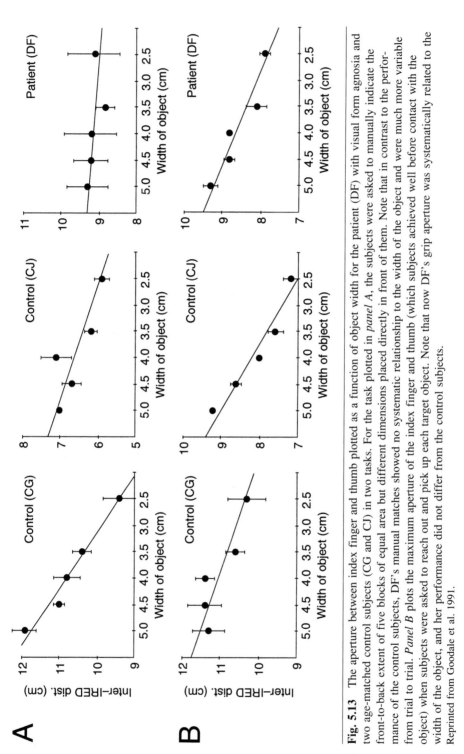

Fig. 5.13 The aperture between index finger and thumb plotted as a function of object width for the patient (DF) with visual form agnosia and two age-matched control subjects (CG and CJ) in two tasks. For the task plotted in *panel A*, the subjects were asked to manually indicate the front-to-back extent of five blocks of equal area but different dimensions placed directly in front of them. Note that in contrast to the performance of the control subjects, DF's manual matches showed no systematic relationship to the width of the object and were much more variable from trial to trial. *Panel B* plots the maximum aperture of the index finger and thumb (which subjects achieved well before contact with the object) when subjects were asked to reach out and pick up each target object. Note that now DF's grip aperture was systematically related to the width of the object, and her performance did not differ from the control subjects. Reprinted from Goodale et al. 1991.

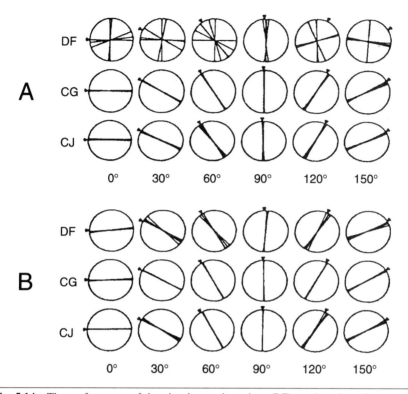

Fig. 5.14   The performance of the visual agnosic patient (DF) on the orientation task contrasted with that of two age-matched control subjects (CG and CJ). *Panel A* shows polar plots that correspond to the orientation of a handheld card the subjects were asked to match with the orientation of a slot in an upright disk. The triangular mark on the circumference of each circle indicates the true orientation of the slot during the depicted trials. Note that DF's performance was much less accurate and more variable than the control subjects. *Panel B* shows polar plots that indicate the orientation of the card just before it contacted the disk in a task in which the subjects were required to post the card into the slot. Note that DF's performance is indistinguishable from the control subjects.
Reprinted from Goodale et al. 1991.

movement-related activity.'' For example, Blum (1989) identified two cell populations in monkey posterior parietal cortex, one of which is active during reaches made without visual guidance and the other during visually guided reaching. In an interesting development, Taira et al. (1990) have shown that some parietal cells are sensitive to the intrinsic object features, such as size and orientation, that determine the posture of the hand and fingers during a grasping movement.

Many well-known motion-sensitive cells in the dorsal pathway are well suited for providing inputs for continually updating information about the disposition and structural features of objects in three-dimensional ego space. Indeed, a subset of these cells seems capable of monitoring limb position during manual prehension (Mountcastle et al. 1984), whereas motion-sensitive cells in the temporal lobe do not respond to such self-produced visual motion (Perrett et al. 1990). Moreover, the posterior parietal region is strongly linked with the premotor regions of the frontal cortex directly implicated in ocular control, reaching movements of the limb, and grasping actions of the hand and fingers. Thus, the parietal cortex is strategically placed to mediate in the visual guidance and integration of prehensile and other skilled actions.

Cells in the ventral stream of projections to the inferotemporal region, unlike those in the dorsal stream, are highly selective for the form, pattern, and color of objects, and many maintain their responsivity over a wide range of size, color, optical, and viewpoint transformations of the object. Such cells, far from providing the momentary information necessary for guiding action, specifically ignore these changing details (for an elaboration, see Goodale and Milner 1992; Milner and Goodale 1993, 1995). Such observations are consistent with the suggestion that networks of cells in the inferotemporal cortex, in sharp contrast to the action systems in the posterior parietal cortex, are more concerned with the enduring characteristics of objects than they are with the moment-to-moment changes in the visual array. The object-centered descriptions that the ventral system delivers would appear to form the raw material for recognition memory and other long-term representations of the visual world. There is extensive evidence for the neuronal encoding of such visual memories in neighboring regions of the medial temporal lobe and related limbic areas (see Brown, Fahy, and Riches 1993; Ono et al. 1993). Moreover, within the ventral system itself, evidence shows that the responsivity of cells can be modulated by the reinforcement history of the stimuli employed to study them (Haenny and Schiller 1988; Richmond and Sato 1987). In short, the ventral stream appears to be a system specialized more for perceiving the world and the significance of objects within it than for controlling actions directed at those objects.

Thus, the human neuropsychology and the monkey electrophysiology converge on the new formulation of the dorsal and ventral stream functions put forward by Goodale and Milner (1992). Considerable work remains to be done in working out the organization of these two systems and their interactions.

Dissociations Between Perception and Action in Normal Subjects

As we indicated at the outset, the nature of the visual information used to program the constituent movements of manual prehension and to control them on-line is not well understood. When confronted with a goal object for the first time, the visuomotor systems mediating prehension must compute the size, shape, orientation, and distance of the object de novo. The temporal constraints on the control of prehension, particularly on the amendments made during its execution, demand that the under-lying computations be both fast and robust. Thus, some cues, such as color, texture gradients, specularities, shading, shadow, and transparency, which are important elements in perception, might not affect the parameters related to the programming and on-line control of action. Others such as optic flow-fields, object boundaries, retinal image size, retinal disparity, and a variety of distance cues might be critical. Some experiments we reviewed lend support to this suggestion (Servos, Goodale, and Jakobson 1992; Savelsbergh, Whiting, and Bootsma 1991). Moreover, the recent work of Goodale and Milner (1992) suggests that the computations involved in transforming visual information into motor output are probably performed independently of visual perception. As such, the computations setting the parameters for the reach trajectory and grip aperture may not be accessible to the usual perceptual or cognitive judgments about the object.

The fact that the patient DF shows intact visuomotor behavior despite her profound perceptual deficits is one of the most compelling examples of this dissociation (Goodale et al. 1991). There are several observations in normal subjects that also lend support to this idea. Under some circumstances, for example, perturbing the position of a target during a manual aiming movement can result in adjustments to the trajectory of the movement even though subjects do not perceive the change in position (Goodale, Pelisson, and Prablanc 1986). Thus, in these experiments, subjects were unable to report, even in forced-choice testing, whether a target had changed position during a saccadic eye movement, though correction saccades and manual aiming movements directed at the target showed near perfect adjustments for the unpredictable shift in the target's position. In other words, an illusory perceptual constancy of target position was maintained despite large amendments in visuomotor control. Similar dissociations between perceived position and manual responses have been reported by Bridgeman and his collaborators (Bridgeman 1987; Bridgeman, Kirch, and Sperling 1981) and by Skavenski and Hansen (1978). In one of Bridgeman's experiments, for example, he found that even though a fixed visual target surrounded by a moving frame appeared to drift in a direction opposite to that of the frame, subjects persisted in pointing to the veridical target location. Similarly, Skavenski and Hansen (1978) showed that when subjects were required to strike with a hammer the location of target lights that were illuminated during a saccade, they were much more accurate than they perceived themselves to be.

Another example of how perception yields different solutions from those generated by action systems was described earlier in the work of Gordon et al. (1991a, 1991b) on the visual calibration of the forces applied during precision grip. In those experiments, subjects applied lower forces to the smaller of a set of objects of the same weight, even though they perceived the smaller object as heavier. Not only does this suggest that perception is not driving the calibration of the required forces, but it also explains the generation of the illusion. If the visuomotor systems use a stored model of the relationship between size and weight (i.e., that the smaller the object the lighter it is) to generate the appropriate forces for lift, then the discrepancy between perceived size and the apparent difficulty in lifting small as opposed to large objects (of equal weight) might create the illusion of greater weight in the smaller object.

Other visuomotor systems in human beings also seem to work outside normal perceptual phenomenology. Lee and Lishman (1975) had subjects stand in a room that was suspended from the ceiling of a larger room and so could be gently oscillated back and forth. Although subjects were unaware of this sway, they did make postural adjustments commensurate with the oscillations of the room. Moreover, they were unaware that they were swaying rhythmically back and forth.

These and several other observations in a variety of visuomotor contexts suggest that perception and visuomotor control often work independently of each other.

Indeed, perception demands different transformations of the incoming visual data than does visuomotor behavior. The primary purpose of perception is to identify objects, classify them, and attach meaning and significance to them. As a consequence, perception is concerned with the enduring characteristics of those objects so they can be recognized when they are encountered again in different visual contexts. To generate these long-term representations, perceptual mechanisms must be object centered (Marr 1982) (i.e., constancies of size, shape, color, lightness, and relative location need to be maintained across different viewing conditions). In contrast, the computations required for action must be viewer centered; both the location of the object and its disposition and motion must be encoded relative to the observer. Moreover, because the position of a goal object in the action space of an observer is rarely constant, such computations must take place de novo every time an action occurs. In short, different transformations are required for perception and action. As we have discussed, these differences lie at the root of the division of labor in the ventral and dorsal projection systems of the primate cerebral cortex.

THE FUTURE

Although it is clear that vision plays an important role in the control of manual prehension, most literature on this subject, as we indicated earlier, is concerned with issues such as speed-accuracy trade-off and the temporal constraints on visual feedback. Instead of going over this well-covered ground, we decided to focus on a neglected topic: the role of specific visual cues in the control of the components of manual prehension. Although only a handful of studies have attempted to address this issue, we already know that certain cues, such as those related to binocularity, play a critical role. What needs to be done now is establish the relative contribution of a range of possible sources of visual information. It is likely that the cues exploited by the visuomotor systems supporting prehension are robust and easily computed. Thus, cues like transparency and shadows may not play an important role, whereas other cues, such as retinal image size and optic flow, will be critical. One interesting direction for future research, therefore, might be to capitalize on the dissociation between cues for perception and cues for action.

Although electrophysiological studies of the visuomotor mechanisms supporting prehension in the monkey have looked in detail at different cues, such as optic flow and object motion, they typically have not related these parameters to the kinematics of limb and hand movement. There have been studies looking at the relationship between this information and the production of pursuit eye movements and goal-directed saccades. Similar studies should be done about prehension.

Although the purpose of prehension can be simply characterized, the necessary computations required to convert information on the retina into a series of appropriate muscle contractions are exceedingly complex. For this reason, few investigators have attempted to address this problem head on. Recently, however, several laboratories are beginning to develop models of how the brain carries out the transformations required to move from one coordinate system (the retina) to another (the arm and hand) during prehension (see for example, Bullock, Grossberg, and Guenther 1993; Flanders, Tillery, and Soechting 1992; Jordan, Flash, and Arnon 1994;

Soechting, Tillery, and Flanders 1990; Stein 1991, 1992). The notion of what constitutes sufficient retinal information for spatial localization in these models has been limited to simple retinal coordinates and has ignored the rich array of cues potentially available. For example, the contributions of stereopsis, optic flow, object motion, and extra-retinal cues such as accommodation and vergence to the control of prehension have largely been ignored. The problem of determining the shape, size, and local orientation of the goal object for shaping of the hand has also not been addressed adequately, although recently, several laboratories have made some headway in incorporating some of these features into their models (Hoff and Arbib 1993; Flanders and Soechting 1995). Such research and model building could clearly benefit from a more detailed analysis of the specific visual cues used in the control of prehension.

REFERENCES

Andersen, R.A. 1987. Inferior parietal lobule function in spatial perception and visuomotor integration. P. 483-518 in *Handbook of physiology*, edited by F. Plum and V.B. Mountcastle. Rockville, MD: American Physiological Society.

Beaubaton, D., Grangetto, A., and Paillard, J. 1979. Contribution of positional and movement cues to visuomotor reaching in split-brain monkey. P. 371-384 in *Structure and function of cerebral commissures*, edited by I. Steele Russell, M.W. Van Hof, and G. Berlucchi. Baltimore: University Park Press.

Blum, B. 1989. Inferior parietal lobule neurones related to eye and hand reach movements in rhesus monkey. *Brain, Behavior and Evolution* 33:104-108.

Bower, T.G., Broughton, J.M., and Moore, M.K. 1970. The coordination of visual and tactual inputs in infants. *Perception and Psychophysics* 8:51-53.

Bridgeman, B. 1987. Separate visual representations for perception and for visually guided behavior. In *Spatial displays and spatial instruments*. N.A.S.A. Conference Publication #10032.

Bridgeman, B., Kirch, M., and Sperling, A. 1981. Segregation of cognitive and motor aspects of visual function using induced motion. *Perception and Psychophysics* 29:336-342.

Brinkman, J., and Kuypers, H.G.J.M. 1973. Cerebral control of contralateral and ipsilateral arm, hand and finger movements in the split-brain rhesus monkey. *Brain* 96:653-674.

Brown, M.W., Fahy, F.L., and Riches, I.P. 1993. Neuronal encoding of information important to visual recognition memory. In *Progress in brain research. The visually responsive neuron: From basic neurophysiology to behavior*, edited by T.P. Hicks, S. Molotchnikoff, and T. Ono. Amsterdam: Elsevier.

Bullock, D., Grossberg, S., and Guenther, F.H. 1993. A self-organizing neural model of motor equivalent reaching and tool use by a multijoint arm. *Journal of Cognitive Neuroscience* 5:408-435.

Castiello, U., Bennett, K.M., and Paulignan, Y. 1992. Does the type of prehension influence the kinematics of reaching? *Behavioral Brain Research* 50:7-15.

Castiello, U., Bennett, K.M., and Stelmach, G.E. 1993. Reach to grasp: the natural response to perturbation of object size. *Experimental Brain Research* 94:163-178.

Chieffi, S., and Gentilucci, M. 1993. Coordination between the transport and the grasp components during prehension movements. *Experimental Brain Research* 94:471-477.

Colebatch, J.G., Deiber, M.P., Passingham, R.E., Friston, K.J., and Frackowiak, R.S. 1991. Regional cerebral blood flow during voluntary arm and hand movements in human subjects. *Journal of Neurophysiology* 65:1392-1401.

Denny-Brown, D., Yanagisawa, N., and Kirk, E.J. 1975. The localization of hemispheric mechanisms of visually directed reaching and grasping. P. 62-75 in *Cerebral localization*, edited by K.J. Zülch, O. Creutzfeldt, and G.C. Galbraith. Berlin: Springer-Verlag.

Elliott, D., and Allard, F. 1985. The utilization of visual feedback information during rapid pointing movements. *Quarterly Journal of Experimental Psychology: Human Experimental Psychology* 37A:407-425.

Felleman, D.J., and Van Essen, D.C. 1991. Distributed hierarchical processing in the primate cerebral cortex. *Cerebral Cortex* 1:1-47.

Ferrera, V.P., Nealey, T.A., and Maunsell, J.H.R. 1991. Magnocellular and parvocellular inputs to macaque area V4. *Investigative Ophthalmology and Visual Science* 32 Supplement 2196:1117.

Ferris, S.H. 1972. Motion parallax and absolute distance. *Journal of Experimental Psychology* 95:258-263.

Fitts, P.M. 1954. The information capacity of the human motor system in controlling the amplitude of movement. *Journal of Experimental Psychology* 47:381-391.

Flanders, M., and Soechting, J.F. 1995. Frames of reference for hand orientation. *Journal of Cognitive Neuroscience* 7:182-195.

Flanders, M., Tillery, S.I., and Soechting, J.F. 1992. Early stages in a sensorimotor transformation. *Behavioral and Brain Sciences* 15:309-362.

Gazzaniga, M.S., Bogen, J.E., and Sperry, R.W. 1967. Dyspraxia following division of the cerebral commissures. *Archives of Neurology* 16:606-612.

Gentilucci, M., Castiello, U., Corradini, M.L., Scarpa, M., Umilta, C., and Rizzolatti, G. 1991. Influence of different types of grasping on the transport component of prehension movements. *Neuropsychologia* 29:361-378.

Gentilucci, M., Chieffi, S., Scarpa, M., and Castiello, U. 1992. Temporal coupling between transport and grasp components during prehension movements: effects of visual perturbation. *Behavioural Brain Research* 47:71-82.

Georgopoulos, A.P. 1986. On reaching. *Annual Review of Neuroscience* 9:147-170.

Gogel, W.C., and Tietz, J.D. 1979. A comparison of oculomotor and motion parallax cues of egocentric distance. *Vision Research* 19:1161-1170.

Gonzalez, E.G., Steinbach, M.J., Ono, H., and Wolf, M.E. 1989. Depth perception in children enucleated at an early age. *Clinical Vision Science* 4:173-177.

Goodale, M.A., and Milner, A.D. 1992. Separate visual pathways for perception and action. *Trends in Neurosciences* 15:20-25.

Goodale, M.A., Milner, A.D., Jakobson, L.S., and Carey, D.P. 1991. A neurological dissociation between perceiving objects and grasping them. *Nature* 349:154-156.

Goodale, M.A., Pelisson, D., and Prablanc, D. 1986. Large adjustments in visually guided reaching do not depend on vision of the hand or perception of target displacement. *Nature* 320:748-750.

Gordon, A.M., Forssberg, H., Johansson, R.S., and Westling, G. 1991a. Integration of sensory information during the programming of precision grip: comments on the contributions of size cues. *Experimental Brain Research* 85:226-229.

Gordon, A.M., Forssberg, H., Johansson, R.S., and Westling, G. 1991b. Visual size cues in the programming of manipulative forces during precision grip. *Experimental Brain Research* 83:447-482.

Haaxma, R., and Kuypers, H.G.J.M. 1975. Intrahemispheric cortical connexions and visual guidance of hand and finger movements in the rhesus monkey. *Brain* 98:239-260.

Haenny, P., and Schiller, P.H. 1988. State dependent activity in monkey visual cortex. I. Single unit activity in V1 and V4 on visual tasks. *Experimental Brain Research* 69:225-244.

Hering, E. 1861. *Beitrage zur physiologie*. Heft 1. Leipzig: Englemann.

Hochberg, J. 1971. Perception II. Space and movement. P. 475-550 in *Woodworth & Schlosberg's experimental psychology*. 3d ed., edited by J.W. Kling and L.A. Riggs. New York: Holt, Reinhart & Winston.

Hoff, B., and Arbib, M.I. 1993. Models of trajectory formation and temporal interaction of reach and grasp. *Journal of Motor Behavior* 25:175-192.

Jakobson, L.S., Archibald, Y.M., Carey, D.P., and Goodale, M.A. 1991. A kinematic analysis of reaching and grasping movements in a patient recovering from optic ataxia. *Neuropsychologia* 29:803-809.

Jakobson, L.S., and Goodale, M.A. 1991. Factors influencing higher-order movement planning: A kinematic analysis of human prehension. *Experimental Brain Research* 86:199-208.

Jakobson, L.S., Servos, P., Goodale, M.A., and Lassonde, M. 1994. Control of proximal and distal components of prehension in callosal agenesis. *Brain* 117:1107-1113.

Jeannerod, M. 1981. Intersegmental coordination during reaching at natural visual objects. P. 153-168 in *Attention and Performance IX*, edited by J. Long and A. Baddeley. Hillsdale, NJ: Erlbaum.

Jeannerod, M. 1984. The timing of natural prehension movements. *Journal of Motor Behavior* 16:235-254.

Jeannerod, M. 1986. The formation of finger grip during prehension: A cortically mediated visuomotor pattern. *Behavioural Brain Research* 19:99-116.

Jeannerod, M. 1988. *The neural and behavioural organization of goal-directed movements*. Oxford: Clarendon Press.

Jeannerod, M., and Biguer, B. 1982. Visuomotor mechanisms in reaching within extrapersonal space. P. 387-409 in *Analysis of visual behavior*, edited by D.J. Ingle, M.A. Goodale, and R.J.W. Mansfield. Cambridge, MA: MIT Press.

Jeannerod, M., and Decety, J. 1990. The accuracy of visuomotor transformation: An investigation into the mechanisms of visual recognition of objects. P. 33-48 in *Vision and action: The control of grasping*, edited by M.A. Goodale. Norwood, NJ: Ablex.

Jeannerod, M., Michel, F., and Prablanc, C. 1984. The control of hand movements in a case of hemianaesthesia following a parietal lesion. *Brain* 107:899-920.

Johansson, R.S. 1991. How is grasping modified by somatosensory input? P. 331-355 in *Motor control: Concepts and issues*, edited by D.R. Humphrey and H.J. Freund. Chichester: Wiley.

Jones, R.K., and Lee, D.N. 1981. Why two eyes are better than one: The two views of binocular vision. *Journal of Experimental Psychology: Human Perception and Performance* 7:30-40.

Jordan, M.I., Flash, T., and Arnon, Y. 1994. A model of the learning of arm trajectories from spatial deviations. *Journal of Cognitive Neuroscience* 6: 359-376.

Lawrence, D.G., and Hopkins, D.A. 1972. Developmental aspects of pyramidal control in the rhesus monkey. *Brain Research* 40:117-118.

Lee, D.N. 1976. A theory of visual control of braking based on information about time to collision. *Perception* 5:437-459.

Lee, D.N. 1980. The optic flow field: The foundation of vision. *Philosophical Transactions of the Royal Society of London* B 290:169-179.

Lee, D.N., and Lishman, J.R. 1975. Visual proprioceptive control of stance. *Journal of Human Movement Studies* 1:87-95.

Lee, D.N., Young, D.S., Reddish, P.E., Lough, S., and Clayton, T.M. 1983. Visual timing in hitting an accelerating ball. *Quarterly Journal of Experimental Psychology* 35A:333-346.

Livingstone, M., and Hubel, D. 1988. Segregation of form, color, movement, and depth: Anatomy, physiology, and perception. *Science* 240:740-749.

Marotta, J.J., Perrot, T.S., Nicolle, D., Servos, P., and Goodale, M.A. 1995. Adapting to monocular vision: grasping with one eye. *Experimental Brain Research* 104:107-114.

Marr, D. 1982. *Vision.* San Francisco: Freeman.

Maunsell, J.H.R., Nealey, T.A., and De Priest, D.D. 1990. Magnocellular and parvocellular contributions to responses in the middle temporal area (MT) of the macaque monkey. *Journal of Neuroscience* 10:3323-3334.

Maunsell, J.H.R., and Newsome, W.T. 1987. Visual processing in monkey extrastriate cortex. *Annual Review of Neuroscience* 10:363-401.

Milner, A.D., and Goodale, M.A. 1993. Visual pathways to perception and action. In *Progress in brain research. The visually responsive neuron: From basic neurophysiology to behavior*, edited by T.P. Hicks, S. Molotchnikoff, and T. Ono. Amsterdam: Elsevier.

Milner, A.D., and Goodale, M.A. 1995. *The Visual Brain in Action.* Oxford: Oxford University Press.

Mishkin, M., Ungerleider, L.G., and Macko, K.A. 1983. Object vision and spatial vision: Two cortical pathways. *Trends in Neurosciences* 6:414-417.

Mountcastle, V.B., Motter, B.C., Steinmetz, M.A., and Duffy, C.J. 1984. Looking and seeing: The visual functions of the parietal lobe. P. 159-193 in *Dynamic aspects of neocortical function*, edited by G.M. Edelman, W.E. Gall, and W.M. Cowan. New York: Wiley.

Muir, R.B. 1985. Small hand muscles in precision grip: A corticospinal prerogative? *Experimental Brain Research* Supplement 10:155-174.

Muir, R.B., and Lemon, R.N. 1983. Corticospinal neurons with a special role in precision grip. *Brain Research* 261:312-316.

Ono, T., Tamula, R., Nishijo, H., and Nakamyra, K. 1993. Amygdalar and hippocampal neuron responses related to recognition and memory in monkey. In *Progress in brain research. The visually responsive neuron: From basic neurophysiology* to behavior, edited by T.P. Hicks, S. Molotchnikoff, and T. Ono. Amsterdam: Elsevier.

Paillard, J. 1982. The contribution of peripheral and central vision to visually guided reaching. P. 367-388 in *The analysis of visual behavior*, edited by D.J. Ingle, M.A. Goodale, and R.J.W. Mansfield. Cambridge, MA: MIT Press.

Paillard, J., Jordan, P., and Brouchon, M. 1981. Visual motion cues in prismatic adaptation: evidence for separate and additive processes. *Acta Psychologica* 48:253-270.

Passingham, R., Perry, H., and Wilkinson, F. 1978. Failure to develop a precision grip in monkeys with unilateral neocortical lesions made in infancy. *Brain Research* 145:410-414.

Paulignan, Y., Jeannerod, M., MacKenzie, C., and Marteniuk, R. 1991. Selective perturbation of visual input during prehension movements. 2. The effects of changing object size. *Experimental Brain Research* 87:407-420.

Paulignan, Y., MacKenzie, C., Marteniuk, R., and Jeannerod, M. 1990. The coupling of arm and finger movements during prehension. *Experimental Brain Research* 79:431-436.

Paulignan, Y., MacKenzie, C., Marteniuk, R., and Jeannerod, M. 1991. Selective perturbation of visual input during prehension movements. 1. The effects of changing object position. *Experimental Brain Research* 83:502-512.

Perenin, M.-T., and Vighetto, A. 1983. Optic ataxia: A specific disorder in visuomotor coordination. P. 305-326 in *Spatially oriented behavior*, edited by A. Hein and M. Jeannerod. New York: Springer-Verlag.

Perenin, M.-T., and Vighetto, A. 1988. Optic ataxia: A specific disruption in visuomotor mechanisms. I. Different aspects of the deficit in reaching for objects. *Brain* 111:643-674.

Perrett, D.I., Mistlin, A.J., Harries, M.H., and Chitty, A.J. 1990. Understanding the visual appearance and consequence of hand actions. P. 163-180 in *Vision and action: The control of grasping*, edited by M. Goodale. Norwood, NJ: Ablex.

Previc, F.H. 1990. Functional specialization in the lower and upper visual fields in humans: Its ecological origins and neurophysiological implications. *Behavioral and Brain Sciences* 13:519-575.

Regan, D. 1986. Visual processing of four kinds of relative motion. *Vision Research* 26:127-145.

Regan, D. 1991. Depth from motion and motion in depth. P. 137-169 in *Binocular vision*, edited by D. Regan. London: Macmillan.

Regan, D. 1993. The divergence of velocity and visual processing. *Perception* 22:497-500.

Regan, D., and Beverley, K.I. 1980. Visual responses to changing size and to sideways motion for different directions of motion in depth: linearization of visual responses. *Journal of the Optical Society of America* 70:1289-1296.

Regan, D., Erkelens, C.J., and Collewijn, H. 1986. Visual field defects for vergence eye movements and for stereomotion perception. *Investigative Ophthalmology and Visual Science* 27:806-819.

Regan, D., and Kaushal, S. 1994. Monocular discrimination of the direction of motion in depth. *Vision Research* 34:163-177.

Richmond, B.J., and Sato, T. 1987. Enhancement of inferior temporal neurons during visual discrimination. *Journal of Neurophysiology* 58:1292-1306.

Savelsbergh, G.J.P., Whiting, H.T.A., and Bootsma, R.J. 1991. Grasping Tau. *Journal of Experimental Psychology: Human Perception and Performance* 17: 315-322.

Savelsbergh, G.J.P., Whiting, H.T.A., Pijpers, J.R., and Van Santvoord, A.A. 1993. The visual guidance of catching. *Experimental Brain Research* 93:148-156.

Schiff, W., Caviness, J.A., and Gibson, J.J. 1962. Persistent fear responses in rhesus monkeys to the optical stimulus of "looming." *Science* 136:982-983.

Schiller, P.H., and Logothetis, N.K. 1990. The color-opponent and broad-band channels of the primate visual system. *Trends in Neurosciences* 13:392-398.

Servos, P., and Goodale, M.A. 1990. The role of stereopsis in prehension. Paper presented at Psychonomic Society Annual Meeting, November, at New Orleans, LA.

Servos, P., and Goodale, M.A. 1992. The role of binocular vision in prehension. *Investigative Ophthalmology and Visual Science* 33:1373.

Servos, P., and Goodale, M.A. 1994. Binocular vision and the on-line control of human prehension. *Experimental Brain Research* 98:119-127.

Servos, P., and Goodale, M.A. 1995. Binocular vision and the kinematics of human interceptive movements. Submitted to *Experimental Brain Research*.

Servos, P., Goodale, M.A., and Jakobson, L.S. 1992. The role of binocular vision in prehension: A kinematic analysis. *Vision Research* 32:1513-1521.

Sheedy, J.E., Bailey, I.L., Buri, M., and Bass, E. 1986. Binocular vs. monocular task performance. *American Journal of Optometry and Physiological Optics* 63:839-846.

Sivak, B., and MacKenzie, C.L. 1991. Integration of visual information and motor output in reaching and grasping: The contributions of peripheral and central vision. *Neuropsychologia* 28:1095-1116.

Skavenski, A.A., and Hansen, R.M. 1978. Role of eye position information in visual space perception. P. 15-34 in *Eye movements and the higher psychological functions*, edited by J. Senders, D. Fisher, and R. Monty. New York: Erlbaum.

Soechting, J.F., Tillery, S.I., and Flanders, M. 1990. Transformation from head- to shoulder-centered representation of target direction in arm movements. *Journal of Cognitive Neuroscience* 2:32-43.

Sparks, D.L., and May, L.E. 1990. Signal transformations required for the generation of saccadic eye movements. *Annual Review of Neuroscience* 13:309-336.

Stein, J.F. 1991. Space and the parietal association areas. P. 185-222 in *Brain and space*, edited by J. Paillard. New York: Oxford University Press.

Stein, J.F. 1992. The representation of egocentric space in the posterior parietal cortex. *Behavioral and Brain Sciences* 15:691-700.

Steinbach, M.J., Ono, H., and Wolf, M.E. 1991. Motion parallax judgements as a function of the direction and type of head movement. *Canadian Journal of Psychology* 45:92-98.

Taira, M., Mine, S., Georgopoulos, A.P., Murata, A., and Sakata, H. 1990. Parietal cortex neurons of the monkey related to the visual guidance of hand movement. *Experimental Brain Research* 83:29-36.

Trevarthen, C.B. 1965. Functional interactions between the cerebral hemispheres in the monkey. P. 24-40 in *Functions of the corpus callosum*, edited by E.G. Ettlinger. London: Ciba Foundation.

Trevarthen, C.B. 1968. Two mechanisms of vision in primates. *Psychologische Forschung* 31:299-337.

Ueno, T. 1977. Reaction time as a measure of temporal summation at suprathreshold levels. *Vision Research* 17:227-232.

Ungerleider, L.G., and Mishkin, M. 1982. Two cortical visual systems. P. 549-586 in *The analysis of visual behavior*, edited by D.J. Ingle, M.A. Goodale, and R.J.W. Mansfield. Cambridge, MA: MIT Press.

von Hofsten, C. 1990. Early development of grasping an object in space-time. P. 65-79 in *Vision and action: The control of grasping*, edited by M. Goodale. Norwood, NJ: Ablex.

Wing, A.M., Turton, A., and Fraser, C. 1986. Grasp size and accuracy of approach in reaching. *Journal of Motor Behavior* 18:245-260.

Woodworth, R.S. 1899. The accuracy of voluntary movements. *Psychological Review Monograph Supplements* 3:1-114.

Zelaznik, H.N., Hawkins, B., and Kisselburgh, L. 1983. Rapid visual feedback processing in single-aiming movements. *Journal of Motor Behavior* 15:217-236.

Chapter 6

Electromyographic Analysis of Performance Enhancement

Daniel M. Corcos
University of Illinois at Chicago and Rush Medical College

Slobodan Jaric
University of Belgrade and Institute for Medical Research, Belgrade

Gerald L. Gottlieb
Boston University Neuromuscular Research Center

Researchers have undertaken the study of motor learning and motor control from different perspectives. Those interested in motor learning have been concerned with the factors that facilitate skill acquisition. Studies have centered around variables such as practice distribution, transfer of learning, the role of demonstrations, and the role of feedback (Schmidt 1988). Little attention has been paid to what is being learned. Researchers in motor control, on the other hand, have been interested in which variables are controlled during movement (Stein 1982). They have advanced several models for how movements are controlled. These models include the equilibrium point hypothesis (Bizzi, Polit, and Morasso 1976; Feldman 1986), dynamical systems theory (Schoner and Kelso 1988), the pulse-step model (Freund and Budingen 1978; Ghez 1979), the impulse-timing model (Wallace 1981), various motor program models (Meyer, Smith, and Wright 1982), the dual-strategy hypothesis (Gottlieb, Corcos, and Agarwal 1989b), and models predicated on minimizing certain variables (Stein, Oguztoreli, and Capaday 1986; Uno, Kawato, and Suzuki 1989). Researchers have conducted few studies to determine how control parameters change as a function of skill acquisition, with the notable exception of a theme issue in the *Journal of Motor Behavior* (Newell 1992) and studies related to schema theory (Schmidt 1975). Even fewer studies have related changes in control parameters to changes in muscle activation patterns.

This chapter will consider myoelectric and kinematic changes from the perspective of the dual-strategy hypothesis of motor control. We will first develop the dual-strategy hypothesis, then discuss kinetic and kinematic changes in performance of movements at a single joint in the context of this theory. We will contrast changes in performance within one experimental session with changes across experimental sessions. This comparison is important because learning is not identical to performance enhancement and can be determined only by some measure of retention. In addition, we will compare changes that occur over one movement distance with those that occur across different movement distances. We will then show that the observed changes can be found in highly skilled individuals who might have already optimized their performance, and in individuals with Down syndrome in whom high levels of motor performance are not expected and who might be considered unable to optimize performance. In both groups, we might not expect the ability to greatly improve performance. We will also consider myoelectric and kinematic changes in the elderly and in children. The chapter will conclude with a review of the electromyographic analysis of performance enhancement in movements that involve multiple degrees of freedom.

DUAL-STRATEGY HYPOTHESIS OF MOTOR CONTROL AND PERFORMANCE ENHANCEMENT

The study of motor control is concerned with understanding how movements are controlled to perform particular movement tasks. A task might consist of moving a load or moving accurately to a position in space. Most studies that have investigated how movements are controlled have been restricted to the control of movements at one joint. Such movements involve only one mechanical degree of freedom and have been studied extensively. The forces involved are simple to understand because the joint torque is directly related to the product of angular acceleration multiplied by the moment of inertia. In addition, single degree-of-freedom movements are normally generated by a small number of agonist and antagonist muscles. The most widely reported electromyographic pattern for such movements has been described as triphasic (Hallett, Shahani, and Young 1975; Wachholder and Altenburger 1926). The idea is that the first burst of activity in the agonist muscle accelerates the limb. The first burst of activity in the antagonist muscle decelerates the limb, and the second agonist burst clamps the limb in position (Hannaford and Stark 1985). Despite the apparent simplicity of the EMG pattern accompanying such movements, the precise manner in which the muscles are activated and how this changes to perform different movement tasks have led to a wide array of findings.

One attempt to reconcile the literature on the control of single degree-of-freedom movements is the dual-strategy hypothesis, which suggests that movements are controlled by one of two sets of rules for activating motoneuron pools (Gottlieb, Corcos, and Agarwal 1989b; Gottlieb, Corcos, and Agarwal 1989a; Corcos, Gottlieb, and Agarwal 1989; Gottlieb et al. 1990; Corcos et al. 1990; Gottlieb et al. 1992). Movements made over different distances and against different inertial loads that have no constraint on movement time are controlled by the speed-insensitive strategy (Gottlieb, Corcos, and Agarwal 1989a). Movements that require specific control over movement speed, such as movements to different-sized targets or movements in specific movement times, are controlled by the speed-sensitive strategy (Corcos, Gottlieb, and Agarwal 1989). Movements performed over different distances without instructions to control movement speed are performed by prolonging the duration (width) of excitation to motoneuron pools and delaying the onset of antagonist muscle activation. Movements performed at different speeds are controlled by increasing the intensity (height) of activation to motoneuron pools and activating the antagonist muscles earlier for faster movements.

To interpret the patterns of muscle activation that accompany different movement tasks, we make the simplifying assumption that the electromyogram is a low-pass filtered version of a rectangular excitation pulse that can be varied in height and width. When this assumption is made, the EMG envelope rises at similar rates for movements that use duration modulation and at different rates when the height is changed. (For a more detailed discussion of the interpretation of the EMG, see Gottlieb, Corcos, and Agarwal 1989b and Gottlieb, Corcos, and Agarwal 1992). These two contrasting patterns of muscle activation can be seen in fig. 6.1, in which movements against different distances, different loads, and at different subject-selected speeds are plotted. The agonist EMGs rise at the same rate for the data set on the left and in the middle, whereas they rise at different rates for the data set on the right.

To quantify how EMG and mechanical parameters change to accomplish different tasks, we have quantified our kinematic and EMG variables as depicted in fig. 6.2. The figure shows position, velocity, and acceleration as well as a typical agonist and antagonist electromyographic pattern for a single degree-of-freedom movement. Four EMG measures are of primary interest. They are the integral of the EMG over the first 30 ms (Q_{30}), the integral of the EMG corresponding to the acceleration phase of the movement (Q_{acc}), the integral of the EMG corresponding to the deceleration phase of the movement (Q_{dec}), and the time difference between the onset of the agonist muscle and the onset of the antagonist EMG (antagonist latency). The logic of choosing these variables is that for speed-sensitive movements, the slope of the rising phase of the EMG should change with speed. As such Q_{30} should increase in value. For speed-insensitive movements, the rising phase of the EMG is constant; therefore, Q_{30} should be independent of distance and load. Movements that require larger forces should have larger EMG quantities and should be associated with larger values of Q_{acc} and Q_{dec}. Finally, movements against larger inertial loads and over longer distances are associated with delayed muscle activation, whereas faster movements are associated with earlier muscle activation. Consequently, the antagonist is delayed for speed-insensitive movements but is activated earlier for speed-sensitive movements.

The EMG measures Q_{30}, Q_{acc} and Q_{dec} are always normalized with respect to the maximum voluntary contraction (MVC), and we will refer to these normalized values as Q^*_{30}, Q^*_{acc}, and Q^*_{dec} in this chapter (for further details, see Corcos et al. 1993). Normalizing the EMG values is important for two reasons. First, it makes the comparison of EMG values across multiple experimental sessions more reliable because the absolute value of the myoelectric signal is dependent on such factors as skin resistance and electrode position, and these can change upon reapplication of electrodes. Second, it makes the EMG signal more meaningful to interpret, because the expected value of the normalized signal lies between 0 and 1. A value of 1 suggests that close to maximal motor unit recruitment is occurring. Values larger than 1 are interpreted to be equal to 1. One cause of values larger than 1 is motor unit synchronization, which can result in a signal disproportionate to the force generated (Basmajian and DeLuca 1985). In addition to quantifying myoelectric parameters, we also quantify various kinematic parameters as shown in fig. 6.2.

One strength of the dual-strategy hypothesis is that it provides an explicit set of rules for how the electromyogram should change when movement speed changes.

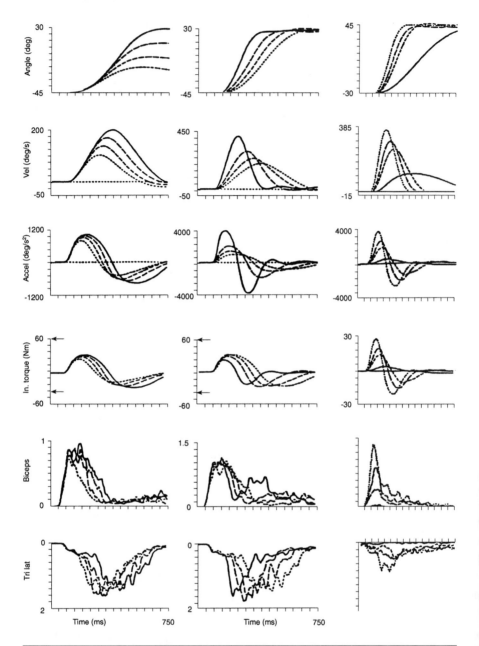

Fig. 6.1 Plotted from top to bottom are averages of joint angle, velocity and acceleration, inertial torque, biceps and triceps EMG (rectified and smoothed with a 30-ms moving average filter). At the *left* are average movements over four different distances (18°,
36°, 54°, 72°). In the *middle* are four sets of 72° movements with four different loads. At
the *right* are 72° movements at four different speeds.
Reprinted from Gottlieb, Corcos, and Agarwal 1992.

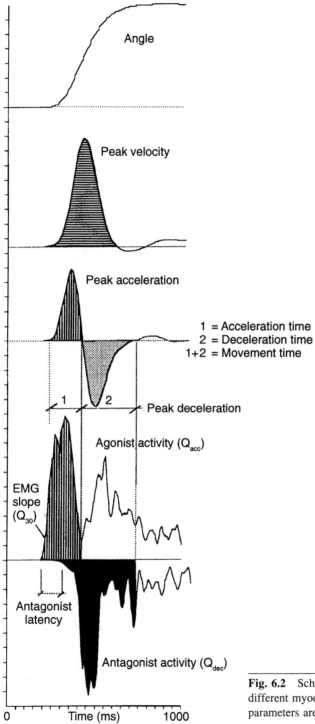

Fig. 6.2 Schematic to illustrate how different myoelectric and kinematic parameters are computed.

As a result, this hypothesis provides a framework to consider changes in movement speed that result from practice.

Performance Enhancement: Changes in Measures of Central Tendency

One of the few sets of experiments that have investigated myoelectric and kinematic correlates of performance enhancement over several experimental sessions was conducted by Corcos and colleagues (Corcos et al. 1993; Jaric et al. 1993), who were interested in how muscle activation patterns changed as a function of practice. As a pretest, five subjects were asked to perform movements over five distances as fast as possible. The subjects were then asked to make 200 movements over one movement distance for seven experimental sessions. Finally, the subjects were asked to repeat the movements over five different distances. The experimental design is depicted in table 6.1. This design enables one to consider performance enhancement from two perspectives. The first perspective is retention of performance enhancement at the same task. The second perspective is performance enhancement in terms of the degree of transfer to a similar task.

Over the course of the first experimental session (part A) and subsequent experimental sessions (part B), subjects improved their performance, as we can see from the plot of peak velocity in fig. 6.3. We chose a logarithmic fit for the data in this study because it has been well established that performance improves rapidly to begin with, then tapers off. We used the following equation to fit the data:

$$Y = a + b \log X \qquad (6.1)$$

where a and b are empirically determined constants.

One interesting observation from our data is that performance changes tapered off in session 1 after about 100 trials (fig. 6.3A, block 5). Previous studies of performance enhancement with one-degree-of-freedom movements (McGrain 1980; Normand et al. 1982) or with multidegree-of-freedom fast movements (Schneider et al. 1989; Schmidtbleicher, Gollhofer, and Frick 1988) did not exceed 100 practice trials per day, so it is not clear how robust this finding is. Physiological muscle fatigue during the experiments can be ruled out as an explanation of this performance

Table 6.1   Experimental Protocol

Session 0	5 distances (18°, 36°, 54°, 72°, and 90°)
Pretest	11 trials at each distance
Sessions 1-7	1 distance (54°)
	10 blocks of 20 trials
Session 8	5 distances (18°, 36°, 54°, 72°, and 90°)
Posttest	11 trial at each distance

Reprinted from Corcos et al. 1993.

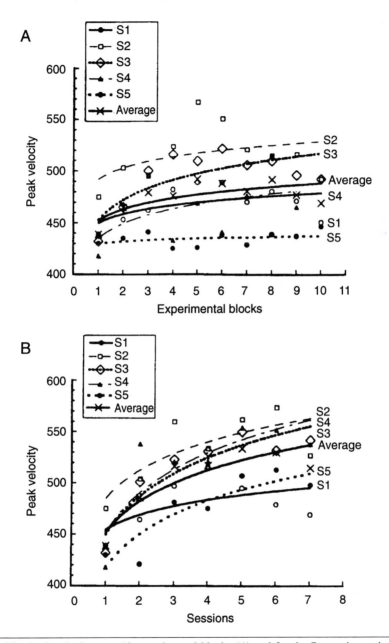

Fig. 6.3   Peak velocity over 10 experimental blocks (*A*) and for the 7 experimental sessions (*B*). The data are for five individual subjects as well as the average of all five subjects (cross). The data have been fitted with a logarithmic relationship.

Note the data in Figure 6.3A are unpublished. Figure 6.3B is reprinted from Corcos et al. 1993.

leveling because, if this were the case, the EMG-force relationship would have changed. For the same level of torque, fatigue would cause an increase in EMG (Bigland-Ritchie et al. 1983), but this was not observed in the three subjects who also performed contractions of 50% of the initial maximum voluntary contraction (MVC) at the beginning and end of the experiment. Some form of psychological fatigue is a possible explanation, and this is consistent with the observation that the EMG signal became smaller as the movements decreased in velocity.

The observation that movement speed increased for this simple task raises the following question. How are muscles activated to achieve this increase in speed? The speed-sensitive strategy suggests that the intensity of activation is increased to both the agonist and the antagonist muscle and that the antagonist muscle is activated earlier. This finding was supported, as we can see in fig. 6.4, which depicts performance change over the first three experimental blocks of session 1. There are substantial differences between subjects in the degree to which we can attribute performance enhancement to changes in the agonist muscle, the antagonist muscle, and the timing of muscle activation. In some subjects, the correlation was highest between measures of EMG quantity and kinematic parameters, whereas in other subjects the correlation was highest between the latency of the electromyogram and a kinematic parameter.

The experimental design used in this study allowed us to determine the extent to which performance changes that occur within an experimental session are similar to those that occur over experimental sessions. This feature of the experimental design is important because it enables us to draw the distinction between performance changes that are temporary and those that are learned. For a change to be considered learned, it must be relatively permanent. The data in fig. 6.5 depict peak velocity (part A) and the standard deviation of the final position (part B). Both data sets show that performance improvement was retained from experimental session to experimental session and as such was learned.

The changes in muscle activation patterns observed over experimental blocks within one experimental session and over experimental sessions were very similar. However, we observed at least one potential difference. One of the five subjects delayed muscle activation across experimental sessions. This finding suggests that prolonged practice can lead to changes in muscle activation patterns that are not consistent with the predictions of the speed-sensitive strategy.

We can determine motor learning in at least two ways. The first is by determining performance enhancement over repeated measurements and showing progressive increments in performance, as we can see in fig. 6.5. An alternative way to consider motor learning is in terms of transfer, which can be defined as "the gain (or loss) in the capability for responding on a transfer or criterion task as a function of practice or experience on a training task" (Schmidt and Young 1987, 48). The use of a transfer task to ascertain the relationship between performance enhancement and muscle activation allows us to extend the findings derived from observations at the same movement distance to findings observed at other movement distances. Because changes of movement distance are made by the speed-insensitive strategy, we can now consider what changes are made to this underlying control scheme. The data in fig. 6.6 depict movements over three distances before and after practice (i.e., the pretest and the posttest). The points to notice are that movement speed

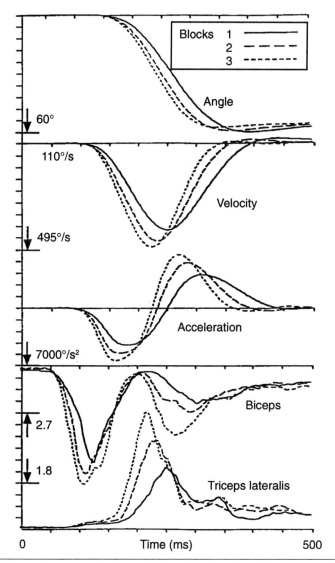

Fig. 6.4 Kinematic and myoelectric variables of the first three blocks of 19 movements of subject 4. The figure depicts angle, velocity, acceleration, and EMGs from biceps and the lateral head of triceps. These variables are an average of approximately 19 trials, aligned in the graph at t = 50 ms on the onset of the biceps EMG.
Reprinted from Corcos et al. 1993.

increased at the nonpracticed distances. In addition, the rise rate of the EMGs in the posttest is steeper and the antagonist EMG is activated earlier. These are the same two changes observed during the performance enhancement over experimental blocks within one experimental session and over experimental sessions.

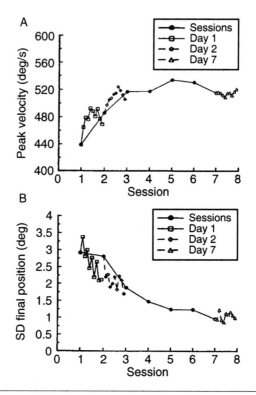

Fig. 6.5   Peak velocity (*A*) and the standard deviation of final position (*B*) for the first block of trials for each of seven experimental sessions (*filled circles*) and all 10 blocks of trials for days 1, 2, and 7 (*open symbols*).
Reprinted from Corcos et al. 1993.

Adaptation and Learning: Changes in Measures of Variability

Performance enhancement can be characterized by the extent to which the movements and the myoelectric signals have become more consistent. The variability of the kinematic data showed a consistent decrease over experimental blocks in the first session and over experimental sessions (e.g., fig. 6.5B). This finding is in accord with the idea that practice leads to consistent, accurate performance. The interpretation of the EMG variability data is less obvious. Whereas the intensity of activation of spinal motoneuron pools increased over both experimental blocks and over experimental sessions, the absolute myoelectric variability (standard deviation of the measures Q^*_{acc} and Q^*_{dec}) remained fairly constant over one experimental session, as we can see in fig. 6.7. This finding differs from studies that have shown either decreased EMG variability (Dugas and Marteniuk 1989; Moore and Marteniuk 1986; Ludwig 1982) or increased variability (Darling and Cooke 1987). The subjects in the study of Darling and Cooke (1987) performed 60 movements, and the myoelectric variability (standard deviation) increased as velocity increased. Their measure of variability was to calculate the variance across successive movements of

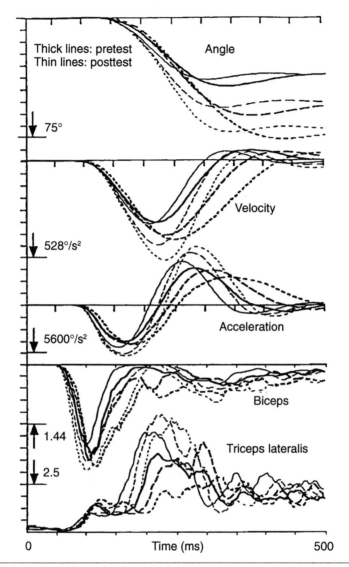

Fig. 6.6   Kinematic and myoelectric variables for 36°, 54°, and 72° movements in the pretest (*darker lines*) and the posttest (*lighter lines*) for one subject (S5) from the practice group. The figure depicts angle, velocity, acceleration, and EMGs from biceps (inverted) and the lateral head of triceps. These variables are an average of approximately 10 trials, aligned in the graph at t = 50 ms on the onset of the biceps EMG.
Reprinted from Jaric et al. 1993.

electromyograms integrated over 10-ms time bins within each record. For example, there would be 20 individual bins for a 200-ms movement. Calculating variability in this manner includes considerably more high frequency content in the myoelectric signal than in the data presented in fig. 6.7, in which the EMG is integrated for at

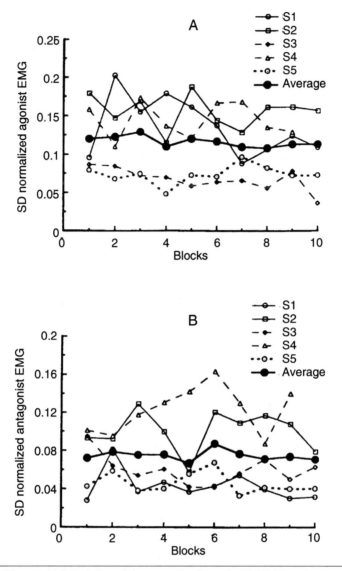

Fig. 6.7 The standard deviation of the normalized agonist EMG (*A*) and antagonist EMG (*B*) for 10 blocks of movement trials. The data are for five individual subjects as well as the average of all five subjects (*black circles*). Unpublished data.

least 100 ms to compute Q^*_{acc} and twice this time to compute Q^*_{dec}. Integration is a low-pass filtering process, and longer time intervals act to decrease the cutoff frequency. In a reanalysis of our data for one of our five subjects, we recalculated the variability of the EMG in bin sizes of 10 ms. When this was done, the EMG variability increased as velocity increased, exactly as reported by Darling and Cooke (1987). The finding that EMG variability increased as movement velocity increased can also be seen in fig. 6.8, in which we plotted a frequency distribution for the variable $Q*_{30}$. The frequency distribution data show that, as movement speed increases from block one to block three, the EMG quantity $Q*_{30}$ increases in value and becomes more variable.

These two observations are consistent. The EMG signal variance emerges from two sources. One is inherent in the generation of the instantaneous EMG interference pattern as a summation of polyphasic motor unit action potentials. This variance component will increase with the number of action potentials or, in terms of our model, with the intensity of the excitation pulse. Variance will decrease in direct proportion to the interval over which the EMG signal is integrated or averaged (whether rectified or not).

A second variance component will exist if, on successive movements, the number of active motor units varies. Short averaging intervals (as used by Darling and Cooke 1987) will be similarly influenced by both components, whereas long averaging intervals (as performed in the study by Corcos et al. 1993) will attenuate the first component. Hence the results of Darling and Cooke (1987) are weighted by the variance of the bioelectrical processes underlying the EMG signal generation and are not in contradiction to ours, which are weighted to extract the variance in the total motor unit recruitment from movement to movement.

The EMG quantity standard deviation showed no consistent change over the seven experimental sessions. The reason for this might be that several competing processes are continually at work. The long integration time intervals that we use extract the variance in total motor unit recruitment from trial to trial. We would expect learning to lead to a decrease in variability. However, as movement speed increases, the intensity of the excitation increases, and this would lead to increased

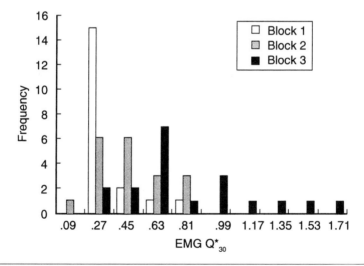

Fig. 6.8 A frequency distribution for the 19 trials in blocks 1, 2, and 3 for subject 4. The data are for the EMG parameter $Q*_{30}$.
Reprinted from Corcos et al. 1993.

variability in the EMG signal due to the additional recruitment of motor units. Any potential decrease in the variability over seven sessions is partially nullified by the fact that the long integration time is shortening from session 1 to session 7 because the movements are made in shorter movement times. This decrease in integration time can increase variability.

Neural Versus Muscular Causes of Performance Enhancement

The evidence discussed in the two previous sections shows that practicing a movement leads to myoelectric and kinematic changes. Because the movements were very rapid and made against a low resistance, no changes in strength were expected and none were found. The data in fig. 6.9 depict the maximal voluntary contraction averaged over the five subjects who took part in the experiment shown in table 6.1.

The absence of a trend in the MVC measurement allows us to conclude that there was no increase in strength due to the muscular exercise associated with the experimental protocol, and increased strength was not the cause of the increase in the kinematic measurements. Had the subjects become stronger by performing the movements, this might have allowed improvements in speed without changes in the neural activation of the muscles. However, even if under some circumstances, changes in movement speed can be partly attributable to changes in muscle strength, it is most likely that such changes in strength would be neurally mediated. The suggestion that performance change is neurally mediated is consistent with a large body of research summarized by Enoka (1988), who argues that the nervous system is of paramount importance in developing strength. Whereas it is true that the

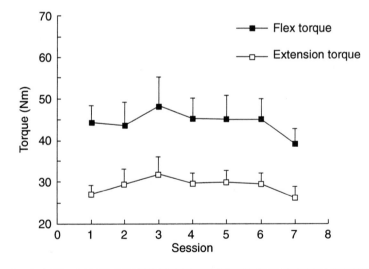

Fig. 6.9 Maximal flexion and extension torque for each of seven experimental sessions. The data are pooled over all five subjects. Unpublished data.

maximal strength a muscle can develop is proportional to its cross-sectional area, a poor relationship exists between increases in muscle strength and muscle size (Jones and Rutherford 1987; Young, McDonagh, and Davies 1985). Changes in strength are consequences of changes in the motor system, which consists of neural, muscular, and mechanical factors. According to Enoka, the consensus is that initial strength gains are due to neural changes, whereas muscle hypertrophy underlies later changes. This suggests that the performance enhancement observed in the studies of Corcos and colleagues (1993) could still be improved upon not only by continuing the training protocol but also by using additional training protocols that would eventually lead to strength gains.

Summary

The findings of the two studies by Corcos and colleagues provide a conceptual framework within which to interpret practice effects on performance changes within and across experimental sessions. When practice of the fastest possible movements leads to a reduction in movement time within an experimental session, the rules for activating motoneuron pools are similar to those that underlie the speed-sensitive strategy. Excitation pulse intensity increases while its duration remains constant. This results in changes in the initial slope of the EMG and in the agonist burst. The duration of the agonist burst will be nearly constant if the duration of the excitation pulse is constant. The antagonist is scaled in a similar way and with decreased latency. The slope of the initial rise in muscle force (or joint torque) will scale with the intensity of the excitation pulse (see fig. 6.1). For constant inertial loads, this implies that acceleration will be proportional to intensity. In addition, when movement velocity and the forces involved in movement production change as a function of practice, there will be a reduction in the variability of kinematic parameters. There may also be changes in EMG variability contingent upon the signal processing methods used.

These rules are consistent with the conclusions of McGrain (1980). He suggested that

- performance is more closely reflected by changes in velocity than EMG,
- when there are no changes in the time course of muscle activation, then integrated EMG will be related to performance changes, and
- if angular velocity increases over practice, there will be an increase in agonist and antagonist electromyographic activity.

The rules of the speed-sensitive strategy suggest that appropriately selected EMG parameters will reflect performance changes, although perhaps with greater variability than will be seen with kinematic measures. When practice leads to changes in the rate at which force is produced, this increase in force production is achieved by increasing the intensity of neural activation to antagonistic muscle groups and decreasing the time delay between them. The fact that neural activation can increase implies that, even at the level of controlling the simplest and most common voluntary movements, there are patterns of motor unit recruitment not immediately available to us. This is most dramatically shown in the frequency distribution data in fig. 6.8, which show increases in the EMG quantity $Q*_{30}$. This increase in the EMG quantity that corresponds to the slope of the EMG is caused by activating the motoneuron pools with increasing intensity. It is only by repetition of the movements and attempts to improve them that these neural patterns become accessible or perhaps *learned.*

PERFORMANCE ENHANCEMENT
IN DIFFERENT GROUPS OF INDIVIDUALS

The studies we presented in the previous section were conducted on young, neurologically normal individuals. We have shown that their movement trajectories change and become more consistent as a function of practice. We have also argued that this trajectory change is related to predictable changes in patterns of muscle activation. In this section, we will consider studies that we have conducted on a baseball pitcher and on individuals with Down syndrome to see whether the same findings hold or whether different rules govern their performance. We chose these two groups of individuals because their performance levels are at the opposite ends of the performance spectrum. Individuals with Down syndrome move more slowly than normal, whereas baseball pitchers move more quickly. These studies will be interpreted in the framework of the dual-strategy hypothesis to determine whether the rules we have developed apply to groups of individuals whose performance levels are outside the normal range. We will conclude with studies that have investigated electromyographic changes in children and in the elderly as a function of practice.

Baseball Pitching[1]

One feature of skilled baseball pitching is the ability to rapidly extend the elbow joint. As such, we decided to investigate the myoelectric and kinematic patterns of elbow flexion and extension movements in a baseball pitcher. The analysis of both flexion and extension movements allowed us to answer two questions. The first question was whether the pitcher would perform rapid elbow flexion movements at similar speeds and use similar patterns of muscle activation as those of normal subjects. This question is of interest because the elbow flexors are not the primary muscles used in pitching and have, presumably, had no more experience in rapid flexion movements than those of normal individuals. Second, to what extent is the performance change in flexion similar to the performance change in extension? We can think of the motion of pitching as extensive prior practice in a similar task. This may lead to enhanced performance in extension compared with control subjects but not leave room for improvement through practice.

In answer to the first question, the performance of the pitcher improved through practice and he reached speeds of 720°/s for 54° flexion movements. His EMG patterns changed in a similar way to those shown in fig. 6.4. The peak velocity of the pitcher contrasts with an average peak velocity of 500°/s for the five subjects whose data are plotted in fig. 6.10 in the next section. There are several possible

---

[1]The results are presented in greater detail in Corcos et al. 1990.

explanations for why his flexion movements are so fast. The first is that an important limiting factor in generating rapid movements is the strength of agonist and antagonist muscles. Colebatch, Gandevia, and Spira (1986) have reported that the maximal elbow flexor torque in males is 62 Nm and the average extensor torque is only half this amount. The maximal flexion torque for the pitcher was 70 Nm and the maximal extension torque was 48 Nm. As such, it is quite possible that he could generate very rapid movements because of the above-average strength of his muscles, particularly the strength of the elbow extensors, which are required to decelerate rapid flexion movements. The second reason his movements are so fast is that pitchers have a high percentage of fast-twitch muscle fibers. This could enable them to exert high forces in agonist muscles during their fast shortening.

In answer to the second question, the pitcher was faster than normal subjects for flexion and extension but did not change his performance over practice trials in the extension movements. The fact that both flexion and extension movements were faster suggests that, in addition to strength and muscle-twitch characteristics, the extensively learned action of rapidly throwing a baseball is transferred to other elbow movements. However, the extensive practice of pitching (an extension movement) left no room for further performance changes in extension but did leave room for improved performance in flexion.

Down Syndrome

Individuals with Down syndrome are often characterized as moving slowly and being poorly coordinated. There are two possible reasons for this. The first possibility is that an underlying deficit exists in the mechanisms responsible for controlling movement (Davis and Sinning 1987; Frith and Frith 1974; Parker and Bronks 1980). Such a deficit could be related to the diminished size of the cerebellum and other brain structures (Woollacott and Shumway-Cook 1986). The alternative point of view suggests that the motor mechanisms are intact but apparent motor deficits are consequences of deficits in other systems such as cognition (Latash and Corcos 1991; Latash 1992). This latter point of view suggests that practice emphasizing motor performance and placing limited demands on cognition should be very effective. To consider this issue, a similar paradigm to that outlined in the section on performance enhancement was used. Eight individuals with Down syndrome were asked to perform movements over four different distances. They then took part in 10 experimental sessions in which they performed 1100 movements at one movement distance. They completed the experiment by repeating the movements over the four distances. On average the peak movement velocity doubled and came close to reaching values similar to those reported for the neurologically normal individuals. These results can be seen in fig. 6.10.

It is worth noting that this comparison underestimates the maximum increase that could be expected, because the Down syndrome group included four males and four females aged 14 to 34, whereas the other group consisted of five males between the ages of 21 and 25. In addition, the individuals with Down syndrome had 300 fewer practice trials and were probably in poorer physical condition because of their lack of experience at generating rapid movements. Nevertheless, repeating the

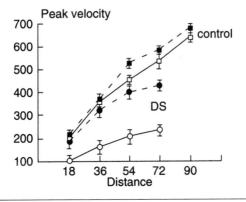

Fig. 6.10   Averaged across the subjects values of peak velocity for the elbow flexion movements performed "as fast as possible" over different distances. Before practice, DS-subjects (*open circles*) were much slower than the control subjects (*open rectangles*). After practice, the DS-subjects improved their performance dramatically (*filled circles*) and became very close to the control group. The control group also improved their performance (*filled rectangles*). Note that the control subjects demonstrated a virtually linear increase in peak speed with movement distance while the DS-subjects deviated down from the linear pattern at longer distances (72°). Scales are in degrees and degrees/second. Standard deviation bars are shown.
Reprinted from Latash 1992.

movement 1100 times led to a dramatic improvement that brought their performance almost to the level of the neurologically normal group.

This dramatic increase in performance at the practiced distance (36°) and the unpracticed distance was accomplished in a manner similar to that described for the neurologically normal group. The data in fig. 6.11 shows position, velocity, acceleration, and the agonist and antagonist EMGs for the pretest and the posttest. The point to notice is that the movements in the pretest are slow and the EMG signal small. The posttest data are normal and should be compared with fig. 6.6. The agonist and antagonist EMG quantities increased and the antagonist latency decreased. We can most easily see this when the data are quantified as in fig. 6.12.

These data show not only that practice can lead to striking changes in performance but also that the EMG can determine the extent to which the performance enhancement is caused by similar patterns of muscle activation to those we have demonstrated for other populations.

Children

Engelhorn (1988) had 7-, 9-, and 11-year-old children perform 60 trials of an elbow-flexion movement. Correct movements consisted of making a 60° movement in 800 ms. Absolute displacement error and movement timing error improved with practice. In addition the agonist, root mean square EMG decreased. Two of the measured parameters showed differences between the age groups. Movement timing

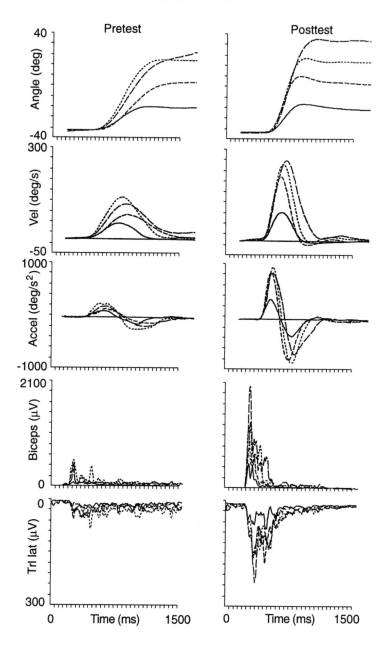

Fig. 6.11 Movements are performed over four distances (18°, 36°, 54°, and 72°) as fast as possible during the pretest and posttest for subject S8. Angle, velocity (vel), acceleration (accel), biceps, and lateral head of triceps (tri lat) are plotted for the pretest and the posttest. The lateral head triceps has been inverted. The onset of the agonist EMG occurs at 200 ms. Reprinted from Almeida, Corcos, and Latash 1994.

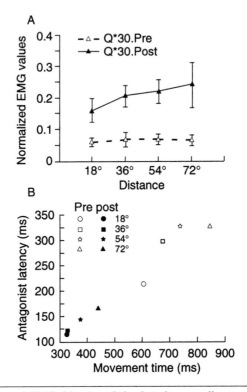

Fig. 6.12   (A) Averaged EMG Q*$_{30}$ (n = 6) is plotted versus distance. The data are for the pretest (*broken line*) and for the posttest (*solid line*). (B) Averaged (n = 5) antagonist latency is plotted versus movement time for the pretest and posttest for four distances. The data are from five individuals with Down syndrome for whom an early and late EMG component could be identified.

Reprinted from Almeida, Corcos, and Latash 1994.

error was less for the 11-year-old children and the time to peak antagonist EMG was delayed. These findings are entirely consistent with other studies that have looked at the effects of practice in tasks that constrain movement time.

Aging

Darling, Cooke, and Brown (1989) investigated the control of step-tracking movements in a group of elderly individuals. They found that the movements of the elderly individuals differed from those of a group of young individuals in the following manner. First, the elderly group displayed greater trajectory variability than the younger group. Second, the pattern of muscle activation consisted of greater tonic activation before the movement, and the antagonist burst was either hard to identify or occurred earlier than in the younger control group. They were also interested in the role of practice and asked the elderly individuals to generate 180 flexion movements and 180 extension movements to determine whether practicing changed how the movements were controlled. The elderly individuals did not increase movement speed as a result of practice. The trajectory and EMG patterns were still variable following practice, but the variability was reduced over that observed during the initial trials. In addition, there was a clear reduction in the antagonist EMG before the movement. The antagonist burst following movement onset became more phasic but was still not correctly timed. These findings are of interest because they suggest that, in some elderly individuals, some aspects of motor performance are modifiable by practice (trial-to-trial consistency), but other aspects are not (speed). Similarly, some characteristics of the patterns of muscle activation are modifiable (tonic activity before the movement and phasic antagonist EMG during the movement), whereas others are not (latencies). The challenge of these findings is to determine the extent to which they are task specific and whether the inability to increase speed and alter the timing of the antagonist muscle is a characteristic of the aging process or indicative of a disease state.

PERFORMANCE ENHANCEMENT IN MULTIDEGREE-OF-FREEDOM MOVEMENTS

The first two sections of this chapter addressed issues related to the EMG analysis of skill acquisition for single degree-of-freedom tasks. This type of analysis is simple to perform because there are a limited number of muscles and a limited number of ways in which muscles can be activated for enhanced performance. This is not true for multidegree-of-freedom tasks in which the challenge for understanding skill acquisition is in ascertaining how the multiple degrees of freedom are coordinated as skill is acquired and performance enhanced. In addition, most studies reviewed in the previous two sections required subjects to generate larger forces to enhance performance. This is not always the case for studies that have investigated the relationship between learning and myoelectric changes. Therefore, in this section we will first review characteristics of different movement tasks. We will then selectively review studies that have analyzed

- the amplitude, slope, and timing of agonist and antagonist muscle activity as a function of joint-specific force requirements,
- the importance of considering interactional forces in understanding the electromyographic patterns of complex movements,
- general patterns of coordination, and
- changes in the activation of postural muscles as a function of movement task and skill level.

Task Characteristics

The dual-strategy hypothesis predicts that if practice leads to increased movement speed, then faster movements will be accompanied by increased EMG quantities, faster rising EMGs, and changes in the timing of muscle activation. This is in contrast to the hypothesis of Payton, Sally, and Meydrich (1976) that ''all the agonists which contribute to a skilled performance begin as a relatively undifferentiated mass of muscle. As learning takes place, the various elements of this muscle mass are differentiated into prime movers and auxiliaries. The prime movers maintain approximately the same level of activity with which they began'' (173). The difference in these two hypotheses is that the dual-strategy hypothesis assumes that performance enhancement related to increased speed is not solely attributable to eliminating extraneous muscle activity but does require increased activation of muscle groups that are the prime movers. One source of the disparate findings in the literature is that many studies that have looked at performance changes and learning have required a constant kinematic criterion, such as propelling a carriage at a criterion velocity of 15 mph (McGrain 1980) or performing a positioning task at velocities of 40° and 200°/s (Engelhorn 1983). Other tasks have been used that either emphasize accuracy (Vorro, Wilson, and Dainis 1978) or hold movement time constant (Engelhorn 1988). The dual-strategy hypothesis has no specific predictions for such studies. However, the assumption is that such tasks do not necessarily require increased force for their successful execution. Instead, they may require less force or a temporal redistribution of the forces. In such cases, no reason exists for any increase in EMG quantity.

Changes in Myoelectric and Kinetic/Kinematic Measures

One of the clearest demonstrations of increased EMG as a function of practice can be found in a study by Finley, Wirta, and Cody (1968). They had subjects perform a tracking task that required flexion, extension, pronation, and supination of the arm muscles. As a result of practice, the muscle activation of agonists and antagonists increased, but the increase was proportionately greater in the agonists. Other studies present a more complex picture as we can see by analyzing a study by Hobart, Kelley, and Bradley (1975). They had subjects learn a novel throwing task involving muscular activity of the pectoralis major, anterior deltoid, posterior deltoid, and triceps brachii. They found that, as a result of practice, one agonist (anterior deltoid) decreased in activity and one (pectoralis major) remained constant. One antagonist remained constant (triceps brachii), whereas the other increased in activity. McGrain (1980) had subjects perform a novel motor task using a knee extension movement preceded by knee flexion, in which subjects had to learn to propel a carriage along a track to a criterion velocity specified by the experimenter. He found increased EMG activity in the knee extensors (rectus femoris and vastus medialis) and biceps femoris (a knee flexor). He found no change in semitendinosus activity (a knee flexor). The speed-sensitive strategy suggests that the rise rate of muscle activity will increase as movement speed increases. Evidence to support this can be found in this study because there was a significant change in the slopes of the two knee extensor muscles, which were functioning as muscle agonists. There was also an increase in speed as the criterion velocity was reached. Normand and colleagues (1982) had subjects perform a bi-articular movement, which consisted of a maximal speed horizontal arm adduction followed by a forearm flexion in the same plane of motion. Subjects increased the speed of both the arm and the forearm movements.

Normand and colleagues analyzed the time for which the muscles were active and the timing of the antagonist muscles. They found that, as a result of training, the antagonist muscles were delayed in activation. This finding is inconsistent with predictions from the speed-sensitive strategy but quite consistent with the idea that movement speed can be increased by delaying the application of a braking force.

General Coordination

Several studies have looked at whole-body movement skills to see how the patterns of muscle activation change as a function of practice. Quantitative analysis of the relationship between EMG parameters and mechanical variables is difficult in such studies because of the large number of muscles and joints involved in acquiring the skill, but we can obtain some qualitative insights into the nature of skill acquisition. Kamon and Gormley (1968) were interested in the patterns of activation for skilled performance during learning the horizontal bar exercise. The movement was broken down into five phases:

- *Phase 1.* Inverted hang—movement of the body forward and slightly upward, accompanied by the start of a forward leg swing
- *Phase 2.* The horizontal position—while continuing the leg swing, the body passes through the horizontal position
- *Phase 3.* Chest opposite the bar—continuation of the trunk movement to bring the chest closer to the bar
- *Phase 4.* Trunk above the bar—continuation of the trunk movement to reach a position on top of the bar and commencement of arm extension
- *Phase 5.* Support position—maintenance of a static balanced position on top of the bar, with the body supported on the arms and the thigh (347)

The data in fig. 6.13 show the EMGs of the same task performed before and after practice. Several features of these data are worth noting. The first is the longer period of activity between stage 3 and 4 in the unpracticed condition. Practice enabled the subject to time the activation of the muscles responsible for elbow extension to take advantage of the angular momentum of the body. This is particularly evident in the much shorter burst of triceps activity. Second, we could characterize the early stages of training by long periods of muscle activation that were overlapping. In the later stage, the bursts shortened. The time to execute the movement also shortened. Similar findings can be seen in a study by Waterland (1970) in which she compared the patterns of muscle activation of a highly skilled gymnast with those of a novice.

Interactional Forces

Most articles we have reviewed so far have used either simple tasks such as single degree-of-freedom flexion movements or simple dependent measures such as movement time and time on target. Such tasks and methods of analysis will not, however, elucidate completely how movements that involve multiple degrees of freedom are controlled and how the movement control changes as a function of practice. As

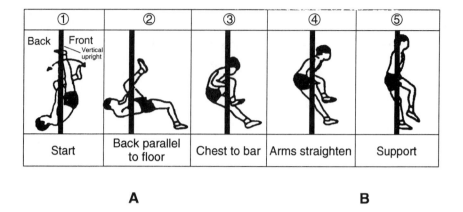

A   **B**

Fig. 6.13   Comparison of electrical activity patterns of the muscles at different stages during training: (A) poorly performed exercise recorded in the early stages of training; (B) fluently performed exercise recorded from the same subject in the final stages of training. The numbers on the myograms refer to the numbering of the sequential phases above. Reprinted from Kamon and Gormley 1968.

pointed out by Schneider and colleagues (1989), the challenge the nervous system confronts when controlling movements is to control "multiple, connected, interacting segmental links in three-dimensional gravitational space" (805). Schneider and colleagues were interested in testing Bernstein's hypothesis that "the secret of coordination lies not only in not wasting superfluous force in extinguishing reactive phenomena but, on the contrary, in employing the latter in such a way as to employ active muscle forces only in the capacity of complementary forces" (Bernstein 1967,

109). To test this hypothesis, they had subjects practice performing an unrestrained movement in the vertical plane. During the upward and downward phases of the motion, the hand had to circumvent a T-shaped barrier midway between the upper and lower target areas. The execution of this task required that the subject perform a series of flexion and extension movements involving the shoulder, elbow, and wrist joints. At each joint, there is a net joint moment composed of gravitational, interactive, and muscle components. Practice caused an increase in movement speed and an increase in the interactive and muscle components. The evidence that muscle forces are employed as complementary forces can be seen in fig. 6.14. The time series data show that as the subjects started the reversal movement, upper arm angular acceleration (a passive interactive moment) caused the shoulder to flex. However, this was counteracted by an almost equal and opposite muscle moment that caused extension at the shoulder.

Support for this idea can be seen in fig. 6.15, which shows the EMG burst patterns used to perform the task. Many features are similar to those that we have described previously in this chapter. After practice, the EMGs are more phasic, there is decreased co-contraction and the bursts are shorter. The important additional observation is that muscle moments are required to overcome passive moments. This can be seen by analyzing the posterior deltoid muscle. In the slow movement, the posterior deltoid was activated and deactivated before entering the target and slowed the shoulder flexion by a lengthening contraction. In the fast movement, the posterior

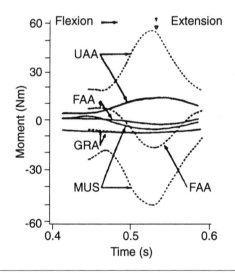

Fig. 6.14   Exemplar time series of the shoulder moments during the reversal phase for the slowest (solid line) and fastest (dashed line) trials for the same representative subject (subject 4): generalized muscle moment (*MUS*); upper-arm-angular acceleration (*UAA*) and forearm-angular acceleration (*FAA*). The changes in shoulder-joint moments that occurred with practice during the reversal were consistent with Bernstein's hypothesis. As subjects decreased their movement times, shoulder-extensor muscle moments (*MUS*) counterbalanced a passive-interactive moment (*UAA*) that caused the shoulder to flex. Reprinted from Schneider 1989.

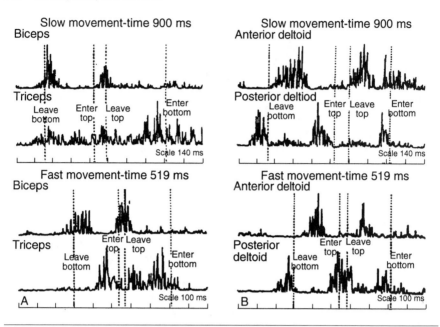

Fig. 6.15 Exemplar EMG burst patterns for (*A*) the biceps brachii (caput longum) and triceps brachii (caput longum) and (*B*) the anterior and posterior deltoids during slowest and fastest trials (subject 5). The *dotted vertical lines* indicate successively when the circular metal plate left the bottom target, entered the upper target, left the top target, and re-entered the bottom target at the end of the movement. The recruitment of the posterior deltoid as the hand approached the upper target occurred significantly sooner in the movement as subjects became faster. Further, co-contraction occurred in anterior and posterior deltoids in early practice, but with practice, the EMG showed only the phasic recruitment of posterior deltoid. During early practice, the absolute and relative durations of all anterior and posterior deltoid bursts decreased significantly.
Reprinted from Schneider 1989.

deltoid was again active before entering the target. However, it was also active during shoulder extension as the hand left the upper target. This increased activity was required to counteract the tendency for the shoulder to flex as a result of the forearm angular acceleration.

Anticipation

The studies that we have so far considered have primarily addressed the question of how EMG patterns change during skill acquisition in movement tasks involving the hand and arm muscles. One can also ask how activation patterns change in postural tasks as a function of practice or training. One such study was performed by Pedotti et al. (1989). They had two groups of subjects perform a task in which the subjects had to bend the head and trunk backward as fast as possible at a given signal, and then return to upright. In addition, they had two groups of subjects (gymnasts and nongymnasts) perform the task while standing on a narrow support. The important finding is that the two groups of subjects responded differently to the task. In the untrained group, the hamstring muscles and soleus muscles were activated simultaneously or even later than the erector spinae (the prime movers). The untrained group of subjects displayed patterns of muscle activation that can be described as *nonanticipated*. This pattern is in sharp contrast to the trained subjects, who activated their calf muscles before the prime movers, which can be described as *distal anticipation*. This finding suggests that practicing a skill can lead to changes in patterns of muscle activation consistent with the dynamic requirements of the task.

CONCLUSION

This chapter has reviewed electromyographic and kinematic changes as a function of practice in single and multiple degree-of-freedom movements in several groups of individuals. The strongest finding is that the relationship between changes in performance and changes in patterns of muscle activation is extremely complex. This finding is hardly surprising because the relationship between EMG and movement kinematics and dynamics is complex (Agarwal and Gottlieb 1982; Agarwal and Gottlieb 1985; Basmajian and DeLuca 1985). Several steps are required to further our understanding of the relationship between changes in performance and changes in patterns of muscle activation. The first step is developing experimentally testable theories that make predictions concerning the relationship between myoelectric and kinematic or kinetic changes. The dual-strategy hypothesis is one such attempt to relate changes in forces and speed to changes in patterns of muscle activation. However, it has many limitations for the study of performance enhancement because (a) it does not account for the observation that muscle activation can be delayed as a function of practice, (b) it does not account for changes in muscle activity when the movement kinematics and dynamics remain constant, and (c) it does not deal explicitly with changes in variability. The second step is to have a clear framework within which to analyze the role of different muscles. Muscles can function as agonists, as antagonists, and as stabilizers. Experimental results must be related to what the muscles were required to do to perform the task and whether their role changed as a function of practice. Finally, because muscles produce forces, the clearest picture of how muscle activation changes to enhance performance will emerge when myoelectric changes are related to changes in force. The development of theories that can relate myoelectric changes to changes in motor performance will prove useful in developing paradigms in which we can identify appropriately determined performance deficits not ameliorated by practice. Such paradigms might have great clinical potential.

REFERENCES

Agarwal, G.C., and Gottlieb, G.L. 1982. Mathematical modeling and simulation of the postural control loop: part I. *CRC Critical Reviews in Biomedical Engineering* 8(2):93-134.

Agarwal, G.C., and Gottlieb, G.L. 1985. Mathematical modeling and simulation of the postural control loop: part III. *CRC Critical Reviews in Bioengineering* 12(1):49-93.

Almeida, G.L., Corcos, D.M., and Latash, M.L. 1994. Practice and transfer effects during fast single-joint elbow movements in individuals with Down syndrome. *Physical Therapy* 74(11):1000-1011.

Basmajian, J.V., and DeLuca, C.J. 1985. *Muscle alive: Their functions revealed by electromyography*. 5th ed. Baltimore: Williams & Wilkins.

Bernstein, N. 1967. *The coordination and regulation of movements*. Oxford: Pergamon Press.

Bigland-Ritchie, B., Johansson, R., Lippold, O.C.J., and Woods, J.J. 1983. Contractile speed and EMG changes during fatigue of sustained maximal voluntary contractions. *Journal of Neurophysiology* 50:313-324.

Bizzi, E., Polit, A., and Morasso, P. 1976. Mechanisms underlying achievement of final head position. *Journal of Neurophysiology* 39:434-444.

Colebatch, J.G., Gandevia, S.C., and Spira, P.J. 1986. Voluntary muscle strength in hemiparesis: distribution of weakness at the elbow. *Journal of Neurology, Neurosurgery and Psychiatry*, 49:1019-1024.

Corcos, D.M., Agarwal, G.C., Flaherty, B., and Gottlieb, G.L. 1990. Organizing principles for single joint movement: IV—Implications for isometric contractions. *Journal of Neurophysiology* 64(3):1033-1042.

Corcos, D.M., Gottlieb, G.L., and Agarwal, G.C. 1989. Organizing principles for single joint movements: II—A speed-sensitive strategy. *Journal of Neurophysiology* 62:358-368.

Corcos, D.M., Gottlieb, G.L., Jaric, S., Cromwell, R.L., and Agarwal, G.C. 1990. Organizing principles underlying motor skill acquisition. P. 251-267 in *Multiple muscle systems: Biomechanics and movement organization*, edited by J. Winters and S. Woo. New York: Springer-Verlag.

Corcos, D.M., Jaric, S., Agarwal, G.C., and Gottlieb, G.L. 1993. Principles for learning single joint movements: I—Enhanced performance by practice. *Experimental Brain Research* 94:499-513.

Darling, W.G., and Cooke, J.D. 1987. Movement related EMGs become more variable during learning of fast accurate movements. *Journal of Motor Behavior* 19(3):311-331.

Darling, W.G., Cooke, J.D., and Brown, S.H. 1989. Control of simple arm movements in elderly humans. *Neurobiology of Aging* 10:149-157.

Davis, W.E., and Sinning, W.E. 1987. Muscle stiffness in Down syndrome and other mentally handicapped subjects: A research note. *Journal of Motor Behavior* 19:130-144.

Dugas, C., and Marteniuk, R.G. 1989. Strategy and learning effects on perturbed movements: an electromyographic and kinematic study. *Behavioral Brain Research* 35:181-193.

Engelhorn, R. 1983. Agonist and antagonist muscle EMG activity pattern changes with skill acquisition. *Research Quarterly for Exercise and Sport* 54(4):315-323.

Engelhorn, R. 1988. EMG and motor performance changes with practice of a forearm movement by children. *Perceptual and Motor Skills* 67:523-529.

Enoka, R.M. 1988. Muscle strength and its development. *Sports Medicine* 6:146-148.

Feldman, A.G. 1986. Once more on the equilibrium-point hypothesis (λ model) for motor control. *Journal of Motor Behavior* 18:17-54.

Finley, F.R., Wirta, R.W., and Cody, K.A. 1968. Muscle synergies in motor performance. *Archives of Physical Medicine and Rehabilitation* 49:655-660.

Freund, H., and Budingen, H.J. 1978. The relationship between speed and amplitude of the fastest voluntary contractions of human arm muscles. *Experimental Brain Research* 31:1-12.

Frith, U., and Frith, C.D. 1974. Specific motor disabilities in Down's syndrome. *Journal of Child Psychology and Psychiatry* 15:293-301.

Ghez, C. 1979. Contributions of central programs to rapid limb movement in the cat. P. 305-319 in *Integration in the nervous system*, edited by H. Asanuma and V. Wilson. Tokyo: Igaku-Shoin.

Gottlieb, G.L., Corcos, D.M., and Agarwal, G.C. 1989a. Organizing principles for single joint movements: I—A Speed-Insensitive strategy. *Journal of Neurophysiology* 62(2):342-357.

Gottlieb, G.L., Corcos, D.M., and Agarwal, G.C. 1989b. Strategies for the control of single mechanical degree of freedom voluntary movements. *Behavioral and Brain Sciences* 12(2):189-210.

Gottlieb, G.L., Corcos, D.M., and Agarwal, G.C. 1992. Bioelectrical and biomechanical correlates of rapid human elbow movement. P. 625-646 in *Tutorials in motor behavior II*, edited by G.E. Stelmach and J. Requin. New York: Elsevier Science.

Gottlieb, G.L., Corcos, D.M., Agarwal, G.C., and Latash, M.L. 1990. Organizing principles for single joint movements: III—The speed-insensitive strategy as default. *Journal of Neurophysiology* 63(3):625-636.

Gottlieb, G.L., Latash, M.L., Corcos, D.M., Liubinskas, T.J., and Agarwal, G.C. 1992. Organizing principles for single joint movements: V. Agonist-antagonist interactions. *Journal of Neurophysiology* 67(6):1417-1427.

Hallett, M., Shahani, B.T., and Young, R.R. 1975. EMG analysis of stereotyped voluntary movements in man. *Journal of Neurology, Neurosurgery and Psychiatry* 38:1154-1162.

Hannaford, B., and Stark, L. 1985. Roles of the elements of the triphasic control signal. *Experimental Neurology* 90:619-634.

Hobart, D.J., Kelley, D.L., and Bradley, L.S. 1975. Modifications occurring during acquisition of a novel throwing task. *American Journal of Physical Medicine*, 54:1-24.

Jaric, S., Corcos, D.M., Agarwal, G.C., and Gottlieb, G.L. 1993. Principles for learning single joint movements: II—Generalizing a learned behavior. *Experimental Brain Research* 94:514-521.

Jones, D.A., and Rutherford, O.M. 1987. Human muscle strength training: the effects of three different regimes and the nature of the resultant changes. *Journal of Physiology* 391:1-11.

Kamon, E., and Gormley, J. 1968. Muscular activity pattern for skilled performance and during learning of a horizontal bar exercise. *Ergonomics* 11(4):345-357.

Latash, M.L. 1992. Motor control in Down syndrome: the role of adaptation and practice. *Journal of Developmental and Physical Disabilities* 4(3):227-261.

Latash, M.L., and Corcos, D.M. 1991. Kinematic and electromyographic characteristics of single-joint movements of individuals with Down syndrome. *American Journal on Mental Retardation* 96(2):189-201.

Ludwig, D.A. 1982. EMG changes during acquisition of a motor skill. *American Journal of Physical Medicine* 61:229-243.

McGrain, P. 1980. Trends in selected kinematic and myoelectric variables associated with learning a novel motor task. *Research Quarterly for Exercise & Sports* 51:509-520.

Meyer, D.E., Smith, J.E.K., and Wright, C.E. 1982. Models for the speed and accuracy of aimed movements. *Psychological Review* 89:449-482.

Moore, S.P., and Marteniuk, R.G. 1986. Kinematic and electromyographic changes that occur as a function of learning a time-constrained aiming task. *Journal of Motor Behavior* 18(4):397-426.

Newell, K.M. 1992. Theme issue on dynamical approaches to motor skill acquisition. *Journal of Motor Behavior* 24(1):2.

Normand, M.C., Lagasse, P.P., Rouillard, C.A., and Tremblay, L.E. 1982. Modifications occurring in motor programs during learning of a complex task in man. *Brain Research* 241:87-93.

Parker, A.W., and Bronks, R.B. 1980. Gait of children with Down syndrome. *Archives of Physical and Medical Rehabilitation* 61:345-351.

Payton, O.D., Sally, S., and Meydrich, E.F. 1976. Abductor digiti quinti shuffleboard: a study in motor learning. *Archives Physical Medicine and Rehabilitation* 57:169-174.

Pedotti, A., Crenna, P., Deat, A., Frigo, C., and Massion, J. 1989. Postural synergies in axial movements: short and long-term adaptation. *Experimental Brain Research* 74:3-10.

Schmidt, R.A. 1975. A schema theory of discrete motor skill motor learning. *Psychological Review* 82:225-260.

Schmidt, R.A. 1988. *Motor Control and Learning: A Behavioral Emphasis*. 2d ed. Champaign, IL: Human Kinetics.

Schmidt, R.A., and Young, D.E. 1987. *Transfer of movement control in motor skill learning*. Orlando, FL: Academic Press.

Schmidtbleicher, D., Gollhofer, A., and Frick, U. 1988. Effects of a stretch-shortening typed training on the performance capability and innervation characteristics of leg extensor muscles. P. 185-189 in *Biomechanics XI-A*, edited by G. Groot, A.P. Hollander, P.A. Huijing, and v.I. Schenau. Amsterdam: Free University Press.

Schneider, K., Zernicke, R.F., Schmidt, R.A., and Hart, T.J. 1989. Changes in limb dynamics during the practice of rapid arm movements. *Journal of Biomechanics* 22(8/9):805-817.

Schoner, G., and Kelso, G. 1988. Dynamic pattern generation in behavioral and neural systems. *Science* 239:1513-1520.

Stein, R.B. 1982. What muscle variable(s) does the nervous system control in limb movements? *Behavioral & Brain Sciences* 5:535-577.

Stein, R.B., Oguztoreli, M.N., and Capaday, C. 1986. What is optimized in muscular movements? P. 131-150 in *Human Muscle Power*, edited by N.L. Jones, N. McMartney, and A.J. McComas. Champaign, IL: Human Kinetics.

Uno, Y., Kawato, M., and Suzuki, R. 1989. Formation and control of optimum trajectory in human multijoint arm movement—minimum torque-change model. *Biological Cybernetics* 61:89-101.

Vorro, J., Wilson, F.R., and Dainis, A. 1978. Multivariate analysis of biomechanical profiles for the corcobrachialis and biceps brachii (caput breve) muscles in humans. *Ergonomics* 21:407-418.

Wachholder, K., and Altenburger, H. 1926. Beitrage zur Physiologie der willkurlichen Bewegung. X. Mitteilung. Einzelbewegungen. *Pflugers Archiv fur die gesamte physiologie des menschen unter der tiere* 214:642-661.

Wallace, S.A. 1981. An impulse-timing theory for reciprocal control of muscular activity in rapid, discrete movements. *Journal of Motor Behavior* 13:1144-1160.

Waterland, J.C. 1970. The harmonies of movement recorded electromyographically. *Perceptual and Motor Skills* 31:1001-1002.

Woollacott, M.H., and Shumway-Cook, A. 1986. The development of postural and voluntary motor control systems in Down's syndrome children. P. 45-71 in *Motor skill acquisition and the mentally handicapped: Issues in research and training*, edited by M.G. Wade. Amsterdam: North-Holland.

Young, K., McDonagh, M.J.N., and Davies, C.T.M. 1985. The effects of two forms of isometric training on the mechanical properties of the triceps surae in man. *Pflugers Archiv* 405:384-388.

Acknowledgments

We thank Kyung Lee, Ronita Cromwell, and Gil Almeida for assistance in performing and analyzing many experiments summarized in this chapter. In addition, we thank Chuck Walter and Howard Zelaznik for their comments on the chapter. This work was supported, in part, by NIH grants NS 01508, NS 28127, AR 33189, and NS 28176, as well as by HHS grant JF-012 through the US-Yugoslav board of scientific cooperation and a grant from the Serbian Research Foundation.

Chapter 7

Dynamic Pattern Perspective of Rhythmic Movement: An Introduction

Stephen A. Wallace
University of Colorado at Boulder

One of my first experiences with nonlinear behavior occurred several years ago in my friend's house during a typical Sunday evening barbecue in Boulder. It was common for my friend, a physicist, and me to share our trials and tribulations of the week at the university and to allow his five-year-old son and my four-year-old daughter to play together for the evening. At one point during our conversation, while our children were playing on the floor with some toy cars in a seemingly civilized fashion, his son suddenly started screaming and rolling all over the floor and kicking his feet, apparently displeased with the way things were going. His son continued this behavior for about 10 seconds, and then, just as suddenly, quieted down and continued playing with my daughter as if nothing out of the ordinary had happened. Dismayed, I looked at my friend for a scientific explanation of his son's behavior, without really needing to ask. With a grin, he turned to me and said, ''Oh, don't worry, he's just going nonlinear!'' My friend didn't have to explain what he meant; it was more or less obvious at the time. Any behavior that suddenly deviates from a previously smooth and predictable trajectory could be categorized as *nonlinear*, but I didn't realize at the time how common these behaviors are in the so-called real world. I do now.

INTRODUCTION TO NONLINEAR BEHAVIOR

Abrupt jumps or discontinuities in behavior, although recognized in many scientific fields, have not been seriously studied until recently. One reason for this lack of serious investigation is that nonlinear behavior has been considered an anomaly and even noise, in the engineering sense, within a given system (i.e., physical, chemical, biological). The smooth, predictable aspects of behavior have garnered most of the attention (Briggs and Peat 1989). Since Newton and his linearly based laws of motion, science has been preoccupied with describing the *order* in nature. Ordered and linear behaviors are predictable (i.e., completely deterministic) in the sense that if I change the known independent variable(s), the value of the dependent variable changes systematically. For example, if $y = x$, then $4y = 4x$, $16y = 16x$, and so on for all values of x and y. In other words, a small change in initial conditions of the

155

independent variable leads to proportionally small changes in the dependent variable, and larger changes in x lead to proportionally larger changes in y. Of course, this type of linear calculation has been useful in many human enterprises, such as measuring the weight of objects, building bridges, and sending astronauts to the moon, to name just a few. But is nature best represented or characterized in such a manner? Gottfried von Leibniz, the coinventor of calculus (with Newton), thought so. Von Leibniz once said, *"Natura non facit saltum"* [Nature does not make jumps]. There is growing evidence that von Leibniz was wrong.

The purpose of this chapter is threefold. First, I would like to provide a perspective for the reader on the development of nonlinear dynamics, a scientific approach that has arisen from chemistry, physics, and mathematics and is making its impact on many scientific disciplines and areas of study. I will argue that nonlinear behavior is prevalent throughout nature, and I will provide several examples to support my claim. Second, I will discuss evidence within the field of motor control that supports a particular theory within nonlinear dynamics, called the *dynamic pattern perspective* (itself grounded in the concepts of synergetics [Haken 1983, 1984]), which holds particular promise in helping us understand movement coordination. I will outline the important features of the theory and document several pieces of evidence that have supported many of its predictions. Finally, I will provide the reader my thoughts on how experiments using synergetic principles might be designed. My objective is not just to show evidence of nonlinear behavior in movement coordination, but to argue that there is a more fundamental cause for its emergence—namely, that nonlinear behavior arises as a normal consequence of self-organization within complex systems. I will also point out that abrupt change in behavior is one small, albeit important, characteristic in nonlinear dynamics. Other characteristics include the concept of pattern formation in complex systems far from equilibrium, stability of behavior patterns, critical fluctuations, the phenomenon of hysteresis, and so on. These characteristcs are well known in the physical sciences and have been extensively explored by my friend and colleague, Professor Scott Kelso, who has greatly contributed to applying nonlinear dynamics to the study of movement coordination. I spent a one-year sabbatical with Dr. Kelso in 1988-89 to learn more about synergetic theory and the dynamic pattern perspective. This chapter represents my attempt to capture the excitement and the challenges I experienced during that wonderful year at the Center for Complex Systems in Boca Raton, Florida.

Complex Systems and the Remarkable Property of Self-Organization

No one would doubt the complexity of a five-year-old's behavior, in the sense that it is difficult to understand. The second definition of the word "complex" in Webster's Dictionary (1977) is "hard to separate, analyze, or solve." Interestingly, the first definition of "complex" is "composed of two or more parts." Thus, a complex system is composed of two or more elements that interact in some way, and understanding this interaction is likely to be more difficult as the number of elements increases. A five-year-old's behavior is a good candidate for a complex system if we agree that several elements or components (genetic contributions, sociocultural influences, current situational factors, etc.) contribute to it.

How do we study complex systems that are, by definition, composed of many parts? A science of complexity is really a science of understanding the relationships among things. It is not, and cannot be, the study of things independent from other things. Poincare (1905) once said, "The aim of science is not things themselves, as the dogmatists in their simplicity imagine, but the relations among things; outside these relations there is no reality knowable." It will not be possible, for example, to understand the personality of a five year old by studying genetic contributions alone, independent of the other factors. Similarly, to understand how movement is coordinated is to appreciate that each subsystem (e.g., biochemical, neural, skeletal, muscular) or level within the human body consists of many interacting components. As such, the human body easily qualifies as a complex system. For example, the human body includes more than 600 individual muscles, but even the simplest act, such as flexion of the elbow joint, requires the coordination of several muscles. How does this coordination arise?

I will argue in this chapter that movement coordination at a given level of analysis arises from self-organization among many contributing components. Self-organization is a property of a complex system living in [what nonlinear dynamical scientists call] *far from equilibrium* conditions. An appreciation of far from equilibrium conditions can be gleaned by examining a complex system under *equilibrium* conditions. Consider a container of water in which the molecules are equally distributed throughout the medium. This complex system is said to be in equilibrium. It is also said to be a *closed* system because, under these conditions, it is not subjected to outside influences (ignoring gravity and environmental temperature changes). However, if we punch a hole in the container, we have established an *open* system, capable of interaction with the surrounding environment. Because of the pressure gradient inside and outside the container and the fact that liquid and gas always move from areas of high to low pressure (called the law of diffusion), the water pours out of the hole. By punching a hole in the container, our complex system, now under non- (or far from) equilibrium condition, can self-organize. No one (or no thing) needs to tell the system how to remove the water molecules from the container through the hole. The law of diffusion takes care of this.

Far from equilibrium conditions can provoke much more elaborate behaviors out of a complex, open system than just water escaping from a container. Consider the phenomenon called the *Benard instability* (first discovered by Henri Benard in 1900) that we can observe by heating a pan of approximately 1 cm of liquid, say vegetable oil, from below. The molecules of oil at room temperature, like the water molecules in the earlier example, are randomly distributed throughout the medium. If we gradually heat the pan from below, at some critical temperature a hexagonal matrix resembling a honeycomb pattern suddenly emerges throughout the medium of oil. The matrix is a result of the temperature gradient between molecules near the surface and those below, and the effects of gravity that pull the cooler molecules down from the upper layer (see Prigogine and Stengers 1984, 142; Coveney and Highfield 1990, 186; or Kelso 1995, 6-9 for an elaboration). If we further increase the temperature to the boiling point, the hexagonal matrix is replaced by turbulence, a qualitatively different pattern of molecule distribution. These patterns of behavior (i.e., random, hexagonal, and turbulent) are caused by changes in an outside variable (what nonlinear dynamical system scientists call a *control parameter*) imposed on the complex system of oil molecules. The control parameter carries no information regarding the nature of the pattern changes of the oil molecules. However, the control parameter helps push the system through the various patterns we observe. These patterns are the result of self-organizing properties of a system far from equilibrium.

Of particular importance in the Benard instability is the behavior of one pattern giving way to another. For example, the hexagonal matrix appears for only a short time before it is replaced by the turbulent motion of the molecules at the boiling point. However, each pattern (hexagonal matrix and turbulence) has a degree of steadfastness or tenacity, such that once the pattern is established there is resistance to change. This resistance is overcome as the control parameter (temperature) is changed, inducing the switch from the hexagonal matrix pattern to turbulence. Nonlinear dynamicists refer to this steadfastness or resistance to change as *stability*, another important feature of nonlinear systems (Campbell 1987). The greater the stability of the pattern, the greater its resistance to change. In some way, the change in the control parameter affects the stability of the patterns. An extremely important scientific breakthrough by nonlinear dynamical theorists has been the successful mathematical modeling of pattern change as a result of loss of stability. The concept of stability (and its loss) lies at the heart of synergetic theory (and the dynamic pattern perspective) and will be discussed later in the chapter.

Another example will illustrate the power of far from equilibrium conditions in producing a variety of behaviors within a complex system. Consider another physical system, a stream of running water (see fig. 7.1) (Briggs and Peat 1989). When the stream is flowing slowly, the molecules of water produce smooth laminar flow around a rock in the middle of the stream. Once the speed of the stream flow reaches some critical value, vortices form behind the rock. Once formed, they remain in the same place for long periods, spinning round and round like small tornadoes (another example of pattern stability!). If the water continues to speed up, these vortices break away on their own and continue downstream. A further increase in speed of the flowing water results in turbulence, not unlike the motion of the oil molecules when they reach the boiling point in the previous example. In this case, however, four major patterns of water flow emerge from the same system: smooth laminar flow, vortices forming behind the rock, vortices breaking away downstream, and turbulence. Each pattern appears suddenly at different water speeds. The control parameter in this example is not temperature, but the speed of water flow in the river.

It is interesting to note that if we were to somehow reverse the speed of water flow in the river, the reemergence of vortices would probably not replace turbulent conditions, as we might expect in a linearly based system. As the speed of water flow is reduced, laminar flow would likely replace turbulent conditions. A similar effect would occur if we reduced the temperature of the oil from the boiling point, in the earlier example. The bubbling oil, a turbulent condition, would not be replaced by the hexagonal matrix before returning to the equilibrium state. The progression of patterns we see as the control parameter is changed (or scaled) in one direction is not necessarily the same when it is changed in the opposite direction, a characteristic of nonlinear systems called *hysteresis* (e.g., Hale and Koçak 1991). Later in

Fig. 7.1   Pattern formation in a flowing stream. From *above* to *below*: laminar flow, formation of vortices, breaking away of the vortices, and finally turbulence (or chaos). The control parameter is the speed of the stream.
Reprinted from Briggs and Peat 1989.

the chapter we will see evidence of pattern changes and hysteresis effects in the coordination of human movement.

Another remarkable property of complex systems, specific to *living* systems, is the ability to adapt to the environment and to learn. It should be clear that living things are not in equilibrium (Ruthen 1993). For example, they metabolize food extracted from the environment, produce energy for the basic life processes, and eliminate waste. They exchange oxygen and carbon dioxide. Their genetic makeup allows them to pass on successful coping strategies to future generations, such as the leaves of a tree orienting themselves for optimal sunlight. Advanced life forms can learn within their own life spans, such as human beings learning to speak a particular language. Nonlinear dynamicists believe that this activity is realized through self-organization at conditions far from equilibrium. Apparent from the previous discussion, pattern formation and pattern change can be achieved at conditions far from equilibrium. In the case of learning, any adaptation is achieved on the backdrop of experience. To achieve a new, qualitatively different behavioral pattern (assumed to possess some degree of stability) requires a loss of stability of a previous behavioral pattern. It should be no surprise then, that learning new modes of movement coordination can be conceptualized as a pattern formation process. This topic is discussed later in the chapter.

When I present the previous examples to beginning graduate students in motor control, they often confront me with the following questions, "These examples are interesting in their own right, but how do they apply to human motor coordination?" or "What does a turbulent stream have to do with motor control?" There is no doubt that bubbling oil and turbulent streams are a far cry from the complex biochemical and neurophysiological interactions of the human body. The behaviors of living and nonliving things can be quite different. Yet under far from equilibrium conditions, living and nonliving things can undergo pattern change, and the principles underlying pattern change in a flowing river are essentially the same as those underlying pattern formation in human movement. These principles are based on the concept of stability and its loss. I hope the connection between Benard convection cells, flowing rivers, and human motor coordination will become clearer by the end of the chapter.

Summary

Complex systems consist of many components and these components interact in many ways. In nonequilibrium conditions, the behavior of the components in an open complex system is influenced by changes in control parameters imposed on the system. In some way changes in the control parameter allow the system to self-organize and to produce patterns with differing degrees of stability. Often, a variety of behavior patterns can be observed by changes in the control parameter. The progression of patterns observed may be dependent on the directionality of changes in the control parameter, a characteristic called hysteresis. Living systems are considered open complex systems that possess the quality of adaptation. This quality allows certain generic features of an organism to remain intact over subsequent generations through genetic transfer. Adaptation also allows new coping strategies to develop but all on the backdrop of existing behaviors. From a nonlinear dynamical view, adaptation and learning are pattern formation processes rooted deeply in the concept of stability.

Nonlinear dynamics embraces the concept of self-organization emphasizing the *macroscopic* behaviors of complex systems as patterns among the individual components of the system. This macroscopic approach to understanding complex systems has its beginnings in chemistry (specifically thermodynamics), mathematics, and physics. As such, nonlinear dynamics is directly at odds with classical Newtonian physics, which emphasizes a *microscopic* approach to understanding the world by trajectory analysis of individual components. In the next section, we examine the limitations of Newtonian physics, followed by the macroscopic approach of thermodynamics. Finally, we outline theoretical physicist Hermann Haken's contributions, which led to the development of the dynamic pattern perspective.

BRIEF HISTORICAL PERSPECTIVE ON SELF-ORGANIZATION IN COMPLEX SYSTEMS

Newton's Laws of Motion

To fully appreciate the development of self-organization in complex systems, we must first appreciate its emergence from traditional and established scientific paradigms. Most historians would agree that science, as we know it today, began with the publication of *Principia* by Isaac Newton in 1686. The book was divided into an Introduction, where Newton defined his famous three laws of motion, Books I and II, where different forces and motions were examined, and Book III, where Newton applied his approach to describing planetary and terrestrial motions (see Fauvel et al. 1988 for a biography of Newton's life and scientific contributions). In addition, Newton (along with Leibniz) developed the calculus used to mathematically express his laws of motion in an exact quantitative manner. I will assume here that the reader is familiar with Newton's laws (i.e., law of inertia, law of acceleration, law of counterforce), which have had a profound effect not only on the methods of scientific inquiry but also on how scientists view the world. Newton's laws attempted to describe the state and motion of a body in space as well as factors that influence its motion. Important in this regard was the development of the concept of the *trajectory* of a body through space. The trajectory of a body can be defined as a series of mathematical solutions describing both the position and the velocity of the body as it travels through space. According to Prigogine (Prigogine and Stengers 1984, 60), Newton's trajectories have three characteristics: *lawfulness*, *determinism*, and *reversibility*. If the initial conditions (i.e., position and velocity) and the forces acting on a body are known, Newton's laws completely govern the resulting trajectory of the body. The trajectory of any body can be lawfully expressed with complete certainty. Every instance of the trajectory is completely deterministic, and therefore it is possible to predict all instances of the trajectory in the future. Furthermore, all instances of the trajectory leading up to its current state can be determined. In this sense we can say that the trajectory of a body is deterministic as well as reversible.

Because of Newton's thinking, an analogy developed that the universe ran like a clock, precisely tuned and mechanistic. Not only could the motion of celestial bodies be determined, but the trajectory of any body, either future or past and regardless of size, could also be known. Marquis Pierre Louis Laplace, an 18th-century mathematician and philosopher, imagined a demon who possessed information about the position and velocity of all the particles in the universe. Laplace's demon, as it has become known, could know the evolution of every particle in the universe. Laplace did not intend to suggest that such a creature would ever exist but to demonstrate man's ignorance about the workings of the universe. If man could possess such information about every particle, the motion of the entire universe would be completely deterministic. The running of our complex planetary system, for example, could be reduced to the independent Newtonian calculations of each planet's orbit.

Also from Newton's work, a *reductionist* philosophy gradually became pervasive throughout the fields of science. If the isolated parts of a complex system could be understood, a simple reassembly of them would result in an understanding of the whole. This reductionist approach is still strong today with microbiologists searching for the missing gene, nuclear physicists smashing the atom to uncover the so-called building blocks of life, neurophysiologists mapping smaller and smaller areas of the brain to explain behavior, and motor control scientists attempting to find the location of central pattern generators and motor programs in the central nervous system. It is important to understand that the reductionist approach has made significant contributions to our understanding of nature. However, the scientific community has a growing realization of its limits.

Newton's laws have allowed scientists to predict the future and past positions of the planets over periods of thousands of years. But recent simulations using powerful computers have shown these predictions break down over longer time scales. Using powerful computers, several scientists have recently shown that if the time scale of prediction is stretched beyond several thousands of years, a mere eye blink in the five-billion-year lifetime of the solar system, accurate prediction of all the planetary motions is impossible (Laskar 1989; Sussman and Wisdom 1992). Furthermore, there can be large periods when the motions become predictable, before again drifting into unforeseeable orbits (Milani and Nobili 1992). These studies indicate that the solar system is *chaotic* if one is willing to investigate its behavior over long time scales. By chaotic I mean that the same complex system can contain both predictable and unpredictable behavior (e.g., Gleick 1987). Why do Newton's calculations fail in accurately predicting the planets' orbits over long time scales? Newton used a mathematical technique in which the small effects of the gravitational pull from a third planet on the solution of the idealized two-body system were added as a series of approximations. Each approximation was smaller than the one before, and the hope was that after a few approximations, the correct solution could be found. However, a brilliant French mathematician, Jules Henri Poincare, in 1889 was the first to show the impossibility of calculating the exact orbits of three or more planets based on Newton's laws. It turned out that the resulting solutions for a three-body system were good in the short term but poor over longer periods.[1] Poincare realized that if Newtonian mechanics could not describe with certainty the motions of three interacting bodies, description of complex systems with many more interacting bodies such as the entire solar system was hopeless. Although the scientific community largely ignored Poincare's work during his own era, modern scientists give him credit for first demonstrating the futility of describing the behavior of a complex system by reducing the system to its individual parts.

Poincare's *Three-Body Problem*, as it has become known, was the first threat to Newtonian mechanics and the reductionist approach. Another threat was also developing in the 19th century. This threat focused on the macroscopic features of a complex system rather than its individual (or microscopic) elements. Strangely enough, this threat to Newtonian mechanics began with an innocent interest in the behavior of heat, but developed into a major area within the field of physics called *thermodynamics*. Thermodynamics focused primarily on closed systems and the macroscopic behaviors of these systems at (or close to) equilibrium. Eventually, the area of *nonequilibrium* thermodynamics in open systems arose out of chemistry, physics, and mathematics. In the next section, we examine the emergence of thermodynamics and nonequilibrium thermodynamics.

Thermodynamics and the Emphasis on Macroscopic Behavior

In this section, I will focus on some major contributions to the emphasis on the macroscopic behavior of complex systems. For a detailed discussion of the development of thermodynamics and the field of nonlinear dynamics see Prigogine and Stengers (1984), Coveney and Highfield (1990), Gleick (1987), and Briggs and Peat (1989).

The development of the modern Industrial Age began with the harnessing of heat. It was known that the application of heat changed the structure of materials. Heat could change water to gas and increase the volume of its molecular composition. Changes in volume could then be used to do work, such as driving steam engines. Fire could ignite fuel, cause combustion, and create heat to warm homes. From a scientific viewpoint, the interest was not so much in the use of heat as in the lawful relations among such variables as heat (or temperature), pressure, and volume.

According to Prigogine and Stengers (1984), the "science of complexity," with its emphasis on macroscopic properties of complex systems, began in 1811 when Baron Jean-Joseph Fourier won the prize of the French Academy of Sciences for his work on the propagation of heat. Fourier's discovery that heat flow was proportional to the temperature gradient was simple yet generalizable to all forms of matter—gas, liquid, or solid. It showed that the distribution of temperature from a

---

[1]This problem was later elaborated on by meteorologist Edward Lorenz, who rediscovered its significance while running computer simulations on weather patterns (see Lorenz 1963). The basic problem, termed *sensitivity to initial conditions*, is that we never know with complete certainty the initial conditions (i.e., instantaneous position and velocity) of a body. This error gets amplified over time, particularly as the body interacts with other bodies, making prediction of the body's trajectory impossible.

heat source continued progressively until thermal equilibrium was reached. The significance of Fourier's work in developing a new field of physics related to heat (or more broadly, energy) flow, called thermodynamics, was twofold. (1) Fourier's work signified the birth of a physical theory just as rigorous as Newton's formulations, focusing not on the behavior of individual bodies, but on the macroscopic behavior of literally millions of molecules of matter. As pointed out by Prigogine and Stengers (1984), "From this time on, mathematics, physics and Newtonian science ceased to be synonymous" (104). (2) Fourier's work introduced the scientific community to the concept of *irreversibility*, an important concept in the history of science, that was later to be incorporated into the second law of thermodynamics. Irreversibility means the evolution of a complex system will never be reversed over time. In other words, time only flows in one direction—always forward and never backward. The concept of irreversibility is foreign to Newtonian mechanics. As mentioned previously, Newton's laws are completely reversible in the sense that if the initial conditions of a body are completely known, both its future and its past trajectory can be determined. Irreversibility means the state of the complex system will never be exactly repeated over time. An ink spot dropped into a pan of water continues to spread throughout the medium until equilibrium is reached. Regardless of what we do to the medium, the molecules of ink will never reverse to their original high concentration within the water molecules. In a true sense, irreversibility introduced humanity to our current concept of time: nature's events always move in a forward direction.

Another prominent figure to arise in the nineteenth century was James Joule, who formulated the concept of energy and provided a means to quantify it. Joule recognized that although matter could be converted so its *potential energy* (i.e., capacity to perform work) is changed, something about it remained the same, namely, its *total energy*. This realization led to the development of the *first law of thermodynamics*, that energy (or more specifically, total energy) can neither be created nor destroyed.

With the advent of the steam engine by John Fulton, incredible interest developed around the construction of the most efficient machine. Some would argue that if all the energy produced by a machine could be preserved, energy could be recycled indefinitely and the machine could, theoretically, run forever. However, the German physicist Rudolf Clausius determined that the transformation from heat to work is not perfect; some heat is lost through friction and other dissipative processes. Clausius realized that the wasted energy could never be recirculated. William Thomson (later Lord Kelvin), an Irish-born mathematician, was quick to recognize the importance of Clausius's discovery, and in 1852 he formulated the *second law of thermodynamics*. Thomson's second law states that in any conversion between heat and work, some energy is irrevocably lost. In 1865, Clausius reformulated the second law using a new concept he dubbed *entropy*, defined as an isolated system's capacity to change. Low entropy means that the system has a considerable capacity to change, whereas high entropy means no capacity to change. In this high-entropy condition, the system has reached a state of equilibrium in which no exchange of energy occurs. It should be understood that, according to the second law, an isolated (or closed) system is always attracted to the final state of maximum entropy. The

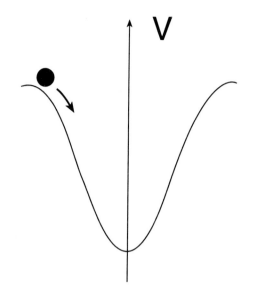

Fig. 7.2   An example of a potential energy (V) function. The black ball represents the current state of the system. The attractor (in this case, high entropy) is located at the bottom of the potential well.

system will evolve from a state of energy exchange among its components to a state of no energy exchange, a condition referred to as equilibrium.

A popular way to model this behavior is to imagine a ball on a landscape containing one well (see fig. 7.2). In this example, the ball represents the current state of potential energy (typically denoted as V) of the complex system. Near the edge of the well, the potential energy of the system is high. If the ball moves (or is pushed) in the direction of the well, it eventually ends up at the bottom of the well where the potential energy is minimal. One can see that the ball has no choice in the matter. Once it leaves its initial condition, it is attracted to a state of equilibrium, in which there is no further exchange in energy. In this example, high entropy can be considered an *attractor*[2]. High entropy is a strong attractor because, once it is reached (the ball settles to the bottom of the well), the system can never return to its initial conditions. Let us see how we might apply the concept of entropy to the ink spot example. When the ink is dropped into the pan of water (an isolated system), entropy is low and the system has a high capacity for change (high potential energy). As the ink spreads throughout the water medium, entropy increases as the ink and water molecules gradually mix. When the ink molecules have completely spread through the water medium, high entropy has been reached—the system no longer

---

[2]A variety of attractors have been discovered in physical and biological systems, such as fixed point, limit cycle, quasi-periodic (or torus), and strange attractors (e.g., see Glass and Mackey 1988 or Kelso and Kay 1987 for more details), a discussion beyond the scope of this chapter.

has the capacity to change (minimal potential energy) and has reached a state of equilibrium.

It was quickly recognized that the second law could be extended to any isolated (or closed) system, and Clausius wasted no time generalizing the principle to the grandest of isolated systems—the universe (after all, by definition, there is nothing beyond the universe as far as can be conceptualized!). Clausius's generalization has led some astrophysicists to theorize that the universe is undergoing a steady increase in entropy—in other words, it is gradually running down until it has no further capacity to change, much like the complete mixing of ink in the pan of water. However, we shall soon see that before high entropy is reached, complex subsystems within the universe—like our solar system, earth's weather, and our own human bodies—have the capacity to change (i.e., exchange energy) in elaborate ways.

The second law of thermodynamics implies that over time a closed (or isolated) complex system will gradually move toward a state of high entropy, to the point of no energy exchange among its components. While Clausius was elaborating on this dismal perspective on the evolution of the universe, Charles Darwin was formulating a different view on the evolution of biological species. With Darwin's theory, biological evolution is characterized by ever-increasing complexity. According to the theory, complex organisms that exist today, such as human beings, evolved from much simpler living structures. Interestingly, both the second law of thermodynamics and Darwin's theory share the concept of irreversibility in that (1) the evolution of a complex system can only move forward, and (2) the initial conditions of the system are lost forever. However, the two conceptualizations predict quite different results—one of increasing randomness (the second law) and the other of increasing complexity (Darwin's theory). How can this be? The answer has to do with the realization that complex systems may be either closed or open; that is, either isolated from outside influences or capable of interacting with other energy sources. When a complex system interacts with outside energy sources, a state far from equilibrium is produced—and amazing things can happen.

Pattern Formation
Under Far From Equilibrium Conditions

If a system is closed, like the pan of water, the second law of thermodynamics prevails. However, if the system is open, an energy exchange can occur from outside the system's boundaries. When this happens, complex structures such as those arising from Benard instability may form as a result of self-organization among the many components within the system. Ilya Prigogine, who in 1977 won the Nobel Prize in chemistry, coined the term *dissipative structures* to describe the various patterns of behavior that can emerge from complex systems under far from equilibrium conditions. Prigogine emphasized that the behavior of open complex systems depends on whether they are in equilibrium, near equilibrium, or far from equilibrium conditions. Far from equilibrium conditions can cause an elaborate array of behavior patterns among the system's components.

Another important figure was German theoretical physicist Hermann Haken, twice nominated for the Nobel Prize for his theory of laser light. Haken described how the incoherent emission of light in a laser device can suddenly switch to a coherent light wave as an outside variable (electric current) is increased. The behavior seen in this system is not unlike that witnessed in our turbulent stream example in that one stable behavioral pattern gives way to another as a control parameter is changed. When a closed complex system is pushed far from equilibrium by an outside variable, other patterns of stability can emerge. Among Haken's contributions to the field of nonlinear dynamics is his emphasis on identifying both control parameters and order parameters in complex systems far from equilibrium. In the laser example, the electric current is the control parameter. As mentioned earlier, the control parameter is any outside variable (or energy source) that can push the complex system into different behavior patterns. Haken has argued that any complex system, chemical, physical, biological, or even sociological, will be sensitive to certain control parameters (Haken 1984). The *order* parameter (also called a collective variable) is the macroscopic description of the actual behavior patterns that emerge. The macroscopic behavior patterns can be quantitatively expressed by the order parameter. The order parameter represents some type of *relationship* among the individual components of the system, because it is the relationship that helps define the patterns. Furthermore, it is the relationship among the components that drastically changes when the behavior patterns switch due to the influence of the control parameter(s). Haken's approach emphasizes the importance of *fluctuations* of the patterns. In each pattern, the system can be near a state of equilibrium, although we see fluctuations of the pattern due to oscillations of the individual components contributing to the pattern. These fluctuations can be modeled as variations of particular mean values of the order parameter describing each pattern. We will examine the importance of fluctuations later in the chapter. Haken also coined the term *slaving principle* to denote that the order parameter dictates the behavior of the individual components. For example, once attracted to the hexagonal matrix in the Benard instability, individual oil molecules have no choice but to stay in the pattern until the temperature increases and the matrix pattern loses stability. The individual components (molecules) are slaves to the order parameter defining the hexagonal matrix pattern. Finally, Haken has emphasized that specific control and order parameters will probably be different across complex systems. For example, the control and order parameters of a given chemical system will likely be different from those in a biological system. However, Haken's challenge to scientists in different fields of study is to find the control and order parameters in their respective systems. Haken dubbed this type of strategy *synergetics*, defined as an interdisciplinary approach to understanding self-organization in complex systems (see Haken 1988). This is the approach Scott Kelso adopted in an attempt to understand the coordination of human movement and the one I will emphasize later in this chapter.

Summary

In this section I have reviewed some major developments of the field of thermo-dynamics, which emphasizes an understanding of the macroscopic features of complex systems. The review started with a description of Newtonian mechanics, which have made a lasting mark on most fields of science. Newton's laws are completely deterministic for describing trajectories of single bodies when the initial conditions (position and velocity) are completely known but become indeterministic when the initial conditions of a body are not known; this becomes prevalent in a three- (or more) body system. Newton's laws can be used successfully for approximating trajectories of interacting bodies, but these approximations eventually lead to large errors. Thermodynamical principles more adequately describe the macroscopic features of complex systems with many interacting components. The review indicated that in closed complex systems, the second law of thermodynamics prevails, and the system is eventually attracted to a state of high entropy. However, if the system is exposed to outside energy sources, a state far from equilibrium is induced, and the system can produce a variety of macroscopic states or behavior patterns. According to the synergetic strategy, outside influences or energy sources are called control parameters, and emerging macroscopic behavior patterns can be described by order parameters. In the next section, I show how the synergetic strategy has been applied to the coordination of human movement.

DYNAMIC PATTERN PERSPECTIVE IN THE COORDINATION OF MOVEMENT

It is an understatement to say that the human body is a complex system (see Haken 1991). At any level (i.e., molecular, cellular, muscular, neuromuscular, systemic, behavioral, biomechanical, psychological), many interacting components can be identified. As scientists, we have a choice to make about how we wish to examine this complexity. We may take the reductionist strategy and undergo the formidable task of identifying all the components at a given level of analysis. Even if we knew the identity of all the components, would we be able to reconstruct the dynamics of their interactions (i.e., could we put Humpty Dumpty back together again)? In my view, a fundamentally different approach is required. My argument is that a strategy based on principles of self-organization is needed to uncover and eventually to understand the complex interactions among the components. The synergetic strategy tells us to look for the patterns among the components and to understand how these patterns change. What types of patterns can we observe within the human body specifically associated with the control and coordination of human movement? Synergetics applied to movement coordination has been termed the *dynamic pattern perspective* (Jeka and Kelso 1989; Kelso 1995; Schoner and Kelso 1988a for reviews). Let us now examine the evidence that movement coordination can be characterized by principles of self-organization, with an emphasis on discovering macroscopic laws for a given level of description.[3]

Kelso's Bimanual Experiments (or the Two-Body Problem)

Any discussion of the dynamic pattern perspective must begin with the bimanual experiments Scott Kelso (1981, 1984) conducted. The original experiments examined

---

[3]Thanks to Scott Kelso for emphasizing this point on an earlier draft of the manuscript.

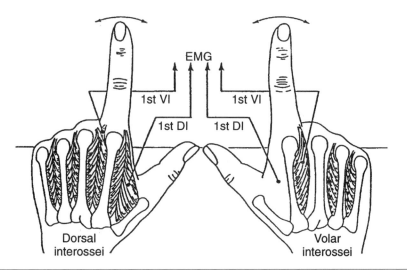

Fig. 7.3 Experimental paradigm used by Kelso (1981, 1984) in the original phase transition experiments. Subjects oscillate the two index fingers in the transverse plane with the same frequency. The movements are monitored by measuring the position of light-emitting diodes attached to the fingertips with a SelSpot camera system. The electromyographic (EMG) activity of the right and left first dorsal interosseous (DI) and first volar interosseous (VI) muscles is obtained with platinum fine-wire electrodes.
Reprinted from Schöner and Kelso 1988.

bimanual finger movements (see fig. 7.3), and the later ones investigated bimanual wrist movements. For simplicity, we will describe only the results of the finger experiments, because the data for the wrist movements were similar. Subjects were required to produce simultaneous and cyclical (oscillatory) movements with the left and right index fingers (or wrists) in the transverse plane. There were two major independent variables in the experiment: the patterning of the movements and the frequency of oscillation. The subjects were required to start a trial in one of two movement patterns. In the *in-phase* pattern, the fingers moved toward each other, then away from each other continuously, with the same (or homologous) muscle groups of the two fingers contracting at the same time. In the *anti-phase* pattern, the fingers moved together in a parallel fashion that required the homologous muscle groups to contract in an alternating fashion. Fig. 7.4 illustrates the displacement of the fingers in the in-phase (7.4A) and anti-phase conditions (7.4B). Kelso was able to quantitatively differentiate these two patterns by calculating a relative phase measure for each. Briefly, moving one finger from maximum adduction to maximum abduction and back represents one complete cycle of finger excursion or 360° in angular coordinates. A single finger's position at a given point on this excursion represents its phase value at that point. Kelso labeled maximal adduction as 0° (or 360°) and maximal abduction as 180° for each finger. From any common point in the cycle, the *relative* phase of the two fingers can be calculated as the difference in their phase values from a common starting position. For example, if both fingers start at maximal adduction, move together to maximal abduction, then return

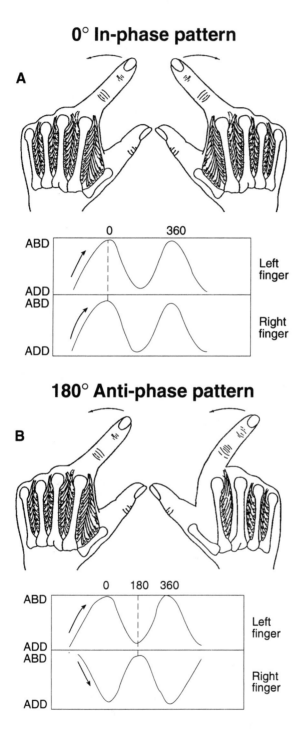

0° In-phase pattern

A

180° Anti-phase pattern

B

Fig. 7.4   In *A*, an example of the 0° in-phase pattern in which maximum abduction of the right index finger is synchronized with maximum abduction of the left index finger. In *B*, the 180° anti-phase pattern in which maximum adduction of the right index finger is synchronized with maximum abduction of the left index finger.

together, the relative phase of the two fingers is 0°, representing the in-phase pattern (fig. 7.4A). However, if the left finger starts at maximal adduction (0° individual phase) and the right finger starts at maximal abduction (180° individual), there is a relative phase difference of 180° if the fingers maintain this difference throughout one complete cycle (fig. 7.4B). The 180° relative phase movement of the two fingers represents the anti-phase pattern. Clearly, there are potentially many relative phase patterns (between 0 and 360°), but Kelso chose to examine subjects' ability to perform only these two patterns (we will learn why later in the chapter).

The other independent variable was frequency of oscillation. Subjects were required to keep pace with an auditory metronome whose frequency (in Hz or beats per s) was systematically increased over the trial. A typical trial might be described as follows. At the beginning of the trial the metronome started at 1 Hz and beeped 15 times before being increased by 0.25 Hz, until a final cycling frequency of 3 Hz was reached. Each set of 15 beeps at a given frequency was called a *plateau*. This manner of manipulating the independent variable of frequency is called *scaling* and is analogous to the systematic temperature increase in the Benard instability demonstration. Clearly, this type of manipulation is different from a randomized treatment method typical in traditional scientific paradigms (e.g., Fisher 1949; Kirk 1968; Thomas and Nelson 1990). Later we will address the advantage of the scaling method used by Kelso. He was able to calculate the mean relative phase and the standard deviation around this mean within each cycling frequency plateau.

The major results of Kelso's experiment can be seen in fig. 7.5. Kelso found that subjects initially prepared in the 0° in-phase pattern could stay in this pattern as cycling frequency was systematically increased. That is, the mean relative phase did not change across all cycling frequencies, and the standard deviation of the relative phase remained consistently small. Different results occurred when subjects were initially prepared in the 180° anti-phase pattern. At low cycling frequencies, subjects had difficulty maintaining the anti-phase pattern reflected in higher standard deviation of relative phase values. At a critical cycling frequency (different for each subject), subjects were unable to continue performing the anti-phase pattern and suddenly switched to the in-phase pattern. Switching from the 180° to 0° pattern is called a *phase transition*. Before switching to the in-phase pattern, the standard deviation of the 180° anti-phase pattern dramatically increased. After switching to the 0° in-phase pattern the standard deviation reduced to the same low value produced during the in-phase preparation. In other experiments by Kelso, cycling frequency was scaled upward to some maximum value, then scaled downward within a single trial. Interestingly, the results showed that following the phase transition from the anti-phase to the in-phase pattern, subjects did not switch back to the anti-phase pattern when cycling frequency was scaled downward. This result is an example of a type of hysteresis effect discussed earlier in the chapter. In summary, I know of nothing in Newton's laws that can predict the phase transition, the increase in standard deviation of the 180° pattern before the phase transition, and the hysteresis effect shown in Kelso's experiment, even though only two components (the fingers) were involved at this level of analysis. My tongue-in-cheek response is to label these results as The Two-Body Problem!

Many features of the Kelso bimanual experiments deserve attention. The scaling of cycling frequency (reminiscent of the method of limits in classical psychophysics

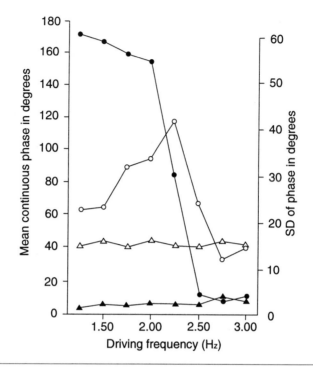

Fig. 7.5   The average mean relative phase for the in-phase (*closed triangles*) and anti-phase (*closed circles*) patterns and the average standard deviation of the relative phase (in-phase = *open triangles*, anti-phase = *open circles*) as a function of cycling frequency. Reprinted from Kelso, Scholz, and Schöner 1986.

experiments, see Massaro 1975, 89-90) allows one to observe how changes in coordination are affected by previous states of the system. The traditional randomization of treatments procedure would have, no doubt, masked many interesting results shown in Kelso's experiments (i.e., phase transition, increase in standard deviation of 180° pattern before phase transition, hysteresis). Another feature worth noting is Kelso's use of two patterns of coordination. From the results it would appear that the in-phase pattern is easier to produce than the anti-phase pattern because subjects can maintain the pattern across all cycling frequencies. That being the case, why investigate the anti-phase pattern? What is gained by investigating both patterns, particularly within the same experiment? The answer has less to do with the practical utility of the experiments and more to do with theory development.

Haken, Kelso, and Bunz (HKB) (1985) Theoretical Model

Our story now turns to the theoretical physicist, Hermann Haken, who eventually learned of Kelso's interesting experiments and invited Kelso to Germany to develop a theoretical explanation of the results based on synergetic theory. The net result was a theoretical paper published in scientific journal *Biological Cybernetics* that has become known as the HKB model (after the authors). The following is a description of the theory and an attempt to show not only how the model explained Kelso's results, but also how it generated new, testable predictions.

Haken, Kelso, and Bunz began by focusing on the main features of Kelso's results: the presence of only two stable coordination patterns, the transition from one pattern to the other, the presence of only one pattern (0°) following the phase transition, and the hysteresis effect—that following the phase transition, the system did not return to the anti-phase pattern as cycling frequency was reduced. These results would be understood within the synergetic framework. Next, they argued that relative phase was an excellent candidate for an order parameter, because this variable reflects the cooperativity among the components (fingers) in this system. It is relative phase that more adequately describes the two patterns, as opposed to the individual kinematic and kinetic measures of each component. That is, knowing the positions and velocities or forces of each component does not adequately distinguish the two patterns. Only a measure like relative phase describes how the fingers move with respect to one another. Finally, as cycling frequency increased, relative phase remained *invariant* longer, and it changed more slowly than the variables describing the behavior of the individual components, a quality characteristic of an order parameter.

The obvious control parameter in Kelso's experiment is cycling frequency. It is an excellent candidate for a control parameter because it is a variable imposed on the two-finger system from the outside, and it can be systematically increased or decreased in value by the experimenter. Finally, the control parameter does not dictate the patterns of coordination to be produced.

Haken, Kelso, and Bunz then modeled the in-phase and anti-phase patterns as attractors, in a nonlinear dynamical sense. They specified a potential function that could describe the layout of the attractor states and how the layout is modified as the control parameter changes. Their first task was to model the attractor landscape using a potential energy (V) function (see fig. 7.5 for an earlier discussion of V). They used the following cosine function to create the valleys and hills of the potential function representing the two attractors at 0 and 180°:

$$V = -a \cos \phi - b \cos 2\phi \qquad (7.1)$$

where a and b are constants with their ratios representing the changes in the cycling frequency, and ϕ is the relative phase. Fig. 7.6A illustrates the resulting potential function when b is set equal to 0. Notice that the deepest part of the well (or basin), where the potential energy is at a minimum, is at the 0° relative phase value between $-\pi$ ($-180°$) and $+\pi$ ($+180°$), a basin of attraction representing the 0° in-phase pattern of coordination. Fig. 7.6B shows the potential function when a is set equal to 0. Notice here that two equivalent basins are generated at $\phi = 0$ and $\phi = \pi$ (the latter equivalent to $\phi = -\pi$).

The next procedure was to insert various values of a and b to form different ratios of b/a in order to simulate changes in cycling frequency. Haken, Kelso, and Bunz changed the b/a ratio from 1 to 0, and fig. 7.7 shows how the potential function V is systematically altered. The upper left corner illustrates the potential function when the b/a ratio is equal to 1, the slowest cycling frequency.

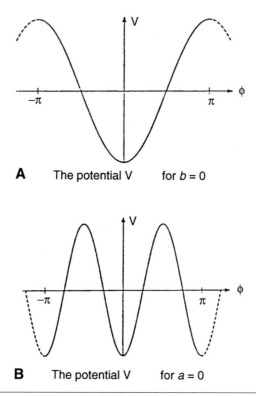

A   The potential V   for *b* = 0

B   The potential V   for *a* = 0

Fig. 7.6 In *A*, the potential V for *b* = 0 from the equation (1) in the text. In *B*, the potential V for *a* = 0. The horizontal axis is relative phase.
Adapted from Haken, Kelso, and Bunz 1985.

Notice at this *b/a* ratio there are two wells, at 180° and 0° relative phase. Also notice that the well at 0° is much deeper and steeper than the one at 180°. The black ball represents the initial status of the two-finger system—in this case, the 180° relative phase (+π). Haken, Kelso, and Bunz showed that as the *b/a* ratio is systematically reduced (i.e., cycling frequency is increased), the potential landscape changes in a most interesting fashion. One major change is that, as cycling frequency increases, the 180° well becomes shallower, and it eventually disappears at the highest cycling frequency. However, the change of the *b/a* ratio has less effect on the shape of the 0° well. The consequences of this change on the black ball representing the two-finger system are that (1) at some critical cycling frequency, the black ball has no choice but to leave the 180° pattern, and (2) the black ball is attracted to the 0° pattern. In nonlinear dynamical terms we say that the 180° pattern is inherently less stable than the 0° pattern because (1) its potential well is shallower than the well representing the 0° pattern, and (2) its potential well is more affected by the change in the control parameter (i.e., its potential becomes shallower and eventually disappears). Furthermore, the change in the control parameter alters the potential landscape to induce a phase transition from the less stable 180° pattern to the more stable 0° pattern, exactly Kelso's results. Although not shown, we can

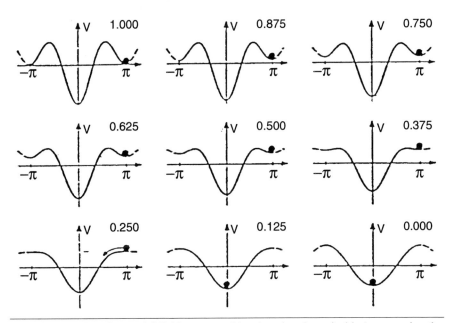

Fig. 7.7   A series of potential fields generated by changing the ratio *b/a* (representing the control parameter of cycling frequency). The *upper left* is the potential at the slowest cycling frequency and the *lower right* is the potential at the fastest cycling frequency. Notice that as cycling frequency increases, the potential well at 180° becomes shallower (less stable) until at a critical frequency the black ball (representing the two-finger system) falls into the potential well of the 0° in-phase pattern signifying a phase transition. Even if cycling frequency were reversed, the black ball would remain in the 0° potential, called hysteresis. Adapted from Haken, Kelso, and Bunz 1985.

easily visualize that if the black ball begins in the 0° well, the change in the control parameter will not affect the system's preference to stay there. The potential well is too deep for the black ball to escape, and the relative phase stays at 0° as the control parameter is changed, again exactly the results of Kelso's experiments.

Another aspect of the HKB model (and an elaboration by Schoner, Haken, and Kelso 1986) addresses the standard deviation of relative phase results from Kelso's experiments. If we assume that our system has some intrinsic fluctuation (or noise) due to variation in the individual components, we can envision the black ball *oscillating* in the 180° basin of attraction (see Zanone and Kelso 1992a for a further discussion of noise within the HKB model). This oscillation would be greater in the 180° basin compared with the 0° basin, and therefore the standard deviation of the relative phase would also be greater. As the control parameter is changed, the 180° basin becomes shallower, allowing oscillation of the black ball to increase until at some critical cycling frequency, it falls into the 0° basin of attraction. This deformation of the potential landscape increases the standard deviation of the relative phase before the phase transition, called an *enhancement of critical fluctuations*. Once the black ball settles in the 0° basin, these fluctuations significantly reduce, and the standard deviation of the relative phase returns to a small value. These effects were demonstrated in the Kelso experiments.

Finally, we turn to the hysteresis effect and the HKB model's explanation of it. Once the black ball falls into the 0° basin following the phase transition, it will stay in that basin even if we decrease cycling frequency (i.e., alter the potential landscape in a reverse manner). It is clear that the 0° basin of attraction does not significantly change, and it remains the most stable pattern in the system. So, similar to the turbulent stream example discussed earlier, pattern changes seen in the two-finger system are not always linear and reversible. Much depends on the relative stabilities of the patterns themselves, where the system is on the potential landscape, and how the control parameter is changed.

In summary, the HKB model describes all the essential features of Kelso's results: phase transitions, enhancement of critical fluctuations, and the hysteresis effect. We can see from the model that when the system is in an unstable pattern and the control parameter is changed, it will be attracted to the more stable pattern. An enhancement of critical fluctuations in the order parameter and the eventual phase transition is also predictable. The HKB model offers a way of describing emerging patterns of coordination as the system is pushed into far from equilibrium conditions by an outside variable, the control parameter. In the next section, we explore another interesting prediction of the model called *critical slowing down*.

Test of the Model: Critical Slowing Down

A fundamental feature of the HKB model is the concept of stability. In the HKB model, stability of the coordination patterns can be related to the shape of the potential landscape (V), which, as we have seen, is directly affected by the current value of the control parameter. If the system is in a stable pattern, we have seen that changes in the control parameter may not necessarily induce a transition to some other pattern. Our black ball is oscillating at the bottom of a deep well (due to inherent noise in the system) and will find it difficult to escape. If the system is in an unstable pattern, changes in the control parameter can induce a phase transition to a more stable pattern. Thus, manipulation of a control parameter is one way to evaluate the relative stabilities of multiple patterns within a complex system. Another way is to perturb the system while it is in each pattern and see how long it takes for the system to return to its pre-perturbation state. Consider fig. 7.8, which shows the black ball at the bottom of the potentials representing the 0° and 180° relative phase patterns.

If we were to push the black ball in one direction, we could measure the time that the system takes, following the perturbation, to return to its pre-perturbation state. In nonlinear dynamical terms, this is called *relaxation time*. Because of the relative shapes of the 0° and 180° potentials, specifically the slope of V (ϕ), the HKB model predicts that the relaxation time following a perturbation from the 0° pattern will be shorter than from the 180° pattern (see Kelso, Ding, and Schoner 1992 for a detailed mathematical derivation of relaxation time). Furthermore, the HKB model predicts that relaxation time should increase in the 180° less stable pattern as cycling frequency increases (see Schoner, Haken, and Kelso 1986 for an

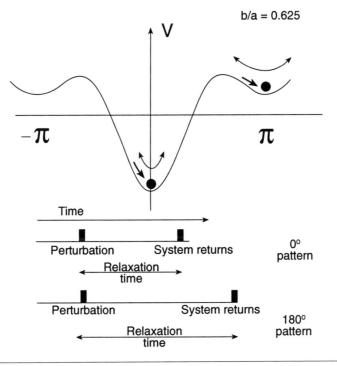

Fig. 7.8 Relaxation time following perturbations (*thick arrows*) to the system during the 0° and 180° patterns. The HKB model predicts shorter relaxation time when the system is in a deep potential well (more stable pattern).

elaboration). An examination of fig. 7.7 shows that the 180° potential at $+\pi$ becomes shallower as cycling frequency increases. Thus, the relaxation time of the black ball following the perturbation should be greater at higher cycling frequencies.

These predictions were tested in a study by Scholz and Kelso (1989). The experimental setup was similar to the original phase transition studies by Kelso. The subject's two index fingers were inserted into metal sleeves attached to potentiometers for measuring each finger's displacement. In addition, a torque motor was connected so it could deliver 50 ms square wave pulses to the fingers. The pulse, which served as a perturbation to either the in-phase pattern or the anti-phase pattern, was randomly delivered throughout the scaling trial, but only to the right finger. Fig. 7.9 illustrates the results from the experiment.

The results strongly supported the predictions from the HKB model. First, relaxation times were greater if subjects were in the anti-phase pattern. Second, relaxation times increased as cyling frequency increased for only the anti-phase pattern. Finally, Scholz and Kelso noted that the perturbations during the anti-phase pattern occasionally induced a transition to the more stable in-phase pattern. This result would be expected if the perturbation was strong enough to push the black ball (see fig. 7.8) out of the shallow potential of the 180° pattern and into the deeper, more stable well representing the 0° pattern.

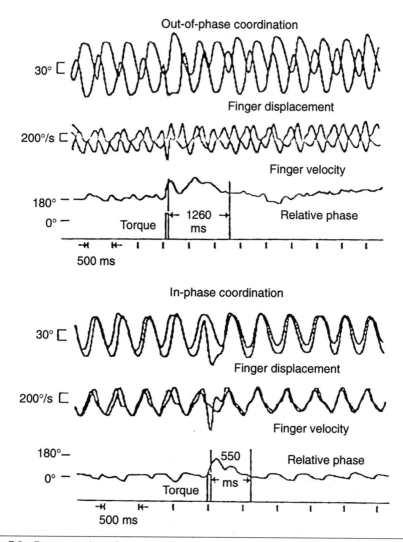

Fig. 7.9   Representation of the relaxation time results from the Scholz and Kelso (1989) study in the out-of-phase (180°) and the in-phase (0°) pattern.
Reprinted from Scholz and Kelso 1989.

In summary, the Scholz and Kelso (1989) results provide complimentary support for the notion that, at least in this two-finger system, there appear to be two patterns of coordination (0° and 180° relative phase) with different relative stabilities. The HKB model was developed to help explain the coordinative behavior exhibited in a simple two-finger system. Can the model be extended to other systems with different movement components (joints, muscles, etc.)? One conclusion from early Kelso experiments was that the most stable patterns of coordination are ones in which homologous (the same) muscles are activated at the same time (see Rosenbaum

1991, 373-374 for an argument). In Kelso's early work, only in the in-phase pattern is this the case. Does homologous muscle activation always define the most stable pattern? This issue was explored while I was on sabbatical at the Center for Complex Systems.

Generalizability to Other Movement Components

Can the HKB model be extended to other movement components? In a recent study (Kelso, Buchanan, and Wallace 1991), we required subjects to coordinate the movements of the wrist and elbow joints in a manner similar to the original Kelso experiments with the two fingers. Fig. 7.10 illustrates the two patterns of coordination investigated.

With the forearm supinated, subjects synchronized either wrist flexion with elbow flexion (homologous muscle groups), defined as the in-phase pattern (fig. 7.10A),

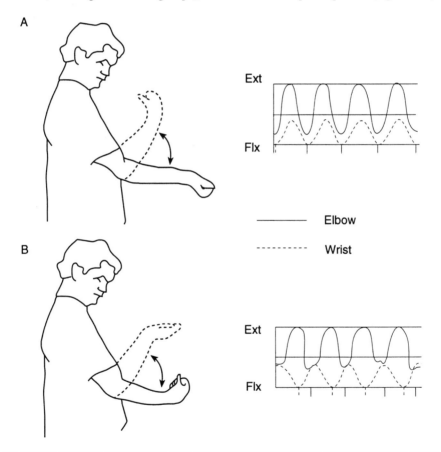

Fig. 7.10   In *A*, the in-phase pattern with maximum wrist flexion synchronized with maximum elbow flexion. In *B*, the anti-phase pattern with maximum wrist extension synchronized with maximum elbow flexion in the Kelso, Buchanan, and Wallace (1991) study.

or wrist extension with elbow flexion (nonhomologous muscle groups), defined as the anti-phase pattern (fig. 7.10B). These movement patterns were investigated with the forearm pronated. To describe the coordination between the elbow and wrist movement we measured the relative phase of peak wrist displacement with respect to one complete cycle of elbow displacement. As in the original Kelso experiments, cycling frequency was scaled (from 1 to 2.25 Hz in steps of 0.25 Hz). The results in this wrist-elbow preparation mirrored those in the two-finger system. When subjects were initially prepared in the in-phase pattern with the forearm supinated, there was no change in the mean relative phase or its standard deviation with increases in cycling frequency. However, in the anti-phase condition, phase transitions were shown in every subject, and there was an enhancement of critical fluctuations before the transition as cycling frequency was increased. When the forearm was pronated, subjects found the wrist flexion-elbow flexion pattern more difficult to coordinate than the wrist extension-elbow flexion condition. Although fewer phase transitions were exhibited with the forearm pronated, there was significant enhancement of critical fluctuations, primarily in the wrist flexion-elbow extension condition, opposite that found with the forearm supinated. Thus, this experiment demonstrated that (1) the basic HKB model can be extended beyond the two-finger system to other components[4] and (2) the stability of the patterns investigated is not necessarily dependent on the simultaneous activation of homologous muscles as Rosenbaum suggested (1991).

Our experiment suggested that the orientation of the forearm may also play a role in determining the stability of patterns in this wrist-elbow system. The possibility that a *spatial* control parameter may influence coordinative movement patterns has been investigated by Buchanan and Kelso (1993). In this experiment, the forearm orientation was systematically manipulated as a control parameter while subjects attempted to coordinate various wrist and elbow movements. The results confirmed the emergence of different patterns of relative stability as a function of the spatial orientation of the forearm. This work suggests that movement coordination may be dependent on at least two control parameters: temporal and spatial. The theoretical modeling for two control parameters in this system has not, to my knowledge, been developed.

There have been other generalizations of dynamic pattern theory to different experimental systems, such as studies on perception-action coupling (Kelso, DelColle, and Schoner 1990), between people coordination (Schmidt, Carello, and Turvey 1990), and speech production (Tuller and Kelso 1991). The reader is encouraged to examine this interesting work. Now we turn to a technique used to examine the stability of various patterns of coordination: the scanning procedure.

Scanning the Dynamics of Movement Patterns

Recall that the HKB model was developed to help explain Kelso's original results and to generate new predictions. Why were these two relative phase patterns, and

---

[4]Some modifications of the basic model are needed when the preferred cycling frequencies (i.e., eigenfrequencies) of the two component oscillators are different, for whatever reasons (see Kelso and Jeka 1992 for a discussion; also see Sternad, Turvey, and Schmidt 1992).

not others, examined in the first place? It turns out that earlier evidence by Yamanishi, Kawato, and Suzuki (1980) using bimanual finger-tapping movements had shown that 0° and 180° relative phase movements were easier to perform than other relative phases. Subjects in this experiment learned to synchronize tapping movements with their index fingers to 10 relative phase patterns dictated by two visual pacing signals. After considerable practice, subjects attempted to produce the different relative phases without the signals. The results suggested that variability in performance was much less at the 0° and 180° relative phases compared with all other relative phases. Tuller and Kelso (1985, 1989) replicated these results with unpracticed subjects who performed exclusively with the aid of visual pacing signals. Fig. 7.11 shows representative data of the results. In fig. 7.11A, plotted on the horizontal axis, is the required relative phase dictated by pacing lights. On the vertical axis is the delta relative phase or the observed minus the required relative phase. Performance close to the horizontal zero line means that the subject was better able to

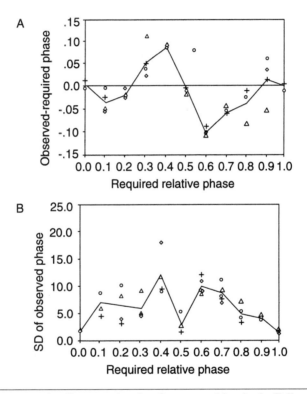

Fig. 7.11   Representative finger-tapping data from one subject in the Tuller and Kelso (1989) study. In *A*, the observed minus the required relative phase (delta relative phase) as a function of the required relative phase. Notice that the constant error is smallest at the 0.0 (0°) in-phase and 0.5 (180°) anti-phase pattern and that surrounding errors are attracted to these patterns. In *B*, the standard deviation (SD) of the observed relative phase as a function of the required relative phase. Notice that variability is less at the in-phase and anti-phase patterns.

Adapted from Tuller and Kelso 1989.

perform the required relative phase. It can be observed that the best performance is at the 0° and 180° relative phases. Also, notice that performance of nearby required phases is attracted toward these two relative phases in that the delta relative phases pass through 0° and 180° required relative phases with a negative slope. In addition, as shown in fig. 7.11B, the standard deviations of the relative phases produced are smallest at the 0° and 180° required relative phase. These scanning procedures, first developed by Yamanishi, Kawato, and Suzuki (1980) and later modified by Tuller and Kelso (1985, 1989), provide further evidence that, at least in these types of bimanual tasks, there are two stable coordination patterns.

Is there anything special about the 0° and 180° relative phase patterns? The answer may depend on the task and how one characterizes the coordination patterns in the task. For example, let us examine a different task—reaching and grasping for an object. In this task, the subject is asked to start with the index finger and thumb in a pinched position, reach forward, and eventually grasp the object. How does one characterize the coordination of the components used in this task? Two major components are the action of the fingers (manipulation component) and of the arm (transport component) (see Jeannerod 1981, 1984). Clearly, one can move the fingers independently of the arm (and vice versa), but in reaching and grasping, the two components need to be coordinated to perform the task effectively without error.

Work in my laboratory with adult subjects has suggested that an important event in this task is the time at which the subject begins final closure of the fingers on the object (Wallace, Weeks, and Kelso 1990). We have shown, for example, that the relative time or the relative phasing of final closure remains invariant across transport speeds (roughly 70% of the total movement time). These data suggest that there may be only one stable coordination pattern in mature reaching and grasping. If true, is this pattern of coordination the same for every subject? A more recent study by Wallace, Stevenson, Spear, and Weeks (1994), using a continuous reaching and grasping task, attempted to explore this issue through a scanning procedure. Adult subjects (N = 6; 3 males and 3 females) were asked to reach out, momentarily grasp an object fixed to a tabletop, and return to the starting position. The subjects were told to synchronize the grasp of the object with the beep of a metronome set at 1.1 Hz, a comfortable pace for all subjects. One complete cycle (from the start, to the grasp, and back to the start) amounted to 360° of arm motion.

The continuous reaching and grasping task allowed us to measure the relative phasing of final closure on the object. Fig. 7.12 shows how we calculated the relative phasing of final finger-thumb closure. To simplify measurement of the fingers, we calculated the aperture (or the resultant distance) between the finger and thumb. Arm motion was represented by the cyclic movement of the subject's wrist to and from the object. In this experiment, we attempted to force subjects to perform different relative phases of final closure in the following manner. We placed an upright dowel along and to the side of the movement path toward the object. This dowel indicated where the subject was to reach a maximum aperture and begin final finger-thumb closure before the grasp (see fig. 7.13). There were 10 target positions spaced in 1 in. increments between the start of the movement and the object (distance from the start to the object was 12 in.). For example, with the target marker in Position 1, nearest the start, the subject had to quickly reach a maximum aperture and begin closing down monotonically on the object. If performed properly, the relative phase of final closure would be 60°. After 10 grasping cycles, we moved

$$\text{Relative phase} = [(t_{close} - t_0) / t_{cycle}] \times 360°$$

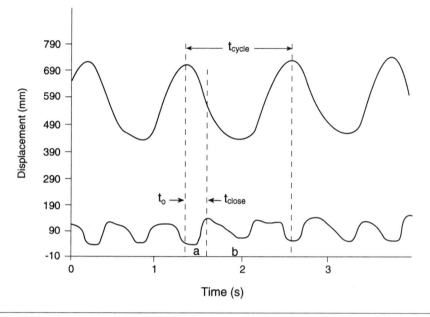

Fig. 7.12 Calculation of relative phase in a reaching and grasping task (Wallace et al. 1994). The *top line* represents displacement of the wrist and the *bottom line* represents displacement of the aperture (i.e., resultant distance between the index finger and thumb). *a* is the time of initial opening and *b* is the time of the grasp in a given cycle. The lowest points in the wrist displacement represent maximum arm displacement and the approximate time of the grasp of the object. The *outside dashed vertical lines* represent one complete cycle of arm motion (from start to start). The *middle dashed vertical line* represents the time of initiation of final aperture closure. Relative phase of final closure is given by the equation shown. Notice that the subject tends to open the hand on the return to the start.

the target marker to Position 2, and so on. Following Position 10 (required relative phase of 156°), the position of the target marker systematically moved back to Position 1. Thus, we were able to scan required relative phases of final closing between 60° and 156° in an increasing and decreasing manner.

If subjects could perform all required relative phases, then we would expect delta relative phase values to be close to zero. However, fig. 7.14 indicates a negative slope of delta relative phase as a function of required relative phase for all six subjects. Notice that the zero crossing is different for each subject. Total variability of the produced relative phase (not shown) was smallest near the point of zero crossing for each subject. Taken together, these results suggest that adult reaching and grasping may be characterized by only one stable coordination pattern. However, each individual has his or her preferred pattern, namely, the individual subject begins final closure at his or her preferred point along the trajectory. In addition, the preferred patterns are not related to either 0° or 180° relative phases, nor could they

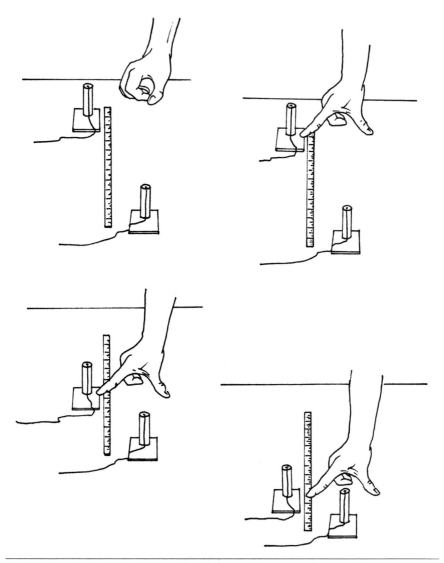

Fig. 7.13 Experimental setup of the Wallace et al. (1994) scanning study on reaching and grasping. The target marker dowel was set up at different points along the movement path toward the object and served as the point where maximum aperture and final finger-thumb closure was to occur. Only three positions are shown here, but in the study 10 positions were used.

be, by definition (at least as defined in this task). A 0° relative phase would require the subject to close at the start of the movement and the 180° relative phase would mean closing at the object, much too late for a successful grasp. Of course, we might be wrong and grasping patterns could be defined in some other way. Thus, depending on the task, coordination patterns can be described in different ways.

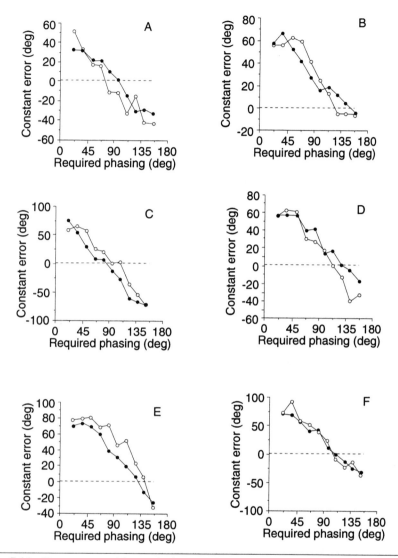

Fig. 7.14 Constant error (observed minus required) relative phase as a function of the required relative phase of the six subjects in the Wallace et al. (1994) study (*open circles* are from increasing required relative phase and *closed circles* are from decreasing required relative phase). Notice that the slope is negative for all subjects although the point of zero crossing is unique for each subject.

Learning of Movement Patterns

Our discussion has focused on the investigation of coordination patterns with different stabilities, the loss of stability due to changes in the potential landscape induced by the control parameter, and phase transitions from one pattern to another. We now turn to the *learning* of new coordination patterns. The focus of this section will be to describe how learning occurs within the context of the HKB model and theoretical extensions of it (Schoner and Kelso 1988b and c).

How is learning conceptualized within dynamic pattern theory? Learning is viewed as a pattern formation process in which the learner acquires new coordination patterns on the background of already existing patterns. When the learner begins a new motor task, we assume he or she already has certain coordination patterns among the components (i.e., joints, muscles) to be used for that motor task. Thus, we assume that the learner does not start the learning process with a "tabula rasa" [blank slate] (to borrow the metaphor from the English philosopher John Locke). The coordination patterns that the learner has and brings to a given motor task are called the learner's *intrinsic dynamics*. These intrinsic dynamics correspond to the attractor layout of the order parameter dynamics. For example, in Kelso's original work, subjects were shown to possess two coordination patterns, the 0° and 180° relative phase patterns of the two fingers. These patterns correspond to the subjects' intrinsic dynamics in this type of motor task.

Intrinsic dynamics can be more specifically defined as the dynamics of the order parameter when *environmental information* is absent (Schoner and Kelso 1988b). Environmental information corresponds to information that defines the task to be learned, that is, the required behavioral pattern. In Kelso's experiments, the subjects were asked to perform the 0° or 180° pattern with no guidance or special instructions provided once the task began. Little environmental information was present that dictated the patterns to produce. Thus, the behavior exhibited by the subjects was primarily due to each subject's intrinsic dynamics. What would happen if we required the subject to learn (or attempt to produce) a pattern that is either similar to or different from the subject's intrinsic dynamics? That is, what type of behavior do we expect when environmental information is imposed onto the subject's intrinsic dynamics? This is precisely the question asked in a recent study by Zanone and Kelso (1992a, also see 1992b for a discussion). For a theoretical answer to the question, let us examine fig. 7.15.

In A, we show the familiar potential landscape of the intrinsic dynamics of the two-finger system when cycling frequency (the control parameter) is slow (1 Hz). This landscape is what we expect when environmental information is absent. To model the landscape in the presence of environmental information, Zanone and Kelso (1992a) added a second term to the original HKB potential equation (1) with the following outcome:

$$V\psi = V(\phi) - c \cos ((\phi - \psi) / 2) \qquad (7.2)$$

where $V(\phi)$ is the potential representing the intrinsic dynamics in equation (1), and the parameter c represents the strength of the environmental information on the intrinsic dynamics. The second term, $- c \cos ((\phi - \psi) / 2)$, is used to attract relative phase toward the required phasing (see Schoner and Kelso 1988b for details). Using this second term, Zanone and Kelso showed what would happen to the potential ($V\psi$) if the required relative phase were either 0°, 180°, or 90° (the latter being a new required pattern different from the intrinsic dynamics). Remember we assume the intrinsic dynamics to be as shown in fig. 7.15A. In B, when the required relative

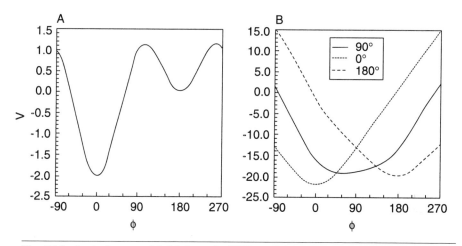

Fig. 7.15   In *A*, the potential (V) from the HKB model at a slow cycling frequency (1 Hz) from equation (1). In *B*, the potential when behavioral information specifies a required relative phase (either 0°, 180°, or 90°). When the behavioral information coincides with the intrinsic dynamics (in *A*), the two minimal potentials remain at 0° and 180°. Notice that when the 90° required relative phase is specified that (1) the resulting minimal potential is shifted away (to the *left*) from the required relative phase implying greater error in performance and (2) the resulting potential well is wider, implying more performance variability. Adapted from Zanone and Kelso 1993.

phase (0° or 180°) is the same as the intrinsic dynamics, the minimum of the potential remains at 0 and 180, respectively. According to the modeling, this is due to the *cooperation* between the intrinsic dynamics and the behavioral information. A close inspection reveals that the 180° potential is slightly more deformed than the 0° potential. Note that the sides of the resulting 180° potential are less steep compared with those of the 0° potential. This represents the differential stability of the two patterns. When the required relative phase is 90°, the resulting minimal potential is close to 90, but attracted toward 0°. Furthermore, the potential is shallow and, according to Zanone and Kelso, is a result of the *competition* between the intrinsic dynamics and the behavioral information. The implications for learning are as follows. If the subject is asked to learn the 90° pattern, it will at first be an unstable pattern (assuming the intrinsic dynamics represented in fig. 7.15A). Attempts at producing this pattern should result in high variability, and the mean relative phase should be attracted closer to the 0° relative phase. As the 90° pattern becomes more stable with practice, the modeling suggests that the 180° pattern will lose stability, and the 0° pattern will likely retain its stability. Thus, the modeling predicts an eventual phase transition in learning when the intrinsic dynamics at the beginning of practice are as shown in fig. 7.15A.

In the experiment Zanone and Kelso had subjects learn the 90° pattern by watching a pair of lights, which could be programmed to produce the desired relative phase, while attempting to synchronize their finger movements with the lights. Over the five days of practice, subjects received feedback about the difference between the desired relative phase of 90° and their produced relative phase after each 20-s trial. Cycling frequency was set at 1.75 Hz. Recall tests were given seven days after the last practice day, requiring the subjects to produce the 90° pattern from memory with feedback. In addition, before and after each day of practice, a scanning procedure was used that required subjects to produce various relative phases. During the scanning runs, no feedback was given. The required relative phases were progressively increased from 0° to 180° by 12 discrete steps of 15°, and each step was 20 s. This insightful addition to the experiment allowed the experimenters to examine the evolution of the attractor landscape as a function of learning.

Not surprisingly, the results showed that subjects learned to produce the 90° pattern as reflected in appropriate changes in the mean relative phase and reductions in variability. The results confirmed the theoretical predictions about changes in the attractor landscape revealed by the scanning runs across the five days of practice. As practice continued, the 90° pattern became more stable and the 180° became less stable, whereas the stability of the 0° pattern remained unchanged. Interestingly, some subjects learned to produce the 90° pattern at the expense of the 180° pattern! I find these results fascinating because it is not necessarily intuitive (unless you know the predictions of the model!) that the 180° pattern would be lost (or become less stable) from the subject's repertoire as a function of learning another pattern. These results suggest that learning is accompanied by phase transitions due to a loss of stability of one pattern and a strengthening of stability in another. One should also recall that the learning behavior is dependent on the initial intrinsic dynamics of the individual subject. If the intrinsic dynamics of the subject are different from those shown in fig. 7.15A, phase transitions may not be experienced (e.g., if the subject starts with intrinsic dynamics similar to the required behavioral information). In my view, dynamic pattern theory, with its emphasis on the relation between intrinsic dynamics and behavioral information, offers a fresh perspective on the learning process that we can experimentally test and generalize to other movement components and movement tasks.

Summary

In this section we have examined the application of synergetic theory (Haken 1983) to movement coordination (called the dynamic pattern perspective). We have explored various aspects of the HKB model (Haken, Kelso, and Bunz 1985) and extensions of it (Schoner and Kelso 1988b) and have seen that the model is useful in characterizing the stability of coordination patterns. We have also seen how stability loss of certain patterns gives rise to other, more stable patterns under conditions far from equilibrium. The emphasis in synergetics is on discovering order parameters that describe patterns among the components and control parameters that effectively alter the potential landscape and push the system in and out of attractive states.

It is not a trivial procedure to discover order and control parameters in any given complex system. As noted by Haken, the order and control parameters will likely be different across systems. However, I believe there is a strategy for finding them, particularly in tasks requiring movement coordination. I will address this topic in my concluding remarks.

CONCLUSIONS: EXPLORING YOUR SYSTEM

Bernstein (1967), a Russian physiologist, first emphasized that the human body possesses an extraordinary number of *degrees of freedom*, or ways in which the body can move. For example, there are roughly 27 behaviorally measurable degrees of freedom in the hand, wrist, elbow, and shoulder joints within a single arm in the human body. The human body, as a whole, possesses hundreds of degrees of freedom, and the diversity of movement is extraordinary. As experimenters, how do we explore movement coordination given this enormous complexity? The first step is to define the system by deciding on the type of coordination and movement components we will study. Are you interested in speech control, upper limb coordination, or gait, for example? Be aware that by selecting the components, you have effectively defined your system, and you must interpret the results of any related experiments within the constraints of the chosen system. Once your system is defined, decide on the task and movement components you will use in the task. One suggestion is to choose components that clearly represent the system in nonredundant ways for a given task. For example, when grasping an object, many motions of the finger joints are correlated. Is it necessary to measure the motions of all the joints in all the fingers? Depending on your question and limitations of recording joint movement, it may not be necessary or even possible to measure all the joint motions of each finger. By making your selections, you have defined the components in your system.

A major difficulty in exploring movement coordination is discovering the order parameter(s). It is likely that the order parameter will be some type of relationship among the components, such as relative phase. Order parameters, by their nature, will be slower moving variables compared with kinematic variables of the individual components. To help identify these slower moving relationships, it is necessary to scale some variable such as motion speed, distance moved, movement direction, or force produced within the chosen task. As you manipulate the scaling variable, the kinematics of the individual components (e.g., position, velocity) will change more rapidly than the potential order parameter.

Once you have identified the slower moving relationships (i.e., potential order parameters), you need to evaluate their dynamics using some type of scanning procedure (e.g., Yamanishi, Kawato, and Suzuki 1980; Tuller and Kelso 1989; Wallace et al. 1994; Zanone and Kelso 1992a). An important consideration is identifying all possible relationships (or patterns) among the components. That is, how many ways can the components move in relation to each other within the task you have chosen? Design the scanning procedure to determine how well subjects can perform these patterns within the same experiment. Both the mean performance of each pattern and the variability around each mean are necessary statistics for determining pattern stability. If you examine only components in a preferred, or most common relationship, you may be investigating only one stable pattern. There may be, and probably are, less preferred patterns. Although there may be many possible relationships among the components, only a few will have some degree of stability. Design the scanning procedure to help identify both preferred and less preferred patterns among the movement components in your system.

Once you have identified patterns, the next step is to verify their relative stability. Choose a control parameter that your system is sensitive to. If the patterns you have chosen have different degrees of stability, changes in the control parameter should induce phase transitions from less stable to more stable patterns. Phase transitions are critical for the identification of patterns with different stabilities. Typically, you should systematically change the control parameter so you can observe critical fluctuations before the transition, the phase transition itself, and possible hysteresis effects if the scaling is reversed. Also, the manner in which you change the control parameter (i.e., the size of the steps or plateaus) can determine the nature of the phase transition. If the control parameter is changed too quickly, you may not observe critical fluctuations of the order parameter. Scale the control parameter over the widest possible range. If the range is too small or limited to a small range of the parameter space, you may not observe phase transitions, only scaling in the kinematics of the individual components within the pattern. The time scale of your experiment should be long enough to observe the phase transitions (if they are there to be observed).

Once you have identified the potential order parameters and have performed experiments that show how your system reacts to changes in the control parameter, it may be possible to model the results mathematically. Of course, if your training in mathematics is as weak as mine, you may need to seek the help of those more gifted! This may allow you to embark on a career of interdisciplinary study with colleagues who can help model your system mathematically while you perform the necessary experiments. It should be pointed out that the mathematics of nonlinear dynamics has a rich and long history, going all the way back to Poincare. To learn it requires years of study, but an appreciation can come from studying nonlinear differential equations. There are several books (e.g., Glass and Mackey 1988; Hale and Koçak 1991; Hirsch and Smale 1974) and self-study computer programs (e.g., Koçak 1989) on the market for this purpose. Once the modeling of your system is complete, you may set up experiments to test the model. For example, does your model predict different relaxation times following perturbations to the stable patterns? Do you expect to find hysteresis effects? Table 7.1 provides a summary of

Table 7.1   Exploring the Coordination of Movement

---

1. Define the system and the joint motions used to perform the task.
2. Scale a parameter within the task (e.g., speed of motion) and identify the slowest moving relationships or patterns among joint motions (potential order parameters).
3. Scan the dynamics of these slower moving relationships.
4. Identify the preferred and nonpreferred patterns.
5. Choose a potential control parameter.
6. Determine the relative stability of the patterns within a phase transition experiment.
7. Mathematically model your system.
8. Test the model.

---

the considerations in adequately exploring movement coordination using a synergetic strategy.

My purpose in this chapter has been to provide an overview of the dynamic pattern perspective and how it may help us better understand the movement coordination. I have not covered all the possible topics, such as asymmetries in order parameter dynamics (e.g., Kelso and Jeka 1992; Schmidt et al. 1991; Sternad, Turvey, and Schmidt 1992; Turvey et al. 1986), or frequency relations among movement components (e.g., DeGuzman and Kelso 1991; Kelso and Jeka 1992). I am hopeful that the reader will consider this chapter a starting point and that I have created enough interest to inspire further exploration of the nonlinear dynamical approach to the study of movement coordination.

REFERENCES

Bernstein, N. 1967. *The coordination and regulation of movements*. New York: Pergamon.

Briggs, J., and Peat, F.D. 1989. *Turbulent mirror: An illustrated guide to chaos theory and the science of wholeness*. New York: Harper & Row.

Buchanan, J.J., and Kelso, J.A.S. 1993. Posturally induced transitions in rhythmic multijoint limb movements. *Experimental Brain Research* 94:131-142.

Campbell, D.K. 1987. Nonlinear science: From paradigms to practicalities. *Los Alamos Science* Special Issue:218-262.

Coveney, P., and Highfield, R. 1990. *The arrow of time: A voyage through science to solve time's greatest mystery*. New York: Columbine.

DeGuzman, G.C., and Kelso, J.A.S. 1991. Multifrequency behavioral patterns and the phase attractive circle map. *Biological Cybernetics* 64:485-495.

Fauvel, J., Flood, R., Shortland, M., and Wilson, R. 1988. *Let Newton be: A new perspective on his life and works*. New York: Oxford University Press.

Fisher, R.A. 1949. *The design of experiments*. Edinburgh: Oliver & Boyd.

Glass, L., and Mackey, M.C. 1988. *From clocks to chaos: The rhythms of life*. Princeton, NJ: Princeton University Press.

Gleick, J. 1987. *Chaos: Making a new science*. New York: Viking.

Haken, H. 1983. *Synergetics: An introduction*. 3d ed. New York: Springer.

Haken, H. 1984. *Synergetics: The science of structure*. New York: Van Nostrand.

Haken, H. 1988. Synergetics. *IEEE Circuits and Devices Magazine* November:3-7.

Haken, H. 1991. Synergetics—Can it help physiology? Vol. 55 in *Rhythms in physiological systems*, Springer Series in Synergetics, edited by H. Haken and H.P. Koepchen. Berlin: Springer-Verlag.

Haken, H., Kelso, J.A.S., and Bunz, H. 1985. A theoretical model of phase transitions in human hand movements. *Biological Cybernetics* 51:347-356.

Hale, J., and Koçak, H. 1991. *Dynamics and bifurcations*. New York: Springer-Verlag.

Hirsch, M.W., and Smale, S. 1974. *Differential equations, dynamical systems, and linear algebra*. New York: Academic Press.

Jeannerod, M. 1981. Intersegmental coordination during reaching at natural visual objects. P. 153-168 in *Attention and Performance IX*, edited by J. Long and A. Baddeley. Hillsdale, NJ: Erlbaum.

Jeannerod, M. 1984. The timing of natural prehension movements. *Journal of Motor Behavior* 16:235-254.

Jeka, J.J., and Kelso, J.A.S. 1989. The dynamic pattern approach to coordinated behavior: A tutorial review. P. 3-45 in *Perspectives on the coordination of movement*, edited by S.A. Wallace. Amsterdam: North-Holland.

Kelso, J.A.S. 1981. On the oscillatory basis of movement. *Bulletin of the Psychonomic Society* 18:63.

Kelso, J.A.S. 1984. Phase transitions and critical behavior in human bimanual coordination. *American Journal of Physiology: Regulatory, Integrative and Comparative Physiology* 15:R1000-R1004.

Kelso, J.A.S. 1995. Dynamic patterns: The self-organization of brain and behavior. International Press.

Kelso, J.A.S., Buchanan, J.J., and Wallace, S.A. 1991. Order parameters for the neural organization of single, multijoint limb movement patterns. *Experimental Brain Research* 85:432-444.

Kelso, J.A.S., DelColle, J.D., and Schoner, G.S. 1990. Action-perception as a pattern formation process. P. 139-169 in *Attention and performance XIII*, edited by M. Jeannerod. Hillsdale, NJ: Erlbaum.

Kelso, J.A.S., Ding, M., and Schoner, G. 1992. Dynamic pattern formation: A primer. P. 397-440 in Proc. Vol. XII, *Principles of organization in organisms*, edited by A.B. Baskin and J.E. Mittenthal. Santa Fe, NM: Addison-Wesley.

Kelso, J.A.S., and Jeka, J.J. 1992. Symmetry breaking dynamics of human multilimb coordination. *Journal of Experimental Psychology: Human Perception and Performance* 18:645-668.

Kirk, R.E. 1968. *Experimental design: Procedures for the behavioral science.* Pacific Grove, CA: Brooks/Cole.

Koçak, H. 1989. *Differential and difference equations through computer experiments.* 2d ed. with diskettes containing PHASER: An animator/simulator for dynamical systems for I.B.M. Personal Computers. New York: Springer-Verlag.

Laskar, J. 1989. A numerical experiment on the chaotic behavior of the solar system. *Nature* 338:237.

Lorenz, E.N. 1963. Deterministic nonperiodic flow. *Journal of Atmospheric Sciences* 20:130-141.

Massaro, D.W. 1975. *Experimental psychology and information processing.* Chicago: Rand McNally.

Milani, A., and Nobili, A.M. 1992. An example of stable chaos in the solar system. *Nature* 357:569.

Poincare, H. [1905] 1952. *Science and hypothesis.* Reprint, New York: Dover.

Prigogine, I., and Stengers, I. 1984. *Order out of chaos: Man's new dialogue with nature.* New York: Bantam Books.

Rosenbaum, D.A. 1991. *Human Motor Control.* New York: Academic Press.

Ruthen, R. 1993. Adapting to complexity. *Scientific American* January:130-140.

Schmidt, R.C., Beek, P.J., Treffner, P.J., and Turvey, M.T. 1991. Dynamical substructure of coordinated rhythmic movement. *Journal of Experimental Psychology: Human Perception and Performance* 17:635-651.

Schmidt, R.C., Carello, C., and Turvey, M.T. 1990. Phase transitions and critical fluctuation in the visual coordination of rhythmic movements between people.

Journal of Experimental Psychology: Human Perception and Performance 16:227-247.

Scholz, J.P., and Kelso, J.A.S. 1989. A quantitative approach to understanding the formation and change of coordinated movement patterns. *Journal of Motor Behavior* 21:122-144.

Schoner, G.S., Haken, H., and Kelso, J.A.S. 1986. A stochastic theory of phase transitions in human hand movement. *Biological Cybernetics* 53:442-452.

Schoner, G.S., and Kelso, J.A.S. 1988a. Dynamic pattern generation in behavioral and neural systems. *Science* 239:1513-1520.

Schoner, G.S., and Kelso, J.A.S. 1988b. A synergetic theory of environmentally-specified and learned patterns of movement coordination. I. Relative phase dynamics. *Biological Cybernetics* 58:71-80.

Schoner, G.S., and Kelso, J.A.S. 1988c. A synergetic theory of environmentally-specified and learned patterns of movement coordination. II. Component oscillator dynamics. *Biological Cybernetics* 58:81-89.

Sternad, D., Turvey, M.T., and Schmidt, R.C. 1992. Average phase difference theory and 1:1 phase entrainment in interlimb coordination. *Biological Cybernetics* 67:223-231.

Sussman, G.J., and Wisdom, J. 1992. Chaotic evolution of the solar system. *Science* 257:56-62.

Thomas, J.R., and Nelson, J.K. 1990. *Research methods in physical activity.* Champaign, IL: Human Kinetics.

Tuller, B., and Kelso, J.A.S. 1985. Coordination in normal and split-brain patients. Paper presented at Psychonomic Society, Boston, MA.

Tuller, B., and Kelso, J.A.S. 1989. Environmentally-specified patterns of movement coordination in normal and split-brain subjects. *Experimental Brain Research* 75:306-316.

Tuller, B., and Kelso, J.A.S. 1991. The production and perception of syllable structure. *Journal of Speech and Hearing Research* 34:501-508.

Turvey, M.T., Rosenblum, L.D., Schmidt, R.C., and Kugler, P.N. 1986. Fluctuations and phase symmetry in coordinated rhythmic movements. *Journal of Experimental Psychology: Human Perception and Performance* 12:564-583.

Wallace, S.A., Stevenson, E., Spear, A., and Weeks, D.L. 1994. Scanning the dynamics of reaching and grasping movements. *Human Movement Science* 13:255-289.

Wallace, S.A., Weeks, D.L., and Kelso, J.A.S. 1990. Temporal constraints in reaching and grasping behavior. *Human Movement Science* 9:69-93.

Webster's new collegiate dictionary. 1977. Springfield, MA: Merriam.

Yamanishi, J., Kawato, M., and Suzuki, R. 1980. Two coupled oscillators as a model for the coordinated finger tapping by both hands. *Biological Cybernetics* 37:219-225.

Zanone, P.G., and Kelso, J.A.S. 1992a. Evolution of behavioral attractors with learning: Non-equilibrium phase transitions. *Journal of Experimental Psychology: Human Perception and Performance* 18:403-421.

Zanone, P.G., and Kelso, J.A.S. 1992b. Learning and transfer as dynamical paradigms for behavioral change. P. 563-582 in *Tutorials in motor behavior II*, edited by G.E. Stelmach and J. Requin. New York: Elsevier Science.

Zanone, P.G., and Kelso, J.A.S. 1993. The coordination dynamics of learning: Theoretical structure and experimental agenda. In *The control and modulation of patterns of interlimb coordination: A multidisciplinary perspective*, edited by J. Massion, P. Casaer, H. Heuer, and S.P. Swinnen. New York: Academic Press.

Acknowledgments

I'd like to thank David Goodman, Scott Kelso, and Edie Stevenson for their helpful comments on an earlier draft of the manuscript.

Chapter 8

Dynamical Perspective on Motor Learning

R.C. Schmidt
Tulane University and University of Connecticut

Paula Fitzpatrick
University of Connecticut

The construction of a theory of motor learning presupposes a theory of motor control. The latter specifies the syntax of the components that underlie the production of coordinated movements (e.g., reflexes and associations in reflex arcs, rules and representations in motor programs), whereas the former specifies how these components become reorganized (e.g., laws of association, hypothesis testing or induction, respectively) through interactions with the environment. This paper is a review of the dynamical theories of motor learning. To introduce this perspective, we will contrast the information-processing, connectionist, and dynamical theories of motor control in terms of their theoretical assumptions. Then we will review the dynamical theory of motor control or dynamical theory of action (as it is called) to provide a basis for understanding the dynamical theory of learning.

INFORMATION-PROCESSING, CONNECTIONIST, AND DYNAMICAL THEORIES OF BEHAVIORAL CONTROL

One can argue that any good theory of behavioral control should have two, not mutually exclusive, properties: (1) it should have theoretical and empirical continuity with its related sciences (biology, physics, chemistry); and (2) it should be non-circular—that is, it should not explain structure of a given complexity with components of equal complexity. Both connectionist (Bullock and Grossberg 1988; Churchland and Sejnowski 1989) and dynamical behavioral control (Turvey and Kugler 1984) theories have criticized contemporary information-processing theories of behavioral control along these lines.

The latter perspective (e.g., Schmidt, R.A. 1982a, 1982b) maintains that control is achieved because the actor has knowledge of a motor program—an internal representation that prescribes the activity of the effector components underlying the movement. The first criticism is based on how the assumptions of the existence of such an internal representation mesh with how the other sciences conceive the structure of action systems. The information-processing perspective on behavior is based on positing a new domain of nature that is not continuous with the other sciences. Information processing rests on the existence of rule-governed, rate-independent processes that manipulate symbol strings (information), not unlike those found in systems of formal logic (Turvey and Kugler 1984). These rate-independent processes are to be contrasted with rate-dependent, law-based processes found in physical systems studied by the other sciences. In fact, Newell and Simon's symbol string hypothesis (1981) suggests that symbolic, rate-independent formal processes are to be found nested within intelligent, physical systems. Further, it has been suggested that these *logic* processes are complementary to the dynamical, rate-dependent physical processes (Pattee 1972, 1977) investigated in the other sciences. Hence, the theoretical foundation of the information-processing view of behavior in general and the motor program view of motor control in particular is the philosophical premise of a new domain of nature in which the processes of intelligent behavior live. The criticism is that this drastic theoretical tactic destroys the continuity between the psychological and physical processes underlying behavior: A qualitatively different theory is required for understanding psychological processes.

The second criticism of the information-processing perspective and theory of motor programs rests on the isomorphic relation between the knowledge structure posited (rules in a motor program) and the motor act it explains. Because rules are basic mechanisms for establishing a process and the positing of a rule has very few constraints on it, what results in theorizing is taking out loans of intelligence (Dennett 1971): Prescriptions for producing an action are proposed rather than principles that let the phenomena (e.g., actions) emerge ''for free'' as an a posteriori consequence of these principles. For example, explanatory concepts, such as motor programs and mental regression, needed for determining the parameters set in motor programs (Schmidt, R.A. 1975) are mechanisms that produce the motor behavior phenomena in question. But how these mechanisms relate to the other constraining details of the system and what deeper principles underlie their existence is not obvious and needs to be determined. The problem is whether such an explanation is forthcoming. Churchland and Sejnowski (1989) think not and suggest that the information-processing theory of mental processes, the so-called Boolean dream (Hofstadter 1982), has the same form of explanation as the homuncular theory of reproduction, in which the structure of the developed neonate is posited as latent in the structure of the sperm. The problem with this kind of theory is that the key structure it is attempting to explain is posited in toto, without determining its origins or its ecology (i.e., how it fits into its context).

By contrast, connectionist theories explain behavioral control in a manner continuous with the biological structure of the computational machinery under study (i.e., the brain) and show how greater (behavioral) complexity emerges from the interaction of simpler biological structures. However, the power of connectionism comes not only from the lower-level complexity and biological nature of the processing units, but also from the processes written over them. In the connectionist theory, information processing is the result of a distributed interaction of microcomponents leading to the greatest constraint satisfaction (McClelland, Rumelhart, and Hinton 1986), or stated another way, states of the greatest harmony (Smolensky 1986). Churchland and Sejnowski (1989) point out that this processing mode is that of a dynamical system: "We model information processing in terms of the trajectory of a complex nonlinear system" (29). How is this? A dynamical system is a system whose components have an "interplay of forces" and "mutual influence" such that the system "tends towards equilibrium or steady states" (Kugler, Kelso, and Turvey 1980, 6). Hence, information processing in a connectionist system can be understood as dynamical and operating in concordance with physical organization strategies found generically in nature. The benefit of such a theory is that the dynamical information processing yields several properties required by any theory of cognitive systems (i.e., graceful degradation, generalization). Best of all, dynamical processing produces these properties for free, without needing specific mechanisms that exclusively produce these properties.

By the criteria for a good theory of behavioral control suggested previously, the connectionist theory is a good theory. It uses dynamical principles of organization found at all scales of nature to form its theory of control and demonstrates how more complex processes emerge from the interaction of simpler components. However, one can argue that the connectionist theory does not go far enough in investigating the dynamical principles underlying behavioral control (Schmidt, Treffner, and Turvey 1991). The argument is as follows. If dynamical principles of organization are generic archetypal themes that nature uses at all scales (Turvey 1990), we not only need to understand the dynamical processes of the nervous system, but also the dynamical processes that neural dynamics are nested within. The nervous system is nested within an action system and the action system within an environment. The perspective of the dynamical theory of behavioral control is that the dynamics of these higher order levels of structure constrain (and at some point determine) the structure of the neural dynamics. Hence, we need a theory of the dynamical processes at these levels and the neural level if we are going to have a complete theory of behavioral control.[1]

The organizations of behavioral systems that are more macroscopic than the level of neural dynamics are in the domain of the dynamical theory of action. It asks the following questions: What are the processes on the level of the action system and its interaction with the environment? What are the physical principles that are harnessed to organize the structured components at this scale of analysis? The dynamical theory of action answers: There are dynamical laws written in terms of the self-organizing, dynamical properties of the effector systems viewed as complex physical systems (Kugler, Kelso, and Turvey 1980; Kugler and Turvey 1987; Schöner and Kelso 1988); and there are laws written at a more macroscopic space/time scale that include the environmental properties and the information that specify them, namely, laws of perceiving and acting (Turvey and Carello 1988).

---

[1] Another criticism of the connectionist perspective is that many current models are general purpose. Many models can be used to generate any type of behavior. Assuming that all connectionist models implement a process of dynamical constraint satisfaction, the problem of being too general purpose is not an intrinsic consequence of the constraint-satisfaction process, but a consequence of choosing which constraints must be dynamically satisfied. One hopes that, with increasing influence from neuroscience and studies of perception and action, the constraints within connectionist models can become more ontologically specific and such models can become more special purpose.

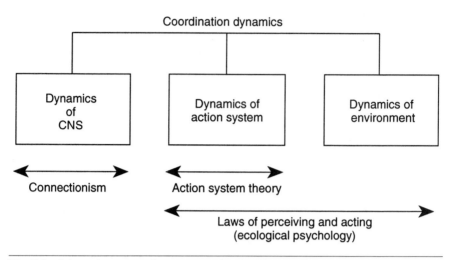

Fig. 8.1   Schematic representing processes involved in coordination dynamics. The coordination and control of an action is determined by the interrelationship of dynamical regularities at the neural, effector, and environmental scales.

Then how do the dynamics of the microscopic nervous system interface with the macroscopic dynamics? It is evident that the dynamics of the central nervous system (CNS) are latent in the organization at these macroscopic scales. However, the dynamical perspective assumes (and this is where the emphasis deviates from connectionist theories) that the processes in the CNS are among many processes that determine the coordination and control of actions and interactions with the environment. In the performance of actions, processes at three levels (CNS, action system, and environment) are necessarily entwined (fig. 8.1). The consequence of this fact cuts both ways. The connectionist must note that the functioning of a neural network underlying an action must deal with the self-organizing tendencies of the action system and its interactions with the environment. Further, the dynamical theorist must bear in mind that the functioning of action systems necessarily involves neural constraints. The dynamical theorist, however, suggests that the cause or responsibility for an action structure is distributed across the three levels. The CNS is not the proprietary level of explanation—the organization of the CNS necessarily depends on how much action organization occurs because of the self-organizing tendencies at the action system and environmental levels.[2]

Consequently, a theory of behavioral control from the dynamical perspective is an interdisciplinary one that aims at continuity across levels of analysis and disciplines (physics, biology, and psychology) and attempts to explain how physical principles (dynamical principles of self-organization) organize a biological organism's behavior. In contrast with the information-processing perspective, knowing how to perform an action is not having a prescription (representation) for producing it, but relating

---

[2]Examples of these self-organizing tendencies at levels macroscopic to the CNS include the mass-spring properties of the action system and the omnipresent constraint of gravitational acceleration.

to the laws of nature so they can be used to create the required organization.[3] Further, to anticipate slightly, the dynamical perspective views learning new behaviors, not as acquiring rules of action encoded in the CNS, but acquiring new relationships to the laws of nature that underlie the action system and the way it relates to environmental properties (Shaw and Alley 1985).

DYNAMICAL THEORY OF MOTOR CONTROL

The organization of an action has been described as consisting of two stages. An organism first assembles an action and second guides the action to its completion. These two stages have been referred to as coordination and control, respectively (Kugler, Kelso, and Turvey 1980). Traditionally, two levels of explanation have been used to understand these processes—one psychological, one physiological. On the psychological or intentional level, the description is of the assembly or coordination of the action system with respect to a goal state or intentional directedness to some aspect of the environment. The control of an action is about applying rules of action based on the occurrent environmental circumstances specified by perceptual information. On the physiological or machine level, the description is of the coordination of the action system with respect to efferent neural signals that appropriately potentiate the necessary effectors and their metabolic resources. In contrast the control of an action is defined in terms of an afferent tuning of the effector system states.

We can view the dynamical theory of action as positing a level of analysis embracing both these descriptions by a common language of explanation operating on the psychological and physiological levels—the language of dynamics. In place of the psychological and neural entities (e.g., motor programs, central pattern generators) traditionally proposed to understand coordination and control, the dynamical approach posits dynamical structures of control spread across several (neural, metabolic, biomechanical, informational, and environmental) levels of analysis and whose functioning is bound by dynamical principles of self-organization. Such a dynamical control regime is a functionally defined entity that describes the configuration of an organism's action system required to pursue a given goal. The evolution of this concept needs to be described.

Such control structures have been referred to over the years by several terms: coordinative structures (e.g., Easton 1972; Turvey 1977), functional synergies (e.g., Bernstein 1967), special-purpose devices (Fowler and Turvey 1978), or task-specific devices (e.g., Bingham 1988). Originally, Bernstein (1967) theorized that control

---

[3]Maintaining that knowing how to perform an act does not require a mental prescription does not deny that some structural correlate exists tantamount to a representation in the knower, but takes issue with what this structural correlate is. There is no doubt that structural changes occur within the actor when a skill is learned. The question is what these changes consist of. The claim of the dynamical perspective is that the structural changes should not be viewed as the addition of a prescription of action components (i.e., a list of what to do when, encoded in symbol strings), but an emergent set of relations between CNS, action system, and environmental properties that form a dynamical system and manifest the action as an aposteriori consequence. Hence, what we propose is that what is learned should be understood as a set of physically encoded dynamical predilections of an action system rather than a motor program.

of an action system as complex as those in a biological organism was possible only because functional synergies—linkages of muscles and joints with each other and external reactive forces—were established in the effector performing a given action. Bernstein and his students maintained that the synergies consisted of *equations of constraint* written over the action system upon the assembly of the action. These equations of constraint specified dependencies of the controllable degrees of freedom on each other, reducing the total number of parameters to be controlled. Hence, the implementation of a synergy left the action system in many ways self-equilibrating and independent from central control.

Dynamical Equations of Constraint

Early research following the Bernstein approach discovered the functional synergies that underlie such coordinations as locomotion (Shik and Orlovskii 1976), aiming at a target (Arutyunyan, Gurfinkel, and Mirsky 1969), and maintaining an upright posture during breathing (Gurfinkel et al. 1971). A second round of Bernstein theorizing in the 1970s and 1980s (Turvey 1990) has sought a basis for equations of constraint in natural physical principles. The goal has been to find how much of the action system organization can be understood in terms of dynamical constraints, in terms of archetypal regimes of self-organization that occur in nature's many scales (Turvey 1988). To understand this second round of Bernstein theorizing, we must explore what is meant by dynamical constraints or regimes.

A dynamical system is a general class of systems which have components that are mutually influencing and settle, tend toward, or relax to equilibrium or attractive states. The study of qualitative dynamics (Abraham and Shaw 1982; Thompson and Stewart 1986) reveals that in nature, attractor states take a limited number of forms. In dynamical analysis of a given system, variables are chosen that represent the possible states the system can enter. The relations of these variables can be represented by geometric models of all possible states, called the *state space* of the system. A *trajectory* represents the evolution or history of a system's states in a state space. Further, special trajectories are used to categorize the kind of dynamic the system displays. These trajectories that represent the asymptotic behavior of the system as time approaches infinity are called limit sets. The most probable limit sets are *attractors*. The simplest state space topology is a point attractor, in which all the trajectories within part of the state space are drawn to a single point. Another common topology is the periodic or limit cycle attractor in which the trajectories are attracted to a closed orbit. Higher order attractors with more complex limit set topologies also exist (e.g., quasiperiodic attractors, chaotic attractors). Though these higher order attractors can take many forms, they can be characterized by a few qualitative features that define them as integral classes of dynamical states.

A dynamical system can be represented by a state space plus a variable that represents a conserved quantity governing the time evolution of the system. This *potential* variable (or just potential, for short) underlies the flow of the system (i.e., the way that the trajectories evolve). Differences in the magnitude of the potential quantity over the state space will cause trajectories in the state space to flow to regions where the potential is less. The regions of the state space where the potential

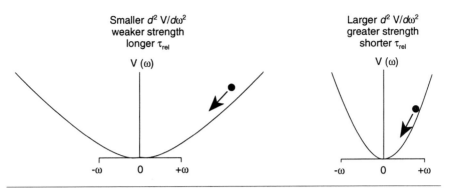

Fig. 8.2 Potential functions representing dynamics with a relatively weak attractive region (*left*) and a strong attractive region (*right*). The minima of the potential wells are dynamical point attractors. The concavity of the well determines the attractor strength.

is least define regions of attraction and are the attractors of the system. The change rate of the potential surrounding the attractive area determines the stability or strength of an attractor. There are two means of measuring the stability or degree of attraction of an attractor. If one knows the potential function, $V(\omega)$, that describes the potential field of an attractor over a single state variable ω, then $d^2V/d\omega^2$ measures the degree of concavity of the attractor's surrounding area (the potential well).[4] The larger the $d^2V/d\omega^2$, the more concave is the potential well, and the more stable or strong is the attractor (see fig. 8.2). Alternatively, stability can be measured empirically by the relaxation time of the system, τ_{rel}—the time it takes the system to return to equilibrium following a perturbation. If one knows τ_{rel}, the concavity of the potential well can be estimated ($d^2V/d\omega^2$); further, if one knows the $d^2V/d\omega^2$, one can estimate the relaxation time (Schöner 1989).

Using the tools of qualitative dynamics, researchers following Bernstein have provided several examples of coordinated movement in which dynamical principles of self-organization are operating. Three classes of coordinated movement have succumbed to a dynamical analysis. Discrete movements in which a limb segment is brought to a specific point in space have been characterized as having the dynamics of a point attractor (Feldman 1966a, b, 1986; Kugler, Kelso, and Turvey 1980; Schöner 1990). Rhythmic movements in which a limb segment is oscillated about a joint have been characterized as limit cycle oscillators having periodic attractors (Beek and Beek 1988; Kay et al. 1987; Kugler, Kelso, and Turvey 1980; Turvey et al. 1988). Further, coordinated interlimb rhythmic movements in which two limb segments are oscillated simultaneously about different joints have been characterized by coupled oscillator regimes that have point attractors at two relative phase angles corresponding to the in-phase (0°) and anti-phase (180°) modes of limb phasing (Haken, Kelso, and Bunz 1985; Schmidt et al. 1991; Schmidt, Shaw, and Turvey 1993; Sternad, Turvey, and Schmidt 1992). We will present examples of specific

---

[4]Just what constitutes the state variable ω is an empirical question. In the work on interlimb coordination, the state variables of the potential function models have been indices of the coordination (e.g., relative phasing or timing).

dynamical control structures that embody these regimes in a later section that explores the dynamical perspective's empirical research on motor learning.

Environmental Sources of Constraint

The second round of Bernstein theorizing has suggested that the equations of constraint underlying functional synergies make use of generic physical principles of self-organization, and that functional synergies can include in their organization noneffector environmental properties. Classically, a functional synergy was a linkage of biomechanical properties constrained to produce a specific goal. Environmental influences on action coordination were deemed external and were viewed merely as inputs to action system control processes. Fowler and Turvey (1978) argued that environmental constraints specified by perceptual information must also be understood as part of the organization of action system synergies. They maintained that for each unconstrained degree of freedom in a muscle linkage, there was an environmental property to constrain its magnitude. The ramification of this proposal is that to understand action, one must understand the functioning of the effectors and the environmental context for the action—namely, those properties in the environment that a coordinated action must refer to in order to accomplish its final state.

Recent work on movement coordination with environmental events has led dynamical researchers to reevaluate where to find the boundary of the dynamical control structures. Research has found that coupled oscillator dynamics operate across a perceptual media (optic array) in the coordination of rhythmic movements between two people (Schmidt, Carello, and Turvey 1990; Schmidt and Turvey 1994) and between a person and an optical metronome (Wimmers, Beek, and van Wieringen 1992). Schmidt, Carello, and Turvey (1990) report that certain properties of dynamical change associated with the breakdown of the alternate phasing of limbs are found in between-person coordination (in which two persons coordinate the swinging of their lower legs) and in within-person bimanual coordination (e.g., Haken, Kelso, and Bunz 1985; Kelso, Scholz, and Schöner 1986). This work highlights the fact that anatomical or neural connections are not necessary to support dynamical control regimes—perceptual media can support these dynamical regimes as well.

The environmental constraints on the functioning of an action system, rather than being seen as an external influence on the dynamic, can be seen as a process intrinsic to the dynamics of the action system control structure. In a manner of speaking, an environmental constraint is one of the multiple constraints that must be dynamically satisfied. A dynamical control structure can contain both action system components and environmental properties specified by perceptual information. So, in terms of the self-organizing processes that underlie action organization, the boundary between the actor and the world functionally does not exist.

In sum, the dynamical theory of motor control maintains that underlying coordinated action are control structures that have the following characteristics. They are governed by the laws of self-organization, *dynamical* principles. The multiple constraints (effector and environmental) on producing the action are mutually influencing, and their interaction brings dynamical steady states that satisfy these constraints. They are *multileveled* entities, in that multiple constraints occur at several nested levels—environmental, biomechanical, metabolic, and neural. These control structures are inherently *informational* entities because they are constrained by environmental properties specified by perceptual information. They are *intentional*, task-specific structures assembled to achieve a particular action goal. They are *soft-assembled*, temporary structures in that many constraints that coordinate the appropriate degrees of freedom are temporary and exist only until the goal or intention is fulfilled.

Finally, because of their dynamical nature, these control structures are relatively *autonomous* from central control in their functioning. One might say that the macroscopic processes of self-organization on the action system and environmental level leave the CNS processing open for other computations. Hence, the macroscopic, self-organizing nature of these control structures may be the basis for the lack of attentional intervention required to perform certain skilled activities. When performing skilled actions, the movements seem to be performed on their own. The perceptual tuning based on occurrent environmental or action system circumstances appears automatic. By participating in the laws of nature, the burden of controlling one's movements is diminished. The apparent ease in performing a skilled action pattern, however, needs to be contrasted with the difficulty of learning a skilled action pattern. From the dynamical point of view, learning a skilled behavior is tantamount to becoming attuned to the laws of dynamical self-organization that govern an effector system. So, by participating in these laws the control of an action becomes effortless.

DYNAMICAL THEORY OF MOTOR LEARNING

What is the process by which the laws of a dynamical control structure are learned so actions can be performed skillfully? If we consider assembling the appropriate functional synergy as the coordination of an action and the functioning of the synergy (maintaining equilibrium) its control, we can understand becoming skillful at producing the action as optimizing this synergy. Fowler and Turvey (1978) have suggested that "learning the laws means that the actor has become attuned (perceptually) to the consequences of different configurations of the multiple constraints on the control structure: An [action] has structure, and discovering an optimal self-organization is in reference to those variables of stimulation corresponding to environmental and biokinematic relations that specify the essential features of the [action] the actor is to perform" (6). They further suggest that such optimization corresponds to the increased use of the effectors' reactive forces, their interaction with the environment in action production (Bernstein 1967), and the increased number of degrees of freedom that are being controlled. The former process increases the control structure autonomy, whereas the latter increases the regime's stability and movement fluidity (Newell and van Emmerik 1989; van Emmerik and Newell 1990).

The description of the control structure optimization is similar to the optimization description in connectionist models of the CNS. We can understand the evolution of the control dynamic to more optimized states as increasing the number of "satisfied constraints" (cf. harmony, Smolensky 1986) that influence the control structure's functioning. The difference between the perspectives is that the constraint satisfaction occurs on multiple levels of organization (neural, metabolic, biomechanic, and environmental) in the dynamical theory, rather than just the level of neural networks in connectionist theory.

By what process are these new constraints satisfied? What guides the actor to new configurations of his or her action system that are more optimal than old configurations? The dynamical perspective's claim is that perceptual information is available that can guide the learner to more optimal states (Fowler and Turvey 1978; Kugler and Turvey 1987; Newell et al. 1989). The basis for this assertion is the ecological theory of perception (Gibson 1979). Any event (either in the environment or in an actor's effector system) has both kinetic and kinematic consequences. An event's kinetics (essentially the structure of its forces) generate kinematic patterns (a geometric representation of the force structure changing over time). If these patterns become manifest in perceptual (visual, auditory, haptic) media, they can be used as information that specifies the generating event and its properties. Much research (e.g., Bingham 1987; Runeson and Frykholm 1981) has demonstrated that kinematic invariants can specify properties of events and their future consequences (for example, time-to-contact [Lee 1980]). The kinematic patterns that specify the latter are particularly important for the prospective control of behavior—coordinating your movements with an event that is in the future.

The performance of an action by an action system is a kinetic event that generates kinematic patterns specific to the properties of the action in the visual and haptic/proprioceptive perceptual media. The kinematic patterns are information that specifies properties, such as the changing stability of the action system during the movement. Each implementation of a control structure (a certain equation of constraint) is characterized by kinematic/perceptual consequences that specify the stability of that execution. The initial implementations of a new action regime have dynamical equations of constraint that are nonstationary—they keep collapsing and need to be reassembled differently. Further implementations on subsequent attempts to produce the same action (e.g., in a learning experiment these are trials or sessions) will be more or less stable. With these stability changes, higher-order kinematic invariants are produced. This is information that specifies prospectively how the control structure needs to be reparameterized (i.e., how the equation of constraint needs to be changed) to increase its stability (i.e., constraint satisfaction) toward an optimally organized control regime (Fowler and Turvey 1978). Because of the reciprocity of action and perception in the evolution of an optimal action system organization, the learning process has been characterized as the exploration of a *perceptual-motor work space* of the nascent control regime (Kugler and Turvey 1987; Newell et al. 1989). In sum, the kinetics (forces) of a motor act generate consequent kinematic invariants in perceptual media. These kinematic patterns specify (a) how well the action is satisfying the task's multiple constraints (its stability), and (b) how the control structure must be changed to increase the stability of the regime through increased constraint satisfaction.

Necessity of a Learning Dynamic

Note that to describe the acquisition of skilled behavior dynamically, one must describe two levels of change or two dynamics—one nested within the other. First we have the dynamic associated with the control structure assembled for producing the action—the coordinative structure or task-specific assembly of an effector system. This dynamic is set up when the action system is assembled under a particular dynamical equation of constraint. It exhibits a series of states that may or may not accomplish its intended goal, depending (more or less) on the optimality of the dynamical constraints employed. This action system control structure is nested within a higher-order dynamic that operates on it and represents the optimization of the control structure's equation of constraint. We can view the functioning of a dynamical control structure and its optimization as two separate dynamical processes. This bipartite organization is analogous to activation rules and learning rules in connectionist models: The former specify how input signals are to be processed in each activation of the network, and the latter specify how the weights between processing units must be changed to process the input information more optimally.

How is this higher-order learning dynamic to be understood? First, it occurs at a longer time scale. If the control structure dynamic proceeds at a time scale of minutes and seconds, then the learning dynamic proceeds at a time scale of hours and days. The index of the former is the relaxation time (τ_{rel}) of the control structure dynamic—the time it takes for the system to return to its equilibrium state from a perturbation. The index for the time scale of the latter is the relaxation time of the learning dynamic—the learning time τ_{learn} (Schöner 1989). This latter quantity is the time it takes for optimization of the action system dynamic to occur. The phenomenon of learning to learn that occurs in learning several related skills would be tantamount to strengthening the learning dynamic, thereby decreasing the relaxation time of the learning dynamic τ_{learn}.

Second, the learning dynamic is intentional in that a future goal state determines the changes it undergoes. This future state is the state of being more skilled—to have an optimal equation of constraint governing the action system. Learning a skilled action must then be doubly intentional. Two intentions must be present: one specifies the goal of the action (e.g., catch the ball, stably produce a 3:2 polyrhythm) and another specifies the goal of the learning (i.e., become more skilled). Related to this point, these two intentions are temporally nested: The former occurs at a shorter time scale than the latter. One can then characterize learning a skill as two temporally nested intentional dynamics.

How does the future state of the system determine its present action or learning behavior? How does this acausal process function? In the traditional cognitive perspective, the future state is available now because it is an internal representation that contains the future in the present. How does the dynamical perspective account for this, given that it eschews internal representation? We have previewed the answer in the discussion of the perceptual-motor work space.

The intention to become more skilled in producing action sets up a learning dynamic to optimize the lower-order action control structure (i.e., coordinative structure). The consequence of this learning dynamic is that information about this optimization process becomes available in the perceptual-motor work space, including information about the learning dynamic's attractor—the optimal organization of the action system control structure. The kinematic flows created in the perceptual media (haptic, visual) can specify the attractor state of the system (e.g., the optimal state of an equation of constraint) even if that system is not at that state.

Where a dynamical system's attractor state is within its state space is specified by the force structure of the system's dynamic and, hence, by the patterning of the system's kinematics generated by the force structure. The kinematic information about the learning dynamic's final state emerges a posteriori from the reparameterization of the control structure's dynamics. From the dynamical perspective, becoming increasingly attuned to the possibilities specified by these kinematic invariants is tantamount to what the information-processing perspective would call building an internal representation of the to-be-learned action. No doubt, this attunement process will cause changes in the structure of the action system that will represent (in some sense of that word) the new coordination potential. This change in the action system's dynamical structure is not a new prescription for the coordination, but a change in the equations of constraint latent in the action system.

DYNAMICAL MODELS OF SKILL LEARNING

The rest of this chapter will review research on the dynamics of motor learning. We follow a theoretical treatment of the formal requirements for a dynamical theory of learning by an examination of several empirical studies that have investigated the dynamics of learning interlimb coordinations.

A Learning Dynamic Formalism

Bob Shaw and colleagues (Shaw and Alley 1985; Shaw et al. 1992) suggest that to model the optimization process in skill learning, the mathematical models need to be advanced beyond those used in modeling the dynamical control structures of action systems. Traditionally, ordinary differential equation (ODE) models have been used to capture the self-organizing dynamics of action systems. Many of these models capitalize on the mass-spring nature of muscles and joints for which ODE models exist. These mass-spring ODEs have been helpful in dynamically modeling both discrete (Feldman, 1966a, b, 1986; Schöner 1990) and rhythmic hand movements (Beek and Beek 1988; Feldman 1966b; Kay et al. 1987). Shaw maintains that to model the changes such control dynamics undergo, a more complex dynamical formalism is necessary, namely, equations of the integro-differential form (Volterra equations). This kind of equation is a higher-order function or *functional* that has one function nested inside another. These equations have been used in hereditary mechanics in which the initial condition of a system is updated to reflect hereditary influences: The hereditary higher-order function sets up the initial conditions of (i.e., reparameterizes) the lower-order control functions.

Note how this nested relationship of the two functions is analogous to that of the learning dynamic and the action system control structure dynamic. Shaw and colleagues use the change in the behavior of a mass-spring system through repeated pulling as an analogy to the evolution of an action system control structure. The Volterra equation that models the hereditary changes of a mass-spring system is found in the following equation,

$$y(t) = kx(t) + \int_0^t k(t, s)x(s) \qquad (8.1)$$

where $y(t)$ and $x(t)$ represent the behavior and the state of the spring, respectively, at time t, k is the spring's initial stiffness, $k(t, s)$ is an operator that represents the hereditary influences on the stiffness and is a function of the pulls on the spring in the interval from 0 to t. The behavior of the spring at any point in time t is a function of (a) the product of its original disposition (k) and present state ($x(t)$), plus (b) the integral of the hereditary changes in its behavior from the time of its original state to time t.

The argument made by Shaw and colleagues is that models similar to this are necessary for modeling the optimization of an action control structure's functioning because they intrinsically capture the evolutionary nature of the system being modeled. As already noted, the structure of the Volterra equations captures the property that the evolving action systems have two nested dynamics—one at a fast time scale (state at time t) and one at a slow time scale (hereditary changes from 0 to t). That the hereditary influence represents a reinitialization of the system's *equation of constraint* (in this case, the mass-spring system's stiffness) allows one to draw the analogy between the hereditary influence and a learning dynamic that parameterizes the action control structure.

In addition, Shaw and colleagues suggest that these Volterra equations cannot only model learning based on historical feedback influences (i.e., increased constraint satisfaction resulting from experience performing the action), but also learning based on anticipatory feedforward influences (i.e., increased constraint satisfaction resulting from the anticipation of prospective future events). These "may manifest themselves as the cumulative effect of expectancies . . . that act on the current state of the learner" (Shaw et al. 1992, 7). In addition to providing a basis for modeling past and future influences on optimizing an action control structure, Shaw suggests that one must model the optimization of both the information pickup (afferent) processes of a dynamical control structure and the optimization of the energy control (efferent) processes. Accordingly, the strategy that he and his colleagues propose is no less than a system of Volterra equations that addresses the optimization of feedback, feedforward, afferent, and efferent subprocesses of a dynamical control structure (fig. 8.3).

Learning a New Bimanual Phasing Pattern

Schöner and colleagues (Schöner 1989; Schöner, Zanone, and Kelso 1992; Zanone and Kelso 1992) have modeled the learning dynamics involved in acquiring a specific skill—a novel bimanual phasing pattern. Bimanual phasing has two natural modes. Limbs can be easily coordinated so they are at the same place in the cycle at the same time (the in-phase mode or 0° relative phase) or so they are in opposite places in the cycle at the same time (the anti-phase mode or 180° relative phase). The two relative phase modes have been found differentially stable: The anti-phase mode is less stable than the in-phase. The bimodality and differential stability of bimanual phasing have been observed in experiments in which the 180° mode breaks down at higher frequencies of oscillation, whereas the 0° mode does not (Kelso 1984;

Organism perspective
(action)
hereditary

Environment perspective
(perception)
anticipatory

Energy control (+ t)

$$y(t) = kx(t) + \int_0^t K_O(t,s)\, x(s)\, ds$$

Equation 1

$$x(t) = ky(t) + \int_0^t K_E(t,s)\, y(s)\, ds$$

Equation 2

Information (observation) (− t)

$$x(t) = ky(t) + \int_0^t K_O^*(s,t)\, y(s)\, ds$$

Equation 3

$$y(t) = kx(t) + \int_0^t K_O^*(s,t)\, x(s)\, ds$$

Equation 4

Fig. 8.3 A system of Volterra equations proposed by Shaw and colleagues of the various subprocesses involved in learning. Equations 1 and 3 represent the optimization of efferent subprocesses, and Equations 2 and 4 represent the optimization of afferent subprocesses. Equations 1 and 2 address optimization of feedback processes, and Equations 3 and 4 address the optimization of feedforward processes. Hence, Equation 1 represents the historical tuning of efferent subprocesses, Equation 2 represents anticipatory tuning of efferent subprocesses, Equation 3 represents the historical tuning of afferent subprocesses, and Equation 4 represents the anticipatory tuning of afferent subprocesses.
Reprinted from Shaw et al. 1992.

Schmidt, Carello, and Turvey 1990) and in experiments that measure the degree of steady state fluctuation of the two modes (Turvey et al. 1986; Schmidt, Shaw, and Turvey 1993).

These properties have been explained as being a consequence of the dynamical nature of the control structure underlying bimanual coordination. The limb effector system acts identically to a regime of two coupled oscillators in which the coupling strength between the oscillators decreases with increasing frequency. Haken, Kelso, and Bunz (1985) have employed a coupled oscillator regime with point attractors at relative phase angles of 0° and 180° to model the bimanual phasing properties. The dynamical description of relative phase angle (ϕ) between the two rhythmic units is defined as the differential equation:

$$\dot{\phi} = -dV(\phi)/d\phi + \sqrt{Q}\varepsilon \tag{8.2}$$

where the rate of change of the relative phase angle ($\dot{\phi}$) is a function of the rate of change of the potential function, $V(\Phi) = -a \cos(\phi) - b \cos(2\phi)$, and a stochastic noise term of magnitude Q. The minima of the potential function (where its rate of change and, hence, $\dot{\phi}$'s rate of change is 0) indicate the stable relative phase patterns attainable by the coupled oscillatory regime. Fig. 8.4 demonstrates that these stable points of the regime appear at $\phi = 0°$ and $\phi = 180°$, and that the stable point at $\phi = 180°$ is less stable (more shallow) than that at $0°$. Increasing the oscillation frequency of the regime will lead to an annihilation of the $180°$ attractor, assuming that the coupling strength a decreases with increasing frequency, when the coupling strengths achieve the ratio of $b/a = 0.25$. In sum, this coupled oscillator dynamic predicts the bimodality and differential stability observed in bimanual limb phasing.

Such an equation of constraint represents the intrinsic dynamic of the bimanual rhythmic movement effector system and provides the foundational initial state that any new, to-be-learned bimanual phasing pattern would build on. Schöner's modeling (1989) and Zanone and Kelso's (1992) experiment capitalize on this in their investigations of learning a new relative phase pattern at $90°$. They are interested in modeling and observing how the behavioral attractor layout evolves as a function of practicing a new relative phase relation at $90°$.

In the empirical investigation, Zanone and Kelso employ a relative timing task (Tuller and Kelso 1989; Yamanishi, Kawato, and Suzuki 1980) in which the index fingers are paced by two visual metronomes, one for each finger. The frequency of the metronomes was fixed, but their relative timing was varied. The subject's task was to flex each index finger in accord with the metronome specific to that hand. Thus, by manipulating relative timing of the two metronomes, the experimenter could control the bimanual relative phasing that the subject was to produce. Past research with the task has demonstrated that the intrinsic dynamic of bimanual phasing constrained subject performance (fig. 8.4). Subject performance was (a) best when the task requirement corresponded to one of the two intrinsic patterns (at $0°$ or $180°$ relative phase), (b) deviated in the direction of the intrinsic phase mode at other required relative phasing values, and (c) showed increasing variability as the required relative phase deviated from the intrinsic phase values.

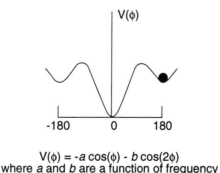

$$V(\phi) = -a\cos(\phi) - b\cos(2\phi)$$
where a and b are a function of frequency

Fig. 8.4   Haken, Kelso, and Bunz (1985) model of the attractors in bimanual, interlimb phasing. The potential function has attractor points (i.e, potential minima) at $0°$ and $\pm180°$ representing the in-phase and anti-phase interlimb phase modes, respectively. The minima at $\pm180°$ are more shallow than at $0°$, denoting the lesser stability of the anti-phase mode of interlimb phasing.
Adapted from Haken, Kelso, and Bunz 1985.

Zanone and Kelso were interested in whether having subjects practice a non-intrinsic relative phase pattern, in this case one at 90°, they could observe an evolution in the underlying attractor layout of the dynamical control structure at the practiced pattern from its initial intrinsic state to one with a new stable point. Note in fig. 8.4 that 90° relative phase is an unstable fixed point—a dynamical repeller. A system initialized to this state will, as a consequence of small perturbations, relax to one of the two stable fixed points at 0° or 180°. Each subject practiced a 90° phasing pattern by tracking the visual metronome for three blocks of five learning trials on five consecutive days. Between learning sessions and at the beginning and end of each day, subjects performed *scanning* trials in which they had to track a changing relative phasing pattern (0° to 180° in 15° steps for 20 s) of the visual metronome in their bimanual movements. With this procedure, the stability of each relative phase pattern, as measured by the deviation from environmentally specified relative phase ($\phi - \psi_E$) and the rate of change of ϕ ($\Delta\phi$), could be evaluated throughout the learning period. The attractive (most stable) regions of the relative phase dynamic could be identified by this method.

Fig. 8.5 is a schematic that represents the changes in stability observed between the first and fifth days of the experiment. Initially, the intrinsic phase patterns (at 0° and 180°) were more stable and the to-be-learned pattern at 90° was least. However, by the fifth day, the practiced phase pattern at 90° was as stable as the intrinsic modes. In some subjects the increase in stability of the 90° pattern was yoked with a decrease in stability of the 180° pattern, suggesting that, not only was a new regime of stability attained, but an old regime of stability was lost.

How are these changes in the stability of relative phase patterns to be understood in terms of the dynamical model of relative phase control structure (fig. 8.4)? Required is a model of the learning dynamic, the higher-order, long time scale dynamic that attracts the bimanual phasing toward the to-be-learned pattern specified by the environment (in this case, the visual metronome). Stated another way, we need a process that reconfigures the control structure governing the relative phasing to have an attractor state at this to-be-learned phase pattern. Schöner (1989) suggests

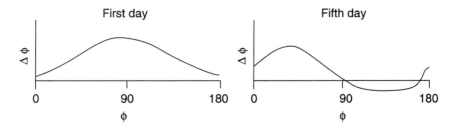

Fig. 8.5   Representation of changes in stability of phase patterns in learning a novel bimanual phasing pattern. The to-be-learned phase pattern at 90° evolves from an unstable phase pattern (large $\Delta\phi$) on the first day to a stable phase pattern (small $\Delta\phi$) on the fifth day. Reprinted from Schöner et al. 1992.

that the learning dynamic in the present task can be represented by the following equation:

$$\dot{\psi} = -\tau_{learn}^{-1}\sin\left((\phi - \psi_{tbl})/2\right) \qquad (8.3)$$

where τ_{learn} is the time scale of the learning, ϕ is the present relative phase angle, and ψ_{tbl} is the to-be-learned relative phase angle. The change rate of acquiring the relative phase pattern ($\dot{\psi}$) is a function of the difference between the present and the to-be-learned pattern and the intrinsic time scale of the learning. This latter magnitude, τ_{learn}, is set by experience with similar tasks (i.e., strength of learning to learn) or strength of information specifying ψ_{tbl}. The consequence of the interaction of the control structure dynamic (Equation 8.2) and the learning dynamic (Equation 8.3) can be represented by a potential function that combines the two dynamics (Zanone and Kelso 1992):

$$V_\psi = V(\phi) - c\,\cos((\phi - \psi)/2). \qquad (8.4)$$

where c is a measure of the strength of the learning dynamic. Fig. 8.6 represents the potential wells of this function with ψ_{tbl} set to 0°, 180°, and 90°. The consequence of the operation of the learning dynamic is a stable relative phase minima at the environmentally specified phase pattern—0°, 180°, or 90°. As Zanone and Kelso point out, the shape of the consequent potential is a product of the competition or cooperation between the intrinsic dynamic and the dynamic necessary to produce the to-be-learned pattern. In fig. 8.6, the wells for $\psi = 0°$ and $\psi = 180°$ have a greater concavity than that for $\psi = 90°$. In addition, the minima of the former two are more singularly defined points, whereas that of the latter is defined more as a

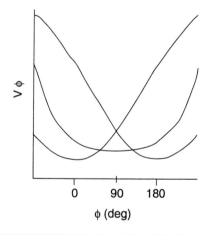

Fig. 8.6 Potential function solutions of Equation 3 that represent the interaction of the control structure dynamic and the learning dynamic when the to-be-learned pattern is at 0°, 90°, and 180° (from *left* to *right*). The consequent concavity of each well denotes the amount of competition or cooperation between the intrinsic dynamics of bimanual phasing (Equation 2) and the dynamics required by the new pattern. See text.
Adapted from Zanone and Kelso 1992.

region. Both properties indicate that the evolution of the $\psi = 90°$ attractor involves a competition between the intrinsic dynamic of the phasing control structure and the to-be-learned dynamic, whereas the evolution of attractors nearer to $\psi = 0°$ and 180° attractor involves more cooperation.

The modeling of the learning dynamic by Schöner (1989) suggests that when competition exists between the intrinsic and the to-be-learned dynamics, there is the possibility that the genesis of a new behavior attractor will annihilate attractor regimes in the original dynamics of the control structure and produce abrupt transitions to new attractive regions. The consequence of the new, emergent equations of constraint is that the original capabilities of the control structure may be eliminated. Zanone and Kelso provide evidence from their experiment that (a) subjects often demonstrated an abrupt acquisition of the 90° relative phase pattern, and (b) after they had acquired this relative phase pattern, the stability of 180° phasing was decreased. Although there were individual differences in these effects, the latter substantiates the idea that a restructuring of the control regime occurs, rather than just another control regime being added. The abrupt transition suggests that this was a process of dynamical change (e.g., a phase transition).

Generally, one can understand the problem of acquiring a skill as "how an extrinsically imposed task [goal] becomes internalized . . . so that [this goal state] acts as an intrinsic rather than an extrinsic constraint" (Shaw et al. 1992, 4). For example, how does the extrinsic constraint of an instructor's movement become internalized by the learner? Zanone and Kelso suggest that the process of learning a new movement pattern is tantamount to transforming environmental information into memorized information. In a different language, the environmental constraint specified in the perceptual media can be used to transform the equation of constraint (in this case, Equation 2) employed by a dynamical control structure. Moreover, Schöner and colleagues provide a dynamical process (Equation 3) that describes this internalization of constraint.

What does this process correspond to in the activity of the organism? How does the equation of constraint get rewritten? One can think about the process as an exploration of a perceptual-motor work space, because the information being memorized at each point is specified in the proprioceptive information that the kinetics of the movement pattern being performed generate. Because the exploration of the work space is a goal-directed, intentional process, the operation of a learning dynamic such as that in Equation 3 can be interpreted as an intentional process that emerges from (a) having the goal to learn the new movement pattern, and (b) using (proprioceptive) information available that specifies how to transform the equation of constraint (i.e., information that specifies the parameterizations of greatest stability) to produce the goal state. The learning process then has two descriptions—one intentional (just stated) and one deterministic (Equation 3). Are these not contradictory? The two descriptions are not contradictory if one countenances the possibility that intentional systems participate in deterministic dynamics, and their nondeterministic intentional behavior emerges from the sheer volume of the deterministic processes interacting across many levels of space/time (Shaw and Kinsella-Shaw 1988).

Learning a New Bimanual Frequency-Locking Pattern

Schmidt et al. (1992) is another example of a study that provides a dynamical analysis of the acquisition of an interlimb coordination pattern. In the Zanone and

Kelso study, the movement pattern to be acquired was coordinating two limbs rhythmically moving at the same frequency (1:1 frequency lock) but with different phase locks or lags. In the Schmidt et al. study, the interlimb pattern to be acquired was the bimanual coordination of effectors moving at different frequencies. What was studied was the 2:1 frequency locking of weighted handheld pendulums swung from the wrist in the sagittal plane. The coordination of such wrist-pendulum systems in a 1:1 frequency lock has been studied to reveal the self-organizing principles underlying the coordination of rhythmic movements (e.g., Kugler and Turvey 1987; Turvey et al. 1988; Schmidt, Shaw, and Turvey 1993). The novelty of such a paradigm lies in the fact that the rhythmic units have well-defined frequency preferences as gravitational pendulums. This allows the experimenter to manipulate environmental constraints on the coordination—for example, how much the intrinsic frequencies of the rhythmic units are competing and how much the frequency competition between the units aids or opposes the coordination required by the task. In the Schmidt et al. experiment, the challenge was to acquire a 2:1 frequency lock with rhythmic units whose ratio of uncoupled frequencies was 1:1.

The intrinsic gravitational predilection of the rhythmic units made performing a 2:1 frequency lock more difficult than other 2:1 coordinations frequently encountered (e.g., finger tapping). The subject's task was to find linkages between the laws of interlimb coordination control structures and the laws that govern the pendulums to be controlled. To put it another way, they were to find the equations of constraint that guide the interaction of these two systems. The tack Schmidt et al. took was (a) to use a measure of mean frequency-locking ratio and stability of frequency locking to estimate the change in the dynamics across the learning sessions, and (b) to describe the property of the equation of constraint that was being tuned to produce this change in stability.

Subjects were instructed to oscillate the pendulum in the right hand so it was at twice the frequency of that in the left hand. They performed this coordination pattern for 20 trials in 12 sessions that were on average 1.5 weeks apart. Both the deviation from a perfect 2:1 frequency ratio (right/left) and standard deviation of this frequency ratio decreased asymptotically across the 12 sessions (fig. 8.7). These measures were used as indices of the topology underlying the dynamics' potential function. The deviation from intended frequency lock indexes the average position of the potential well's minima. Assuming a constant amount of stochastic noise emerges from the microstructure of the effector system, the standard deviation of the behavior can be used as an index of the concavity of the potential well governing the control structure dynamic producing the behavior: the less steep the sides of the well, the greater the standard deviation (Schöner 1989). The argument is that a stochastic perturbation of a given magnitude of force will travel through the force field of the potential well less far when the rate of change of the potential is less steep. Assuming these relations, the evolution of the attractor governing the 2:1 frequency lock can be estimated (fig. 8.8).

Presumably, the subjects are attuned to information in a perceptual-motor work space that specifies how the manipulation of certain parameters of the control structure's equation of constraint will affect the control structure's stability. But what are the parameters being manipulated to cause the optimization? Schmidt et al. examined the relative phasing of the two limbs to answer this question. Intuitively,

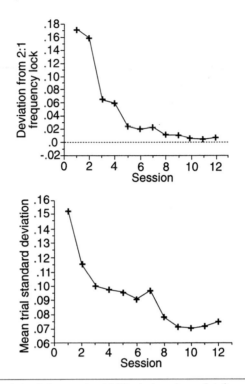

Fig. 8.7   Representation of changes in stability in learning a 2:1 frequency-locking pattern with wrist-pendulum systems. Experimental mean data from four subjects representing the deviation from 2:1 frequency lock (*top*) and fluctuation in frequency-locking behavior (*bottom*) across 12 learning sessions.

the 2:1 frequency-locking task requires specific relative movements of the two wrist-pendulum systems. Accordingly, Schmidt et al. examined a measure that captures the macroscopic space/time order of the 2:1 task—the pattern of oscillator phase velocities. The oscillator phase velocity is the change rate of its phase angle around its limit cycle. In perfectly 2:1 frequency-locked oscillators the phase velocity of the faster oscillator is always twice that of the slower oscillator; hence, the phase velocity ratio (PVR) will be a constant value of 2. By calculating the time series of the PVR for the learning trials, an index of the relative movements of the limbs was attained. Neither at the beginning nor at the end of their training were the relative movements like those of perfectly frequency-locked oscillators. The time series exhibited an oscillation about the criterial value of 2 with greater deviation in oscillation in the first compared with the last session. A spectral analysis of the PVR across the 12 sessions revealed a gradual evolution of spectral peaks at integer multiples of the frequency of oscillation (fig. 8.9). Such a consequent spectral pattern indicates that, although phase locking per se was never achieved, phase entrainment was. This is consistent with previous research on 1:1 frequency locking, which demonstrates that even when the rhythmic units are at the same tempo their relative phase is not at a constant value (i.e., for 1:1 frequency lock, PVR = 1 or ϕ =

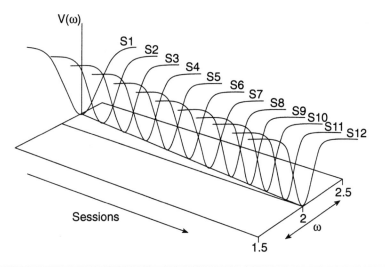

Fig. 8.8 Schematic representation of the evolution of the movement control structure's potential field across learning sessions. The position of the potential minima was estimated using the deviation from a 2:1 frequency lock, and the concavity of the attractive regions was estimated using the fluctuation in frequency-locking behavior. See text. Reprinted from Schmidt et al. 1992.

constant). Further, 1:1 frequency-locked limbs exhibit a similar spectrum of relative phase with peaks at integer multiples of the frequency of oscillation (e.g., Schmidt et al. 1991).

Just what is underlying these spectral peaks and why their topology changes under certain conditions is still a question. Two hypotheses have been ventured: (a) the peaks correspond to specific rhythmic subprocesses of perceptual constraint, for example, perceptual anchor points (Beek 1989; Schmidt et al. 1991), or (b) the peaks are a manifestation of the different oscillatory dynamics of the component oscillators—for example, the left hand is a harmonic oscillator and the right hand a van der Pol (Schmidt, Shaw, and Turvey 1993). Whichever explanation is forthcoming given the evolution of the PVR spectrum across learning trials, the case can be made that the subject learning to perform a 2:1 frequency-locking pattern is manipulating certain parameters of a dynamical equation of constraint about a specific phase entrainment pattern. The parameters may be becoming attuned to certain kinds of perceptual information needed for the entrainment pattern (Hypothesis 1) or may be the adjusting of the weights on the various friction and stiffness functions (Beek and Beek 1988) underlying the oscillatory behavior of the rhythmic units (Hypothesis 2).

The Schmidt et al. (1992) study demonstrates that acquiring a movement pattern can be understood in terms of learning the intrinsic lawful regularities of a movement control structure and how they must be reparameterized to produce the successful control of certain environmental objects (in this case, the pendulums) that have their own dynamics. This study highlights that, necessarily, the coordination dynamics underlying an action result from the interplay of organismic, environmental, and

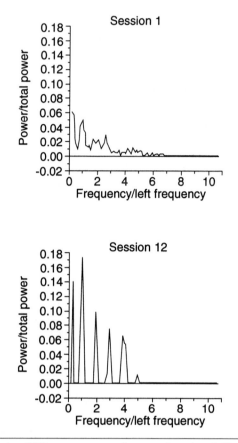

Fig. 8.9 Representative PVR power spectra from sessions 1 and 12. As the frequency-locking pattern is learned, the power comes to be packaged at integer multiples of the frequency of oscillation.
Reprinted from Schmidt et al. 1992.

task constraints (Newell 1986). Hence, the emergent control structure is written across both the actor and his or her environment, and the glue that binds them is the dynamical law of coupled oscillators harnessed by the intention associated with the task goal.

Learning to Cascade Juggle

Another skill in which the dynamics of coordination are obviously written across the actor and the environment is in juggling. In this activity, the actor must countenance not only the constraints of his effector system (organismic) and those of the environment (balls in the gravitational field), but more important, those associated with the task of juggling. The bimanual oscillatory movements of a juggler's hands are under severe temporal and spatial task constraints (Beek 1989; Beek and Van

Santvoord 1992). The first is expressed in the equation of the common juggle, which governs the order of all balls and both hands. The timing of the juggling hands and juggled balls must be such that the "ratio of hand cycle times to ball cycle times must (on average) be equal to the ratio of the number of hands to the number of balls" (Beek and Van Santvoord 1992, 87). In symbols:

$$\text{Number of hands/number of balls} = t_{\text{hand}}/t_{\text{ball}} \tag{8.5}$$
$$= (t_1 + t_u)/(t_1 + t_f)$$

where t_1 is the time that the hand is loaded, t_u is the time that the hand is unloaded, and t_f is the time that the ball is in the air. This is a temporal constraint that must be satisfied to perform any juggling task.

In addition, Beek (1989; Beek and Turvey 1992) has argued that more microscopic task constraint must be satisfied, one that expresses the internal organization of a juggling hand cycle time. What must be satisfied is a stable mode-locking relation between the dynamical regime responsible for the subtask of transporting the ball and the one responsible for the longer task of rhythmically moving the hand. Beek maintains that the stablest mode locking between these two regimes is attained when the ratio of the time that the ball is loaded to the time of a full hand cycle is .75. In symbols, $t_1/t_{\text{hand}} = .75$. This ratio indexes a "preferred point in the dynamical work space of cascade juggling" (Beek and Van Santvoord 1992, 87). This latter constraint was confirmed with expert cascade jugglers. In juggling five and seven balls, the ratio of the time the ball is in the hand to the total cycle time of the hand was very close to .75 on average across different hands. In juggling three balls, the observed ratios were close to but not exactly .75 ($\bar{x} = .70$) and were more affected by t_{hand}. The variability in the ratio when juggling three balls suggests, Beek maintains, that skilled jugglers often prefer less stable points in the work space because they offer a flexibility not available at the stable points; and that operating close to but not in stable mode lock is a property of skilled behavior. The deviation of the t_1/t_{hand} ratio from .75 can be interpreted as a measure of the frequency modulation or quasiperiodicity in the mode locking of the two regimes and may map onto the flexibility or flair of the juggle. In Beek's words, the actor "seeks the best of two worlds: stability and reliability on the one hand (mode locking), and adaptability and flexibility on the other hand (modulation)" (Beek and Van Santvoord 1992, 93).

Beek contends that the process of learning to juggle is three staged. Each stage employs a greater degree of constraint satisfaction. In the first stage, the actor must satisfy the basic constraints of the common juggle equation. The degree of satisfaction of this constraint can be measured by an index

$$z = \{[(N/H) - 1] \, (t_1/t_f)\} + (Nt_u/Ht_f) - 1, \tag{8.6}$$

derived from Equation 5 using the experimentally acquired t_1, t_f, and t_u. In an experiment in which 20 previously unskilled subjects were taught to juggle in 10 half-hour sessions, the z values decreased to near 0 as the number of cycles juggled increased in the first 5 sessions.

The second stage of juggling corresponds to optimizing the internal organization of the juggling hand cycle, that is, developing a t_1/t_{hand} ratio of .75. In the same experiment, Beek found that for the slow learners, the t_1/t_{hand} ratio was greater than

.75 at session 4 but not significantly different from .75 at session 7 or 10. Alternatively, the faster learners had already achieved $t_1/t_{hand} = .75$ by session 4 but by session 10 their ratio was significantly less than .75 ($t_1/t_{hand} = .73$). These results indicated that the slower learners reached stage 2 of learning to juggle between session 4 and session 7, and the faster learners reached it by session 4. Finally, the third stage of juggling was revealed only in the faster learner group in that they had a t_1/t_{hand} ratio that was significantly less than the theoretically derived preferred ratio of .75 by session 10. This suggests that these jugglers could maintain a stable juggle with a degree of flexibility. The subjects had learned to modulate the mode locking and to explore the space around the mode lock at $t_1/t_{hand} = .75$. In so doing, they could balance the stability of their performance with adaptability, the hallmark characteristic of the third stage of juggling.

Learning to juggle is tantamount to reconfiguring the intrinsic dynamics of the bimanual rhythmic movement control structure to function in accord with the required task constraints. Notice that in achieving this goal the actor has to satisfy the intrinsic constraints of the bimanual control structure, the environmental constraints of the balls, and the task constraints of the action. The dynamical process of constraint satisfaction involved here is identical in the abstract to that described in learning in connectionist machines (Churchland and Sejnowski 1989; Smolensky 1986). Satisfaction of the multiple constraints means the discovery of an equilibrium or steady state relation between the necessary constituents of an action. This process of constraint satisfaction underlies the evolution of the attractor layout of the control structure dynamics. However, the constraint satisfaction processes discussed here are at the macroscopic level of the eco-niche rather than that of the neural net. This is not to suggest that constraint satisfaction on the neural level doesn't occur or is irrelevant, but only that it is part of a constraint satisfaction process that includes the properties of the action system and the environment.

SUMMARY

The dynamical theory of motor learning is based on the dynamical theory of motor control. Rather than provide a prescription for the organization of an action, this approach to motor control seeks to understand how action emerges based on generic dynamical principles that precipitate self-organization. The dynamical theory of motor control is similar in this respect to many connectionist theories that seek to give a principled account of the presence of behavioral order. Contrary to connectionist theories, the dynamical theory does not suppose that the nervous system is the proprietary level of explanation of action. In addition to neural components, the organization of an action is constrained by components and dynamical processes at the level of the action system (e.g., coordinative structures) and at the level of the environment (e.g., the laws of perceiving and acting).

Instead of rules of action being encoded in the CNS, the dynamical theory of motor learning proposes that acquiring a skilled action requires becoming attuned to the physical laws that govern a dynamical control structure. These laws are not housed in a specific mechanism (like the CNS), but are distributed across all the components of the action system and environment, and as such, are (in a manner of speaking) incorporeal. Because perceptual information is available about the state of the dynamical control structure and how it changes over reparameterizations of the control structure, information exists in a perceptual-motor work space about the direction the reparameterizations should take to reach an optimally configured equation of constraint. Learning the laws that govern an effector system results from exploring this perceptual-motor work space with the intention of achieving a more stably configured control structure. This long time scale, intentional process can also be given a deterministic description in terms of the operation of a learning dynamic—a higher-order process of dynamical relaxation to an optimal state in which multiple constraints are uniquely satisfied so the functioning of the control structure can be referred to as skilled.

REFERENCES

Abraham, R.H., and Shaw, C.D. 1982. *Dynamics—The geometry of behavior. Pt. 1: Periodic behavior.* Santa Cruz, CA: Ariel Press.

Arutyunyan, G.H., Gurfinkel, V.S., and Mirsky, M.L. 1969. Investigation of aiming at a target. *Biophysics* 13:536-538.

Beek, P.J. 1989. Juggling dynamics. PhD diss., Free University Press, Amsterdam.

Beek, P.J., and Beek, W.J. 1988. Tools for constructing dynamical models of rhythmic movement. *Human Movement Science* 7:301-342.

Beek, P.J., and Turvey, M.T. 1992. Temporal patternings in cascade juggling. *Journal of Experimental Psychology: Human Perception and Performance* 18:934-947.

Beek, P.J., and Van Santvoord, A.A.M. 1992. Learning the cascade juggle: A dynamical systems analysis. *Journal of Motor Behavior* 24:85-94.

Bernstein, N. 1967. *The coordination and regulation of movements.* London: Pergamon.

Bingham, G.P. 1987. Kinematic form and scaling: Further investigations on the visual perception of lifted weights. *Journal of Experimental Psychology: Human Perception and Performance* 13:155-177.

Bingham, G.P. 1988. Task-specific devices and the perceptual bottleneck. *Human Movement Science* 7:225-264.

Bullock, D., and Grossberg, S. 1988. Neural dynamics of planned arm movements: Emergent invariants and speed accuracy properties during trajectory formation. *Psychological Review* 95:45-90.

Churchland, P.S., and Sejnowski, T.J. 1989. Neural representation and neural computation. In *Neural connections, neural computation,* edited by L. Nadel, L.A. Cooper, P. Culicover, and R.M. Harnish. Cambridge, MA: MIT Press.

Dennett, D.C. 1971. Intentional systems. *The Journal of Philosophy* 68:87-106.

Easton, T.A. 1972. On the normal use of reflexes. *American Scientist* 60:591-599.

Feldman, A.G. 1966a. Functional tuning of the nervous system with control of movements or maintenance of a steady posture—II. Controllable parameters of the muscles. *Biophysics* 11:498-508.

Feldman, A.G. 1966b. Functional tuning of the nervous system during control of movements or maintenance of a steady posture—III. Mechanographic analysis of the execution by man of the simplest motor tasks. *Biophysics* 11:667-675.

Feldman, A.G. 1986. Once more on the equilibrium-point hypothesis (lambda model) for motor control. *Journal of Motor Behavior* 18:17-54.

Fowler, C.A., and Turvey, M.T. 1978. Skill acquisition: An event approach with special reference to searching for the optimum of a function of several variables. In *Information processing in motor control and learning*, edited by G.E. Stelmach. New York: Academic Press.

Gibson, J.J. 1979. *The ecological approach to visual perception.* Boston: Houghton Mifflin.

Gurfinkel, V.S., Kots, Ya. M., Paltsev, Ye. I., and Feldman, A.G. 1971. The compensation of respiratory disturbances of the organization of interarticular interaction. In *Models of the structural-functional organization of certain biological systems*, edited by I.M. Gelfand, V.S. Gurfinkel, S.V. Fomin, and M.L. Tsetlin. Cambridge, MA: MIT Press.

Haken, H., Kelso, J.A.S., and Bunz, H. 1985. A theoretical model of phase transitions in human hand movements. *Biological Cybernetics* 51:347-356.

Hofstadter, D.R. 1982. *Metamagical themas: Questing for the essence of mind and pattern.* New York: Basic Books.

Kay, B.A., Kelso, J.A.S., Saltzman, E.L., and Schöner, G. 1987. Space-time behavior of single and bimanual rhythmical movements: Data and limit cycle model. *Journal of Experimental Psychology: Human Perception and Performance* 13:178-192.

Kelso, J.A.S. 1984. Phase transitions and critical behavior in human bimanual coordination. *American Journal of Physiology: Regulatory, Integrative and Comparative Physiology* 15:R1000-R1004.

Kelso, J.A.S., Scholz, J.P., and Schöner, G.S. 1986. Non-equilibrium phase transitions in coordinated biological motion: Critical fluctuations. *Physics Letters* A118:279-284.

Kugler, P.N., Kelso, J.A.S., and Turvey, M.T. 1980. On the concept of coordinative structures: I. Theoretical lines of convergence. P. 3-47 in *Tutorials in motor behavior*, edited by G.E. Stelmach and J. Requin. Amsterdam: North-Holland.

Kugler, P.N., and Turvey, M.T. 1987. *Information, natural law, and the self-assembly of rhythmic movement.* Hillsdale, NJ: Erlbaum.

Lee, D.N. 1980. Visuomotor coordination in space-time. P. 281-295 in *Tutorials in motor behavior*, edited by G.E. Stelmach and J. Requin. Amsterdam: North-Holland.

McClelland, J.L., Rumelhart, D.E., and Hinton, G.E. 1986. The appeal of parallel distributed processing. P. 3-44 in *Parallel distributed processing, explorations of the microstructure of cognition. Volume 1: Foundations*, edited by J.L. McClelland and D.E. Rumelhart. Cambridge, MA: MIT Press.

Newell, A., and Simon, H.A. 1981. Computer science as empirical inquiry: Symbols and search. In *Mind design: Philosophy, psychology, artificial intelligence*, edited by J. Haugeland. Cambridge, MA: MIT Press.

Newell, K.M. 1986. Constraints on the development of coordination. P. 341-360 in *Motor development in children: Aspects of coordination and control*, edited by M.G. Wade and H.T.A. Whiting. The Hague: Nijhoff.

Newell, K.M., Kugler, P.N., van Emmerik, R.E.A., and McDonald, P.V. 1989. Search strategies and the acquisition of coordination. P. 85-122 in *Perspectives on the coordination of movement*, edited by S.A. Wallace. Amsterdam: North-Holland.

Newell, K.M., and van Emmerik, R.E.A. 1989. The acquisition of coordination: Preliminary analysis of learning to write. *Human Movement Science* 8:17-32.

Pattee, H.H. 1972. Laws and constraints, symbols and language. In *Towards a theoretical biology*, edited by C.H. Warrington. Chicago: Aldine.

Pattee, H.H. 1977. Dynamic and linguistic modes of complex systems. *International Journal of General Systems* 3:259-266.

Runeson, S., and Frykholm, G. 1981. Visual perception of lifted weight. *Journal of Experimental Psychology: Human Perception and Performance* 7:733-740.

Schmidt, R.A. 1975. Schema theory of discrete motor skill learning. *Psychological Review* 82:225-260.

Schmidt, R.A. 1982a. More on motor programs. P. 187-217 in *Human motor behavior: An introduction*, edited by J.A.S. Kelso. Hillsdale, NJ: Erlbaum.

Schmidt, R.A. 1982b. The schema concept. P. 219-235 in *Human motor behavior: An introduction*, edited by J.A.S. Kelso. Hillsdale, NJ: Erlbaum.

Schmidt, R.C., Beek, P.J., Treffner, P.J., and Turvey, M.T. 1991. Dynamical substructure of coordinated rhythmic movements. *Journal of Experimental Psychology: Human Perception and Performance* 17:635-651.

Schmidt, R.C., Carello, C., and Turvey, M.T. 1990. Phase transitions and critical fluctuations in the visual coordination of rhythmic movements between people. *Journal of Experimental Psychology: Human Perception and Performance* 16(2):227-247.

Schmidt, R.C., Shaw, B.K., and Turvey, M.T. 1993. Coupling dynamics in interlimb coordination. *Journal of Experimental Psychology: Human Perception and Performance* 19:397-415.

Schmidt, R.C., Treffner, P.J., Shaw, B.K., and Turvey, M.T. 1992. Dynamical aspects of learning an interlimb rhythmic coordination. *Journal of Motor Behavior* 24:67-82.

Schmidt, R.C., Treffner, P.J., and Turvey, M.T. 1991. Neural networks and the first and second rounds of theorizing on Bernstein's problem. *Human Movement Science* 10:117-131.

Schmidt, R.C., and Turvey, M.T. 1994. Phase-entrainment dynamics of visually coupled rhythmic movements. *Biological Cybernetics* 70:369-376.

Schöner, G. 1989. Learning and recall in a dynamic theory of coordination patterns. *Biological Cybernetics* 62:39-54.

Schöner, G. 1990. A dynamic theory of coordination of discrete movement. *Biological Cybernetics* 63:257-270.

Schöner, G., and Kelso, J.A.S. 1988. Dynamic pattern generation in behavioral and neural systems. *Science* 239:1513-1520.

Schöner, G., Zanone, P.G., and Kelso, J.A.S. 1992. Learning as change of coordination dynamics: Theory and experiment. *Journal of Motor Behavior* 24:29-48.

Shaw, R.E., and Alley, T.R. 1985. How to draw learning curves: Their use and justification. In *Issues in the ecological study of learning*, edited by T.D. Johnson and A.T. Pietrewicz. Hillsdale, NJ: Erlbaum.

Shaw, R.E., Kadar, E., Sim, M., and Repperger, D. 1992. The intentional spring: A strategy for modeling systems that learn to perform intentional acts. *Journal of Motor Behavior* 24:3-28.

Shaw, R.E., and Kinsella-Shaw, J. 1988. Ecological mechanics: A physical geometry for intentional constraints. *Human Movement Science* 7:155-200.

Shik, M.L., and Orlovskii, G.N. 1976. Neurophysiology of locomotor automatism. *Physiological Reviews* 56:465-501.

Smolensky, P. 1986. Information processing in dynamical systems: Foundations of harmony theory. P. 194-281 in *Parallel distributed processing: Explorations in the microstructure of cognition, Volume 1: Foundations*, edited by D.E. Rumelhart and J.L. McClelland. Cambridge, MA: MIT Press.

Sternad, D., Turvey, M.T., and Schmidt, R.C. 1992. Average phase difference theory and 1:1 phase entrainment in interlimb coordination. *Biological Cybernetics* 67:223-231.

Thompson, J.M.T., and Stewart, H.B. 1986. *Nonlinear dynamics and chaos*. Chichester, England: Wiley.

Tuller, B., and Kelso, J.A.S. 1989. Environmentally-specified patterns of movement coordination in normal and split-brain subjects. *Experimental Brain Research* 75:306-316.

Turvey, M.T. 1977. Preliminaries to a theory of action with reference to vision. In *Perceiving, acting, and knowing: Toward an ecological psychology*, edited by R. Shaw and J. Bransford. Hillsdale, NJ: Erlbaum.

Turvey, M.T. 1988. Simplicity from complexity: Archetypal action regimes and smart perceptual instruments as execution-driven phenomena. In *Dynamic patterns in complex systems*, edited by J.A.S. Kelso, A.J. Mandrell, and M.F. Schlesinger. Singapore: World Scientific.

Turvey, M.T. 1990. Coordination. *American Psychologist* 45:938-953.

Turvey, M.T., and Carello, C. 1988. Exploring a law-based ecological approach to skilled action. In *Cognition and action in skilled behavior*, edited by A.M. Colley and J.R. Beech. Amsterdam: Elsevier Science.

Turvey, M.T., and Kugler, P.N. 1984. An ecological approach to perception and action. In *Human motor actions: Bernstein reassessed*, edited by H.T.A. Whiting. Amsterdam: North-Holland.

Turvey, M.T., Rosenblum, L.D., Schmidt, R.C., and Kugler, P.N. 1986. Fluctuations and phase symmetry in coordinated rhythmic movements. *Journal of Experimental Psychology: Human Perception and Performance* 12:564-583.

Turvey, M.T., Schmidt, R.C., Rosenblum, L.D., and Kugler, P.N. 1988. On the time allometry of coordinated rhythmic movements. *Journal of Theoretical Biology* 130:285-325.

van Emmerik, R.E.A., and Newell, K.M. 1990. The influence of task and organismic constraints on intralimb pen-point kinematics in a drawing task. *Acta Psychologia* 73:171-190.

Wimmers, R.H., Beek, P.J., and van Wieringen, P.C.W. 1992. Phase transitions in rhythmic tracking movements: A case of unilateral coupling. *Human Movement Science* 11:217-226.

Yamanishi, T., Kawato, M., and Suzuki, R. 1980. Two coupled oscillators as model for the coordinated finger tapping by both hands. *Biological Cybernetics* 37:219-225.

Zanone, P.G., and Kelso, J.A.S. 1992. Evolution of behavioral attractors with learning: Nonequilibrium phase transitions. *Journal of Experimental Psychology: Human Perception and Performance* 18:403-421.

Acknowledgments

During the writing of this paper, R.C. Schmidt was supported by National Science Foundation Grant BNS 9109880, a Tulane University Committee of Research Summer Grant, and a Lousiana Board of Regents Grant RD-A-23. Paula Fitzpatrick was supported by a National Science Foundation Predoctoral Fellowship. Correspondence concerning this article should be addressed to R.C. Schmidt, Department of Psychology, Box 176A, 1 College Street, College of the Holy Cross, Worcester, MA 01610-2395.

Chapter 9

Trajectory Formation in Arm Movements: Minimization Principles and Procedures

Mitsuo Kawato

ATR Human Information Processing Research Laboratories, Kyoto, Japan

Recent studies of computational neuroscience and robotics reveal the computational difficulty involved in voluntary movement control. The problems to be solved even for simple, visually guided reaching movements are not only computationally intensive but also require general principles to resolve their inherent ill-posedness. It was in the mathematical theory of partial differential equations that the notion of well-posed and ill-posed problems was developed. A problem is well posed when its solution exists, is unique, and depends continuously on the parameters that define the problem. Ill-posed problems, on the contrary, fail to satisfy one or more of these criteria. Most people cannot execute difficult movements, such as those encountered in advanced sports, because of limitations in their motor control skills and physical limitations in their biomechanical apparatus. This is the first kind of ill-posed problem (nonexistence of solution). We sometimes observe abrupt behavior changes induced by subtle changes in parameters defining motor tasks. For example, Rosenbaum (1992) systematically examined the choice of overhand grip versus underhand grip with subjects asked to grasp a handle and rotate it to a target orientation. The choice of grip was consistent within a certain range of the initial handle orientation and the target orientation, but it abruptly changed at the boundary of these regions. This is the third kind of ill-posed problem (discontinuous changes of solutions induced by small changes in parameters defining the task). Most frequently, we observe the second kind of ill-posed problem: the solution to the problem is not uniquely determined. This has been called by different names in psychology, neuroscience, and robotics: synergy problem (Bernstein 1967), degrees-of-freedom problem (Saltzman 1979), overcompleteness (Pellionisz and Llinas 1980), and redundancy problems (Paul 1981). Jordan (1990) called the second kind of ill-posed problem indeterminacy problems.

The problem of controlling goal-directed limb movements can be conceptually made into an information-processing sequence involving trajectory planning, coordinate transformation (from extracorporal space to intrinsic body coordinates), and motor command generation. These elements are required in order to translate the spatial characteristics of the movement target or goal into an appropriate pattern of muscle activation (Saltzman 1979, Hollerbach 1982). Although we do not know whether the brain solves these problems step by step or simultaneously, the three problems are all ill posed in the sense that the solution is not unique. Let us illustrate this difficulty with a simple example from a visually guided reaching movement (fig. 9.1). Consider a thirsty person reaching for a glass of water. Here, the goal of the task is to control the arm movements toward the glass to reduce thirst. To

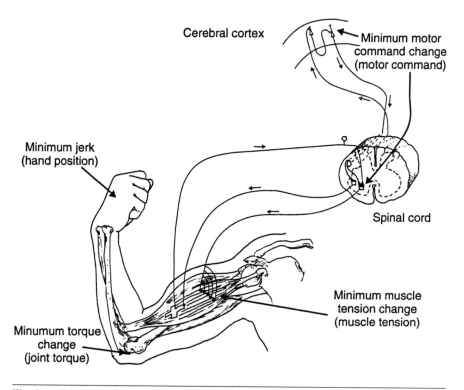

Cerebral cortex

Minimum motor command change (motor command)

Minimum jerk (hand position)

Spinal cord

Minimum muscle tension change (muscle tension)

Minumum torque change (joint torque)

Fig. 9.1 Schematic diagram to illustrate components involved in visually guided reaching movements and different spaces where variables are represented. Four different spaces are considered to represent movement conditions, movement trajectories, and motor commands. The positions of the target or obstacles are represented in three-dimensional Cartesian space. The hand position in this coordinate system can be measured by the visual system. For movements, joint torques are generated from muscle tensions. Muscle activation levels are controlled by the nervous system. The minimum jerk model is defined in the Cartesian coordinates of the hand position, and can solve the trajectory formation problem. The minimum torque change model is defined in the joint torque coordinates, and can solve the trajectory formation problem, the inverse kinematics problem, and the inverse dynamics problem up to the joint torque. The minimum muscle tension change model is defined in the muscle tension coordinates, and solves the previous three problems up to the muscle tension. The minimum motor command change model is defined in the motor command coordinates of the central nervous system, and can solve the previous three problems up to the motor commands in the brain. It is possible to impose a smoothness constraint on motor commands at different levels such as a motor neuron firing in the spinal cord, or a pyramidal tract neuron firing in the cerebral motor cortex.

achieve this goal, the brain should select one desirable trajectory in task-oriented coordinates from the infinite number of possible trajectories that lead to the glass, whose spatial coordinates are provided by the visual system (determination of trajectory). Second, the spatial coordinates of the desired trajectory are transformed in terms of a corresponding set of body coordinates, such as joint angles or muscle lengths (coordinate transformation). Finally, motor commands are generated to coordinate the activity of many muscles so the desired trajectory is achieved (control problem).

First, consider the trajectory formation problem. In visually guided reaching movements, the position of the target object is provided by the visual system. The current position of the hand is measured by the visual and/or the somatosensory system. The time required to travel from the initial position to the target position should be selected within a reasonable range, say from several-hundred milliseconds to a few seconds depending on the task conditions (i.e., whether accurate final positioning or speed is required). For simplicity, let us assume that the movement duration has already been selected. An infinite number of possible trajectories connect the initial and target positions within that time. Here, by the word trajectory we mean velocity profiles as well as path shapes. If subjects are asked to trace a curve written on a paper, for example, the path is already determined as the task requirement. Still, there are an infinite number of possible choices regarding what proportion of movement time is devoted to a given segment of the curve (i.e., velocity profile). Consequently, the trajectory formation problem is ill posed.

Second, consider the coordinate transformation problem to calculate joint angles from the desired hand position given in Cartesian coordinates. The level (task space, intrinsic body space, or motor command space) at which a desired trajectory is planned is still an open question. In visually guided reaching, a mathematical theory for trajectory planning, which will be explained later, and intuition both suggest that the trajectory is first planned in the task space. In this case the task-space coordinates of the whole trajectory should be transformed into those in the intrinsic body coordinates so muscle activation can achieve the trajectory. On the other hand, if the trajectory is planned in the body space or in the motor command space, the target coordinates should first be transformed into the coordinates in these spaces. Thus, regardless of where the trajectory is planned, coordinate transformation is essential. This problem is called the inverse kinematics problem in the robotics field. The mapping from the body coordinates to the task coordinates is called forward kinematics of the controlled object (arm and hand in fig. 9.1) because it describes the kinematic relationship. For control, the inverse of this mapping is necessary and is called the inverse kinematics problem. This problem becomes ill posed in the second sense if the number of degrees of freedom of the body coordinates is larger than the degrees of freedom of the task coordinates. In this case, it is said that the controlled object is redundant or has excess degrees of freedom. The degrees of freedom of a system is the number of variables that can be independently changed. For positioning and orienting the hand in three-dimensional Cartesian space, the degrees of freedom of the task space is 6, because we need 3 degrees of freedom each for positioning and orienting. We have at least 7 degrees of freedom for the arm and the hand: 3 at the shoulder, 1 at the elbow, and 3 at the wrist. To be precise, we have 13 overall and 9 at the shoulder. Thus, the upper extremity has at least

1 extra degree of freedom. It can easily be demonstrated by grasping an object firmly and fixing the position and orientation of the hand while still freely moving the elbow with a fixed shoulder position. This capability is helpful when trying to manipulate objects while avoiding obstacles. However, because the forward kinematics is a many-to-one mapping, the inverse kinematics cannot be determined uniquely.

Third, consider a control problem. Muscles should generate the appropriate tension for producing the desired time course of changes of joint angles. This problem is called the inverse dynamics problem in the robotics field. The forward dynamics of a controlled object is generally described by a set of ordinary differential equations with some control variables as inputs. For example, if we regard joint torques generated around the shoulder, elbow, and wrist as control inputs, changes in joint angles and joint angular velocities can be described as nonlinear functions of joint angles, joint angular velocities, and joint torques. Using the Lagrange equation in analytical mechanics, ordinary differential equations of motion can be written for arms or robot manipulators. Based on the forward dynamics, we can predict the time evolution of the state of the controlled object from its initial state and time course of control inputs. Conversely, we can view the same ordinary differential equations as a computational mechanism for calculating the control inputs required to produce a desired trajectory when the input and output are exchanged. That is, if we determine a desired trajectory, its velocity and acceleration, the necessary joint torques are uniquely determined using the same nonlinear equations. This problem is called inverse dynamics and can be solved uniquely for joint torques. However, if we regard muscle tensions as control inputs, they are not uniquely determined. A joint torque is calculated as the summation of agonist and antagonist muscle tensions around the joint, weighted by their moment arms. The infinite number of muscle tension combinations give the same joint torque, for example, well known as coactivation. Consequently, muscle tensions cannot be determined uniquely, even when the joint torque or, equivalently, when the desired trajectory in the body coordinates is specified.

Finally, in the central nervous system, there exists a vast number of neurons involved in motor control. Even if the muscle tensions are all specified, we cannot assume that the firing patterns of motor neurons in the spinal cord, corticomotoneuronal neurons in the motor cortex, rubrospinal neurons in the red nucleus, and deep cerebellar nucleus neurons in the cerebellum are uniquely determined. Here, we observe overwhelmingly excess degrees of freedom in highly distributed parallel control systems.

APPROACHES TO RESOLVING ILL-POSED PROBLEMS

Several approaches have been proposed for resolving the indeterminacy problems (see Saltzman 1979; Jordan and Rosenbaum 1989 for review). Here, we review some of them in relation to the optimization approach, which is the subject of this chapter. Bernstein (1967) proposed that connections, physical or physiological, between muscle groups can serve to partition degrees of freedom. He proposed that there are *synergies* among muscle groups that help reduce the degrees of freedom to be managed (see Turvey, Shaw, and Mace 1978, Saltzman 1979 for related concepts of coordinative structures). These theoretical predictions were recently supported by physiological evidence that the axon of a single pyramidal tract neuron in the motor cortex has multiple branches at different levels of the spinal cord (Shinoda, Yokota, and Futami 1981; Shinoda, Yamaguchi, and Futami 1986). Thus, there exists a neurophysiological coupling mechanism among activities of different muscles. The use of a feedback controller also reduces the number of degrees of freedom in the motor control network. Introducing couplings between potentially independent variables decreases the number of degrees of freedom (see the example by Saltzman 1979). Feedback controllers and coordinative structures are examples of such couplings. A hierarchical control strategy, such as the virtual trajectory control (Bizzi et al., 1984; Hogan 1984) or the task dynamic approach (Saltzman and Kelso 1987) provides specific design principles to introduce couplings between the high-level task space, the low-level body space, and the motor comand space.

If the objective of motor control is merely to decrease the degrees of freedom of the system, it is easily achieved by introducing strong couplings among all independent variables so the system behaves in a stereotyped, single fixed-action pattern. However, this is not at all desirable. The solutions adopted by the motor control network should be flexible and should adapt to various environmental conditions; otherwise, humans would not have the capacity for *motor equivalence*—the ability to achieve the same physical objective in more than one way.

In engineering, an objective function (performance index) is frequently used to select a unique solution for a problem. This is the fundamental concept of the optimal control theory (Bryson and Ho 1975). This optimal control concept was also explored in biological motor control (Hogan 1984, Nelson 1983). Nelson, for example, examined cost functions related to movement time, distance, peak velocity, energy, peak acceleration, and rate of acceleration (jerk) change. How are the optimization models that can resolve the indeterminacy problems related to these proposals of synergies, coordinative structures, feedback controllers, virtual trajectory control, task dynamics control, and so on? Are they mutually exclusive? Is one a generalization of the other? Are they partly overlapped? In my opinion the two classes of theories are different in their levels of explanation. Marr (1982), a pioneer in the field of computational neuroscience, pointed out that an information-processing device (e.g., the brain) must be understood at the following levels:

1. Computational theory
2. Representation and algorithm
3. Hardware implementation

Whereas the optimization model provides a theory at the computational level, the first class of theories provides an explanation mainly at the hardware-implementation level. The task dynamics approach or the virtual trajectory control hypothesis also provides an explanation at the second level. If one considers only the third level, the hardware-implementation level, it sometimes seems useless to discuss the degrees-of-freedom problem, redundancy, or solution uniqueness. At any given time, the central nervous system has a fixed synaptic connection pattern. Thus, if some pattern of sensory events is input to this system, it will produce a unique pattern of action. The central nervous system does not need to struggle to solve an indeterminate problem. Such problems are made up by researchers who are used to thinking that a problem in physics or engineering must have a unique solution—the nervous system is under no such constraint. A similar discussion can be found in a recent paper by Anastasio and Robinson (1990). My answer to this criticism of the main idea treated in this chapter is that such criticism neglects the first and the second levels of Marr (1982), and at the same time ignores how some nervous system connectivity pattern has been acquired during the phylogenetic and ontogenetic development. Jordan (1990) showed that the synaptic weights in a recurrent neural network can be learned from an optimization principle so the network can generate a smooth hand trajectory. It is possible to train a neural network based on the optimization principle. If one simply looks at the trained network with learned weights, one might be tempted to interpret that the wiring in the recurrent network solves the ill-posed trajectory formation problem. This explanation is certainly as true as that at the hardware level. However, it would be misleading to say that there exists no such problem as excess degrees of freedom. As a computational theory explanation, one should say that the optimization principle solves the indeterminacy problem. This is the rationale for including a chapter on the optimization principle in this volume.

In this chapter, we introduce several optimization models that are experimentally confirmed. In particular, we show that optimization at some specific space can solve the ill-posed motor control problem at that level (fig. 9.1). The minimum jerk model defined at the task space can resolve the ill-posed trajectory formation problem. The minimum torque change model defined at the intrinsic body coordinates can resolve the ill-posed inverse kinematics problem. The minimum muscle tension change model defined at the muscle level can resolve the ill-posed inverse dynamics problem. Finally, the minimum motor command change model defined in the central nervous system can resolve indeterminate motor control problems. We also introduce optimization procedures that produce various optimization trajectories. In particular, several neural network models that solve optimization problems will be highlighted.

INVARIANT FEATURES
OF A MULTIJOINT ARM TRAJECTORY

Nelson (1983) compared velocity patterns for the same movement time and distance that are optimum with respect to different objective functions. The controlled object was a simple point mass system with a linear frictional force. Cyclic movement between two targets was examined. The following performance indices were examined: minimum peak acceleration, minimum physical energy, minimum jerk, constant stiffness, minimum peak velocity (impulses), minimum time, and maximum distance. In this case, the velocity patterns of the minimum jerk, constant stiffness, and minimum energy were similar. Thus, it is difficult to choose a single optimization model by comparing predicted velocity profiles with experimental data. Multijoint arm trajectories for discrete point-to-point movements need to be examined to discriminate the predictions based on different optimization models.

One beautiful feature of human multijoint arm movement is that the hand paths between two points are roughly straight, and the hand-speed profiles are bell shaped (Kelso, Southard, and Goodman 1979; Morasso 1981; Abend, Bizzi, and Morasso 1982; Atkeson and Hollerbach 1985; Flash and Hogan 1985; Uno, Kawato, and Suzuki 1989).

We reexamined human multijoint arm movements using the OPTOTRAK (Northern Digital Inc.) position measurement system. Subjects (three males aged 28-39) were asked to move their hands from one point to another using elbow and shoulder joint rotations while their wrists were braced. Arm movement was constrained in the horizontal plane at the shoulder level. We tested the following three methods for constraining the movement in the horizontal plane: (1) hanging the elbow by a long strap from the ceiling, (2) attaching a cuff made of a low-friction material to the wrist (the table was covered by a low-friction Teflon sheet), and (3) asking subjects to hold their arms above the table about 5 cm to 10 cm before, during, and after the movement. The three methods gave essentially the same results, but the third one gave the smoothest and most comfortable movement execution. Thus, we report here the results obtained under the third condition. The path data shown in fig. 9.2 have already been published in Japanese (Koike and Kawato 1994), but the velocity and acceleration data shown in fig. 9.3 have not. Similar but more noisy data using the long strap (method 1) were previously published (Kawato et al. 1993).

Durations for movement were not given; instead, subjects could select their own comfortable duration, which ranged from 500 to 750 ms depending on the distances moved. Fig. 9.2 shows hand paths for five movements (T1→T3, T2→T6, T3→T6, T4→T1, T4→T6) taken from one subject. The hand position was sampled at 400 Hz, and each point in fig. 9.2 corresponds to one sampled position. Paths generated

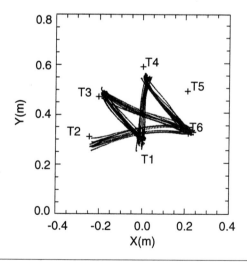

Fig. 9.2   Hand paths for five discrete point-to-point movements (T3 → T6, T2 → T6, T1 → T3, T4 → T1, T4 → T6) measured with the OPTOTRAK position measurement system.

Reprinted from Koike and Kawato 1994.

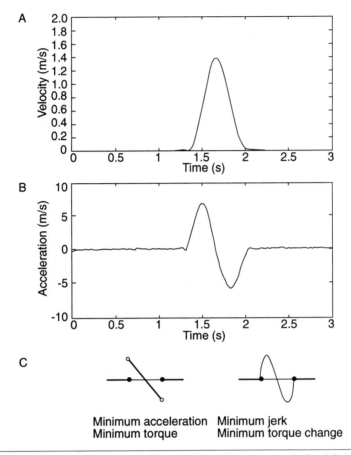

Fig. 9.3 Velocity and acceleration profiles for T2 to T6 movement in fig. 9.2. *A,* the velocity profile, *B,* the acceleration time course, and *C,* theoretical predictions of the acceleration profile by the minimum acceleration model and minimum torque model (*left*) and by the minimum jerk model and the minimum torque change model (*right*).

under 10 trials for each movement were overwritten. The positions of the initial and target points were the same as those used in Uno, Kawato, and Suzuki (1989). The origin of fig. 9.2 is the shoulder position, the X-axis is toward the right, and the positive direction of the Y-axis is forward away from the body. One can see that the trajectories are usually straight, but they are significantly curved for some movements (e.g., T2→T6). The observation that transverse paths are significantly curved but radial paths (paths away from the frontal plane of the body) are straighter will play an important role in discriminating different computational theories.

We also calculated hand tangential velocities and accelerations. Fig. 9.3A and B show them for the movement from T2 to T6 shown in fig. 9.2. Note that velocity and acceleration profiles of other movements are very similar (see fig. of Uno, Kawato, and Suzuki 1989 for velocity profiles for different paths). A second-order

Butterworth filter with a cutoff frequency of 10 Hz was used to make numerical calculations of the velocity from the position data. The same filter was again used to obtain the acceleration from the velocity.

The shape of the velocity profile agrees with previous studies and is characterized by a single peak and bell-shaped profile. The acceleration profile is more noisy because of numerical differentiation, but reveals important characteristics that can be used to reject some computational models for trajectory planning and control. When the hand is in a static state either before or after the movement, the acceleration is zero. During the movement, it is not zero except at the time of peak velocity, as we can see from fig. 9.3B. It should be emphasized that the acceleration gradually increased from zero at the beginning of the movement, and that it gradually increased (decreased in magnitude) to zero at the end of the movement (conceptually depicted in the right column of fig. 9.3C). It was not discontinuous at the beginning or the end of the movement. Consequently, optimization models such as minimum acceleration or minimum torque, which predict the discontinuity of acceleration at the beginning and end of movement, are rejected.

The end point control hypothesis (Bizzi, Polit, and Morasso 1976) is also rejected because it predicts the discontinuity of acceleration at the beginning of movement. In this hypothesis the equilibrium position jumps from the start posture to the target posture at the initiation of movement. The force or torque generated in this hypothesis is the difference between the actual position and the equilibrium position multiplied by the mechanical stiffness of the motor apparatus. Because the force jumps from zero just before movement initiation to a big value just after the movement, the acceleration that covaries with the force has a big discontinuity at the beginning of the movement.

MINIMUM JERK MODEL

To account for the kinematic features of human multijoint arm movements such as those explained in the previous section, Flash and Hogan (1985) proposed a mathematical model, the minimum jerk model, which assumes that the trajectory followed by a subject's arm minimizes the square of the movement jerk (rate of change in acceleration), integrated over the entire movement:

$$C_J = 1/2 \int_0^{t_f} \left\{ \left(\frac{d^3X}{dt^3} \right)^2 + \left(\frac{d^3Y}{dt^3} \right)^2 \right\} dt. \qquad (9.1)$$

eHere, (X, Y) are Cartesian coordinates of the hand, and t_f is the movement duration. Flash and Hogan (1985) showed that the unique trajectory predicted by this equation agreed well with data on movements made in front of the body. Let us explain this in more detail.

It can be mathematically shown that the optimal solution of the minimum jerk model for each coordinate axis has the form of a fifth-order polynomial in time using the Euler-Poisson equation. The fifth-order polynomial function has six unknown parameters that should be specified to determine the solution. In the case of a discrete, point-to-point movement, the six parameters are uniquely determined from the six boundary conditions at the beginning and the end of movement. The velocity and acceleration of the hand are zero before and after the movement (4). The initial and final hand positions are given (2). Consequently, the following pair of equations is derived as the time course of X and Y coordinates of the hand position:

$$X(t) = X_0 + (X_0 - X_f)(15\tau^4 - 6\tau^5 - 10\tau^3), \qquad (9.2)$$
$$Y(t) = Y_0 + (Y_0 - Y_f)(15\tau^4 - 6\tau^5 - 10\tau^3).$$

Here, $\tau = t/t_f$ is a normalized time ($0 \leq \tau \leq 1$), and (X_0, Y_0) and (X_f, Y_f) are the Cartesian coordinates of the initial and final hand positions. Readers are encouraged to ascertain that each of these equations satisfies the six boundary conditions. The predicted trajectory for a discrete point-to-point movement is a straight line because the temporal dependence of X and Y are identical as expressed in the second term of the equations. The trajectory is characterized also by a perfectly symmetrical bell-shaped speed profile. Thus, the prediction is in qualitative agreement with the data shown in fig. 9.2 and 9.3.

The minimum jerk model can predict hand trajectories for via-point movements (fig. 9.4) and point-to-point movements. The model reproduced not only the qualitative features of trajectories but also the quantitative details. The minimum jerk

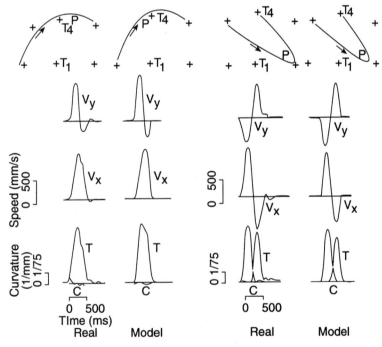

Fig. 9.4 Comparison of real data (*left, Real*) and theoretical prediction based on minimum jerk model (*right, Model*) for two kinds of via-point movements.
Reprinted from Flash and Hogan 1985.

model was the first optimization model that was experimentally confirmed and thus epoch making in the field of trajectory optimization in biological motor control. It also has important implications for trajectory planning and motor control. The minimum jerk model was based solely on the kinematics of movement, independent of the dynamics of the musculoskeletal system. It is successful only when formulated in terms of the hand motion in extracorporeal space, and fails when defined in terms of, for example, the joint angles. This is because the minimum jerk model predicts straight trajectories in the space where the objective function is defined. The minimum jerk model defined in joint angle space predicts straight paths in the joint angle space, but these are overly curved in Cartesian space when compared with the experimentally observed data. Thus, the minimum jerk model implies that the trajectory is first planned in extrinsic space. It also implies that the brain should adopt a hierarchical control strategy: trajectory planning at the task space, and motor control in the body space.

The minimum jerk model requires a smooth hand trajectory (i.e., the smoothest possible movement in the sense of the third derivative of the position). One natural question here is whether other smoothness criteria such as minimum acceleration or minimum snap (fourth-order temporal derivative of the position) can predict real data equally well. Using the Euler-Poisson equation, it can be shown that if the nth-order derivative of the position is minimized, the optimal solution becomes the $(2n-1)$ order polynomial function of time. Thus, the minimum acceleration trajectory becomes a third-order polynomial. Then the acceleration profile of this trajectory becomes a straight line and must have large discontinuities at the beginning and the end of the movement, as shown in fig. 9.3C. Thus, the lower-order smoothness model is rejected from the experimental data such as that in fig. 9.3B, which did not show large discontinuities of acceleration either at the beginning or the end of the movement. Note that for the single-joint cyclic movement, predictions by the minimum jerk model and the minimum acceleration model cannot easily be discriminated (Nelson 1983). The minimum snap trajectory, on the other hand, becomes a seventh-order polynomial function and has eight parameters to be specified. Thus, we need to specify the trajectory jerk at the beginning and the end of the movement as well as other boundary conditions regarding position, velocity, and acceleration. If the boundary values of the jerk were chosen in the same manner as those of the minimum jerk trajectory, the minimum snap trajectory would be identical to the minimum jerk trajectory. For parsimonious reasons, we prefer the minimum jerk model to the minimum snap model or any other higher-order model because it contains the smallest number of unknown parameters.

MINIMUM TORQUE CHANGE MODEL

The minimum jerk model is simple and beautiful, and quite powerful in reproducing experimental data. It is also attractive in that a unique optimal solution can be analytically obtained when only the movement time and kinematic positions of the initial, via-, and target points in the task space are provided. Simplicity and uniqueness are virtues of this model but, at the same time, its possible drawbacks. That is, the uniqueness of the solution might be too strong in the sense that the model predicts a single unique trajectory regardless of various conditions in the environment or in the motor task itself.

If a major objective of motor control is merely to decrease the degrees of freedom in the system, this can be easily achieved by introducing strong couplings among all independent variables so the system behaves in a stereotyped, single fixed-action pattern. However, this is not at all desirable. The solutions adopted by the motor control network should be flexible and should adapt to various environmental conditions; otherwise, humans would not have the capacity for *motor equivalence* or *equi-finality*—the ability to achieve the same physical objective in more than one way. However, because the minimum jerk model is a kinematic model, it cannot adapt planned trajectories in extrinsic space to different dynamic aspects involved in the motor task, environment, and motor apparatus, such as the inertial characteristics of manipulated objects, force field, or physical parameters of the arm.

Based on the idea that movement optimization must be related to movement dynamics, Uno, Kawato, and Suzuki (1989) proposed the following alternative quadratic measure of performance:

$$C_\tau = 1/2 \int_0^{t_f} \sum_{i=1}^{m} \left(\frac{d\tau_i}{dt}\right)^2 dt, \qquad (9.3)$$

where, τ_i is the torque fed to the ith of m actuators. Here, the performance measure (objective function) is the sum of the square of the change rate of the torque, integrated over the entire movement. One can see that C_τ (Equation 9.3) is related to C_J (Equation 9.1) because the change rate of torque is locally proportional to the jerk. In particular, if the controlled object is a point mass, then the force is equal to the product of the mass and acceleration. Thus, minimum jerk (rate of change of acceleration) is identical to minimum force change (minimum torque change). For a multijoint, nonlinear controlled object, the two criteria are different. In particular, it must be emphasized that C_τ depends critically on the dynamics of the musculoskeletal system, not just on the kinematics.

Here, I note that using the minimum torque change model is much more difficult than using the minimum jerk model. In the minimum jerk model, the user can be ignorant of the actual values of joint torques or physical parameters of arm dynamics, but the minimum torque change model requires the user first to estimate physical parameters of the arm, then numerically estimate the joint torques. In more detail, we need to execute the following three steps to derive predictions of the minimum torque change model. First, we need to develop a dynamical model of the arm. For example, Lagrangean equations of the two-link model of the upper arm and the forearm should be derived. Second, we need to estimate physical parameters of this dynamical model based on a subject's arm geometry. Lengths, masses, center of masses, inertia moments of the two links, and viscosity values at joints should be estimated. We estimated these values before we measured trajectories of a subject. Thus, parameter estimation is by no means parameter fitting to the observed kinematic data. We cannot predict beforehand how changes in estimated physical parameters affect calculated trajectory shapes. Third, based on the derived dynamical model with the estimated physical parameter values, we should calculate a unique trajectory using some numerical program. This computation is exactly the solution to the nonlinear optimization problem that has long been studied in optimal control engineering. Thus, many efficient computer programs are available for solving the problem. However, the user needs to understand the numerical method.

I must emphasize that there exists no parameter fitting in the previous procedure when physical parameter estimation is based only on a subject's arm geometry. Because the dynamical model of the arm is determined beforehand, the predicted minimum torque change trajectory is automatically and uniquely derived. Thus, one can disprove the model if predicted trajectories are significantly different from the observed trajectories.

For movements between pairs of targets in front of the body, predictions made by both these models have agreed well with experimental data. However, movement trajectories under the minimum torque change model (Equation 9.3) are different from those under the minimum jerk model (Equation 9.1) in four other behavioral situations. In one situation, data already support the minimum torque change model (Atkeson and Hollerbach 1985). The other three situations were not examined until recently. However, Uno, Kawato, and Suzuki (1989) dealt with them and found that the minimum torque change model accounted for the data better than did the minimum jerk model.

The first result by Uno, Kawato, and Suzuki (1989) concerned what happened when the starting point of an arm was to the side of the body and the end point was in front. Here the movement path was curved under the minimum torque change model, but always straight under the minimum jerk model. The hand paths of 16 human subjects were all curved, supporting the minimum torque change model (Uno, Kawato, and Suzuki 1989).

The second result by Uno, Kawato, and Suzuki (1989) concerned movements between two points while resisting a spring, one end of which was attached to the hand while the other was fixed. Here, the minimum jerk model always predicted a straight movement path regardless of external forces. The minimum torque change model predicted a curved path and an asymmetrical speed profile for the movement with the spring. The latter predictions agreed closely with the data, further supporting the minimum torque change model.

Third, Uno, Kawato, and Suzuki (1989) examined vertical movement affected by gravity. The minimum jerk model always predicted a straight path between two points. The minimum torque change model predicted curved paths for large up-and-down movements, but essentially straight paths for small fore-and-aft movements. The speed profiles were bell shaped for both movements. This outcome agrees closely with data of Atkeson and Hollerbach (1985), as one would expect from the minimum torque change model.

Another source of evidence supporting the major role of link dynamics in observed curvature comes from comparing curvatures within the horizontal plane (e.g., fig. 9.2) and within the vertical plane (Atkeson and Hollerbach 1985). For movements shown in fig. 9.2, only shoulder and elbow extension and flexion were involved.

Transverse movements were curved but radial movements were straighter. Atkeson and Hollerback (1985) also examined movements in which only the elbow and shoulder flexion and extension were involved. They found that up-and-down movement paths are outwardly convex, whereas fore-and-aft movement paths are straight. If we rotate the vertical plane 90° around the anterior-posterior axis passing through the shoulder joint, it exactly matches the horizontal plane at the shoulder level. This rotation can be achieved by 90° shoulder abduction. Then, fore-and-aft movements in the vertical plane correspond to radial movements in the horizontal plane, and up-and-down movements in the vertical plane correspond to transverse movements in the horizontal plane. This conceptual yet interesting coincidence of observed curvatures by 90° shoulder abduction makes perfect sense if the curvature difference associated with different paths comes from dynamic interactions between the forearm and upper arm. For this discussion we neglected the effect of gravity on path shapes based on a previous computer simulation (Uno, Kawato, and Suzuki 1989), and additionally adopted the theoretical argument that uniform force field does not influence shapes of optimal trajectories.

Finally, the most compelling evidence obtained by Uno, Kawato, and Suzuki (1989) concerned a pair of via-point movements (fig. 9.5). These movements involved two subcases, with identical start and end points, but with mirror-image via-points. Because of objective function C_J's invariance under translation, rotation, and roll, the minimum jerk model predicted identical movement paths with respect to roll and identical speed profiles for the two subcases. On the other hand, the minimum torque change model predicted two different paths. For the concave path, the speed profile should have two peaks. However, for the convex path, the speed profile should have only one peak. The latter predictions agree closely with the data (Uno, Kawato, and Suzuki 1989).

Summarizing these comparisons, we see that the trajectory derived from the minimum jerk model is determined only by the geometric relationship of the initial, final, and intermediate points on the movement trajectory. The trajectory derived from the minimum torque change model depends not only on the relationship among these three points, but also on the arm posture (in other words, the location of the shoulder relative to the three points) and on external forces. Empirical data suggest that the latter dependence is in fact the case. Wann, Nimmo-Smith, and Wing (1988) found that the minimum jerk model fails because of its lack of information about movement dynamics.

There are other conceptual reasons to favor the minimum torque change model over the minimum jerk model. The minimum jerk model postulates the smoothest possible trajectory in task-oriented Cartesian coordinates, whereas the minimum torque change model postulates the smoothest possible trajectory in the motor command space. This induces a difference in the model's capability to resolve the ill-posed motor control problems discussed earlier. The minimum jerk model can only determine the desired trajectory in task-oriented coordinates, and hence cannot resolve the ill-posed inverse kinematics or inverse dynamics problems for redundant manipulators. Thus, a combination of this and other approaches is needed to resolve all three ill-posed problems. Many researchers have recently taken the needed

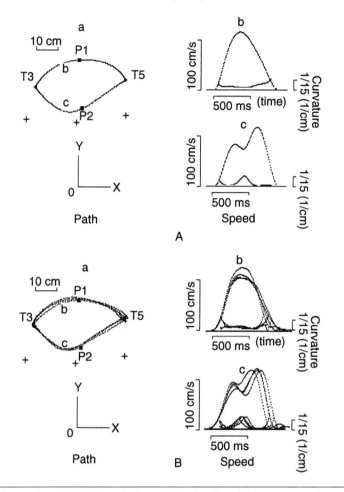

Fig. 9.5 Comparison of (A) theoretical prediction by the minimum torque change model and (B) real data for via-point movements. Free movements passing through a via-point, either P1 or P2 are considered. P1 and P2 are located symmetrically with respect to the line connecting T3 and T5. (A) Hand trajectories predicted by the minimum torque change model. *a* shows the convex path (b: T3 → P1 → T5) and the concave path (c: T3 → P2 → T5). Figs. *b* and *c* show the corresponding speed profiles (*dotted curves*) and curvature profiles (*solid curves*). (B) Hand trajectories observed in human arm movements. Four trials are depicted for each movement. *a* shows the hand paths, and figs. *b* and *c* show the corresponding speed profiles (*dotted curves*) and curvature profiles (*solid curves*). Reprinted from Uno, Kawato, and Suzuki 1989.

step-by-step computational approach (Hogan 1984; Flash 1987; Mussa-Ivaldi, Morasso, and Zaccaria 1988; Massone and Bizzi 1989). However, the minimum torque change model can resolve the ill-posed trajectory formation and inverse kinematics problems simultaneously when the locations of the desired end point, desired via-points, and obstacles are given in task-oriented coordinates.

MINIMUM MUSCLE TENSION CHANGE MODEL

Musculoskeletal systems possess muscle-tension sensors (Golgi tendon organs) as well as muscle-length and velocity sensors (muscle spindles) but no direct joint-torque sensors; joint capsule mechanoreceptor afferents are not sensitive to intermediate joint angles, but are sensitive to extremes of joint angles (Kandel, Schwartz, and Jessell 1991). Considering these physiological constraints, Uno, Suzuki, and Kawato (1989) proposed a minimum muscle tension change model, in which the following objective function is minimized.

$$C_F = 1/2 \int_0^{t_f} \sum_{i=1}^{n} \left(\frac{dF_i}{dt}\right)^2 dt, \qquad (9.4)$$

where F_i is the muscle tension generated by the ith of n muscles. Generally, the number of muscles n is much larger than the number of joints m. Here, the performance measure (objective function) is the sum of the square of the change rate of the muscle tension, integrated over the entire movement. One can see that C_F (Equation 9.4) is related to C_τ (Equation 9.3) because the joint torque is the summation of muscle forces weighted by their moment arms for the joint. If the joint torque were generated by only one muscle and if its moment arm were constant regardless of the joint angle and the same for all muscles, then the minimum muscle tension change model would become identical to the minimum torque change model. Of course, the joint torque is generated by several muscles; their moment arms are different and moment arms do depend on joint angles. Thus, the minimum muscle tension change model is different from the minimum torque change model.

Using the minimum muscle tension change model requires a more sophisticated model of the arm than the minimum torque change model. We should take into account not only the link dynamics but also the muscle geometry for the dynamic modeling of the arm. Specifically, we must determine which muscles effectively contribute to the considered movements, then estimate the moment arms of these muscles, which change with varying postures. This sounds like a formidable task, and laborious, but can be done independent of the measurement of movement trajectories. Thus, although the minimum muscle tension model possesses more parameters (related muscles and their moment arms) than the minimum torque change model, it by no means guarantees a better fit to the observed trajectories, because the muscle parameters are estimated from literature of biomechanical studies or dissection experiments and are perfectly independent of the observed trajectories.

Uno, Suzuki, and Kawato (1989) simulated discrete point-to-point trajectories (fig. 9.2) based on the minimum muscle tension change model. We used a two-link manipulator with six muscles (elbow flexor and extensor, shoulder flexor and extensor, and double-joint flexor and extensor) as a model of the human arm. We found that the minimum muscle tension change model can reproduce human data.

Dornay et al. (1995) reexamined minimum muscle tension change trajectories while using a dynamic model of a monkey's arm, which was based on biological measurement. The arm model was based on an anatomical study using Rhesus monkeys done in Bizzi's laboratory at MIT (Dornay 1991). Attachments of 17 shoulder, elbow, and double-joint muscles were marked on the skeleton. The skeleton was reassembled to the natural configuration of a monkey during horizontal arm movements. X-ray analysis was used to create a simplified horizontal model of the arm.

Dornay et al. (1995) simulated seven horizontal arm movements, including four of the five movements shown in fig. 9.2, using the monkey's model. Fig. 9.6 shows

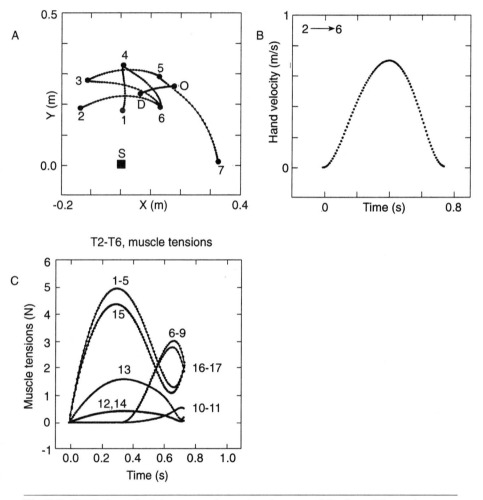

Fig. 9.6 Predictions of minimum muscle tension change model using a 17-muscle-arm model. (A) Hand paths for seven discrete point-to-point movements (T2 → T6, T3 → T5, T3 → T6, T4 → T6, T7 → T5, T4 → T1, O → D). (B) Hand tangential velocity for T2-T6 movements. (C) 17-muscle tension time courses for T2-T6 movement for the 17-muscle model of the monkey arm predicted by the cascade neural network model. 1 to 5, shoulder extensors; 6 to 9, shoulder flexors; 10 to 11, elbow extensors; 12 to 14, elbow flexors; 15, double-joint extensor; 16 to 17, double-joint flexors.
Adapted from Dornay et al. 1992.

the hand paths (A), the hand tangential velocity profiles (B), and time courses of 17 different muscles (C) for the movement from T2 to T6. The start and target point locations shown in A were selected according to those in Uno's experiment (Uno, Kawato, and Suzuki 1989). The location of T4 in human experiments was readjusted so it could be mapped onto the monkey arm geometry. The movement duration was always 0.75 s. As can be seen, roughly straight hand paths and bell-shaped speed profiles were reproduced, with minute details similar to real data. That is, the hand path was not strictly straight, unlike the minimum jerk model, but was convex for T7 to T5, and somewhat convex for T2 to T6. However, the path from T4 to T1 is straighter than the other paths. These results agree with the experimental data by Uno, Kawato, and Suzuki (1989). The speed profile was not perfectly symmetrical, unlike the minimum jerk model. This is a known characteristic of human data as shown in figs. 9.2 and 9.3. I emphasize that here a smaller and appropriate inertia value, which was properly scaled for the monkey arm, was used in the simulation.

In fig. 9.6C, typical tri-phasic muscle activities were seen for the shoulder and double-joint flexors and extensors. First, about 0.3 s after the start of the movement, the shoulder extensor and the double-joint extensor generated large tensions. Then, from 0.4 s to 0.7 s after the movement onset, these extensor tensions decreased while the shoulder flexors and double-joint flexors increased their activities. Just before the end of the movement, these extensors and flexors were coactivated to stop the arm movement. This is a well-known characteristic of human ballistic movement.

MINIMUM MOTOR COMMAND CHANGE MODEL

The evolution of the minimum torque change model to the minimum muscle tension change model can be interpreted as a proximal shift of the space where the smoothness constraint is given (see fig. 9.1) from more extrinsic space (joint torques) to more intrinsic space (muscle tensions). Because of several theoretical and computational reasons given later, this proximal shift seems to be further extended so the smoothness constraint is defined in the intrinsic space, even for the brain.

I proposed the minimum motor command change model (Kawato 1992) where the following criterion is minimized:

$$C_M = 1/2 \int_0^{t_f} \sum_{i=1}^{n} \left(\frac{dM_i}{dt}\right)^2 dt, \tag{9.5}$$

where M_i is the ith motor command out of n commands. Several definitions of motor commands are possible. At the lowest level, we could define the ith muscle motor command by the instantaneous frequency of nerve pulses arriving at the ith muscle. At the spinal cord level, we could denote the firing frequency of each alpha-motoneuron by M_i. In this case summation in the equation is taken over all motor neurons related to the investigated movements. Thus, both the rapid change in individual firing rate and rapid recruitment are penalized. At an even higher level, we could represent firing frequencies of corticomotoneuronal neurons in the cerebral motor cortex by M_i.

To understand the theoretical reasons for the preference of the minimum motor command change model, recall that all three computational problems involved in visually guided reaching movements (trajectory planning, coordinates transformation, motor command generation) encounter computational difficulty: the redundancy problem. The previous optimization principles were proposed to resolve the ill-posedness of these problems. It is important to realize that if we define the smoothness criterion of some optimization model at a specific space, then the model can solve only ill-posed computational problems defined at or above that level (fig. 9.1). The minimum jerk model defined at the task space can thus resolve only the ill-posed trajectory formation problem. Because the minimum torque change model specifies the smoothness criterion at the joint-torque coordinates, it can determine unique torque waveforms when the target position is specified. Because joint angles and the corresponding Cartesian coordinates are uniquely determined from the torque waveforms, both the ill-posed inverse kinematics problem (coordinates transformation from visual to joint space), which is formulated between the joint space and the visual space, and the trajectory formation problem are simultaneously solved by the minimum torque change model. Similarly, the minimum muscle tension change model, which specifies the smoothness criterion at the muscle level, can resolve the ill-posed inverse dynamics problem (the problem of determining muscle tensions from desirable joint motions) as well as the inverse kinematics problem and trajectory formation problem. Finally, the minimum motor command change model, which specifies the smoothness criterion in the central nervous system, can resolve excess degrees of freedom at that motor command level and the previous three problems (trajectory formation, inverse kinematics, and inverse dynamics).

The following gives three reasons for extending the minimum muscle tension change model to the minimum motor command change model. First, to solve the ill-posed problem of the enormous excess degrees of freedom in the central nervous system (larger numbers of motor or corticomotoneuronal neurons than the number of muscles), we need to use the smoothness principle in the state space of the central nervous system (i.e., firing frequency of neurons).

Second, in view of the nature of the neural network hardware, which executes trajectory planning and control (see several neural network models for trajectory formation in later sections), we can say that the origin of the smoothness resides in the central nervous system rather than in the periphery. Thus it seems more plausible to impose the smoothness constraint at the central nervous system level rather than the peripheral level.

Finally, Uno and Kawato (1994), in response to Flash's (1990) criticism of the link inertia parameter values used in Uno, Kawato, and Suzuki (1989), found that the minimum torque change model can reproduce human data well if measured dynamic viscosity values (Bennett et al. 1992) in combination with correct inertia parameter values are used in the simulation. But if zero viscosity values are assumed as in Flash (1990), the predicted hand paths are too concavely curved from the body compared with the human data. Because the musculoskeletal system's viscosity properties arise mainly from muscle velocity-tension relationships and spinal reflex characteristics, the measured viscosity coefficients used cannot be interpreted as a visco-elastic component of the dynamical properties of the arm. Thus, if we are really talking about the torque that is generated at the joint, there is only a little viscosity in the controlled object. Consequently, we should interpret the torque in this simulation as the motor command arriving at the muscles determining muscle-generated torques. In this sense, the original minimum torque change model should be renamed the minimum *commanded* torque change model.

Flash (1990) criticized the minimum torque change model based on her simulation of the minimum torque change trajectory. The criticism regarded link inertia moment values assumed in Uno, Kawato, and Suzuki (1989). Let the subscript 1 denote physical parameter values of the upper arm (link 1), and 2 denote those of the forearm (link 2). The values assumed in Uno, Kawato, and Suzuki (1989) are as follows: mass $M_1 = 0.9$[kg], $M_2 = 1.1$[kg]; length $L_1 = 0.25$[m], $L_2 = 0.35$[m]; center of mass from joint $S_1 = 0.11$[m], $S_2 = 0.15$[m]; inertia moment around joint $I_1 = 0.065$[kg m^2], $I_2 = 0.100$[kg m^2]; coefficient of viscosity around joint $b_1 = 0.08$[kg m^2/s], $b_2 = 0.08$[kg m^2/s]. Although we used the moment value I_2 experimentally obtained by Cannon and Zahalak (1982), it was about double a reasonable value based on the other physical parameters of the links: mass, length, and center of mass used in the simulation. When a reasonable, smaller inertia moment value was assumed with 0 viscosity value, the hand path for point-to-point movement in front of the body was too concavely curved compared with the human data (Flash 1990).

Recent direct measurements of elbow viscosity value during movements by Bennett et al. (1992) suggest a higher value, such as the average of 0.4 [kg m^2/s] and the range from 0.2 [kg m^2/s] to 0.8 [kg m^2/s]. Our current best estimate of parameter values is summarized as follows: $M_1 = 0.9$[kg], $M_2 = 1.1$[kg]; length $L_1 = 0.25$[m], $L_2 = 0.35$[m]; center of mass from joint $S_1 = 0.12$[m], $S_2 = 0.15$[m]; inertia moment around joint $I_1 = 0.0201$[kg m^2], $I_2 = 0.0453$[kg m^2]; coefficient of viscosity around joint $b_1 = 0.4$[kg m^2/s], $b_2 = 0.4$[kg m^2/s]. For this set of parameter values, the minimum torque change model predicts trajectories that are similar to human data. We can conclude that the minimum torque change model is still an attractive model that can reproduce human movement data with the realistic inertia moment values and measured viscosity values (Uno and Kawato 1994).

Again, I must note the trade-off between the computational potential of different optimization models and their ease of use or ease of examination. The minimum jerk model deals with only the trajectory formation problem, but the user need not know even the kinematics of the arm. We can easily calculate its solutions as fifth-order polynomials. On the other hand, the minimum torque change model can resolve the trajectory formation problem, the inverse kinematics problem and the inverse dynamics problem; thus, it can provide joint-torque values. However, the user must derive ordinary differential equations for the arm dynamics and must estimate physical parameters included in these equations. We saw earlier that estimation is not simple and could become a source of dispute. With the minimum muscle tension change model, the user can determine muscle tensions, but must describe the muscle geometry as well as the link dynamics and specify the moment arms of the muscles. We can discuss the neural coding of the motor program at the spinal or brain level with the minimum motor command change model. Here we must specify how neural firing patterns are transformed into muscle tensions. Thus, the user confronts a difficult problem of modeling the nervous system with the arm system. Actually, this is a short history of efforts made by our group for past years. We have just established a good quantitative model of transformation from EMG to movement (Koike and Kawato 1995) and are planning to examine the minimum motor command change model based on it.

NEURAL NETWORK MODELS

We introduced several optimization models in the previous sections, but we have not yet discussed how optimization problems can be solved. Optimization models correspond to the computational theory for understanding the brain proposed by Marr (1982). Optimization procedures address the algorithm- and hardware-level understandings for the same problem. As Marr pointed out, many different algorithms and different hardware can form a single computational theory. For example, Uno, Kawato, and Suzuki (1989) used a Newton-like method for calculating the minimum torque change trajectory. In the field of optimal control theory, first-order and second-order gradient methods were developed to compute numerically the optimal solutions of two-point boundary value problems based on the Euler-Lagrange equation (see, for example, Bryson and Ho 1975). We can use any of these engineering methods to calculate the optimal trajectory and motor commands. However, most of them cannot be regarded as biologically plausible procedures to solve optimal trajectory formation problems. For example, matrix inversions or solving adjoint equations in the backward direction of time, which we used in the previous schemes, seem difficult to implement neuronally. In this chapter, we do not discuss efficient numerical methods to compute optimal trajectories on digital computers, although they are necessary for research purposes. Readers are encouraged to refer to Uno, Kawato, and Suzuki (1989) or textbooks on numerical methods of optimal control theory, such as Bryson and Ho (1975).

In this section, rather, we introduce several neural network models that can solve the optimization problems explained in earlier sections. We hope that we can ultimately propose biologically and psychologically plausible models for trajectory planning in the brain. Unfortunately, most neural network models introduced in this section have several artificial characteristics that are difficult to implement neuronally. Accordingly, we evaluate different neural network models to determine whether they are practical in biologically plausible manners.

Dynamic optimization models, such as the minimum torque change, minimum muscle tension change or minimum motor command change models have important implications for computations done in the central nervous system. If we adopt one of them as a computational scheme, it leads to two important computational constraints. First, the brain needs to acquire, by training, an internal model of the controlled object and continuously use it for trajectory formation. This is because the smoothness criterion is applied to the motor command space (either joint torque, muscle tension, or neural firings), which is more central than the task-oriented coordinates in which movement conditions such as target locations or via-point locations are represented. To calculate optimal solutions, the smoothness constraint and task requirement represented in the two spaces must be combined. Consequently, either a forward or an inverse model of the motor apparatus must be used to transmit information from the motor command space to the task space (forward model) or from the task space to the motor command space (inverse model). Second, the brain must simultaneously solve all three ill-posed problems: the trajectory formation, coordinate transformation, and control problems. This is because the inverse kinematics and inverse dynamics problems must be addressed to determine joint torques, muscle tensions, or motor commands.

Simple Recurrent Network Model
for Minimum Jerk Trajectory

As the simplest example of a neural network model that can generate optimal trajectories, a recurrent network that generates a minimum jerk trajectory is first introduced. It is easy to analytically calculate the minimum jerk trajectory. The optimal solution is expressed as a fifth-order polynomial function in time. Coefficients of this polynomial function are determined from boundary conditions and the movement time by solving a simple algebraic equation. However, it is extremely difficult to assume that this computational procedure is adopted in the brain. Instead of such an algebraic procedure, Hoff and Arbib (1993) proposed a network model that can generate a minimum jerk trajectory. Their model is based on an optimal feedback controller design known in optimal control theory. The model can be implemented as a recurrent neural network model, which receives the movement duration, the target location, and the current position and velocity information, and can generate position and velocity at the next time step. Thus, it calculates the minimum jerk trajectory in Cartesian coordinates.

Jordan's Recurrent Network for Optimal Trajectory

Jordan (1990) showed that a recurrent network can be trained to generate a minimum jerk virtual trajectory. A simple mass-spring model of a single joint is used as a controlled object. First, a forward dynamics model of this joint is trained in a recurrent network. Then, another recurrent network for motor control is attached to the motor command input channel of the previously trained forward dynamics model. The motor control network is assumed to calculate a virtual trajectory (Bizzi, Accornero, Chapple, and Hogan 1984; Hogan 1984). Two objective functions are minimized during training. One corresponds to the minimum jerk criterion of the virtual trajectory (Flash 1987). The other corresponds to the target location error at the end of movement. The first function is the smoothness constraint and is regarded as a soft constraint to the optimization problem. The second function is the movement condition constraint and is regarded as a hard constraint to the optimization problem. The weighted summation of these two error signals is used to modify synaptic weights in the motor control recurrent network. Jordan (1990) showed that this combined recurrent network can generate a minimum jerk virtual trajectory. We can regard the learning process as embedding the two constraints into the synaptic weights of the motor control recurrent network.

Jordan's network is attractive in several respects. First, it was shown that a network can be trained as a trajectory formation and control device. Second, the recurrent network generates trajectories in real time. Third, the movement time is naturally represented as time in the dynamics of the recurrent network. He stated that the learning scheme can readily be applied for a minimum torque change trajectory.

Related to Jordan's approach, Massone and Bizzi (1989) trained a recurrent neural network to produce minimum jerk trajectories for a simple two-link, six-muscle arm model. In the learning, perfect teaching information of a desired trajectory was given. Thus, it was shown that a minimum jerk trajectory motor command can be stored in a recurrent network by simple supervised learning.

Cascade Neural Network Model
for a Dynamically Optimized Trajectory

The cascade neural network model calculates the optimal trajectory and the corresponding necessary motor command from information about the locations of the target point, via-points, and obstacles, which are given by the higher motor center (Kawato et al. 1990). It was originally proposed for the minimum torque change model but can be applied to the minimum muscle tension change model or the minimum motor command change model without any change. The cascade structure of the model corresponds to the dynamic properties of the controlled object; it provides a forward model of the controlled object as a whole. The minimum torque change criterion is embedded as hardware (electrical synapses) in the model. That is, neurons representing motor commands at a neighboring time are connected by an electrical resistance so their states can be brought to a common value. This is why time should be represented spatially in the cascade network model. During use, the network first acquires a forward model of a controlled object by training, and then calculates motor commands by relaxation, using the learned forward model. Backpropagation (Rumelhart, Hinton, and Williams 1986) of position and velocity errors in the task space through the forward dynamics model in the cascade structure is used for transformation of these errors into the motor command space.

We can show mathematically that the cascade neural network executes a steep descent motion with respect to the objective function of the optimal control and will reach a stable equilibrium point where the summation of the smoothness criterion multiplied by the electrical conductance of the gap junction and the error in movement conditions is minimum. Consequently, the torque time course required to generate the minimum torque change trajectory can be calculated by relaxation. An appropriate delay line should be inserted between the first layer of the cascade neural network and the controlled object so this calculated motor command moves the controlled object.

Hirayama, Kawato, and Jordan (1993) proposed a hybrid neural network model of aimed arm movements, which consists of a feedforward controller and a postural controller. The cascade neural network was employed as a computational implementation of the feedforward controller. This network computes feedforward motor commands based on a minimum torque change criterion. If the weighting parameter of the smoothness criterion is fixed and the number of relaxation iterations is small, the cascade model cannot calculate the exact torque, and the hand does not reach the desired target using the feedforward control alone. Thus, one observes an error between the final position and the desired target location. By simulating target-directed arm movements using a fixed weighting parameter value and a limited iteration number, they found that the cascade model generated a planning time-accuracy tradeoff, and a quasi-power-law type speed-accuracy tradeoff.

Meyer et al. (1990) found that power functions with varying exponents, a family for which the logarithm is the asymptote, fit the speed-accuracy data discernibly better than the logarithm function. These quasi-power laws with the exponent n are expressed as follows:

$$MT = a_n + b_n \, (A/W)^{1/n} \qquad (9.6)$$

where MT is the movement time, A is the amplitude of movement, W is the width of a target, and a and b are constants that depend on behavioral situations. We note that this equation is approximately the same as the linear law if n is 1, and to the log law if n is infinity.

The cascade model provides a candidate neural mechanism to explain the stochastic variability of the time course of the feedforward motor command. The approach also accounts for several invariant features of multijoint arm trajectories, such as roughly straight hand paths and bell-shaped speed profiles. They suggest that part of the movement speed-accuracy trade-off may be explained by the difficulty in the neural computation of a feedforward ballistic motor command. For larger and faster movements, amplitudes of necessary motor commands and their change rates are larger. Thus, it gets more difficult to calculate the motor commands in the feedforward mode.

Trajectory Formation Based on Forward and Inverse Models

Because humans need only a few hundred milliseconds' planning time for movements, the large number of iterations required by the relaxation methods seems to disprove their biological plausibility in the brain. To resolve the disadvantages of the cascade network and propose biologically plausible optimization procedures, we had the novel idea of using both forward and inverse models of the motor apparatus during optimization calculation. By introducing both the forward and inverse models of the motor plant, we can reduce the relaxation time dramatically. The backpropagation calculation becomes unnecessary, and the movement time can be represented as the network dynamics time. Thus, we can resolve all three disadvantages of the cascade network.

Fig. 9.7 shows the structure of the new model, which consists of four subnetworks: a feedforward network for the inverse dynamics and kinematics model of the controlled object, a recurrent network for the forward dynamics and kinematics model of the controlled object, a network that executes smoothing of the motor commands, and a network that calculates an approximate trajectory of the nonlinear optimization problem. Let us explain the fundamental relaxation procedure in this model. First, the approximate trajectory formation mechanism generates a suboptimal trajectory. Although this suboptimal trajectory does not attain optimal performance, it satisfies

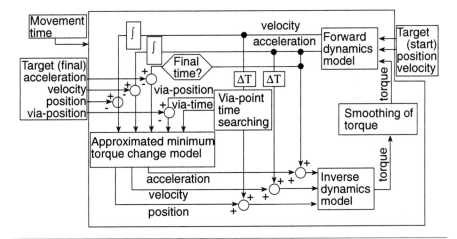

Fig. 9.7   The neural network structure proposed for arm trajectory formation based on minimum torque change model using forward and inverse models of the controlled object. The network consists of five main components: the forward dynamics model, the inverse dynamics model, the suboptimal trajectory formation mechanism, the torque smoother, and the via-point time search. They can all be implemented as biologically plausible neural networks. Mainly circular information flow in the model can be seen (approximated minimum torque change model → inverse dynamics model → smoothing of torque → forward dynamics model → via-point time searching → approximated minimum torque change model). The inputs of the proposed neural network are positions, velocities, and accelerations at the start and the end times, movement time, and via-point positions. Because the target position is used in real time during trajectory formation and control, the new model can deal with a target change experiment. It is also possible to use feedback information about the current position and velocity of the controlled object in the forward dynamics model. Thus, the new model can accommodate simultaneous feedback and feedforward control.
Reprinted from Wada and Kawato 1993.

the multiple-point boundary conditions. Second, the inverse model of the controlled object calculates the motor command necessary to produce the suboptimal trajectory. Then, the pair (the trajectory and the motor command) satisfies the dynamic relationship for the controlled object as well as the task specifications for the target point and via-points. Third, the motor command smoothing circuit smooths the motor command waveform. Here, the smoothing operation corresponds exactly to the steepest descent motion with respect to the summation of the smoothness criterion and the task constraint, because the boundary conditions and the dynamic relationship between the trajectory and the motor command are rigorously satisfied. After this smoothing operation, however, neither the boundary conditions nor the dynamic relationship is satisfied. Fourth, the forward model of the motor apparatus operates on the smoothed motor command and calculates the resulting trajectory. The new trajectory and the smoothed torque give a valid pair, which satisfies the dynamic relationships. However, the boundary conditions are still violated. Finally, the approximate trajectory formation mechanism generates a corrective suboptimal trajectory that compensates for the error in the boundary conditions. This corrective trajectory is summed with the previous trajectory. At this point the boundary conditions are satisfied. However, the dynamic relationships are violated. Returning to step 2 and using the inverse model, the correct motor command is calculated. After this, the four operations—inverse dynamics, motor command smoothing, forward dynamics, and corrective trajectory formation and summation—are repeated in this order until a satisfactory solution is obtained.

Here, we explain how each of the four components in the new model can be implemented as biologically plausible neural network models. The inverse model of the controlled object can be obtained by feedforward neural network models by using the feedback-error-learning scheme (Kawato, Furukawa, and Suzuki 1987; Kawato 1990). The forward model of the controlled object can be obtained by a recurrent neural network model as shown by Jordan (1990). We can implement the motor command smoothing mechanism in several ways. For example, a neural network can get a simple high-cut temporal filter. Finally, as the Hoff-Arbib network and Jordan's sequential network show, an approximately optimal trajectory formation mechanism can also be obtained by recurrent neural networks.

Let us intuitively explain why the new model resolves the three disadvantages of the cascade neural network model. First, backpropagation is not needed because both the forward dynamics and inverse dynamics models are used in the new model. In the cascade or Jordan's model, only the forward model was used, and hence backpropagation through it was essential to transform the terminal error condition into the motor command space. In the new model, the inverse dynamics model executes this operation. Second, the iteration number is dramatically reduced because of the overall structure of the model. Finally, because a simple temporal filter can execute the motor command smoothing, spatial representation of time is not needed.

Wada and Kawato (1993) simulated the new model for a simple two-link model of the human forearm and upper arm. The simulated hand paths are shown in fig. 9.8, and they are close to the exact solutions obtained by the Newton-like method. The number of iterations required was typically 1 to 5. Furthermore, they show that a simple minimum jerk trajectory in the joint space is sufficient as an approximately optimal solution to obtain the minimum torque change trajectory. Thus, we can use the Hoff-Arbib network as an approximate trajectory generation mechanism.

For a difficult movement under this new neural network model, in which the forward dynamics model is not accurate and the movement planning time is not sufficient, a one-shot calculation based on the approximate trajectory formation mechanism and the inverse model of the motor apparatus is supposedly used in the brain just once. This is a step-by-step hierarchical control strategy. However, if the forward model is accurate and the planning time is sufficient, the total network relaxes its states a few times so the minimum motor command change trajectory is generated.

We hypothesize that the relaxation computation exemplified by the new neural network model is used for very skilled movements, with step-by-step computation used for difficult and less-skilled movements. That is, the computational scheme adopted by the brain may change with motor learning. Some of our experimental data support this idea. First, in human arm movements perturbed by an external spring force (Uno, Kawato, and Suzuki 1989), subjects generated trajectories of

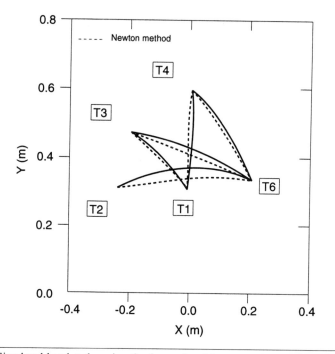

Fig. 9.8 Simulated hand paths using the forward and inverse trajectory formation network. Five discrete point-to-point trajectories in front of the body are shown. The coordinates are the same as in fig. 9.2. The trajectories generated by the new model (*solid curves*) are compared with those (*broken curves*) generated by the Newton-like method of Uno, Kawato, and Suzuki (1989). The two kinds of trajectories are similar and gently curved. Reprinted from Wada and Kawato 1993.

various shapes when they were still not accustomed to the spring. After tens of repetitions, however, they consistently generated a curved hand path, which is the minimum torque change trajectory. Second, Uno (unpublished observation) introduced a nonlinear coordinate transformation between the hand position on a two-dimensional position digitizer and the CRT coordinates displaying the end point, the start point, and the hand position. Because of the nonlinear transformation, a straight line on the CRT corresponded to a curve on the digitizer, and vice versa. Here, subjects first generated roughly straight hand paths on the CRT, approximating the minimum jerk trajectory in the visual task space (CRT coordinate). After several periods of training, however, they generated roughly straight hand paths on the digitizer (i.e., curved paths on the CRT), conforming to the minimum torque change trajectories.

These data suggested that step-by-step computation is replaced by more accurate computation of the optimal trajectory using relaxation computation after appropriate motor learning is carried out. In the first case, with the external spring, the forward-dynamics model of an arm combined with the spring must be relearned. In the second case, with artificial coordinate transformation, the forward-kinematics model of an arm combined with an imposed nonlinear transformation between the digitizer and the CRT must be relearned. Thus, step-by-step computation is used temporarily until the forward model is relearned.

This is consistent with findings by other investigators. Schneider and Zernicke (1989) reported a decrease of jerk cost during practice. Their results might be explained as improved control performance caused by an intensive learning of forward dynamics and kinematics of the arm for a special task. In contrast, other motor control schemes, such as the equilibrium trajectory approach (Hogan 1984; Flash 1987), do not support efficient movement refinement during practice.

From a broader viewpoint, the forward dynamics and kinematics model of a controlled object and an environment may be regarded as a world simulator. Similarly, the inverse dynamics and kinematics model may be regarded as an action controller. Third, the approximate trajectory generation mechanism is considered a fixed-action pattern generator. Thus, relaxation computation using the world simulator, the action controller, and the action pattern generator could be understood as internal simulation of the action-response chain, which leads to better behavioral planning and motor control.

Articulatory Movement
and Motor Theory of Speech Perception

Although the minimum muscle tension change criterion was found and ascertained for arm movement, it does not depend on any special feature of the arm as a controlled object. I believe that a computational principle, such as the minimum motor command change model, must be independent of the controlled object, but inherent in the central nervous system itself. The structure of the cascade network (gap junction) or the new model with forward and inverse models (motor command smoother) also suggests that the computational principle has its origin in the central nervous system rather than in the periphery. Thus, it is natural to explore whether the minimum muscle tension change model might be applicable to other controlled objects such as an articulator. It is well known that an articulator shows a very smooth movement, whereas the phoneme sequence sounds discrete and distinctive to us. These kinds of data support that a smoothness constraint such as the minimum muscle tension change model exists also for articulatory movement, that is speech.

In speech synthesis, a long series of phonemes must be uttered continuously. From the trajectory formation standpoint, this implies that many via-points are specified for one continuous trajectory. Our neural network models can autonomously find the best time to pass through many via-points. This intrinsic timing control capability is one of the most attractive features of our network models.

It is straightforward to apply the cascade network model to speech synthesis. However, it is extremely difficult to obtain a good quantitative dynamical model of the articulator. Hirayama et al. (1992) have trained a forward dynamics model of a speech articulator in a three-layer perceptron using an electromyogram as the control input, and generated articulator trajectories with multiple via-points.

The attractiveness of a smoothness constraint, such as the minimum muscle tension change model, in speech motor control and speech perception is at least threefold. First, the smoothness constraint can explain coarticulation; at any point during an utterance, we can discern the influences of gestures associated with several adjacent segments in acoustic or articulatory measurements. Second, it can resolve the redundancy that exists in motor control of speech at the dynamics and kinematics levels. This is another aspect of the first point. The smoothness constraint resolves the ill-posed inverse kinematics and inverse dynamics problems in a way that leads to coarticulation. Third, it can explain casual speech if the hard constraint is not strictly satisfied. That is, the trajectory does not accurately pass through the via-points, and the trajectory and the motor command are smoother than the rigorous minimum muscle tension change trajectory. It might be tempting to regard this dominance of the smoothness as casualness of speech.

Kawato (1989) showed that we can apply the cascade network not only to speech synthesis, but also to continuous speech recognition, as first hypothesized in "motor theory of speech perception" (Liberman et al. 1967). This theory emphasizes the role of the motor control neural network in speech perception to decode the sound signal into articulatory gestures. It is more plausible to assume that the intended gestures or the desired via-points are estimated by the motor control neural network rather than by the articulatory gesture itself. Recently, Wada et al. (1995) showed that the new network with forward and inverse models can solve pattern recognition of movement trajectory as well as the trajectory formation problem.

Jordan (1990) and Bailly, Laboissière, and Schwartz (1991) studied coarticulation phenomena using recurrent neural network models. In these studies, the smoothness of speech comes either from the smooth state change of the network dynamics or the kinematic optimization model. Considering the different speeds of the tip of the tongue and the jaw, it seems reasonable to explore, for the speech articulator, the dynamic optimization models explored for the multijoint arm.

Minimum Jerk Model Combined With Virtual Trajectory Control Hypothesis

One bit of experimental data supporting the minimum torque change model rather than the minimum jerk model is curved trajectories for movements whose starting point is an outstretched arm to the side and end point is in front of the body. One may notice that even the trajectory from T2 to T6 in fig. 9.2 is curved. Flash (1987) explained these slight curvatures observed in data by combining the minimum jerk model with the virtual trajectory control hypothesis (Bizzi et al. 1984; Hogan 1984). That is, the virtual trajectory, and not the real trajectory, was assumed to be planned as the minimum jerk trajectory. Although the virtual trajectory is straight, the real trajectory is slightly curved because of imperfect control by the virtual trajectory control. However, the stiffness values assumed in Flash's simulation (1987) could be controversial. Bennett et al. (1992) recently found that mechanical stiffness during movement was much smaller than assumed by Flash (1987). Then, based on these measured values of stiffness during movement, Katayama and Kawato (1993) showed that the virtual trajectory is wildly curved to reproduce roughly straight hand paths. We can understand the differences between Flash's and Katayama's simulations if we recall that the required joint torques are generated as the product of mechanical stiffness and the difference between the virtual and real trajectories in the virtual trajectory control hypothesis. If physical parameters such as the moment of inertia, mass, and link length are given, and the desired hand trajectory is fixed, the required joint torques are uniquely determined from the inverse dynamics equation. When the stiffness is large, the difference between the virtual and real trajectories is small, but if the stiffness is small, this difference becomes large. Human multijoint hand paths are roughly straight for point-to-point movements. Consequently, in Flash's simulation in which high stiffness was assumed, the virtual trajectory could be close to the real trajectory; that is, it could be a simple straight trajectory. In Katayama's simulation, however, in which low stiffness was assumed, the virtual trajectory was different from the real trajectory and was wildly curved. Conversely, if the virtual trajectory is planned as the minimum jerk trajectory, real trajectories are overly curved and do not get close enough to the target points if the measured dynamic stiffness values during movements are used (Katayama and Kawato 1993). Thus, if we consider the low mechanical stiffness values recently measured during movement (Bennett et al. 1992; Gomi, Koike, and Kawato 1992; Gomi and Kawato 1996), it seems difficult to reproduce slightly curved hand paths by combining the virtual trajectory control hypothesis and the minimum jerk model (see Kawato et al. 1993 and Gomi and Kawato 1996 for review).

Temporal and Spatial Couplings and Adaptive Significance

It is well known that the concurrent performance of two manual tasks results in a tight temporal coupling of the limbs. Franz, Zelaznik, and McCabe (1991) investigated whether a similar coupling exists in the spatial domain; subjects produced continuous drawings of circles and lines, one task at a time or bimanually. They found temporal coupling and concomitant accommodation in the movement path for the conditions under which the hands were producing different shapes. As one of the spatial constraint mechanisms, they suggested the minimum torque change model. However, for two arms, there exists only weak physical coupling. Thus, the minimum motor command change model at either the motor cortex, the premotor cortex, or the supplementary motor area, seems to be a more plausible mechanism for the bimanual spatial and temporal coupling.

Finally, we discuss the adaptive advantages of smoothness constraints. Flash and Hogan (1985) first suggested that a smoothness constraint such as the minimum jerk model possibly reduces the wear and tear of the motor apparatus. If the wear and tear at the joint level are important, the minimum torque change model is better than the minimum jerk model. This is because we know that joint-torque waveforms for the minimum jerk model are sometimes quite jerky, especially for difficult movements near the work space boundary or with multiple via-points. If the muscles need to be protected, the minimum muscle tension change model seems the most reasonable. On the other hand, the central nervous system has long time constants ranging from a several-millisecond membrane time constant to a few-hundred-millisecond network time constant. The minimum motor command change model in the central nervous system might be compatible with these long time constants and the resulting smooth temporal behaviors, and beneficial for reducing the computational intensiveness of motor planning and control. I hope, ultimately, that the optimization models we discussed in this chapter might be understood from the optimization principle at the organism level such as the maximum fitness. However, at this moment, discussions on the adaptive implications of the smoothness models remain speculative.

CONCLUSION

Three computational problems to be solved for visually guided reaching movements, trajectory formation, coordinate transformation, and calculation of motor commands, are all ill posed in redundant biological motor control systems. These problems are ill posed in the sense that there exist an infinite number of possible solutions. Because humans effortlessly solve these ill-posed problems, past computational studies sought principles to resolve these difficulties.

Multijoint point-to-point arm movement trajectories are characterized by roughly straight hand paths and bell-shaped speed profiles. Mathematical models that can reproduce these data have been examined.

At the computational understanding level of Marr, only an optimization model can provide a solution to these theoretical and empirical questions. Kinematic and dynamic optimization principles have been proposed to account for those invariant features of human movement data so far. Experimental data has been found to support the dynamic optimization theory, which requires both forward and inverse models of the motor apparatus and the external world.

We show that three optimization models, the minimum jerk model, minimum torque change model, and minimum motor command change model, can resolve these three ill-posed problems. We also introduced several neural network models proposed to solve these optimization problems.

In the future, optimization models and neural network models for visually guided reaching movements will be extended to treat more complicated sequential movements such as speech or cursive handwritings. They will be expanded to deal with integration of different vision modules, learning new behaviors by imitation, and even to consciousness.

REFERENCES

Abend, W., Bizzi, E., and Morasso, P. 1982. Human arm trajectory formation. *Brain* 105:331-348.

Anastasio, T.J., and Robinson, D.A. 1990. Distributed parallel processing in the vertical vestibulo-ocular reflex: Learning networks compared to tensor theory. *Biological Cybernetics* 63:161-167.

Atkeson, C.G., and Hollerbach, J.M. 1985. Kinematic features of unrestrained vertical arm movements. *Journal of Neuroscience* 5:2318-2330.

Bailly, G., Laboissière, R., and Schwartz, J.L. 1991. Formant trajectories as audible gestures: an alternative for speech synthesis. *Journal of Phonetics* 19:9-23.

Bennett, D.J., Hollerbach, J.M., Xu, Y., and Hunter, I.W. 1992. Time-varying stiffness of human elbow joint during cyclic voluntary movement. *Experimental Brain Research* 88:433-442.

Bernstein, N. 1967. *The Coordination and Regulation of Movements*. London: Pergamon.

Bizzi, E., Accornero, N., Chapple, W., and Hogan, N. 1984. Posture control and trajectory formation during arm movement. *Journal of Neuroscience* 4:2738-2744.

Bizzi, E., Polit, A., and Morasso, P. 1976. Mechanism underlying achievement of final head position. *Journal of Neurophysiology* 39:435-444.

Bryson, A.E., and Ho, Y.C. 1975. *Applied Optimal Control*. New York: Hemisphere.

Cannon, S.C., and Zahalak, G.I. 1982. The mechanical behavior of active human skeletal muscle in small oscillations. *J. Biomech* 15:111-121.

Dornay, M. 1991. Static analysis of posture and movement, using a 17-muscle model of the monkey's arm. *ATR Technical Report*, TR-A-0109. Kyoto, Japan: ATR.

Dornay, M., Uno, Y., Kawato, M., and Suzuki, R. 1995. Minimum muscle tension change trajectories. *Journal of Motor Behavior*. In press.

Flash, T. 1987. The control of hand equilibrium trajectories in multi-joint arm movements. *Biological Cybernetics* 57:257-274.

Flash, T. 1990. The organization of human arm trajectory control. P. 282-301 in *Multiple Muscle Systems: Biomechanics and Movement Organization*, edited by J.M. Winters and S.L.Y. Woo. New York: Springer.

Flash, T., and Hogan, N. 1985. The coordination of arm movements: An experimentally confirmed mathematical model. *Journal of Neuroscience* 5:1688-1703.

Franz, E.A., Zelaznik, H.N., and McCabe, G. 1991. Spatial topological constraints in a bimanual task. *Acta Psychologica* 77:137-151.

Gomi, H., and Kawato, M. 1996. The change of human arm mechanical impedance during movements under different environmental conditions. *Society for Neuroscience Abstracts* 21:686.

Gomi, H., Koike, Y., and Kawato, M. 1992. Human hand stiffness during discrete point-to-point multi-joint movement. *Proceedings of IEEE Engineering in Medicine and Biology Society*, 1628-1629.

Hirayama, M., Kawato, M., and Jordan, M.I. 1993. The cascade neural network model and a speed-accuracy trade-off of arm movement. *Journal of Motor Behavior* 25:162-174.

Hirayama, M., V-Bateson, E., Kawato, M., and Jordan, M.I. 1992. Forward dynamics modeling of speech motor control using physiological data. P. 191-198 in *Advances in Neural Information Processing Systems 4*, edited by R.P. Lippmann, J.E. Moody, and D.S. Touretzky. San Mateo, CA: Morgan Kaufmann.

Hoff, B., and Arbib, M.A. 1993. Models of trajectory formation and temporal interaction of reach and grasp. *Journal of Motor Behavior* 25:175-192.

Hogan, N. 1984. An organizing principle for a class of voluntary movements. *Journal of Neuroscience* 4:2745-2754.

Hollerbach, J.M. 1982. Computers, brains and the control of movement. *Trends in Neuroscience* 5:189-192.

Jordan, M.I. 1990. Motor learning and the degrees of freedom problem. P. 796-836 in *Attention and performance XIII*, edited by M. Jeannerod. Hillsdale, NJ: Erlbaum.

Jordan, M.I., and Rosenbaum, D.A. 1989. Action. P. 727-767 in *Foundations of cognitive science*, edited by M.I. Posner. Cambridge, MA: MIT Press.

Kandel, E.R., Schwartz, J.H., and Jessell, T.M., eds. 1991. *Principles of Neural Science*. 342-349, 3d ed. New York: Elsevier.

Katayama, M., and Kawato, M. 1993. Virtual trajectory and stiffness ellipse during multijoint arm movement predicted by neural inverse models. *Biological Cybernetics* 69:353-362.

Kawato, M. 1989. Motor theory of speech perception revisited from minimum-torque-change neural network model. *Proceedings of 8th Symposium on Future Electron Devices*, 141-150.

Kawato, M. 1990. Computational schemes and neural network models for formation and control of multijoint arm trajectory. P. 197-228 in *Neural networks for control*, edited by T. Miller, R. Sutton, and P. Werbos. Cambridge, MA: MIT Press.

Kawato, M. 1992. Optimization and learning in neural networks for formation and control of coordinated movement. P. 821-849 in *Attention and Performance, XIV: Synergies in Experimental Psychology, Artificial Intelligence, and Cognitive Neuroscience—A Silver Jubilee*, edited by D. Meyer and S. Kornblum. Cambridge, MA: MIT Press.

Kawato, M., Furukawa, K., and Suzuki, R. 1987. A hierarchical neural-network model for control and learning of voluntary movement. *Biological Cybernetics* 57:169-185.

Kawato, M., Gomi, H., Katayama, M., and Koike, Y. 1993. Supervised learning for coordinative motor control. P. 126-161 in *Computational Learning & Cognition, SIAM Frontier Series*, edited by E.B. Baum. Philadelphia: Society for Industrial and Applied Mathematics.

Kawato, M., Maeda, M., Uno, Y., and Suzuki, R. 1990. Trajectory formation of arm movement by cascade neural-network model based on minimum torque-change criterion. *Biological Cybernetics* 62:275-288.

Kelso, J.A.S., Southard, D.L., and Goodman, D. 1979. On the nature of human interlimb coordination. *Science* 203:1029-1031.

Koike, Y., and Kawato, M. 1994. Trajectory formation from surface EMG signals using a neural network model. *The Transactions of the Institute of Electronics, Information and Communication Engineers, DII* 77:193-203 (in Japanese).

Koike, Y., and Kawato, M. 1995. Estimation of dynamic joint torques and trajectory formation from surface electromyography signals using a neural network model. *Biological Cybernetics* 73:291-300.

Liberman, A.M., Cooper, F.S., Shankweiler, D.P., and Studdert-Kennedy, M. 1967. Perception of the speech code. *Psychological Review* 74:431-461.

Marr, D. 1982. *Vision*. New York: Freeman.

Massone, L., and Bizzi, E. 1989. A neural network model for limb trajectory formation. *Biological Cybernetics* 61:417-425.

Meyer, D.E., Smith, J.E.K., Kornblum, S., Abrams, R.A., and Wright, C.E. 1990. Speed-accuracy tradeoffs in aimed movement: Toward a theory of rapid voluntary action. P. 173-226 in *Attention and performance XIII*, edited by M. Jeannerod. Hillsdale, NJ: Erlbaum.

Morasso, P. 1981. Spatial control of arm movements. *Experimental Brain Research* 42:223-227.

Mussa-Ivaldi, F.A., Morasso, P., and Zaccaria, R. 1988. Kinematic networks—A distributed model for representing and regularizing motor redundancy. *Biological Cybernetics* 60:1-16.

Nelson, W.L. 1983. Physical principles for economies of skilled movements. *Biological Cybernetics* 46:135-147.

Paul, R. 1981. *Robot Manipulators: Mathematics, Programming, and Control.* Cambridge, MA: MIT Press.

Pellionisz, A., and Llinas, R. 1980. Tensorial approach to the geometry of brain function: Cerebellar coordination via a metric tensor. *Neuroscience* 5:1125-1136.

Rosenbaum, D.A. 1992. Plans for object manipulation. P. 803-820 in *Attention and Performance, XIV: Synergies in Experimental Psychology, Artificial Intelligence, and Cognitive Neuroscience—A Silver Jubilee*, edited by D. Meyer and S. Kornblum. Cambridge, MA: MIT Press.

Rumelhart, D.E., Hinton, G.E., and Williams, R.J. 1986. Learning representations by back-propagating errors. *Nature* 323:533-536.

Saltzman, E.L. 1979. Levels of sensorimotor representation. *Journal of Mathematical Psychology* 20:91-163.

Saltzman, E.L., and Kelso, J.A.S. 1987. Skilled actions: A task-dynamic approach. *Psychological Review* 94:84-106.

Schneider, K., and Zernicke, R.F. 1989. Jerk-cost modulations during the practice of rapid arm movements. *Biological Cybernetics* 60:221-230.

Shinoda, Y., Yamaguchi, T., and Futami, T. 1986. Multiple axon collaterals of single corticospinal axons in the cat spinal cord. *Journal of Neurophysiology* 55:425-448.

Shinoda, Y., Yokota, J., and Futami, T. 1981. Divergent projection of individual corticospinal axons to motoneurons of multiple muscles in the monkey. *Neuroscience Letters* 23:7-12.

Turvey, M.T., Shaw, R.E., and Mace, W. 1978. Issues in the theory of action: Degrees of freedom, coordinative structures and coalitions. P. 557-595 in *Attention and Performance VII*, edited by J. Requin. Hillsdale, NJ: Erlbaum.

Uno, Y., and Kawato, M. 1994. Dynamic performance indices for trajectory formation in human arm movements. *ATR Technical Report*, TR-H-071. Kyoto, Japan: ATR.

Uno, Y., Kawato, M., and Suzuki, R. 1989. Formation and control of optimal trajectory in human multijoint arm movement—minimum torque-change model. *Biological Cybernetics* 61:89-101.

Uno, Y., Suzuki, R., and Kawato, M. 1989. Minimum muscle-tension-change model which reproduces human arm movement. *Proceedings of the 4th Symposium on Biological and Physiological Engineering*, 299-302 (in Japanese).

Wada, Y., and Kawato, M. 1993. A neural network model for arm trajectory formation using forward and inverse dynamics models. *Neural Networks* 6:919-932.

Wada, Y., Koike, Y., V-Bateson, E., and Kawato, M. 1995. A computational theory for movement pattern recognition based on optimal movement pattern generation. *Biological Cybernetics* 73:15-25.

Wann, J., Nimmo-Smith, I., and Wing, A.M. 1988. Relation between velocity and curvature in movement: Equivalence and divergence between a power law and a minimum-jerk model. *Journal of Experimental Psychology: Human Perception and Performance* 14:622-637.

Acknowledgments

I thank Dr. Yoh'ichi Tohkura of ATR Human Information Processing Research Laboratories for his continuing encouragement. I am grateful to Drs. Yoji Uno, Menashe Dornay, Yasuhiro Wada, Yasuharu Koike, Masazumi Katayama, Makoto Hirayama, and Hiroaki Gomi for allowing me to duplicate their results and for discussing subjects treated in this chapter. Preparation of this manuscript was supported by a Human Frontier Science Project Grant to Mitsuo Kawato.

Chapter 10

Neural Network Modeling
of Sensory-Motor Control in Animals

Daniel Bullock, Stephen Grossberg, and Frank Guenther

Boston University

Neural network research spans many fields, including studies of vision, speech perception and production, reinforcement learning, memory, pattern recognition, and movement control. Within each of these areas, neural network researchers use many approaches to accomplish many goals. The purpose of this chapter is to introduce that subset of neural network modeling that seeks to understand the computations and neurophysiological bases of movement control in animals. To understand where this approach fits in with other approaches to using neural networks for control, as well as with other approaches in psychology, it will be useful to consider three potential goals of movement control studies:

1. Detailed characterization of the input-output functions of animal and/or human behavior or inferred components of such behavior
2. Detailed characterization of the anatomy and physiology of biological sensory-motor control
3. Technological applicability of the system

Many neural network researchers studying movement control are primarily interested in technological applicability, while only loosely pursuing goals 1 and 2. Much of the utility of neural networks in this research derives from their ability to learn complex nonlinear mappings. Examples of this approach can be found in Barto (1990), Jordan (1988), Kuperstein (1988), Miller (1987), Narendra (1990), and Ritter, Martinetz, and Schulten (1989). To the extent that biological systems are better at a task than current technology, these researchers attempt to mimic their performance. However, they make little attempt to account for details of animal performance not necessary for technological applications. Furthermore, the networks used in this approach show only a superficial resemblance to neurophysiology. The networks are massively parallel and composed of neuron-like units, but little or no attempt is made to relate the processing units to particular neural populations existing *in vivo*.

Traditional cognitive psychology, on the other hand, focuses on goal 1 with little concern for detailed characterization of the anatomical loci of model components and with almost no concern for technological applicability. Connectionist modeling (e.g., McClelland and Rumelhart 1981) represents a partial departure from this tradition by using neuron-like elements and massive parallelism. Like the engineering approach just described, the resemblance to neurophysiology is only superficial, and comparison to specific neural populations is rarely carried out.

By contrast, the approach exemplified in the following sections strongly emphasizes goals 1 and 2 and places tertiary emphasis on goal 3. Proponents of this approach attempt to ''open up the black box'' (i.e., to build a model of the biological system that captures its constituent structure and the elementary functions describing interactions among the constituents—neural populations or subsystems). This is done by explaining not only psychophysical data, but also by using anatomical and neurophysiological data to constrain the model. Unlike connectionist approaches, the resulting model has a necessarily nonhomogenous structure that reflects the task specificity of neural circuitry; brain regions that perform different tasks have evolved both phylogenetically and ontogenetically to use different structure and connectivity. An accurate model computes the overall input-output function as a composition of these distinct, more elementary functions. This research strategy adheres to the slogan of the Swiss structuralist Piaget, that to understand is to reconstruct. The description of the constituent structure taken with the local laws of interaction provide an understanding of the mechanisms by which the aggregate input-output function is generated *in vivo*.

Examples of this approach can be found in Calabrese, Angstadt, and Arbas (1989), Grossberg and Kuperstein (1986, 1989), Houk and Gibson (1987), Ito (1984), Kawato, Furukawa, and Suzuki (1987), and Selverston and Moulins (1986). These models differ in the scope of the sensory-motor problems they address and the detail with which they describe the neural mechanisms involved. The remainder of this chapter describes a collection of interrelated neural models that cover a wide range of the field of neural networks for biological sensory-motor control. Readers unfamiliar with neural network models may at this point benefit from reading the appendix, which reviews elementary concepts in the analysis of neural networks as dynamical systems.

INTEGRATIVE EXAMPLE: REACHING TO A VISIBLE TARGET, OR HOW LIGHT GETS INTO THE MUSCLES[1]

One of the most studied tasks in the motor control literature is reaching to targets in space. Many neural network modelers have concentrated on a subset of the computations involved in the chain of events spanning from visually perceiving a target to issuing commands to the motoneurons involved in moving the arm to the target (e.g., Houk and Gibson 1987; Ito 1984; Zipser and Andersen 1988). Other researchers have attempted to model the entire task with simple network models (e.g., Kuperstein 1988; Ritter, Martinetz, and Schulten 1989; Gaudiano and Grossberg 1991). The remainder of this chapter reviews a research program concerned with describing this process in detail with a collection of neural network

---

[1]In the late 1970s, Michael Turvey often began his colloquia with the provocative question: ''How does light get into the muscles?''

models that each perform a subtask in the larger task of visually guided reaching. Four networks, motivated by anatomical, physiological, and psychological data, collectively perform the following tasks:

- Neural representation of a visually perceived target within a head-centered coordinate frame
- Transformation of this representation into a body-centered coordinate frame
- Formation of a spatial trajectory from current hand position to the target
- Transformation of this spatial trajectory into joint angle commands (inverse kinematics)
- Invariant production of the commanded joint angle time courses despite large changes in muscle tension (inverse dynamics)

These models were formulated with strict attention to internal consistency; this includes several kinds of consistency within and between networks. First, because these networks are interconnected to form an integrated sensory-motor system, the representations used at the interfaces between the networks must be consistent. Second, because this collection of networks is formulated as a partial model of the human sensory-motor control system, the model must be consistent with motor control tasks other than reaching that will use many of the same subsystems. That is, the proposed solution for visually guided reaching should be constrained so the resulting model is compatible with the solution of other motor tasks such as handwriting. Third, because these networks are meant as mechanistic models of biological sensory-motor control, there must be consistency of model component types across networks, and consistency of these components with available neurophysiological data. The lowest-level components of these models correspond to neurons or populations of neurons, and many model cell types have been identified with neuron types *in vivo* whose properties closely match those of the model cells.

Strict attention is also paid to the role of learning within these models. Mechanical properties of biological systems change with time. For example, the lengths of arm segments and strengths of muscles change with age. To assure accurate reaching, parameter values in the sensory-motor control system (e.g., the weighting of synaptic connections) must be *adaptive*, not prewired at birth. However, performance of a reaching task under temporarily constraining conditions, such as blocked movement of a particular joint, should not require new learning to restructure the motor control system. Two later sections describe networks that generate the desired trajectories for reaches. These networks use information from an action-perception cycle in order to adaptively organize mappings that transform a head-centered representation of target positions into a body-centered representation, transform spatial movement commands into joint angle movement commands, and transform joint angle position information into spatial position information. The control system adaptively finds parameters that implicitly account for the relations among body segments and strengths of muscles, but do not use new learning to solve movement problems under temporary environmental constraints.

These networks were also formulated with attention to robust performance. The DIRECT model of trajectory formation and inverse kinematics, reviewed later, was motivated by motor equivalence data suggesting that humans can generate a spatial movement trajectory in many ways, depending on environmental constraints. These data point to movement trajectory formation in spatial, rather than motor, coordinates, and this constrains the form of the head- and body-centered representations of space described in later sections. The DIRECT model provides robust performance of movement trajectories under conditions of visual shift, a blocked joint, or reaches with a tool, rather than the hand, as the end effector. The model performs these reaches automatically (i.e., without reverting to special performance modes and without requiring new learning under the different conditions). The FLETE network design, also described later, models spinal circuits that ensure the invariant production of commanded joint angle time courses in the face of conditions that lead to large variations in muscle tension.

To summarize, the collection of networks described in the following sections uses only information available in an ongoing action-perception cycle to learn the transformations necessary for an extremely flexible system capable of successfully performing several tasks under a variety of environmental conditions. Rather than optimizing performance for abstract criteria such as minimum jerk or minimum torque change (c.f. Flash and Hogan 1985; Uno, Kawato, and Suzuki 1987) by learning a set of model parameters specific to a single task, we believe that the optimization criterion of biological sensory-motor control systems is the rapid, successful performance of many motor tasks in a constantly changing environment.

FORMING A HEAD-CENTERED
REPRESENTATION OF TARGET POSITION

The bilaterally symmetric organization of the body provides a simple and direct source of information for computing absolute position of a fixated target with respect to the observer's head and body. When both eyes binocularly fixate a target, the angle of intersection of the lines of gaze, which is a function of the eyes' attitudes in their orbits, may be used to compute the absolute distance and direction of the fixation point with respect to the head. Such extraretinal information may also be used to complement visual processing to derive better estimates of the absolute distance and direction of visually detected but nonfixated objects (see Grossberg et al. 1993).

Fig. 10.1 describes the geometry of three-dimensional target localization in terms of spherical coordinates that closely relate to the three-dimensional representation proposed here. The origin of this coordinate system, called the cranial egocenter, lies at the midpoint between the two eyes. Thus, the representation is *cyclopean*. The head-centered horizontal angle or azimuth, θ_H, and the vertical angle or elevation, ϕ_H, measure deviations from straight-ahead gaze. The radial distance R_H in the spherical coordinate frame of fig. 10.1 is replaced by vergence in the representations of three-dimensional space described herein.

Greve et al. (1993) and Guenther (1992) give evidence for such a coordinate system and a full description of a neural network model that forms a neural representation of target position based on this coordinate system. A less formal description of this network and the neurally generated representation follows.

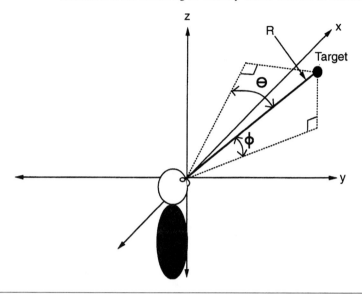

Fig. 10.1   Spherical coordinate frame for specifying a target position with respect to the head. This coordinate frame is related to the head-centered representation of space.

The head-centered representation neural network, shown in fig. 10.2, binocularly combines outflow signals from tonically active cells that control the position of each eye to form a head-centered representation of a foveated target. Forming such a representation is possible because the vector of command signals needed to orient two eyes to foveate a single point contains all the information needed to specify that point's three-dimensional location relative to the cranial egocenter. The extraction of this implicit information can be done in just two stages of opponent processing. First, opponent interactions combine the outputs of the cells that control the agonist and antagonist muscles of each eye. These opponent interactions give rise to opponent pairs of cells the sum of whose activity is approximately constant, or normalized (see Greve et al. 1993). The following equations define the resulting normalized internal representations of the horizontal angle of each eye:

$$l_1 + l_2 = 1 \tag{10.1}$$

$$\theta_L = -90° + 180° \times l_2 \tag{10.2}$$

$$r_1 + r_2 = 1 \tag{10.3}$$

$$\theta_R = -90° + 180° \times r_2 \tag{10.4}$$

where l_i indicates the activity of left eye cell population i, and r_i indicates the activity of right eye cell population i. Internal representations for the vertical angles of left and right eyes may be defined similarly. Thus

$$l_3 + l_4 = 1 \tag{10.5}$$

$$\phi_L = -90° + 180° \times l_4 \tag{10.6}$$

$$r_3 + r_4 = 1 \tag{10.7}$$

$$\phi_R = -90° + 180° \times r_4. \tag{10.8}$$

Next, the normalized outputs from both eyes are combined in two ways to generate a head-centered spatial representation of the binocular fixation point. In particular, opponent cells from each eye generate inputs of opposite sign (excitatory and inhibitory) to their target cells at the next processing stage. As illustrated in fig. 10.2, one combination gives rise to a cell population whose activity h_2 approximates the angular spherical coordinate θ_H. The other combination gives rise to a cell population whose activity h_5 approximates the binocular vergence γ, which can be used to estimate the radial distance R_H. The two combinations generate head-centered coordinates by computing a sum and a difference of the normalized opponent inputs

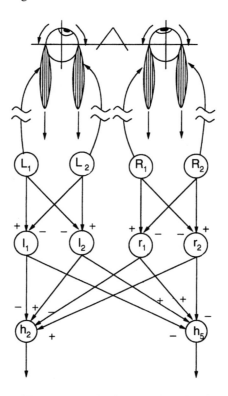

Fig. 10.2   Network for combining corollary discharges from both eyes, via two stages of opponent processing, into a head-centered representation of three-dimensional target position.

from both eyes. Such a general strategy for combining signals is well known in other neural systems, such as color vision. For example, a sum $L + M$ of signals from two color-vision channels estimates luminance, whereas a difference $L - M$ estimates color (DeValois and DeValois 1975; Mollon and Sharpe 1983). Thus, computations that may be used to control reaching in three-dimensional space are derived from a broadly used principle of neural computation. The following paragraphs describe the mathematical details of the combination of left and right eye muscle signals to produce a head-centered representation of space.

Let the cell populations h_i, $i = 1, 2, \ldots, 6$, form the basis for this head-centered spatial representation. These populations are arranged in antagonistic pairs. First we define cell activities h_1, h_2, h_3, and h_4 that linearly approximate the following estimates of θ_H and ϕ_H:

$$h_1 + h_2 = 1 \tag{10.9}$$

$$\theta_H = -90° + 180° \times h_2 \tag{10.10}$$

$$h_3 + h_4 = 1 \tag{10.11}$$

$$\phi_H = -90° + 180° \times h_4. \tag{10.12}$$

These head-centered binocular representations of θ_H and ϕ_H emerge by simply averaging the corresponding monocular components derived from the left and right eye muscle command corollary discharges using a shunting on-center off-surround network. Specifically,

$$\frac{d}{dt}h_2 = -Bh_2 + (1 - h_2)(l_2 + r_2) - h_2(l_1 + r_1), \tag{10.13}$$

where B is a non-negative decay rate. Solving this equation at equilibrium ($dh_2/dt = 0$) yields

$$h_2 = \frac{l_2 + r_2}{B + l_1 + r_1 + l_2 + r_2}. \tag{10.14}$$

Since $l_1 + l_2 \cong 1$ and $r_1 + r_2 \cong 1$, choosing a near-zero decay parameter B, such that $0 < B \ll 1$, leads to the approximation:

$$h_2 \cong \frac{l_2 + r_2}{2}. \tag{10.15}$$

Likewise,

$$h_1 \cong \frac{l_1 + r_1}{2}. \tag{10.16}$$

so that, by (15) and (16),

$$h_1 + h_2 \cong 1. \tag{10.17}$$

To see how opponent computation leads to a representation of target distance, note that vergence is equal to the difference between r_1 (the normalized outflow command to the medial rectus of the right eye) and l_1 (the normalized outflow command to the lateral rectus of the left eye). Define antagonistic cell populations with activities h_5 and h_6 for internal representation of vergence. Let h_5 receive excitatory inputs l_2 and r_1 from cells controlling the medial recti of both eyes and inhibitory inputs l_1 and r_2 from cells controlling the lateral recti of both eyes (fig. 10.2). Then its activity will be governed by

$$\frac{dh_5}{dt} = -Ch_5 + (1 - h_5)(r_1 + l_2) - (h_5 + D)(l_1 + r_2), \tag{10.18}$$

where C and D are both non-negative. Here C is the decay rate and $-D$ is the lower bound on cellular activity h_5. At equilibrium,

$$h_5 = \frac{r_1 + l_2 - Dl_1 - Dr_2}{C + r_1 + r_2 + l_1 + l_2}. \tag{10.19}$$

Because $r_1 + r_2 = 1$ and $l_1 + l_2 = 1$, equation (19) can be rewritten as

$$h_5 = \frac{1 - D}{C + 2} + \frac{1 + D}{C + 2}(r_1 - l_1). \tag{10.20}$$

If $D = 1$ and $C = 0$, then

$$h_5 = r_1 - l_1. \tag{10.21}$$

In this case, which might be considered ideal, subjective vergence equals physical vergence. A small departure from this ideal would occur if C were near zero but positive, and if D were slightly less than unity (i.e., if $0 < C \ll 1$ and $0 \ll D < 1$). Then the slope $(1 + D)(C + 2)^{-1}$ of h_5 versus $r_1 - l_1$ is less than 1, and the intercept $(1 - D)(C + 2)^{-1}$ of the function is positive. Such values are biologically plausible and compatible with the Foley (1980) estimate from psychophysical data of the internal representation of target distance.

FORMING A BODY-CENTERED
REPRESENTATION OF TARGET POSITION

This section addresses the formation of a body-centered representation of three-dimensional target positions using the head-centered representation described in the previous section, coupled with information concerning the head position with respect to the torso. This work is described in detail in Guenther et al. (1994) and Guenther (1992). The adaptive computational strategy embodied by this network uses signals generated automatically during the typical behavioral sequence associated with changes of visual fixation. In a typical episode

1. the representation of a novel, initially nonfoveal visual target wins an internal competition that determines the next target to be foveated, and a saccade is made to this target;
2. information regarding head-centered target location is combined with information about neck muscle states to yield a stored estimate of target location relative to the body;
3. neck muscles rotate the head (either randomly or to point the nose toward the target) while the eyes make a vestibular ocular reflex (VOR)-mediated counterrotation to ensure continued foveation during the head movement; and
4. during the head movement and ocular counterrotation, both internal representations of the target's location in head coordinates and internal representations of neck angles change while the stored representation of target position in body coordinates remains constant.

If the network that combines head-centered representation and neck angle information to yield an estimate of target location in body coordinates is well tuned, then its estimate will remain invariant during the head rotation and ocular counterrotation. If it is not well tuned, then a discrepancy will develop during the head rotation between this network's current estimate and the estimate stored before the head rotation. This discrepancy may then serve as an error signal capable of directing a learning process that improves the network's knowledge, stored in its synaptic weights, about how to combine neck angle and head coordinate signals to estimate target positions relative to the body. The stage that registers the discrepancy in our model is called a difference vector (DV) stage, because errors are registered on a component-by-component basis. The Vector Associative Map (VAM) of Gaudiano and Grossberg (1991) is a neural mechanism that carries out DV-based learning; the current network uses a variant of VAM learning. The learning process described for this transformation requires no teacher and combines mechanisms known to be separately available *in vivo*.

The body-centered representation approximates a spherical coordinate frame that is similar to the spherical coordinate frame of fig. 10.1. The relationship between the head-centered and body-centered spherical coordinate frames is shown in fig. 10.3. The origin of the body-centered system is the same as the origin of the head-centered system when the head is pointed straight ahead. The body-centered frame also uses the same three spherical coordinates as the head-centered system, denoted by (θ_B, ϕ_B, R_B) in the body-centered frame. When the head points straight ahead, the head-centered representation (θ_H, ϕ_H, R_H) is identical to the body-centered representation (θ_B, ϕ_B, R_B). When the head moves from straight ahead, however, the head-centered frame moves with the head while the body-centered frame remains stationary.

The choice of these coordinate frames results from an investigation of the physiology of the head-neck systems of humans and many other vertebrates. The biomechanics of the neck vertebrae favor rotations of the head around preferred axes (Vidal et al. 1988). Movements along one of these preferred axes correspond to changes in θ_N (i.e., side-to-side or horizontal movements), whereas movements along the other preferred axis correspond to changes in ϕ_N (i.e., vertical movements). Movements along other axes, for example tilting the head to one side, are much more

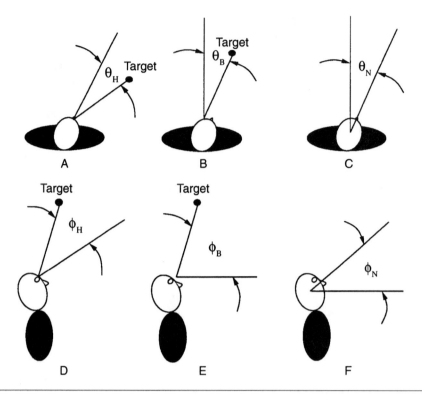

Fig. 10.3   Top view (*a, b, c*) and side view (*d, e, f*) showing relationships between the head-centered coordinates (*subscript H*), body-centered coordinates (*subscript B*), and head angles with respect to the body (*subscript N*).

constrained by the biomechanics of the neck. Further evidence for the biological importance of these preferred axes comes from Masino and Knudsen (1990), who showed that separate neural circuits controlled horizontal and vertical head movements in the barn owl.

The importance of these results in the current context is as follows. Learning to discount head movements in the body-centered representation consists of compensating for changes in head position by negating the resulting changes in the head-centered representation of a fixed target position. In other words, $(\theta_B, \phi_B) = (\theta_H, \phi_H) + (\theta_{correction}, \phi_{correction})$, where $(\theta_{correction}, \phi_{correction})$ is a learned correction based on neck muscle information. (The third coordinate in the two representations, distance from the head, changes little with head movement; see Guenther 1992, and Guenther et al. 1994, for further discussion of corrections to the vergence component.) When the transformation network is properly tuned, this correction is nearly linearly related, in fact nearly equal, to the head movement defined according to the preferred axes (i.e., θ_N, ϕ_N). This linear relation between head movements and the required correction to the head-centered representation allows very fast and accurate learning of the correction. The relationship between head movements and other head- and body-centered coordinate frames, such as Cartesian, is much more complex, making the transformation from a head-centered representation to a body-centered representation far more difficult to learn.

Although head position (θ_N, ϕ_N) can be derived from neck muscle length information, an organism cannot, without learning, use this neck muscle information accurately to compensate for head movements when forming a body-centered representation. This is because the relationship between any neck muscle length and head position is dependent on details of the neck anatomy that vary from individual to individual and can change with time (e.g., growth). Therefore, the organism must *adaptively* find parameters that allow neck muscle length information to compensate for changes in head position. The network described in the following paragraphs rapidly and successfully finds these parameters without an external teacher. Instead, network construction capitalizes on the fact that the positions of fixed objects with respect to the body do not change while the head moves, allowing the organism to internally generate teaching signals. We briefly describe this process in the following paragraphs.

Fig. 10.4 illustrates the network used for the simulations. We omit populations corresponding to representations of R_H and R_B in this section due to the relative independence of these variables with respect to neck movements. In this network, there are five main neural population types:

1. Neck muscle length populations with activities n_{ij} $(1 \leq i \leq 9, 1 \leq j \leq 2)$
2. Head coordinate representation populations with activities h_i $(1 \leq i \leq 4)$
3. Head-neck Difference Vector (DV) populations with activities x_i $(1 \leq i \leq 4)$
4. Unnormalized body coordinate representation populations with activities $b_i^{(1)}$ $(1 \leq i \leq 4)$
5. Normalized body coordinate representation populations with activities $b_i^{(2)}$ $(1 \leq i \leq 4)$

Each head-centered representation population projects with a fixed-weight connection to the corresponding DV population. Each neck muscle length population projects to every DV population through an adaptable-weight synaptic connection, indicated by filled semicircles in fig. 10.4. Furthermore, VOR-mediated gating modulates the interactions between the DV populations and the unnormalized body-centered representation populations. The learning law in the simulations is as follows:

$$\frac{d[z_{ijk}]}{dt} = -\varepsilon x_k[-Ez_{ijk} + n_{ij}] \tag{10.22}$$

where z_{ijk} is the weight of the synaptic connection between neck muscle length activity n_{ij} and DV population activity x_k, ε is a learning rate parameter with a small positive value, and E is a decay rate parameter. Thus, learning is local (i.e., it depends only on the pre- and post-synaptic cell activities, not on activities or activity changes at distant points in the network).

The following steps were used to train the network:

1. Initialize all weights to 0.0.
2. Choose a random initial head position (θ_N, ϕ_N).
3. Choose a random target position (θ_T, ϕ_T).

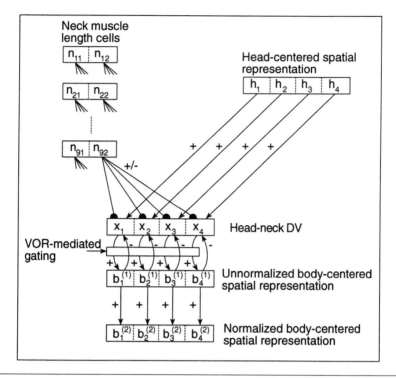

Fig. 10.4 Network for learning transformation from a head-centered spherical coordinate representation to a body-centered spherical coordinate representation of target position.

4. Foveate a new target (i.e., adjust h_i so that $\theta_H = \theta_T - \theta_N$ and $\phi_H = \phi_T - \phi_N$) and store this target into the body coordinate populations $b_i^{(1)}$ and $b_j^{(2)}$. This step corresponds to the breaking of VOR fixation to foveate and store a new target. Storing the target is presumed to be carried out by the transient opening of the gated excitatory pathways from the populations x_i to the populations $b_j^{(1)}$. This gating action is presumed to occur each time VOR fixation is broken.

5. Choose a new head position while remaining foveated on the current target (i.e., change n_{ij} and adjust h_i accordingly to keep $\theta_H + \theta_N = \theta_T$ and $\phi_H + \phi_N = \phi_T$). This step corresponds to moving the head while using VOR to keep the target foveated.

6. Adjust the weights from the neck muscle length populations to the head-neck DV populations according to equation (22).

7. If more trials remain, repeat steps 3 through 7.

Despite the use of simple, local learning laws and no external teacher, the system globally self-organizes to perform the required transformation from a head-centered to a body-centered representation of three-dimensional target positions. Fig. 10.5A shows the internal representation (left side) and actual target position (right side) during a head movement after 20 learning trials. As the head moves, the internal representation of the target position also moves, even though the actual target

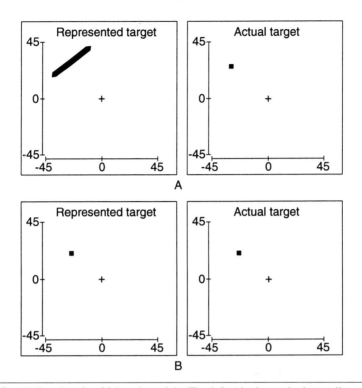

Fig. 10.5   (*A*) Results after 20 learning trials. The *left side* shows the internally represented body-centered target position as the head is moved through over 30° of both horizontal and vertical angle. The *right side* shows the actual target position. The change in represented target position as the head is moved indicates that the network has not yet learned to invariantly represent body-centered target position. (*B*) Results after 200 learning trials. The *left side* shows the internally represented body-centered target position as the head is moved through over 30° of both horizontal and vertical angle. The *right side* shows the actual target position. The internal representation is now invariant under head movements.

position with respect to the body remains fixed. After foveating only 200 targets, however, the network has learned to invariantly represent the body-centered target position despite large head movements, as shown in fig. 10.5B.

DIRECT: TRAJECTORY FORMATION AND INVERSE KINEMATICS

Once the position of a target relative to the body is known, a trajectory from the current hand position to the target must be formed. The phenomenon of motor equivalence (i.e., the ability to realize a movement goal using motor means that vary from trial to trial) implies that trajectory formation is controlled in spatial, rather than motor, coordinates. For example, it is well known that the overall spatial shape of written letters remains remarkably consistent when produced with entirely different effector systems (Merton 1972; Raibert 1977). Spatial trajectory formation is also supported by psychophysical data, which show that the spatial characteristics of movements to targets remain invariant across movements despite large variations in the joint angle characteristics from movement to movement (e.g., Morasso 1981) or changes in the end effector used to reach to the target (e.g., Lacquaniti, Soechting, and Terzuolo 1982). The ability to produce a desired movement trajectory in many ways results in robustness of movement performance under a variety of environmental conditions.

The representation of target positions described earlier is consistent with trajectory formation in spatial coordinates. The Vector Integration to Endpoint (VITE) model (Bullock and Grossberg 1988a, 1991) is a neural network model of trajectory formation that exhibits key kinematic properties of human movements, including asymmetric bell-shaped velocity profiles (e.g., Nagasaki 1989; Zelaznik, Schmidt, and Gielen 1986). As shown in fig. 10.6, this model has three stages, each of which computes a vector much like the body-centered representation (b_1, b_2, . . . , b_6): a target position vector (*TPV*), which specifies the desired joint angles that define the end goal of a movement, a present position vector (*PPV*), which specifies the current joint angles, and a difference or direction vector (*DV*) formed by subtracting the *PPV* from the *TPV*. The *DV* thus specifies the desired movement direction and magnitude. In the VITE model, it is fundamental that the *DV* be computed before movement and stored until movement initiation. This precomputation and storage is called motor priming, an important precursor of deliberate action and fully voluntary movement (Busemeyer and Townsend 1993; DeJong et al. 1990). The phenomenon of voluntary release of a primed movement implies that there must be an internal signal whose activation allows the *DV* to be expressed. This signal is called the *GO* signal, and its action is analogous to opening a gate between the primed *DV* and the effector apparatus. Closing and opening of this gate is captured in the model

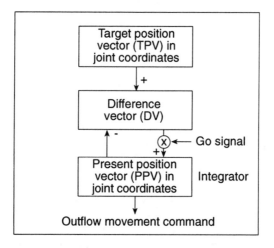

Fig. 10.6   Block diagram of the VITE model.

by assuming that the *GO* signal is zero during the priming interval but positive during movement, and that *GO* multiplies the *DV* before the latter affects the effector apparatus via the *PPV* stage. Then $DV \times GO$ specifies desired movement velocity, and making *GO* positive serves the dual function of releasing movement and scaling its speed. If the $DV \times GO$ signal is integrated at the *PPV* stage, a process we call *PPV* updating, then the *PPV* moves toward the *TPV* after *GO* becomes positive, and the *PPV* specifies desired position in joint coordinates.

Taken together, $DV \times GO$ and *PPV* give the desired movement trajectory, which evolves gradually. Because of the inhibitory feedback from the *PPV* to the *DV* stage, the *DV* is driven to zero by *PPV* updating. When *PPV* reaches *TPV*, $DV = 0$. Therefore, $DV \times GO = 0$ even if *GO* remains large, and the movement self-terminates at the target coordinates. If the onset of *GO* is gradual, such that *GO* exhibits growth through much of the movement time, then velocity profiles have the smooth, bell-like form characteristic of human and animal movement.

However, VITE falls short as a comprehensive model of movement control—even for elementary visually guided movements. It does not explain how to compute the *TPV* in joint coordinates assumed by the model. Thus, it does not solve the inverse kinematics problem: how can a goal specified in three-dimensional spatial coordinates be realized by movements involving changes in joint coordinates, which may have many more than three dimensions? As noted earlier, the conservation of spatial form across movements made with varying effectors (the motor equivalence phenomenon) suggests that three-dimensional spatial computations are a critical aspect of the process of trajectory formation. The **DI**rection-to-**R**otation Effector Control Transform (DIRECT) model (Bullock, Grossberg, and Guenther 1993; Guenther 1992), schematized in fig. 10.7, extends the VITE model to allow spatial trajectory formation with motor equivalent movement production. The motor coordinates *TPV* and *PPV* of VITE are replaced by a spatial target position vector (TPV_s) and spatial present position vector (PPV_s). The PPV_s is then subtracted from the TPV_s to form a difference vector (DV_s), which represents the desired movement magnitude and direction in spatial coordinates.

Once this desired movement direction has been formulated, the problem of mapping into motor coordinates to control the joint angles, or the inverse kinematics problem, must still be solved. The DIRECT model learns a solution, which transforms DV_s into a motor direction vector (DV_m) specifying joint rotations. This transformation from directions in three-dimensional space into joint rotations plays a key role in producing motor equivalent reaching (see Bullock, Grossberg, and Guenther 1993). The DV_m components are then integrated by a motor present position vector (PPV_m) that specifies commanded joint angles. As in VITE, signals from the DV_m to the PPV_m stage can be gated by a *GO* signal.

The DIRECT model contains two learned transformations, indicated by filled semicircles in fig. 10.7: the spatial-to-motor transformation, which commands the motor actions needed to carry out a spatially defined trajectory, and a motor-to-spatial transformation, which allows motor information regarding end effector position to be used in place of visual information when performing reaches without visual feedback. As in the previous networks, learning in the DIRECT model is achieved through autonomously generated repetition of an action-perception cycle, which generates the associative information needed to learn these transforms. Piaget

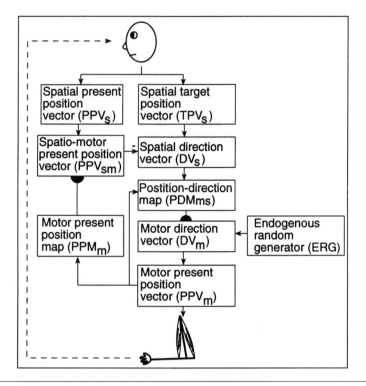

Fig. 10.7   Block diagram of the DIRECT model.

(1963) called this cycle a *circular reaction*. A circular reaction endogenously creates movements in babies during a *motor babbling* phase, and leads to learning transformations among representations correlated through these movements. After learning takes place, the movements may be carried out in an intentional, or goal-oriented, manner.

Motor babbling is energized by an Endogenous Random Generator, or ERG, whose activations are integrated to generate movement commands (Gaudiano and Grossberg 1991). In the DIRECT model, ERG activations excite the DV_m stage, which encodes motor commands for rotating the joints, causing spontaneous arm movements during the motor babbling stage. The network uses the information generated by these spontaneous arm movements in several ways. Visual feedback provides information about the positions and directions of movements in three-dimensional space. Internal feedback provides information about the joint configurations that generate these movements. The network is designed to combine these multiple sources of information in a manner that solves the motor equivalence problem.

During motor babbling, the endogenously moving end effector is a salient visual target. As the system visually tracks its own end effector, information regarding the direction of end effector movement, represented at the DV_s stage during motor babbling, drives learning of the spatial-to-motor transformation. To convert DV_s

activations into effective reaching behaviors, each DV_s must be transformed into a DV_m, which produces movement in the corresponding spatial direction; that is, spatial directions need to be converted into joint rotations. The appropriate DV_m to learn depends on the configuration of the arm when the DV_s is computed. The conjoint activation of the PDM_{ms} stage by both the PPV_m stage and the DV_s stage activates a few cells in the PDM_{ms} map. Topographic maps such as the PDM_{ms} are found in many areas in the brain, and self-organizing neural networks that form such maps have been extensively studied (e.g., von der Malsburg 1973; Grossberg and Kuperstein 1986, 1989; Kohonen 1984). This map architecture allows the PDM_{ms} cells to learn the babbled DV_m activity that is producing the motion direction registered at the DV_s stage. Learning takes the form of a local, Hebbian learning law with gated decay called the *outstar* learning law (Grossberg 1968, 1982; Levine 1991).

A motor-to-spatial transformation is also learned during motor babbling. The goal of this transformation is to convert a motor representation PPV_m of the present end effector position into a visual representation (i.e., in the same coordinate frame as PPV_s) of present end effector position. The vector representation PPV_m is transformed into a map representation PPM_m via a self-organizing feature map, and the PPM_m cells learn corresponding PPV_s vectors at the PPV_{sm} stage via outstar learning. In this way, a configuration coded at the PPV_m stage learns to predict the corresponding spatial position of the end effector as represented through vision at PPV_s.

In summary, during motor babbling, the *ERG* spontaneously generates motor vectors DV_m that are integrated into arm movements by the PPV_m stage. The arm movements draw visual attention to the end effector. As a result, spatial DV_s vectors are computed that, conjointly with PPV_m feedback signals, enable the PDM_{sm} map to learn an appropriate DV_m with which to move in the corresponding spatial direction DV_s when the end effector is at PPV_m. Simultaneously, joint configurations coded by the PPM_m stage are associated through learning at the PPV_{ms} stage with the corresponding spatial positions PPV_s of the end effector perceived through vision.

These movements and learning events during motor babbling are not goal oriented. The babbled movements are endogenously activated, and the learning events correlate spatial and motor representations coactivated by the babbled movements. During subsequent goal-oriented reaching movements, the target is not typically the end effector, so the information coded at TPV_s and at PPV_s is not the same. The DIRECT model is designed such that, after motor babbling ends, when a target other than the end effector activates TPV_s, the difference between present position of the end effector at PPV_{sm} and the target position at TPV_s is computed at DV_s, and the arm is steered toward the target by activating an appropriate series of DV_m vectors to move the arm in the desired direction. If visual feedback of the end effector is not available during the reach, then the motor pathway $PPV_m \rightarrow PPM_m \rightarrow PPV_{sm}$ is used to estimate end effector position, rather than the visual pathway $PPV_s \rightarrow PPV_{sm}$. In particular, after learning, the DIRECT model uses gating signals to direct the flow of visual information to the PPV_s block if the visually attended spatial position corresponds to the end effector, or to the TPV_s block if the visually attended spatial position corresponds to a goal-oriented movement target. This requires the developing system to incorporate some mechanism for differentiating between self-generated movements of the hand and other potential targets of visual attention (moving or stationary) in the visual field. For a thorough discussion of these gating signals and a possible mechanism for providing this self versus other distinction, see Guenther (1992).

DIRECT model simulations of a three-joint arm performing reaches in two-dimensional space verify the model's performance of unconstrained reaches to targets, reaches with one joint blocked during the reach, reaches using a tool or pointer as the end effector, reaches with visual input shifted by 30°, and reaches with no visual feedback of end effector position during the reach. It is important to note that training was done only in normal mode (i.e., with no blocked joints, no tools, and no shifted visual input). Yet because of the direction-to-rotation inverse kinematic mapping, the model automatically compensates for these different conditions to perform the reach successfully on the first try. Fig. 10.8 shows the model performing reaches using a tool as the end effector. The target is the small box at the end of the effector, and the tool is the fourth segment of the effector projecting from the box at the hand to the target. By simply representing tool tip position rather than hand position at the PPV_s block (corresponding to visually attending to the tool tip during the reach), the model automatically produces accurate reaches with this novel fourth effector segment of arbitrary length and angle with respect to the hand.

As with the networks reviewed earlier, the DIRECT model components correspond to neurons or populations of neurons, and synaptic learning uses only information available at the pre- and post-synaptic cells. Because of this, the DIRECT model

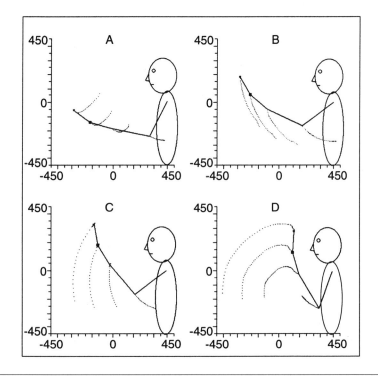

Fig. 10.8   Trajectories formed by the model using a pointer for reaching.

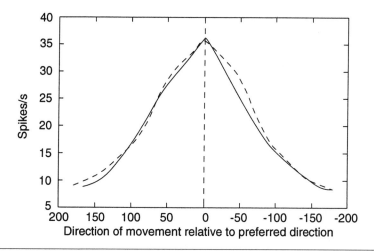

Fig. 10.9 Directional tuning curve averaged over 500 measurements of the joint velocity cells in different parts of joint space for the simulated model (*solid line*) and corresponding data from Kalaska et al. (1989) (*broken line*). Model data has been scaled to cover the same range as the Kalaska et al. data.

may provide insights regarding neurophysiological data. Many neurophysiologists have reported that motor cortical cells seem to be broadly tuned to desired direction of movement (e.g., Georgopoulos et al. 1982; Kalaska et al. 1989). That is, a motor cortical cell fires with maximal response rate for movement in a preferred direction, and at progressively lower rates for movement directions farther from the preferred direction. Fig. 10.9 compares the averaged tuning curve of the DIRECT model DV_m cells to neurophysiological data from the motor cortex. The solid line in fig. 10.9 indicates the average form of DV_m tuning curves in the model after training. The broken line in fig. 10.9 shows an averaged tuning curve obtained from single cell measurements in primate motor cortex by Kalaska et al. (1989). Based on the similarities in these curves and several additional comparisons, including the time course of real cell and model cell activities during movement, we believe that the DIRECT model provides insights about how and why these tuning curves might arise in motor cortical cells.

Ideas from the VITE and DIRECT models have recently been used to model behavior with serial structure. In particular, the DIVA model of Guenther (1992, 1994) treats speech production, whereas the VITEWRITE model of Bullock, Grossberg, and Mannes (1993) treats handwriting production. Both treatments demonstrate that we can replace many older ideas about stored motor programs once we recognize that movement properties can be better understood as emergent characteristics of adaptive dynamical systems.

FLETE: ACCURATE REACHING
DESPITE VARIATIONS IN TENSION

The networks described so far give an account of the transformations from visual localization of a target to issuing joint angle commands that move the arm to the target. However, successful performance of these joint angle commands requires the answer to many questions that fall under the heading of inverse dynamics, or how to generate the forces needed to realize kinematic goals. How can a limb be rotated to, and stabilized at, a desired angle? How can joint stiffness be varied independently of joint angle? How can the movement speed from an initial to a desired final angle be controlled under conditions of low joint stiffness? How can launching and braking forces be generated to compensate for inertial loads? Simultaneous achievement of these abilities requires a complex neuromuscular system, with several identifiable subsystems.

These tasks require that each muscle be able to generate a wide range of tensions at any length it may assume as the limb (into which it inserts) rotates. More stringently, these tasks require Factorization, or independent control, of muscle LEngth and muscle TEnsion. This overarching theme led to the acronym "FLETE" for an original mathematical model of the neuromuscular system described in Bullock and Grossberg (1988b, 1989). The components of the FLETE model will be briefly introduced here; see Bullock and Contreras-Vidal (1993) and Bullock, Contreras-Vidal, and Grossberg (1993b) for a complete description of the motivation for these components, their functionality, and simulation results verifying their contribution to model performance.

The first question we will address concerns how a limb can be rotated to, and stabilized at, a desired angle. Fig. 10.10A schematizes a system in which two opposing muscles insert into a distal limb segment connected by a rotary or hinge joint to a more proximal limb segment, similar to the human forearm's connection to the upper arm. Suppose such a forearm segment is initially at rest and that $F_1 = F_2$, where the F_i, $i = 1, 2$ denote the pulling forces exerted by the opponent muscles. Then the limb can be set in motion by making the forces F_1 and F_2 unequal. The limb can be halted and stabilized at a new joint angle if the forces re-equilibrate as it approaches that angle and if the system can automatically generate whatever new muscle force imbalance may be needed to return it to the desired angle after any deviation (e.g., after the rotating limb initially overshoots the desired angle).

As many observers have noted (Cooke 1980; Feldman 1986; Polit and Bizzi 1979), muscle itself seems to have evolved to help provide this basic functionality. Essentially, muscle is springy tissue with a neurally controllable contractile component, which gives it a neurally modifiable threshold length for force development (Rack and Westbury 1969). To highlight this essence, at risk of oversimplification,[2] we can assume that the force F_i developed by a muscle is a threshold-linear function of its length L_i, its fixed resting length Γ_i, its stiffness, k, and its neurally modifiable contractile state, C_i:

$$F_i = k[L_i - (\Gamma_i - C_i)]^+ \tag{10.23}$$

where notation $[w_i]^+$ means max $(0, \omega_i)$. So if $\omega_i = L_i - (\Gamma_i - C_i) > 0$, $F_i = k \cdot \omega_i$; if $\omega_i \leq 0$, $F_i = k \cdot 0 = 0$.

---

[2]A better approximation to real muscle, whose stiffness also varies with contractile state, is gotten by replacing (23) with $F_i = k \cdot g([L_i - (\Gamma_i - C_i)]^+)$, where $g(x)$ is nonlinear (e.g., quadratic). See Bullock and Contreras-Vidal (1993) for further treatment.

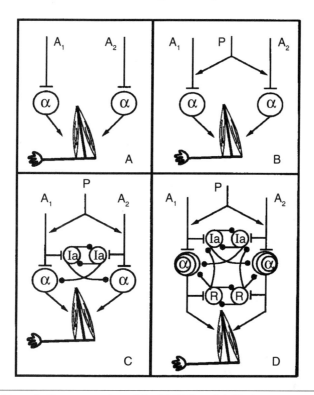

Fig. 10.10   Stages in the construction of the FLETE model. Excitatory connections are indicated by *flat bars*, inhibitory connections by *filled circles*. (A) Opponent alpha-motoneuron pools provide neural control over muscle contractile states and thereby the balance of forces acting across the joint. A motor intention can take the form of a pattern of descending signals (A_1, A_2) to the α-MN pools. (B) Joint stiffness can be controlled by adding descending signal P to both signals A_1 and A_2. The signal P is capable of producing high levels of co-contraction of the opponent muscles. (C) Design for alleviating saturative loss of sensitivity by α-MN pools to the difference $A_1 - A_2$ when signal P becomes large. The added model interneurons have the same connectivity as *Ia* interneurons known to exist *in vivo*. (D) Alpha-motoneurons have different sizes, which correspond to different thresholds for recruitment, and Renshaw cells "tap the cables" running from α-MN pools to muscles. Their negative feedback to α-MNs can compensate for distortion introduced by the size principle.

Equation (23) shows that a muscle is springlike in that it develops a force only when stretched to a length L_i greater than the effective threshold length, $\Gamma_i - C_i$. However, it also shows that muscle is more versatile than an ordinary spring, because this threshold can be neurally adjusted by varying the muscle's state of contraction, C_i.

To gain control over contractile states C_1 and C_2, there must exist (see fig. 10.10A) opposing alpha-motoneuron pools α-MN_1 and α-MN_2, whose axons project to, and allow differential activation of, the opposing muscles. Let the activation levels of the opposing motoneuron pools be designated by M_1 and M_2. Then, as shown in fig. 10.10A, a motor intention—a neural state corresponding to specification of a desired joint angle—can take the form of a pattern of signals (A_1, A_2) suitable for inducing a differential pattern of activation (M_1, M_2) across the motoneuron pools. This creates a pattern (C_1, C_2) of contractile states, thereby creating a new stable point (L_1, L_2) for the limb. So if nothing goes wrong along the way, motor intention (A_1, A_2) will invariably lead to desired joint angle $\theta(L_1, L_2)$. We now show that many things can go wrong along the way, and all the circuitry that distinguishes fig. 10.11 from fig. 10.10A will be motivated by the animal's need to reduce errors of motor realization to a minimum.

Historically, analyses of what can go wrong in motor realization have focused on how nonmuscular forces imposed by the external world can complicate the story we kept simple by assuming that only muscular forces were acting on the limb. We now supplement such analyses by turning our attention inward, to neural, neuromuscular, and musculoskeletal sources of error variance.

Suppose that we want to improve on the fig. 10.10A system by adding the ability to stiffen a joint in varying degrees while holding joint angle constant. Such joint

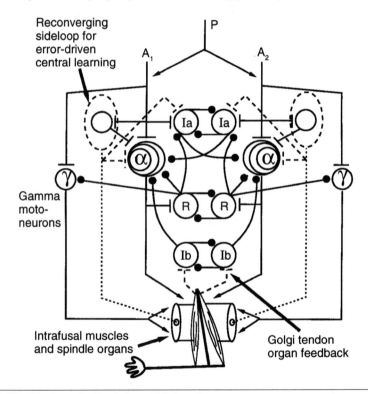

Fig. 10.11 The force feedback from Golgi tendon organs can compensate for muscle fatigue, and a parallel neuromuscular system comprising γ-MNs, intrafusal muscles, and spindle receptors allows measurement of residual positioning errors. Spindle feedback signals act locally via the stretch reflex, but also project to the higher brain, where they may guide recalibration of descending commands.

stiffening is known (e.g., Humphrey and Reed 1983) to involve simultaneous increments to the contractile states of the joint's opponent muscles, which results in
co-contraction.

The simplest way for the higher nervous system to effect a co-contraction is to
add a signal, whose magnitude we will denote by P, to both components of the
signal pattern (A_1, A_2). Then the net input to the opponent $\alpha\text{-}MN_s$ would be $(A_1 +
P, A_2 + P)$. This modification is shown in fig. 10.10B. If variations in P always
have the same effect on muscle-force production in both opponent channels, then
a limb initially at equilibrium at a desired angle θ will remain there as P varies:
Though F_1 and F_2 will both increase or decrease, their difference will remain
unchanged. Such an invariant relationship between (A_1, A_2) and θ under variations
of co-contraction signal P can be summarized by

$$\theta(A_1, A_2) = \theta(A_1 + P, A_2 + P). \tag{10.24}$$

Threats to this desirable invariance property arise due to the property of physical
neurons called *saturation*, or loss of sensitivity to input differences near the upper
bound of neuronal activity. Grossberg (1973) noted decades ago that saturative loss
of sensitivity to differences existing across pattern processing channels can be
prevented by allowing the channels to interact laterally via inhibitory signals. *In
vivo*, inhibitory interneurons called *IaINs* are known to exist with the signed connectivity, vis-a-vis $\alpha\text{-}MNs$ and each other, shown in fig. 10.10C. Sherrington, in his
experiments on the stretch reflex, demonstrated the need for a pathway to mediate
reciprocal inhibition between opponent muscle channels. The *IaINs* of fig. 10.10C
are known to receive feedback from stretch receptors and from Renshaw cells (both
of which we introduce into the model in later paragraphs). Our remarks on the
computational necessity for *IaINs* are compatible with, but also extend prior proposals regarding their function. In particular, we agree that for rapid movements to
be energetically efficient, it is important to prevent an antagonist muscle from
retarding the action of an agonist muscle. This would be difficult if the only process
for lowering $\alpha\text{-}MN$ activation levels were a passive decay process, especially with
the small passive decay rates seen *in vivo*. Reciprocal inhibition via *IaINs* allows
rapid decrementing of activity in antagonist alpha-motoneuronal pools.

We next need to ask whether the pattern (M_1, M_2) induced by motor intention
$(A_1 + P, A_2 + P)$ is faithfully registered in the pattern (C_1, C_2) of contractile states
induced by activities M_1, M_2. To see why it would not be, in the absence of further
structure, consider a simple differential equation describing changes in contractile
state through time:

$$\frac{d}{dt}C_i = (B_i - C_i)M_i - \delta C_i \tag{10.25}$$

This says that a sufficiently large neural input M_i can push contractile state C_i up
to the limit B_i, and that contractile state relaxes at rate δ. *In vivo*, B_i corresponds to
the maximal number of muscle fibers that can be simultaneously activated.

The presence of an upper bound B_i means that the ability of the C_i to remain
sensitive to differences across the M_i can saturate if the range of M_i is too large
relative to B_i. This problem can be avoided, given the neural provisions that avoid

M_i saturation in fig. 10.10C, if B_i is itself a function of M_i. In fact, this is assured *in vivo* by a motor unit design principle with a progressive recruitment rule. Motor units are composed of distinct alpha-motoneurons that project to distinct sets of contractile fibers. Moreover, within the motoneuron pools, there exist distributions of activation thresholds such that larger net excitatory inputs to the pool recruit larger numbers of motor units. Because smaller α-*MNs* are recruited earlier and larger later, this rule has been called the size principle of motoneuron recruitment (Henneman 1957). Fig. 10.10D schematizes the addition of a size principle to our model by showing a stacked series of α-*MN* cells with increasing diameter.

Unfortunately, introduction of the size principle by itself causes a loss of independent control of joint angle by (A_1, A_2) and of joint stiffness by signal P. To see this, note that under all initial choices of (A_1, A_2) other than $A_1 = A_2$, signal P will cause deeper recruitment in one muscle channel than the other. Because of the size principle, part of the signal P is subjected to greater amplification in that channel where recruitment is deeper, and a resultant force imbalance develops in that channel's favor. In consequence, the animal who had hoped to stabilize its limb at its initial posture by stiffening the joint would instead experience a large, unwanted, limb rotation!

Such an unequal amplification could be neurally compensated if it could be measured. Because the α-*MNs*, which are directly linked to muscle, are usually looked upon as the last stage of the nervous system, we might suppose that the unequal amplification could be measured only by its effect on muscle (e.g., by way of stretch receptors embedded in the opponent muscles). However, because muscle contraction is slow relative to the unequal neural amplification, a significant rotation error could develop before it could be halted by feedback from stretch receptors.

In fact, the α-*MNs* project directly to muscle and directly to a class of cells called Renshaw cells, whose function has not been well understood. In Bullock and Grossberg (1988b, 1989), we proposed that these Renshaw cells were perfectly situated to measure and to compensate for unequal amplifications of a co-contractive signal P sent to both opponent muscle channels. As shown in fig. 10.10D, each muscle control channel has its own Renshaw cell pool, which receives excitatory inputs from its channel's α-*MN* pool. The Renshaw pool sends inhibitory signals to its own channel's α-*MN* and *IaIN* pools, as well as to the opponent channel's Renshaw pool.

Consider the consequences of this signed connectivity under conditions of unequal recruitment. When P causes deeper recruitment in α-*MN* pool 1, the Renshaw population in channel 1 becomes much more active than in channel 2. This causes α-*MN*$_1$ to be subjected to greater Renshaw inhibition than α-*MN*$_2$, thus partially correcting channel 1's expected force advantage. Simultaneously, α-*MN*$_2$ is disinhibited by two pathways:

$$R_1 \rightarrow R_2 \rightarrow \alpha\text{-}MN_2 \tag{10.26}$$

and

$$R_1 \rightarrow IaIN_1 \rightarrow \alpha\text{-}MN_2. \tag{10.27}$$

This further compensates for channel 1's expected force advantage by increasing the force developed by channel 2. Simulations reported by Bullock and Grossberg (1988b, 1989) showed that Renshaw-mediated compensation could virtually eliminate undesired joint rotations associated with variations in P for any given choice of (A_1, A_2). In our theory, then, Renshaw cells play a key role in ensuring the invariance principle formalized by equation (24).

The fully expanded FLETE model is shown in fig. 10.11 on page 282. This figure contains three more modifications to fig. 10.10D that we briefly touch on here. First, consideration of muscle fatigue and the imbalances it can introduce led to including Golgi tendon organs and Ib interneurons in the expanded FLETE model of fig. 10.11. Force feedback from the Golgi tendon organs to Ib interneurons compensates for muscle fatigue by inhibiting the $\alpha\text{-}MN$ in the same channel and the $IbIN$ in the opposing channel; the addition of these pathways to the model has been shown through simulations to improve performance even without muscle fatigue.

Second, the realization that truly high performance of the motor control system cannot rely solely on the automatic, feedforward compensatory mechanisms described so far has led to the inclusion of error feedback mechanisms. This includes the well-known stretch reflex arc, consisting of γ motoneurons projecting to the intrafusal muscles, whose spindle organs in turn project to the $\alpha\text{-}MN$ and $IaIN$. Discrepancies between commanded muscle length at the $\gamma\text{-}MN$ and actual length of the extrafusal muscles result in spindle organ excitation, which in turn results in $\alpha\text{-}MN$ excitation or inhibition to correct this discrepancy.

Third, consideration of changes in mechanical advantage of antagonistically paired muscles depending on joint angle has led to including a reconverging sideloop pathway, which incorporates error-driven learning into the command issued to the $\alpha\text{-}MN$. Bullock and Grossberg (1990, 1991) follow in a tradition of work by Albus (1975), Ito (1984), Grossberg and Kuperstein (1986, 1989), and Kawato, Furukawa, and Suzuki (1987) by summarizing how such a central adaptive process sensitive to spindle feedback signals can learn an intended angle-dependent, preemptive compensation for angle-dependent variations in mechanical advantage. A key neural site for this and other instances of context-dependent adaptation of motor commands is the cerebellum, whose basic circuit we have begun to model at a level of detail similar to fig. 10.11 (see Bullock, Contreras-Vidal, and Grossberg 1993a; Contreras-Vidal 1994).

This completes the conceptual reconstruction of the peripheral neuromuscular system as a module that affords independent control of muscle length and joint stiffness. See Bullock and Contreras-Vidal (1993) for a summary of experimental evidence for all the cell types and connections (including sign) assumed in the model, as well as simulation results verifying the functionality we describe here. Since Bullock and Grossberg (1992), it has been known that variants of FLETE can also produce realistic transient muscle activations, such as the triphasic EMG pattern often observed during rapid, self-terminated movements (Lestienne 1979).

CONCLUDING REMARKS

This chapter has focused on the subset of neural network research concerned with explaining biological sensory-motor control. This approach seeks to explain detailed psychophysical data on movement performance and identify neural substrates of the system components. Insights gained from psychophysics, anatomy, and physiology are formulated into models whose components derive from neural network and dynamical systems theory. This chapter has concentrated on a collection of interrelated neural networks, which form a system for performing the transformations from visually perceiving a target to specifying commands to the muscles that carry out a reach to the target. These networks resolve key problems in the theory of motor planning, inverse kinematics, and inverse dynamics. The VITE or DIRECT model can generate a kinematic trajectory with a uniphasic velocity profile, and therefore needs no preformed kinematic motor program. Similarly, the FLETE model can generate a multiphasic force profile, and therefore needs no preformed dynamic motor program. These networks highlight issues of autonomy, flexibility, and generativity in movement. They learn without an external teacher, optimize performance over a wide range of tasks, and automatically compensate for potential disruptions in movement performance. Many model cell types have been identified with *in vivo* neural populations that have similar operating characteristics and/or connectivity. We suspect that only through continued elaboration of such a model framework will there emerge a clear understanding of how the perceiving brain controls movement in animals.

REFERENCES

Albus, J.S. 1975. A new approach to manipulator control: The cerebellar model articulation controller (CMAC). *Transactions of the ASME Journal of Dynamic Systems, Measurement, and Control* 97 (September):220-227.

Barto, A.G. 1990. Connectionist learning for control. P. 5-58 in *Neural Networks for Control*, edited by W.T. Miller, III, R.S. Sutton, and P.J. Werbos. Cambridge, MA: MIT Press.

Bullock, D., and Contreras-Vidal, J.L. 1993. How spinal neural networks reduce discrepancies between motor intention and motor realization. P. 183-221 in *Variability and Motor Control*, edited by K.M. Newell and D.M. Corcos. Champaign, IL: Human Kinetics.

Bullock, D., Contreras-Vidal, J.L., and Grossberg, S. 1993a. Cerebellar learning in an opponent motor controller for adaptive load compensation and synergy formation. P. 481-486 in *Proceedings of the World Congress on Neural Networks, Portland, IV*. Hillsdale, NJ: Erlbaum.

Bullock, D., Contreras-Vidal, J.L., and Grossberg, S. 1993b. Equilibria and dynamics of a neural network model for opponent muscle control. P. 439-458 in *Neural Networks in Robotics*, edited by G. Bekey and K. Goldberg. Boston: Kluwer Academic.

Bullock, D., and Grossberg, S. 1988a. Neural dynamics of planned arm movements: Emergent invariants and speed-accuracy properties during trajectory formation. *Psychological Review* 95(1):49-90.

Bullock, D., and Grossberg, S. 1988b. Neuromuscular realization of planned trajectories. *Neural Networks* 1, Supplement 1:329.

Bullock, D., and Grossberg, S. 1989. VITE and FLETE: Neural modules for trajectory formation and tension control. P. 253-297 in *Volitional Action*, edited by W. Hershberger. Amsterdam: North-Holland.

Bullock, D., and Grossberg, S. 1990. Spinal network computations enable independent control of muscle length and joint compliance. P. 349-356 in *Advanced Neural Computers*, edited by R. Eckmiller. Amsterdam: Elsevier.

Bullock, D., and Grossberg, S. 1991. Adaptive neural networks for control of movement trajectories invariant under speed and force rescaling. *Human Movement Science* 10:1-51.

Bullock, D., and Grossberg, S. 1992. Emergence of tri-phasic muscle activation from the nonlinear interactions of central and spinal neural network circuits. *Human Movement Science* 11:157-167.

Bullock, D., Grossberg, S., and Guenther, F.H. 1993. A self-organizing neural model of motor equivalent reaching and tool use by a multijoint arm. *Journal of Cognitive Neuroscience* 5:408-435.

Bullock, D., Grossberg, S., and Mannes, C. 1993. A neural network model for cursive script production. *Biological Cybernetics* 70:15-28.

Busemeyer, J.R., and Townsend, J.T. 1993. Decision field theory: A dynamic-cognitive approach to decision making in an uncertain environment. *Psychological Review* 100:432-459.

Calabrese, R.L., Angstadt, J.D., and Arbas, E.A. 1989. A neural oscillator based on reciprocal inhibition. P. 33-50 in *Perspectives in Neural Systems and Behavior*, edited by T.J. Carew and D.B. Kelley. New York: Liss.

Carpenter, G.A., and Grossberg, S. 1987. A massively parallel architecture for a self-organizing neural pattern recognition machine. *Computer Vision, Graphics, and Image Processing* 37:54-115.

Cohen, M.A., Grossberg, S., and Pribe, C. 1993. A neural pattern generator that exhibits arousal-dependent human gait transitions. P. 285-288 in *Proceedings of the World Congress on Neural Networks, Portland, IV*. Hillsdale, NJ: Erlbaum.

Contreras-Vidal, J.L. 1994. Neural networks for motor learning and regulation of posture and movement. PhD diss. Boston University, Department of Cognitive and Neural Systems.

Cooke, J.D. 1980. The organization of simple, skilled movements. P. 199-212 in *Tutorials in Motor Behavior*, edited by G.E. Stelmach and J. Requin. Amsterdam: North-Holland.

DeJong, R., Coles, M.G.H., Logan, G.D., and Gratton, G. 1990. In search of the point of no return: The control of response processes. *Journal of Experimental Psychology: Human Perception and Performance* 16:164-182.

DeValois, R.L., and DeValois, K.K. 1975. Neural coding of color. In *Handbook of Perception. Vol. 5: Seeing*, edited by E.C. Carterette and M.P. Friedman. New York: Academic Press.

Feldman, A.G. 1986. Once more on the equilibrium-point hypothesis (λ model) for motor control. *Journal of Motor Behavior* 18:17-54.

Flash, T., and Hogan, N. 1985. The coordination of arm movements: An experimentally confirmed mathematical model. *Journal of Neuroscience* 5(7):1688-1703.

Foley, J.M. 1980. Binocular distance perception. *Psychological Review* 87:411-434.

Gaudiano, P., and Grossberg, S. 1991. Vector associative maps: Unsupervised real-time error-based learning and control of movement trajectories. *Neural Networks* 4:147-183.

Georgopoulos, A.P., Kalaska, J.F., Caminiti, R., and Massey, J.T. 1982. On the relations between the direction of two-dimensional arm movements and cell discharge in primate motor cortex. *Journal of Neuroscience* 2:1527-1537.

Greve, D., Grossberg, S., Guenther, F.H., and Bullock, D. 1993. Neural representations for sensory-motor control, I: Head-centered 3-d target positions from opponent eye commands. *Acta Psychologica* 82:115-138.

Grossberg, S. 1968. Some nonlinear networks capable of learning a spatial pattern of arbitrary complexity. *Proceedings of the National Academy of Sciences* 59(2):368-372.

Grossberg, S. 1973. Contour enhancement, short-term memory, and constancies in reverberating neural networks. *Studies in Applied Mathematics* 52:217-257.

Grossberg, S. 1982. *Studies of Mind and Brain*. Dordrecht, Holland: Reidel.

Grossberg, S., Guenther, F., Bullock, D., and Greve, D. 1993. Neural representations for sensory-motor control, II: Learning a head-centered visuomotor representation of 3-d target positions. *Neural Networks* 6:43-67.

Grossberg, S., and Kuperstein, M. 1986. *Neural Dynamics of Adaptive Sensory-Motor Control: Ballistic Eye Movements*. Amsterdam: North-Holland.

Grossberg, S., and Kuperstein, M. 1989. *Neural Dynamics of Adaptive Sensory-Motor Control, Expanded Edition*. Elmsford, NY: Pergamon Press.

Guenther, F.H. 1992. *Neural Models of Adaptive Sensory-Motor Control for Flexible Reaching and Speaking*. PhD diss., Boston University, Department of Cognitive and Neural Systems.

Guenther, F.H. 1994. A neural network model of speech acquisition and motor equivalent speech production. *Biological Cybernetics* 72:43-53.

Guenther, F.H., Bullock, D., Greve, D., and Grossberg, S. 1994. Neural representations for sensory-motor control, III: Learning a body-centered representation of 3-d target position. *Journal of Cognitive Neuroscience* 6:341-358.

Henneman, E. 1957. Relation between size of neurons and their susceptibility to discharge. *Science* 26:1345-1347.

Houk, J.C., and Gibson, A.R. 1987. Sensorimotor processing through the cerebellum. P. 387-416 in *New Concepts in Cerebellar Neurobiology*, edited by J.S. King. New York: Liss.

Humphrey, D.R., and Reed, D.J. 1983. Separate cortical systems for control of joint movement and joint stiffness: Reciprocal activation and coactivation of antagonist muscles. P. 347-372 in *Motor Control Mechanisms in Health and Disease*, edited by J.E. Desmedt. New York: Raven Press.

Ito, M. 1984. *The Cerebellum and Neural Control*. New York: Raven Press.

Jordan, M. 1988. Supervised learning and systems with excess degrees of freedom. Technical Report COINS 88-27, Computer and Information Sciences, University of Massachusetts at Amherst, MA.

Kalaska, J.F., Cohen, D.A.D., Hyde, M.L., and Prud'homme, M. 1989. A comparison of movement direction-related versus load direction-related activity in primate cortex, using a two-dimensional reaching task. *Journal of Neuroscience* 9(6): 2080-2102.

Kawato, M., Furukawa, K., and Suzuki, R. 1987. A heirarchical neural-network model for control and learning of voluntary movement. *Biological Cybernetics* 57:169-185.

Kohonen, T. 1984. *Self-Organization and Associative Memory.* New York: Springer-Verlag.

Kuperstein, M. 1988. An adaptive neural model for mapping invariant target position. *Behavioral Neuroscience* 102(1):148-162.

Lacquaniti, F., Soechting, J.F., and Terzuolo, C.A. 1982. Some factors pertinent to the organization and control of arm movements. *Brain Research* 252:394-397.

Lestienne, F. 1979. Effects of inertial load and velocity on the braking process of voluntary limb movements. *Experimental Brain Research* 35:407-418.

Levine, D.S. 1991. *Introduction to Neural and Cognitive Modeling.* Hillsdale, NJ: Erlbaum.

Masino, T., and Knudsen, E.I. 1990. Horizontal and vertical components of head movement are controlled by distinct neural circuits in the barn owl. *Nature* 345:434-437.

McClelland, J.L., and Rumelhart, D.E. 1981. An interactive activation model of context effects in letter perception: Part 1. Account of basic findings. *Psychological Review* 88(5):375-406.

Merton, P.A. 1972. How we control the contraction of our muscles. *Scientific American* 226:30-37.

Miller, W.T. III. 1987. Sensor-based control of robotic manipulators using a general learning algorithm. *IEEE Journal of Robotics and Automation* RA-3(2):157-165.

Mollon, J.D., and Sharpe, L.T. 1983. *Colour Vision.* New York: Academic Press.

Morasso, P. 1981. Spatial control of arm movements. *Experimental Brain Research* 42:223-227.

Nagasaki, H. 1989. Asymmetric velocity and acceleration profiles of human arm movements. *Experimental Brain Research* 74:319-326.

Narendra, K.S. 1990. Adaptive control using neural networks. P. 115-142 in *Neural Networks for Control*, edited by W.T. Miller III, R.S. Sutton, and P.J. Werbos. Cambridge, MA: MIT Press.

Piaget, J. 1963. *The Origins of Intelligence in Children.* New York: Norton.

Polit, A., and Bizzi, E. 1979. Characteristics of motor programs underlying arm movements in monkeys. *Journal of Neurophysiology* 42:183-194.

Rack, P.H.M., and Westbury, D.R. 1969. The effect of length and stimulus rate on the tension in the isometric cat soleus muscle. *Journal of Physiology* 204:443-460.

Raibert, M.H. 1977. Motor control and learning by the state space model. Technical Report AI-M-351, Massachusetts Institute of Technology. NTIS AD-A026-960.

Ritter, H.J., Martinetz, T.M., and Schulten, K.J. 1989. Topology-conserving maps for learning visuo-motor-coordination. *Neural Networks* 2:159-168.

Selverston, A.I., and Moulins, M., eds. 1986. *The Crustacean Stomatogastric System.* New York: Springer-Verlag.

Uno, Y., Kawato, M., and Suzuki, R. 1987. Formation of optimum trajectory in control of arm movement: Minimum torque-change model. Technical report, Japan IEICE.

Vidal, P.P., de Waele, C., Graf, W., and Berthoz, A. 1988. Skeletal geometry underlying head movements. P. 228-238 in *Representation of Three-Dimensional Space in the Vestibular, Oculomotor, and Visual Systems*, Volume 545 of *Annals of the New York Academy of Sciences*, edited by B. Cohen and V. Henn. New York: New York Academy of Sciences.

von der Malsburg, C. 1973. Self-organization of orientation sensitive cells in the striate cortex. *Kybernetik* 14:85-100.

Zelaznik, H.N., Schmidt, R.A., and Gielen, C.C.A.M. 1986. Kinematic properties of rapid aimed hand movements. *Journal of Motor Behavior* 18:353-372.

Zipser, D., and Andersen, R.A. 1988. A back-propagation programmed network that simulates response properties of a subset of posterior parietal neurons. *Nature* 331:679-684.

Appendix

Modeling Neural Networks as Dynamical Systems

Neural networks are ubiquitous in animals and form the basis of natural intelligence. Since the time of the pioneering neurobiologists Cajal and Sherrington, we have known these networks are composed of excitable cells called neurons, which often communicate with other neurons across physical discontinuities known as synapses. To describe neurons as excitable is to say that they are active elements, and that the fluctuations in their *activation level* are at least partly dependent on inputs, whether from other cells or from outside the network. We also know that the *efficacy* of trans-synaptic communication between some kinds of cells changes, again at least partly dependent on inputs. We can think of both neural activation level and synaptic efficacy as continuous variables of the neural network.

To understand how activation patterns and synaptic efficacies within these networks can evolve and generate intelligent behavior, it is necessary to describe the biophysical laws governing both types of variables. A mathematical rule describing a lawful relation between some dependent variable and factors that cause continuous changes in that dependent variable is a *differential equation*. Thus, differential equations provide the natural language for describing neural networks. If we can use a differential equation to describe all the important factors that determine changes in a dependent variable, and if we can determine the value of that variable at some initial time and know the time histories of the controlling factors after that initial time, then we can compute the time history of the dependent variable for all subsequent times. Performing such a computation is known as solving an *initial value problem*: we start the dependent variable at its initial value, then compute its changes under the influence of the determining factors. If we want to track the evolution, or time history, of many variables (e.g., the activation levels of many cells in a neural network), then we need a differential equation for each distinct cell, and we will have to solve the initial value problem for an entire system of differential equations. Such systems of differential equations are known as dynamical systems, a term often used to refer to the natural systems described or modeled by systems of differential equations.

An inherent characteristic of neural networks is that the cells in a network communicate with one another. Each cell's activation level can therefore be a determining factor for other cells. In such cases, we do not know the time histories of the controlling factors in advance. All the cellular activation levels, and their determining factors, which include other cells' activation levels, are evolving at once. Can we still solve the initial value problem? The answer is yes, but accurate solution requires that we continuously and simultaneously update each cell's set of determining factors as time proceeds. It will not suffice to trace one cell's entire time history, then the next cell's, and so forth. This would represent a serial evolution, not the parallel, simultaneous evolution characteristic of neural networks. With a serial, digital computer, the best we can do is to approximate continuous and simultaneous updating of all cell activation levels. We do this by slicing time into very small steps, and letting the determining factors act on each (simulated) cell for only a brief time before updating the next cell. Though this is a serial process, it is virtually parallel, because all cells are updated within so short a time that updating is almost simultaneous. Methods that do such updating by computer are known as numerical methods for solution of differential equations. Because such methods add up, or integrate, the net effect of all the changes to a variable through time, they are also called numerical integration routines. These methods range from fast, simple, but error-prone routines, such as Euler's simple method, to more sophisticated, less error-prone, but slower methods, such as Euler's improved method, the Runge-Kutta method, and Gear's method.

One of the most desirable properties of differential equation modeling is the natural way it allows us to represent the idea that the time it takes for a dependent variable to evolve from some initial value to some final value depends on the net strength of the determining factors pushing the dependent variable from the initial value toward the final value. As an example, consider the following facts about between-neuron communications and neuronal activation dynamics. When one cell releases an excitatory transmitter into a synapse, this transmitter diffuses across to the adjacent cell, where it opens gates in the target cell's membrane. This allows an increased flow, or current, of certain ions into the target cell, a physical process that takes time. The amount of transmitter determines how many gates open and therefore the upper bound on flow per unit time, the flow rate. The total amount of flow determines how much the target cell's activation is raised above its initial value, and the rate of flow determines how quickly this net change occurs. In real cells, the ionic flow will always stop when the cell reaches an inherent upper bound on its activation level, and the flow slows as the cell approaches this upper bound, even if a large amount of excitatory transmitter is bombarding the cell's membrane. These properties are captured by the following differential equation:

$$dX/dt = (B - X)I \tag{A1}$$

where X is the cell's activation level, B is the fixed upper bound on the cell's activation level, and I is the amount of excitatory transmitter (more precisely, the net conductance, or openness to current flow, of the gates affected by the transmitter). This equation tells us that the instantaneous rate, dX/dt, at which the neuron's activation level X can be driven from an initial value of 0.0 toward activation level B is partly determined by the amount, I, of excitatory transmitter. More transmitter will reduce the time needed for the neuron to go from 0 to B, just as more gas will reduce the time needed for a car to go from 0 to 200 kph. The equation also tells us that once X becomes equal to B, the rate, dX/dt, at which the neuron gains activation becomes zero, because then $B - X = 0$, and $dX/dt = 0 \times I = 0$, however large the value of I. Thus, the equation captures the properties of neuronal activation dynamics described previously.

Extensions of these elementary ideas have led to systematic treatment of many rate-dependent behavioral phenomena, such as voluntary control of movement speed and speed-accuracy tradeoffs (Bullock and Grossberg 1988a; 1991), control of gait transitions in locomotion (Cohen, Grossberg, and Pribe 1993), and control of learning rate (Carpenter and Grossberg 1987).

Acknowledgments

Daniel Bullock is supported in part by the National Science Foundation (NSF IRI 90-24877 and NSF IRI 87-16960) and the Office of Naval Research (ONR N00014-92-J-1309).

Stephen Grossberg is supported in part by the Air Force Office of Scientific Research (AFOSR F49620-92-J-0499), the National Science Foundation (NSF IRI 90-24877 and NSF IRI 87-16960), and the Office of Naval Research (ONR N00014-92-J-1309).

Frank Guenther is supported in part by the National Science Foundation (NSF IRI 90-24877 and NSF IRI 87-16960) and the Air Force Office of Scientific Research (AFOSR F49620-92-J-0499).

Credits

Figure 5.2 Reprinted, by permission, from L.S. Jakobson and M.A. Goodale, 1991, "Factors influencing higher-order movement planning: A kinematic analysis of human prehension," *Experimental Brain Research* 86.

Figure 5.3 Reprinted, by permission, from L.S. Jakobson and M.A. Goodale, 1991, "Factors influencing higher-order movement planning: A kinematic analysis of human prehension," *Experimental Brain Research* 86.

Figure 5.4 Reprinted, by permission, from L.S. Jakobson and M.A. Goodale, 1991, "Factors influencing higher-order movement planning: A kinematic analysis of human prehension," *Experimental Brain Research* 86.

Figure 5.5 Reprinted from *Vision Research*, vol. 32, P. Servos, M.A. Goodale, and L.S. Jakobson, The role of binocular vision in prehension: A kinematic analysis, Copyright 1992, with kind permission of Pergamon Press Ltd, Headington Hill Hall, Oxford, OX3 0BW, United Kingdom.

Figure 5.6 Reprinted from *Vision Research*, vol. 32, P. Servos, M.A. Goodale, and L.S. Jakobson, The role of binocular vision in prehension: A kinematic analysis, Copyright 1992, with kind permission of Pergamon Press Ltd, Headington Hill Hall, Oxford, OX3 0BW, United Kingdom.

Figure 5.7 Reprinted from *Vision Research*, vol. 32, P. Servos, M.A. Goodale, and L.S. Jakobson, The role of binocular vision in prehension: A kinematic analysis, Copyright 1992, with kind permission of Pergamon Press Ltd, Headington Hill Hall, Oxford, OX3 0BW, United Kingdom.

Figure 5.8 Reprinted, by permission, from L.S. Jakobson and M.A. Goodale, 1991, "Factors influencing higher-order movement planning: A kinematic analysis of human prehension," *Experimental Brain Research* 86.

Figure 5.9 Reprinted, by permission, from P. Servos and M.A. Goodale, 1994, "Binocular vision and the on-line control of human prehension," *Experimental Brain Research* 98: 119-127.

Figure 5.10 Reprinted, by permission, from P. Servos and M.A. Goodale, 1994, "Binocular vision and the on-line control of human prehension," *Experimental Brain Research* 98: 119-127.

Figure 5.11 Reprinted, by permission, from P. Servos and M.A. Goodale, 1994, "Binocular vision and the on-line control of human prehension," *Experimental Brain Research* 98: 119-127.

Figure 5.12 Reprinted, by permission, from Mishkin et al., 1983, "Object vision and vision: Two cortical pathways," *Trends in Neuroscience* 6.

Figure 5.13 Reprinted by permission for *Nature* vol. 349, pp. 154-156; Copyright 1991 Macmillan Magazines Limited.

Figure 5.14 Reprinted by permission for *Nature* vol. 349, pp. 154-156; Copyright 1991 Macmillan Magazines Limited.

Figure 6.1 Reprinted, by permission, from G.L. Gottlieb, D.M. Corcos, and G.C. Agarwal, 1992, "Bioelectrical and biomechanical correlates of rapid human elbow movement." In *Tutorials in Motor Behavior II*, edited by G.E. Stelmach and J. Requin (New York: Elsevier Science Publishing Company, Inc.).

Figure 6.3B From D.M. Corcos et al., 1993, "Principles for learning single-joint movements: I - Enhanced performance by practice," *Experimental Brain Research* 94: 499-513. Copyright © 1993 by Springer-Verlag New York, Inc. Reprinted with permission.

Figure 6.4 From D.M. Corcos et al., 1993, "Principles for learning single-joint movements: I - Enhanced performance by practice," *Experimental Brain Research* 94: 499-513. Copyright © 1993 by Springer-Verlag New York, Inc. Reprinted with permission.

Figure 6.5 From D.M. Corcos et al., 1993, "Principles for learning single-joint movements: I - Enhanced performance by practice," *Experimental Brain Research* 94: 499-513. Copyright © 1993 by Springer-Verlag New York, Inc. Reprinted with permission.

Figure 6.6 Reprinted, by permission, from S. Jaric et al., 1993, "Principles for learning single-joint movements II. Generalizing a learned behavior," *Experimental Brain Research* 94.

Figure 6.8 From D.M. Corcos et al., 1993, "Principles for learning single-joint movements: I - Enhanced performance by practice," *Experimental Brain Research* 94: 499-513. Copyright © 1993 by Springer-Verlag New York, Inc. Reprinted with permission.

Figure 6.10 Reprinted, by permission, from M.L. Latash, 1992, "Motor control in down syndrome: The role of adaptation and practice," *Journal of Developmental and Physical Disabilities* 4.

Figure 6.11 Reprinted from *Physical Therapy*. Almeida, G.L., Corcos, D.M., and Latash, M.L. "Practice and transfer effects during fast single-joint elbow movements in individuals with down syndrome." 1994: 74: 1012 with permission of the American Physical Therapy Association.

Figure 6.12 Reprinted from *Physical Therapy*. Almeida, G.L., Corcos, D.M., and Latash, M.L. "Practice and transfer effects during fast single-joint elbow movements in individuals with down syndrome." 1994: 74: 1012 with permission of the American Physical Therapy Association.

Figure 6.13 Reprinted, by permission, from E. Kamon and J. Gormley, 1968, "Muscular activity pattern for skilled performance and during learning of a horizontal bar exercise," *Ergonomics* 11(4).

Figure 6.14 Reprinted from *Journal of Biomechanics*, 22, K. Schneider, "Changes in limb dynamics during the practice of rapid arm movements," Copyright 1989, with kind permission from Elsevier Science Ltd, The Boulevard, Langford Lane, Kidlington OX5 1GB, UK.

Figure 6.15 Reprinted from *Journal of Biomechanics*, 22, K. Schneider, "Changes in limb dynamics during the practice of rapid arm movements," Copyright 1989, with kind permission from Elsevier Science Ltd, The Boulevard, Langford Lane, Kidlington OX5 1GB, UK.

Table 6.1 From D.M. Corcos et al., 1993, "Principles for learning single-joint movements: I - Enhanced performance by practice," *Experimental Brain Research* 94: 499-513. Copyright © 1993 by Springer-Verlag New York, Inc. Reprinted with permission.

Figure 7.1 From *Turbulent mirror: An illustrated guide to chaos theory* by John Briggs and F. David Peat. Copyright © 1989 by John Briggs and F. David Peat. Reprinted by permission of HarperCollins Publishers, Inc.

Figure 7.3 Reprinted, by permission, from G. Schöner and J.A.S. Kelso, 1988, "Dynamic pattern generation in behavioral and neural systems," *Science* 239: 1514.

Figure 7.5 Reprinted, by permission, from J.A.S. Kelso, J.P. Scholz and S. Schoner, 1986, "Nonequilibrium phase transitions in coordinated biological motion: Critical fluctuations," *Physics Letters A* 118 (6): 283.

Figure 7.6 Adapted, by permission, from H. Haken, J.A.S. Kelso and H. Bunz, 1985, "A theoretical model of phase transitions in human hand movements," *Biological Cybernetics* 51: 350.

Figure 7.7 Adapted, by permission, from H. Haken, J.A.S. Kelso and H. Bunz, 1985, "A theoretical model of phase transitions in human hand movements," *Biological Cybernetics* 51: 350.

Figure 7.9 *Journal of Motor Behavior*, Volume 21, No. 2, p. 130, 1989. Reprinted with permission of the Helen Dwight Reid Educational Foundation. Published by Heldref Publications, 1319 Eighteenth St., N.W., Washington, D.C. 20036-1802. Copyright 1989.

Figure 7.11 Adapted, by permission, from B. Tuller and J.A.S. Kelso, 1989, "Environmentally-specified patterns of movement coordination in normal and split brain subjects," *Experimental Brain Research* 75: 310.

Figure 7.15 Adapted, by permission, from P.G. Zanone and J.A.S. Kelso, 1993, "The coordination dynamics of learning: Theoretical structure and experimental adenda." In *The Control of Modulation Patterns of Interlimb Coordination: A Multidisciplinary Perspective*, edited by J. Mission et al. (New York: Academic Press).

Figure 8.3 *Journal of Motor Behavior*, Volume 24, 1992. Reprinted with permission of the Helen Dwight Reid Educational Foundation. Published by Heldref Publications, 1319 Eighteenth St., N.W., Washington, D.C. 20036-1802. Copyright 1992.

Figure 8.4 Adapted, by permission, from H. Haken, J.A.S. Kelso, and H. Bunz, 1985, "A theoretical model of phase transitions in human hand movements," *Biological Cybernetics* 51.

Figure 8.5 *Journal of Motor Behavior*, Volume 24, 1992. Reprinted with permission of the Helen Dwight Reid Educational Foundation. Published by Heldref Publications, 1319 Eighteenth St., N.W., Washington, D.C. 20036-1802. Copyright 1992.

Figure 8.6   Adapted, by permission, from P.G. Zanone and J.A.S. Kelso, 1992, "Evolution of behavioral attractors with learning: Nonequilibrium phase transitions," *Journal of Experimental Psychology: Human Perception and Performance* 18.

Figure 8.8   *Journal of Motor Behavior*, Volume 24, 1992. Reprinted with permission of the Helen Dwight Reid Educational Foundation. Published by Heldref Publications, 1319 Eighteenth St., N.W., Washington, D.C. 20036-1802. Copyright 1992.

Figure 8.9   *Journal of Motor Behavior*, Volume 24, 1992. Reprinted with permission of the Helen Dwight Reid Educational Foundation. Published by Heldref Publications, 1319 Eighteenth St., N.W., Washington, D.C. 20036-1802. Copyright 1992.

Figure 9.2   Reprinted, by permission, from Y. Koike and M. Kawato, 1994, "Trajectory formation from surface EMCT signals using a neural network mode," *The Transactions of the Institute of Electronics, Information and Communication Engineers* J77-D-II (1).

Figure 9.4   Reprinted, by permission, from T. Flash and N. Hogan, 1985, "The coordination of arm movements: An experimentally confirmed mathematical model," *Journal of Neuroscience*: 1697.

Figure 9.5   Reprinted, by permission, from Y. Uno, M. Kawato, and R. Suzuki, 1989, "Formation and control of optimal trajectory in human multijoint arm movement," *Biological Cybernetics*: 95.

Figure 9.6   Adapted, by permission, from M. Dornay et al., 1995, "Minimum-muscle-tension-change," *Society of Instrument and Control Engineers* '92 Kunamoto: 1133.

Figure 9.7   Reprinted from *Neural Networks*, 6, Y. Wada and M. Kawato, "A neural network for arm trajectory formation using forward and inverse dynamics models," Copyright 1993, with kind permission from Elsevier Science Ltd, The Boulevard, Langford Lane, Kidlington OX5 1GB, UK.

Figure 9.8   Reprinted from *Neural Networks*, 6, Y. Wada and M. Kawato, "A neural network for arm trajectory formation using forward and inverse dynamics models," Copyright 1993, with kind permission from Elsevier Science Ltd, The Boulevard, Langford Lane, Kidlington OX5 1GB, UK.

Index

Underwood, B.J., 42
Ungerleider, L.G., 106, 107, 108, 109
Uno, Y., 123, 232, 236, 237, 238, 239, 240,
242, 243, 244, 245, 251, 264
Up-and-down arm movements, 238

V

VAM (Vector Associative Map), 269
Van Assche, E., 40
Vandenberghe, J., 40
Vander Linden, D.H., 43
Van Donkelaar, P., 27
van Emmerik, R.E.A., 203
Van Essen, D.C., 106
Van Galen, G.P., 29
VanMier, H., 28, 29
Van Santvoord, A.M., 38, 216-217
van Wieringen, P.C.W., 202
V-Bateson, E., 252
Vector Associative Map (VAM), 269
Vector Integration to Endpoint (VITE), 274-275
Verschueren, S.A., 38
Via-point arm movements, 238
Vidal, F., 18, 22
Vidal, P.P., 269
Vighetto, A., 108
Virtual trajectory control, in arm movements,
229, 253-254
Visible targets, in neural network models,
262-264
Visual agnosia, 108
Visual information: cortical systems for, 106-
108; cues in, binocular, 95-104; —,
monocular, 104-105; in object manipulation,
94-95; perception-action dissociations in,
112-114; studies of, electrophysiological,
109-112; —, neuropsychological, 108-109;
—, open and closed-loop, 92-94; transport
and grasp components of, 88-92
VITE model, of trajectory formation, 274-275
VITEWRITE model, of trajectory formation,
279
Volterra equations, in skill learning, 206
von der Malsburg, C., 277
von Hoften, C., 88
von Leibniz, Gottfried, 156
Vorro, J., 144

W

Wachholder, K., 124
Wada, Y., 249, 250, 251
Wade, M.G., 4
Walicke, P.A., 78
Wallace, S.A., 4, 7, 123, 155, 179, 182-185
Walter, C.B., 38, 42, 44, 45, 46, 50-51, 54,
58, 59, 60
Wang, J., 68
Wang, Y.T., 49
Ward, S.L., 20
Waterland, J.C., 145
Watsmart technique, in trajectory recording, 5

Webster's New Collegiate Dictionary, 156
Weeks, D.L., 182
Weiner, M.J., 73
Welsh, J.P., 81
Westbury, D.R., 280
Westling, G., 103
White, M.A., 50
Whiting, H.T.A., 104, 113
Wickens, C.D., 57
Wickens, D.D., 21
Wickstrom, R.L., 4, 6
Wilkinson, F., 88
Williams, H.G., 6, 10
Williams, R.J., 247
Willingham, D.B., 79
Wilson, F.R., 144
Wilson, R., 161
Wimmers, R.H., 202
Wing, A.M., 92
Winstein, C.J., 42, 43, 45, 51
Wirta, R.W., 144
Wisdom, J., 162
Wolf, M.E., 105
Woollacott, M.H., 6, 10, 139
Woods, J.J., 130
Woodworth, R.S., 1-3, 91
Worringham, C.J., 67, 75, 79
Wright, C.E., 4, 21, 123, 248
Wright, D.L., 49
Wulf, G., 46, 51
Wyatt, E.P., 17, 18, 20, 24
Wyke, M., 69, 70

X

Xu, Y., 243, 244, 253, 254

Y

Yamaguchi, T., 229
Yamanishi, J., 57, 181, 182, 209
Yamashita, H., 70
Yanagisawa, N., 88
Yao, W.X., 49
Yeo, C.H., 68
Yeo, R.A., 78
Yokota, J., 229
Young, D.E., 10, 49, 55, 130
Young, K., 137
Young, R.R., 124
Yu, J., 68

Z

Zaccaria, R., 239
Zahalak, G.I., 244
Zaidel, W.W., 69
Zanone, P.G., 38, 59, 186-188, 207-208, 211-
213
Zelaznik, H.N., 1, 3, 4, 18, 19, 22, 37, 40, 56,
93, 254, 274
Zernicke, R.F., 147, 252
Zipser, D., 262
Zuo, C.-C., 72

About the Contributors

Daniel Bullock is an associate professor in the cognitive and neural systems department at Boston University. He received his PhD in experimental psychology from Stanford University. He has been awarded research grants by the National Science Foundation and the Office of Naval Research. His interests include racquetball, hiking, and reading.

Daniel M. Corcos is an associate professor in the School of Kinesiology at the University of Illinois at Chicago. He earned his PhD in motor control from the University of Oregon. Dr. Corcos has received three research awards from the National Institutes for Health. He enjoys running, swimming, and cycling.

Carol L. Cross is a PhD candidate at the University of Michigan. The topic of her dissertation is error correction and detection in motor learning. She is in charge of a program for children with coordination problems at the Willow Run school district in southeast Michigan.

Paula Fitzpatrick received her PhD in experimental psychology from the University of Connecticut. She is currently a research specialist with the Center for the Ecological Study of Perception and Action, also at the University of Connecticut. She is a member of the Society for Research in Child Development and the International Society for Ecological Psychology. Gardening, cooking, and furniture refinishing are among her hobbies.

Melvyn A. Goodale is a professor in the Department of Psychology at the University of Western Ontario, where he also received his PhD. He is a member of the Association for Research in Vision and Ophthalmology and the Society for Neuroscience. He enjoys hiking, reading, and spending time with his family.

Stephen Grossberg is director of the Center for Adaptive Systems at Boston University. He is also a Wang professor and chairman of the cognitive and neural systems department. He received his PhD in mathematics from Rockefeller University. He worked with Dr. Bullock to formulate the Vector Integration to Endpoint (VITE) model of arm movement control and the DIRECT model of motor equivalent reaching. Dr. Grossberg likes spending leisure time at his beach house on Cape Cod.

Frank Guenther is an assistant professor of cognitive and neural systems at Boston University. He received the Alfred P. Sloan Research Fellowship in neuroscience and is a member of the Society for Neuroscience and the International Neural Network Society. His interests include billiards and furniture design.

Slobodan Jaric chairs the research laboratory of the Faculty for Physical Culture at the University of Belgrade, Yugoslavia, where he is an associate professor. Jaric, who obtained his PhD in biophysics, established a course on motor behavior and learning at the university. He is a member of the International Society of Biomechanics and the Yugoslav Society for Neurosciences. In his free time he enjoys running, swimming, and reading.

Mitsuo Kawato heads the ATR Human Information Processing Research Laboratories in Kyoto, Japan. He earned his PhD in biophysical engineering from Osaka University. He serves as editor-in-chief of *Neural Networks* and is a member of the Japanese Neural Network Society. His hobbies include gardening, baseball, and tennis.

Kyoung-nae Kim is an instructor of physical education at Yonsei University in Seoul, South Korea. He is one of Korea's leading figures in tae-kwon-do.

Stuart T. Klapp is a professor of psychology at California State University, Hayward. He received his PhD in psychology from the University of California, Berkeley. Dr. Klapp is a member of the Psychonomics Society. He enjoys hiking and camping.

Monique McMillan is a professional dancer and teacher of dance. She is currently residing in Knoxville, Tennessee, with plans to attend occupational therapy school.

R.C. Schmidt is currently an associate professor in the Department of Psychology at the College of the Holy Cross. He received his PhD in psychology from the University of Connecticut in 1988 and completed post-doctoral work at that university's Center for the Ecological Study of Perception and Action. He serves as consulting editor for the *Journal of Motor Behavior* and is a member of the American Psychological Society and the International Society for Ecological Psychology.

Philip Servos earned his PhD in psychology from the University of Western Ontario. He is currently a post-doctoral fellow in the Department of Psychology at Stanford University. As a PhD candidate, he conducted many of the experiments described in chapter five. Reading, music, and soccer are among his interests.

Ann L. Smiley-Oyen is currently an assistant professor of motor control at the University of Pittsburgh. She received her PhD in motor behavior from the University of Michigan where as a graduate student she worked with neurologically impaired subjects. She enjoys downhill skiing and playing with her children.

Stephan P. Swinnen heads the motor control laboratory and is a professor of kinesiology at Katholieke Universiteit, Leuven. He was the principle organizer of a multidisciplinary conference on interlimb coordination sponsored by the Human Frontier Science Program Organization in 1992. His hobbies include nature walks and animal observation.

Stephen A. Wallace is an associate professor in the Department of Kinesiology at the University of Colorado, Boulder. He received his PhD in physical education-motor control from the University of Wisconsin, Madison. Dr. Wallace served as a visiting research scientist at the Center for Complex Systems at Florida Atlantic University in 1988-1989. He enjoys playing guitar and listening to music.

Charles J. Worringham is an associate professor of kinesiology at the University of Michigan. He earned his PhD in physical education from the University of Wisconsin, Madison. He is a member of the North American Society for the Psychology of Sport and Physical Activity and the Society for Neuroscience. In his free time Dr. Worringham likes to orienteer.

Howard N. Zelaznik served as the executive editor of the *Journal of Motor Behavior* from 1989 to 1996 and is president-elect of the North American Society for the Psychology of Sport and Physical Activity. He earned his PhD in physical education from the University of Southern California in 1978. He is a professor in the Department of Health, Kinesiology, and Leisure Studies at Purdue University and a fellow of the American Psychological Society. His interests include running and coaching youth baseball and soccer.

The international journal for the multidisciplinary study of voluntary movement

Motor Control

Available January 1997

Mark Latash, PhD, Editor

Motor Control is designed to provide a multidisciplinary forum for the exchange of scientific information on the control of human movement across the lifespan, including issues related to motor disorders.

In addition to publishing research papers, *Motor Control* will publish review articles, quick communications, commentaries, target articles, and book reviews. When warranted, an entire issue may be devoted to a specific topic within the area of motor control.

Subscription Information

Frequency: Quarterly (January, April, July, October)
Current Volume: 1 (Beginning January 1997)
Subscription Rates: (including shipping):

	Individual	Institution	Student
U.S.	$40.00	$90.00	$24.00
Canada—surface	$60.00 Cdn	$128.00 Cdn	$38.00 Cdn
Canada—air	$82.00 Cdn	$150.00 Cdn	$60.00 Cdn
*Other—surface	$44.00	$94.00	$28.00
*Other—air	$60.00	$110.00	$44.00

*Other international customers should direct orders and requests for information to Human Kinetics' U.S. office.

Student rates are available for up to 3 years; along with payment indicate name of institution, year in school, and advisors' name.

Item: JMC • ISSN: 1087-1640

To place your order, U.S. customers **call TOLL FREE 1-800-747-4457**. Customers outside the U.S. place your order using the appropriate telephone number/address shown in the front of this book.

Prices are subject to change.

Human Kinetics
The Information Leader in Physical Activity
http://www.humankinetics.com/

2335